WHA ABOUT
THE FIRST EDITION OF THIS FILM GUIDE

"Authoritative, exhaustive, and essential, *Blood Moon's Guide to Gay and Lesbian Film* is the queer ˜irl's and queer boy's one-stop resource for what to add to their feature-film queue. The film synopses ł the snippets of critic's reviews are reason enough to keep this annual compendium of cinematic formation close to the DVD player. But the extras--including the Blood Moon Awards and commen- ˙y on queer short films—are butter on the popcorn."

Books to Watch Out For (www.btwof.com)

"̇his 400-page first edition of everything fabu in movies for 2005 is an essential guide for both the casu- ι˙ viewer and the hard-core movie watching homo. It's comprehensive and entertaining, with an intro- ˙˙ction that announces the **Blood Moon Awards** (they call them the "Bloody Moons"), an amazingly ˙horough look at their best picture winner, *Brokeback Mountain*, as well as a conclusion packed with sexy ˙ːs of three hunks that played gay last year: Colin Farrell, Jake Gyllenhaal and Heath Ledger. While it ˙ems *Brokeback* is all over this book — from the cover to the last pages — there are over 135 feature ˙ns and 60 shorts discussed, including big ones like *Transamerica* and *The Family Stone*, as well as ˙ser-known releases like *D.E.B.S.* and *Hubby/Wifey*. This year's Gay and Lesbian Film festival movies ˙ in it, too. Scattered throughout the listings are "Special Features;" tongue-in-cheek essays about the ˙t and worst mishaps in film last year. Case in point: the essay explaining how Farrell's full frontal ˙, err, cut from *Alexander*. Blood Moon plans on publishing a new edition every year, so here's hop- ˙for a good, gay 2007."

Bay Windows (Boston)

"˙mething new that's a lot of fun is *Blood Moon's Guide to Gay and Lesbian Film*. It's like having ˙ ˙ess to a feverishly compiled queer film fan's private scrapbook. This first edition gives a snapshot of ˙ ˙ere we are in Hollywood now, which should be updated with each further annual edition. It's valu- ˙˙ și and a lot of fun and, like screen representations of us, it verges wildly between tribute and titilla- tiᴄˑ. Now, I'm ready for my closeup..."

Gay Times (London)

"Startling. This exhaustive guide documents everything from the mainstream to the obscure, detailing dozens of queer films from the last few years."

HX (New York)

Blood Moon's Guide to Gay and Lesbian Film

Second Edition

BY *Darwin Porter and Danforth Prince*

Blood Moon Productions, Ltd.

www.BloodMoonProductions.com

Cover designs by Richard Leeds (www.BigWigDesign.com)
Layouts by Nicole Mathison

ISBN13 978-0-9748118-7-1
Copyright © 2007 Blood Moon Productions, Ltd.

SECOND EDITION PUBLISHED AND RELEASED October 2007

1 3 5 7 9 10 8 6 4 2

Publisher's Cataloging-In-Publication Data
(Prepared by the Donohue Group, Inc.)

Porter, Darwin.
  Blood Moon's guide to gay and lesbian film / by Darwin Porter and Danforth Prince.-- 1st ed. (2006)-

  p. : ill. ; cm.
  Annual

1. Gay men--Film catalogs. 2. Lesbians--Film catalogs. 3. Homosexuality in motion pictures--Catalogs. 4. Homosexuality, Male, in motion pictures--Catalogs. 5. Lesbianism in motion pictures--Catalogs. 6. Motion pictures--Catalogs. I. Prince, Danforth. II. Title. III. Title: Guide to gay and lesbian film.

PN1995.9.H55 P67
791.43/653

**Announcing winners of *The Blood Moon Awards*®
("The Bloody Moons")**

Honoring Merit and Excellence in GLBT Films.

**For other titles from Blood Moon,
Please turn to the final pages of this guidebook.**

The authors wish to thank Monica Dunn
for her tireless editorial assistance with this guidebook.

The authors dedicate this book to the filmmakers, actors, writers,
distributors, technicians, and publicists
who made the films reviewed in this book possible.

With apologies to those whose names were inadvertently omitted,
and with regrets for anything which we might have misinterpreted,
we salute the filmmakers and actors whose works are reviewed within this guide.
We wish them luck and strength in the challenges and adversities ahead.

Gay Films

"*The sorry state of American Gay Cinema has for too long been a source of frustration for many in our community; Typically horrible production values, poor scripts, inane plots, bad performances, and lousy direction have combined over the years to create very low expectations among LGBT filmgoers. We as a group have been so desperate to see images of our lives portrayed on the silver screen that we have tossed out the high expectations that we as a community have a reputation for in such areas as art, creativity, and style to tolerate and even embrace garbage cinema as long as it was gay themed. So it is refreshing and exciting that American Gay Cinema seems to finally be improving.*"

Herb Krohn

"*I won't be directed by a fairy! I have to work with a real man.*"

Clark Gable, snarling about his then-director, George Cukor, on the set of *Gone With the Wind*

"*I am prepared to believe that the sense of romance in those of our brothers and sisters who incline towards love of their own sex is heightened to a more blazing pitch than in those who think of themselves as normal.*"

Lord Laurence Olivier

"*Half the people in Hollywood are dying to be discovered. The other half are afraid they will be.*"

Lionel Barrymore

TABLE OF CONTENTS

PART THREE: SHORT GAY FILMS

PART FOUR: HOLLYWOOD'S HOTTEST HOTTIES

The Year of the Queer in Cinema

First, let's get the bad news out of the way: 2006 and early 2007 saw no individual break-through film with the emotional power of *Brokeback Mountain.*

But the good news is that gay films, or gay characters within mainstream films, are now a deeply entrenched fixture within post-millennium America, where we trust they will stay for-ever now that Jerry Falwell is no longer around to protest. And the swelling numbers of gay films, and the increasing quantities of gay characters within so-called straight films, reminded us of a bloated Elvis busting out of his breeches.

In 2006, actors continued to Out themselves. The already-Out Rupert Everett published his memoir, *Red Carpets and Other Banana Skins.* He told the press that coming out was a mixed blessing as his film career seemed stalled. "I really think people are more prejudiced than ever against gays, and I also think there is more race hatred than ever. So I give up trying to look for straight leading-man roles." He was heading for Sydney where he'd been asked to be the "Queen of the Mardi Gras."

Everett's assessment may be uneccesarily bleak. Some actors, including Neil Patrick Harris and T.R. Knight, continue to play horny straights even though they are gay in private life.

That heartthrob of the 1940s and 50s, Farley Granger, also outed himself in 2007 with the publication of *Include Me Out* with Robert Calhoun. Actually, Granger outed himself as a bisexual, since he'd had brief affairs with Barbara Stanwyck and Ava Gardner—he turned down Joan Crawford—and a long-running sexual battle with Shelley Winters. He came to know Leonard Bernstein intimately, Arthur Laurents very intimately. Granger met his co-author at the time of the assassination of President Kennedy and the happy pair have been an item ever since.

Chad Allen, who stars as a gay detective in *Shock to the System*, told the press that until *Brokeback Mountain*, "There was a huge fear or belief that you couldn't tell a story with a gay hero and have it make money. A well-made movie with a good story trumps everything. It's not just a victory for gay rights; it's a victory for humanity."

Gay men by the millions flocked during the summer of 2007 to see John Travolta in a dress in the newest film version of *Hairspray.* Despite the fact that various tabloids have tried to Out him in "Second Coming" headlines, Travolta still had the balls to dress in drag, donning latex and a wig. He plays a role previously inhabited by such gay icons as Divine, Harvey Fierstein, and Bruce Vilanch.

Travolta showed more guts than the very heterosexual Tom Cruise, fellow Scientology buff, in taking on such a role. In spite of the rumors, Cruise continues to play things "super macho," grabbing that poor girl, Katie Holmes, and practically fucking her in front of cameras every time he spots the paparazzi.

Concerning the role he was about to interpret, Travolta told his director, "I want to show cleavage. I want to show a waist. I want to show that this woman still has some sense of wom-anliness left in her."

Before the world premiere of *Hairspray,* the casting of Travolta revolted some gay activists, who weren't at all happy about the former star of *Grease* squeezing into the house dress of Edna Turnblad. The chief charge is that Travolta's church of Scientology is homophobic.

Its founder, L. Ron Hubbard, in his 1950 best-seller *Dianetics*, referred to gays as "very ill physically" and "sexual perverts." In a lawsuit filed in 1998, a former Scientologist, Michael Pattinson, charged that the church had deceived him by using Travolta as an example of a gay man who'd happily gone straight. Travolta has been married to Scientologist Kelly Preston for 13 years as of 2007. The church called Pattinson's charges "hogwash."

Because of the homophobia built into Scientology, Kevin Naff, editor of the respected gay newsmagazine *The Washington Blade*, has urged gays to boycott *Hairspray*. What's a gay moviegoer to do? Everyone will have to decide for him/herself.

Fortunately, there are dozens of other films on the horizon whose dilemmas are associated with their plots, rather than in moral issues associated with how they were made. A good example is MGM's *Death at a Funeral*. Two brothers confront a blackmailer at their father's funeral. He claims to be the deceased patriarch's hitherto secret gay lover. You get Peter Dinklage cast as gay, and Alan Tudyk running around *sans* wardrobe.

Any crop of films will include the inevitable tales of straight men being pressured to play gay for a reason, and in 2007, Universal released its big summer comedy about same-sex marriage, *I Now Pronounce You Chuck and Larry*. Firemen Adam Sandler and Kevin James create, with much aimiable buffoonery, the illusion of being a bona-fide gay couple as a means of applying for domestic partner benefits. Gays along with millions of straights flocked to see this film, which on its opening weekend outpaced --at least in terms of sales--the latest Harry Potter movie. We're happy to report that this otherwise butch, mass-market, and very mainstream film ends on a note that pleads for tolerance for gays. And in its back-handed, "*aw-shucks*" kind of way, it even endorses same-sex marriage.

Fortunately, some members of the gay press are pressuring mainstream studios, expressing their visual expectations in ways that are Out and Proud: *Instinct* magazine published a gay-perspective and amusing preview of *Hostel II,* saying, "We don't think it's necessarily torture to watch Jay Hernandez tied up again! We'd start by ripping off his shirt, then tearing off his pants." For *The Bourne Ultimatum*, the writer said, "Matt Damon, here's your ultimatum: Get naked in this one, or else!" Damon didn't listen.

The outlook at the latest Sundance Festivals in 2007 looked a bit bleak for queer titles. Even *The Advocate* asked the question, "Has Sundance gone postgay?" Ironically, despite that assessment, there were more Out gay filmmakers at Sundance than ever before. We're talking the likes of Tommy O'Haver (*Billy's Hollywood Screen Kiss*) and Gregg Araki (*Mysterious Skin*). Historically the festival has been known for its ground-breaking release of gay-themed cinema titles. Not so any more. Many of the latest films from directors as well known as those noted above contain virtually no gay content.

"The coming-out story is no longer the fresh story," John Cooper, Sundance Festival director, told the press. "Neither is what I call the 'gays-are-people too' story. Those movies are still going to be made, and I think they need to be made, but at the time, the focus is on what's fresh, what makes your hair stand up?"

Helmer Ian Iqbal Rashid, known for his *Touch of Pink* (2004), had a slightly different point of view. "I do believe that a film can have a queer sensibility without necessarily being explicitly about LGBT characters or storylines. But I also believe there's still a need for stories where queerness is named and explicitly articulated—and yes, I still believe there's a need for coming-out stories."

Making Love (1982), now considered a Golden Oldie for gay men, was the first gay-friendly romance to come out of a major Hollywood studio. Back in 1982, many movie-goers, not necessarily having understood the content of the film, walked out, especially when Michael Ontkean and Harry Hamlin kissed. *Making Love's* failure at the box office postponed the production of most other mainstream gay films for years. Fortunately, we've come a long way, baby, since those dark days.

Sherry Lansing, president of Fox when *Making Love* was released, still stands by her decision, even though the film made only $12 million at the box office. "I absolutely fell in love with the script, and I thought it was going to be one of the biggest movies in the history of film."

Michael Douglas turned down the role, even gay-friendly Richard Gere cabled his regrets. Hamlin claimed that *Making Love* paralyzed his movie career, but says he still has no regrets.

Movie trivia note: Originally the set designer on *Making Love* had decorated the inside of Hamlin's house with a full-length blow-up of Judy Garland above the fireplace. Get it? If you loved Garland, you just had to be gay . . . at least back in 1982.

Regrettably, gay men in the coming months will get more screen exposure than lesbians. But all is not lost. *Desert Hearts* from 1986, which has been hailed as the greatest lesbian drama ever made, was recently re-released as a DVD. At the time of its filming, the stars of *Desert Hearts*, Patricia Charbonneau and Helen Shaver, were warned about career suicide if they "played nakedly lesbian."

"We went ahead anyway," Shaver told the press. "And that was long before lesbian chic. Donna Deitch, the director, had guts." *Good news on the lesbian film front*: Deitch is writing a long-awaited sequel to *Desert Hearts,* this one set in the 1970s.

The emerging technologies of DVD, coupled with the hunger for gay-themed entertainment and increased willingness on the part of film studios to invest in restoration and re-digitalization, has led to the release of many marvelous classics. These have included *The Lost Language of Cranes* (1991) in which both a father and a son come out to each other. A film ahead of its time also has been released in DVD. *The Naked Civil Servant* (1975) is based on the witty memoirs of the eccentric Quentin Crisp as he struggles to maintain his artfully personalized brand of flamboyance. Crisp's refusal to compromise, despite "fag-bashing" attacks and mass intolerance during an era when (male) homosexuality was still illegal in Great Britain, led to his elevation to a role as a gay icon and international celebrity. In a vivid portrait, John Hurt plays Crisp in the film.

"Lost films" of yesterday are also coming back, with restorations. An example includes Gus van Sant's *Mala Noche* (Bad Night) from 1985 with a new 35mm print. Even the gay classic, *Mommie Dearest*, an ungrateful and jealous adopted daughter's libelous portrait of Joan Crawford, came back as a restored version in 2007. After all, a whole new generation of gay men and women have emerged since some of these golden oldies first came onto the market. *"And Everything Old is New Again"* as the song blithely says.

The queer presence in current cinema crosses a wide spectrum of the rainbow flag—tragic star-crossed lesbian lovers in *Imagine Me & You*; "well-heeled" and deeply politicized crossdressers in *Kinky Boots*; an effeminate author (Truman Capote) in *Infamous*.

"During the past couple of years," said Lisa Daniel, director of the Melbourne Queer Film Festival, "films have leaned further away from the whole angst-ridden life of a gay or lesbian, or the coming-out sagas, and we're seeing interesting stories about queers. We're growing up. It has been said that a film is a reflection or mirror of society and its social realities. It's a two-way street as well; sometimes society is a reflection of what's in film, but more often film reflects what is going on in society at that time. We are seeing an increased acceptance of queer life in general. That is, as long as it's not too scary or confronting."

Although unheard of only a few years ago, films with gay themes are appearing in less-developed and relatively conservative countries which include Peru, Serbia, Korea, Singapore, Turkey, Argentina, and the Philippines. One film from Israel, for example, deals with an Israeli soldier falling for a (male) Palestinian. Many of them share a theme about the difficulties that queer people face in homophobic societies. Some even tackle such sensitive subjects as what to do about trannies incarcerated in prison.

There aren't many "happy ever after" stories. Most films show that despite good intentions, things do go wrong for gay men and lesbians. The impact that AIDS has on the worldwide community continues to be a dominant feature. Another hot topic is gay marriage, an idea which so utterly horrifies our soon-to-be-retired president.

Hundreds of gay or lesbian films are released every year but only a fraction of them are shown in movie houses, even in such cities as Los Angeles or New York. Many gay-themed movies are shown at film festivals, events where producers hope they'll be able to find a distributor. Regrettably, only a small percentage are ever picked up by a major, or even a medium-sized distributor.

That's where this guidebook comes in: It exists as a means of documenting the wide range of queer films out there, the increasing politicization of the subject matter, and the explosion of the art form worldwide.

With respects to the filmmakers, particularly those taking risks within inhospitable terrains, I urge all of you to let the entertainment begin.

Danforth Prince, President
Blood Moon Productions

SHOULD WE *SWISH* OR SHOULD WE *SWAGGER*?

In his book, *Becoming the Kind Father*, author Calvin Sandburn wrote, "Society used to assign certain characteristics to men, including power, aggressiveness, professional success, and autonomy. Other, shall we say, swishier traits were expected of women such as the ability to create and nurture connections, kindness, and communication."

In their race to compete, women have sometimes rejected some of these more "feminine" attributes, in favor of something more macho and "testosterone-pumped."

But perhaps things are changing. Role model Johnny Depp in his third reprise as the sexually ambiguous Captain Jack Sparrow in *Pirates of the Caribbean: At World's End* seems just as gay as ever. His mascara is thick, his gestures are regal, and as a Beau Brummel clone inspired by Regency England, he sports jewelry, an elaborate sense of protocol, and a wisp of white lace tied just above his left hand.

So what's a guy to do? Stay manly or start acting like the straight world's version of what it is to act gay?

Laura Sessions Stepp wrote: "Increasing numbers of young men bend the gender role freely, especially if their buds are doing the same. A preppy guy in high school might pair a

lime-green Polo by Ralph Lauren shirt with light yellow J. Crew pants, a Lily Pulitzer belt and Rainbow flip-flops. And whereas men used to greet each other with a handshake, now it's a hug."

Her words are echoed by William Albert, deputy director of a pregnancy prevention group in Washington, D.C. "Guys who are virgins are still more troubled by their virginity than are virgin girls. Not as many teenage males are having intercourse as in the past, but more of them are having oral sex."

"Maybe Depp with his *Pirate* movies is teaching us something," Stepp said. "There's not longer a defined line between *swish* and *swagger*. Maybe it's both!"

Let's face it. When all is said and done, and in spite of the queer content appearing more and more in mainstream cinema, there's nothing quite like watching a gay film with a gay audience.

Announcing This Edition's Winners of
THE BLOOD MOON AWARDS

FOR EXCELLENCE AND MERIT
IN GAY AND LESBIAN FILMS

Let's call them
"The Bloody Moons...."

There are Oscar Awards, there are SAG awards, there are awards from the Rotarians and the Knights of Columbus, and awards from universities.

WHY NOT AWARDS FOR OUTSTANDING
GAY AND LESBIAN FILM VENUES TOO?

In the pages that immediately follow,
with respect and admiration for each of the films, filmmakers, and creative visions celebrated within this guidebook,
Blood Moon is pleased to announce *its winners* and *its runners-up*
in the following categories of film achievement:

1. Best Picture
2. Best Director
3. Best Actor
4. Best Actress
5. Best Supporting Actor
6. Best Supporting Actress

THE BLOOD MOON AWARDS.
OUT, OUTRAGEOUS, AND PROUD.

Winners!

Best Picture

Infamous

Stephen Frears
The Queen

Best Director

Best Actor

Toby Jones
Infamous

Marion Cotillard
La Vie en Rose

Best Actress

Best Supporting Actor

Ian McKellen
The Da Vinci Code

Judi Dench
Notes on a Scandal

Best Supporting Actress

... and the Runners-Up!

Best Picture

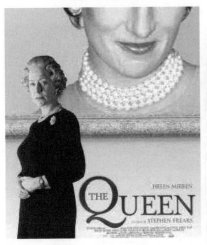

Best Director

The Queen

Auraeus Solito

The Blossoming of Maximo Oliveros

Best Actress

Best Actor

Annette Bening

Running With Scissors

John Malkovich

Color Me Kubrick

Best Supporting Actress

Best Supporting Actor

Hilary Swank

The Black Dahlia

Richard Griffiths

The History Boys

Part One:

Superheroes, Gay Iconography, and the Movies

Gay and American--my comic book collection probably defined me as a gay kid even before I understood what that meant.   Now they're putting Superman in the sociology textbooks, talking about his crotch, and defining him as a gay icon. Go figure...

Reader Ted Messner, Age 34
Nashville, Tennessee

SUPERMAN RETURNS

In Tight, Tight Blue Tights & a Bulging Red Bikini

Superman Returns is a gorgeously crafted epic only because of its gorgeously crafted star, Brandon Routh, one of the greatest of all movie heartthrobs. Straight women and gay men fell in love with this prime specimen of male beauty in most countries of the world.

When the movie opened, gay papers claimed that the two must-see homo movie events of the summer were *The Devil Wears Prada* and *Superman Returns*. "What a treat," wrote one gay reviewer, "to go from a black comedy with Meryl Streep channeling Anna Wintour to the giant screen adventures of Brandon Routh's Superbulge."

It's asking the impossible, especially for a man with gay DNA, to take his eyes off Brandon for even a second. Especially since, although the film is super-sized, it lacks a super story.

In this newest version, Superman has returned to Earth after having mysteriously vanished—according to the story line—for five years. Actually, Superman hasn't appeared in any new movies in more than 20 years, when he was the focal point of *Superman IV: The Quest for Peace,* in 1987. In advance of its 2007 version, some of the suits at Warner Brothers worried that Superman was too retro—too sincere, too simple, too *good* for modern audiences. The newest version's director, the openly gay Bryan Singer didn't think so. "He's the ultimate immigrant. He represents what America is. We don't always get it right, but Truth and Justice—those are Superman's ideals."

Of course, Singer knew that a little box office razzmatazz never hurts, either.

In the newest version, Superman (alias Brandon Routh) finds the world a very different place from what it was when inhabited by Christopher Reeve. His ex-flame, Lois Lane, as blandly played by Kate Bosworth, has a four-year-old son and a fiancé, the handsome James Marsden. It's not made clear just who the daddy is or was. Perhaps Superman? Single mom Lois isn't prepared to give the recently returned Superman a hero's welcome. In fact, she's bitchy, writing in the *Daily Planet*: "The world does-

n't need a savior. And neither do I."

In his Clark Kent disguise, Superman gets his old job back at the *Daily Planet*. He's hired by Perry White, as played by Frank Langella. On his first day on the job, Superman proves Lois wrong: The world still needs him, perhaps more than before. He rescues Lois when a space shuttle launched from the back of a jet fails to disengage and rockets into space with the jet still attached. Naturally, Lois is on board.

Through fire and molten debris, our hero brings the disintegrating plane in for a soft landing in a crowded baseball stadium. Once rescued, he and Lois lock eyes for the first time in five years. Why can't other so-called straight men get a girl's attention this dramatically?

Despite the theatricality of this rescue, it's obvious that Brandon and Kate Bosworth will not be the screen's next version of Spencer Tracy and Katharine Hepburn (both of whom, incidentally, were bisexuals). But in spite of this, the relatively plain Lois must have some superpower not evident to mere mortals to have kept a stud like Superman chasing after her all these years. One wonders what he did for sex during the time he's been away? Another girlfriend or friends? A boy perhaps? His trusty fist?

Since his reincarnation, Superman has changed. He seems very different from the mega-butch George Reeves, a former amateur boxer, who was TV's first Man of Steel flying around between 1951 and 1958.

Replacement Supermen have included the late Christopher Reeve, whose chiseled good looks first made headlines beginning around 1978. Unlike his "stiffer" predecessor from TV's black-and-white days, Reeve had an openness about him that included an ability to cuddle with Lois Lane in the 1980s *Superman II*. Dean Cain, the star of the hit TV series *Lois & Clark*, which ran for 87 episodes between 1993 and 1997, wound up marrying Teri Hatcher's Lois. And beginning in 2001 and running for seven consecutive seasons, Tom Welling played a confused, adolescent Clark Kent in *Smallville*, another TV

Supermen, *left to right*: George Reeves, Christopher Reeve, Dean Cain, and Tom Welling

series. Its tagline—"*His journey, their battle, our future*"—is a slogan that tragic heroes since the days of Homer might have applied to their particular quests.

In Brandon Routh's interpretation of Superman, some editorial columnists found him radically different from each of his predecessors, one writer even daring to suggest a "feminized icon." Others more charitably suggested that the young actor had found Superman's soft side.

McG (*né* Joseph McGinty Nichol, best known for having directed the movie version of *Charlie's Angels*) was originally slated to direct *Superman Returns*. But he lost the role because of his refusal to fly to Australia for location shots. "I don't really freak out that we're gonna crack, but I freak out when everything's great and you're at 40,000 feet and then you realize you're in a steel tube and you can't get out of there and there's nothing but water everywhere when you look down."

After McG, along came director Bryan Singer. Born in 1965 in New York City, he claims to have re-imagined the Man of Steel as a sensitive guy dealing with typical "chick flick" romantic problems. Enigmatically, he ordered his screen writers to strive for "a kind of civilized masculinity...and emotional Kryptonite." This brought a response from a blogger: "I thought 'emotional Kryptonite' when used regarding men was an oxymoron . . . oh, yeah, unless they are gay."

Singer before Superman was mostly noted for his direction of many of the *X-Men* movies. At presstime, he was involved in a movie treatment of the hit TV series *Football Wives*. His production company, Bad Hat Harry, is named after a line in the shark flick, *Jaws* (1975).

In addition to having to endure rumors that he was hung like a Brontosaur, the rookie actor, Brandon, had to endure rumors that he was Singer's private boy toy as well.

Simon Halls, one of Brandon's publicists, claimed that Singer had been "totally professional" with his *Superman* star, noting that Brandon has a longtime girlfriend. In spite of bloggers, rumors of a casting couch audition have been ruled out. "It never happened," said a source at WB who didn't want to be named.

When Singer directed the movie version of Stephen King's *Apt Pupil* in 1998, several male extras filed lawsuits. In their claim, they said that the helmer had "bullied" them into stripping naked for a shower scene. Singer, it was alleged, also staged private screenings of the film's soapy, frontal nude

Director Bryan Singer

"Did director Bryan Singer's penchant for casting with the lensman in his pants influence his choice of Brandon Routh to play the Man of Steel in *Superman Returns*? Ever since the unknown 26-year-old actor whose career highlights consist of a season on *One Life to Live* and an episode of *Will & Grace* landed the part over Warner Brothers' reported favorite, Jim Caviezel, fanboy bloggers have been wondering whether the famously beefcake-friendly filmmaker's decision had more to do with his libido than his director's eye."

Radar Online

Superheroes Spread-Eagled?

TRUST A FEW
FEAR THE REST

X-MEN

Bloggers, as represented by the Radar website with those casting-couch accusations, have been particularly cruel with Singer. We've never been beneath Singer's bed, so we don't know the truth of these widely published rumors. But according to the site, and allegedly coming from actor Alex Burton, he got the role of Pyro in Singer's *X-Men* "after a hot-tub session with the director at a homo-heavy Hollywood party."

We don't even know if Burton really said that, or if the hot tub session actually happened, but the quote has been distributed around the world.

Just Imagine:

Leonardo DiCaprio as the young **Darth Vader**? Haley Joel Osment as **Harry Potter**? What about Nicolas Cage as **Superman**? Each of those possibilities almost happened.   But if Cage had landed the role, would media have speculated as wildly about his bulge—or lack thereof—as they did with Brandon Routh's package? And whereas Lisa Marie Presley, Elvis's daughter, wasn't particularly helpful when Howard Stern asked her about former husband Michael Jackson's crotch, in the case of Cage, we wonder what insights she might have provided.

A final irony associated with the casting of S-Man? The soulful and exceptionally handsome James Caviezel, to some degree already graced with superhero status thanks to his associations with Jesus, wanted to play Superman but Singer wouldn't cast him, citing that he was already "too famous" because of his role in Mel Gibson's *The Passion of the Christ.*

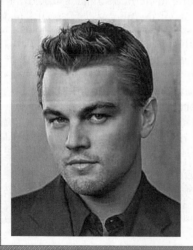

footage at his home.

After all the brouhaha and measurements associated with the film's MALE, star, how did they come up with a Lois Lane? Singer cast Bosworth after watching her play the alcoholic 1950s star, Sandra Dee, in *Beyond the Sea,* the Bobby Darin biopic, as directed by Kevin Spacey. Ironically, as if to prove that Hollywood is a cliquish and incestuous place, Spacey played the villain, Lex Luthor, in *Superman Returns.* Scarlett Johansson, who would probably have been better, or at least sexier, was considered for the role of Lois, but as often happens in La-La Land, things didn't work out.

Brandon is soulful, aesthetically glorious, and appealingly vulnerable as Superman, but it's Spacey as the demented villain, Lex Luthor, who steals the film. Recently released from prison, and hell-bent on world domination, he'll use radioactive crystals from Superman's home planet, Krypton, as weapons against him. Kryptonite, 'natch, is our hero's Achilles' heel. As an actor, Spacey brilliantly bridges the gap between the whimsical and the sinister.

Spacey (as Luthor) controls the technology that

Kate Bosworth

For yet another take on Superman, the 1950s George Reeves version, and to see Ben Affleck in a Superman costume, turn within this guidebook to our review of *Hollywoodland,* a film that also starred Adrien Brody.

will catalyze the immediate formation of a new land mass in the Atlantic that will swamp North America and whittle out an all-new, all-virgin continent that will be completely under Luthor's control. Such are the ways of evil. Thank God for Superman.

Even an actor as strong and powerful as Spacey loses out when his on-screen girlfriend appears with a Betty Boop wig and two yippy and vicious little dogs. Parker Posey plays Kitty Kowalski as a boozy floozy. As such, she provides a welcome comic relief from Brandon's sincerity and Bosworth's dullness.

The film opens one dark and stormy night within the palatial mansion of a dying billionairess. The old lady, about to bequeath her estate to an attentive young paramour, Lex Luthor, is portrayed by the vintage camp actress Noel Neill. "I love you, Lex Luthor," she gasps with her final breath. Presumably, it's from the estate she bequeaths him that Lex Luthor is able to create the persona that leads to his return as malefactor *numero uno.* Could the screenwriter have been thinking of Doris Duke?

A trained singer and dancer, Ms. Neill played Lois Lane briefly in 1948, and then more extensively in the

Parker Posey

Kevin Spacey as Lex Luthor

TV series, *Adventures of Superman*, at the debut of that series' second season in 1953. When *Adventures of Superman* ended in 1957, Neill for the most part retired from show biz.

As for the film's supporting actors, some were living and some were dead. *Superman Returns* features archival footage of the late superstar Marlon Brando, who played Superman's father, Jor-El, in the 1980 Chrisopher Reeve version. Brando, who was paid an huge stipend for his very brief appearance, delivers a hambone performance that's bizarre at best, mumbling interplanetary mumbo jumbo. This stock footage was originally shot by *Superman II* director Richard Donner in 1978. Had that dusty old Brando footage not become available, Johnny Depp was originally considered for the role of Jor-El.

The still lovely Eva Marie Saint, who appeared with Brando in 1954s *On the Waterfront*, plays Superman's mother, and does so with her brilliant charm. She is, in fact, the most gracious actor in the film. For her onscreen efforts in *Waterfront*, she won an Oscar, as did Brando himself.

Superman Returns was also technically innovative, opening at 90 IMAX theaters and featuring 20 minutes of footage converted from 2-D to 3-D. This was the first live-action feature film to use this process and in the vanguard of a new 3-D boom. For twenty years prior to the release of this film, 3-D technologies had for the most part been used within IMAX nature documentaries. Those who were of movie-going age in the 1950s will remember a primitive form of 3-D when the scary *House of Wax* broke box office records and ushers handed out cardboard-rimmed eyeglasses to everyone in the audience.

OR MAYBE HE'S JUST SENSITIVE?

During the media buildup associated with the release of this film, nearly every outlet in media, including both *The New York Times* and *The Advocate*, dealt with the question, "IS SUPERMAN GAY, OR JUST SENSITIVE?"

Www.defamer.com weighed in with this:

"Joel Schumacher and George Clooney might have made great strides by re-imagining Batman as a rubber-nippled, impressively cod-pieced bondage queen, but we don't think the tag-team of Bryan Singer and the previously obscure Brandon Routh are quite up to the task of delivering gay Superman until at least the second installment of the revived franchise. Still, it is quite generous of *The Advocate* to preemptively include the new, still-unproven Man of Steel in its summer "Gay Superhero" issue. Placing his image above the names of established big-screen, homosexual presences like Ian McKellan and Kevin Spacey ensures that he won't be forgotten while he decides on the right time to come out of the phone booth."

Just Who Is Brandon Routh?

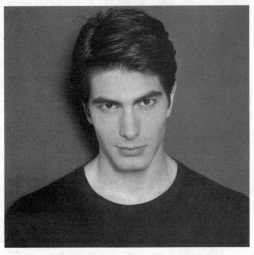

Famous for his blue tights and unforgiving red shorts, the American actor, Brandon James Routh, burst into the world one chilly autumn morning on October 9, 1979 in Des Moines, Iowa, land of high literacy rates and corn-fed boys. His mother, Katie, was a teacher; his father, Ron, a carpenter. But in their spare time his artistically inclined parents showed a devotion to music. Brandon's sister, Sara Routh, in fact, is a professional singer.

Boy Routh grew up 100 miles from the hometown of George Reeves, the ill-fated actor who played Superman on the small, black-and-white TV sets of the 1950s. Early in life, Brandon thought about an acting career, but didn't think a young boy growing up in Iowa had much of a chance at Hollywood.

Sometimes identified as a "momma's boy," he was not popular at school and often spent time in his room reading *Superman* comic books. He learned to play both the trumpet and piano when he attended Norwalk High School in Norwalk, Iowa. There, he enjoyed sports and studied theater. He went to bed in his Superman pajamas, perhaps replicating a fantasy of Michael Jackson.

When others dreamed of girls, young Brandon tended to dream about blue tights. His mother, Katie, said: "I remember asking him why he didn't go out with the others. He turned to me and said, 'But they are doing drink and drugs, and I'm not into that.' I never asked him again. He was a very good-looking kid, but he did not date."

Immediately after mama's comments hit the papers, bloggers went to work to alter the conversation:

MAMA ROUTH: *Son, why is it you never go on dates, but stay home and watch old Joan Crawford movies?*
BRANDON: *Well, Mom, they all do drink, and I plan on making it in Hollywood!*
MAMA ROUTH: *Oh, thank goodness. Your father and I thought you might be . . . I can't utter the word.*
BRANDON: *Not at all, Mom. Now could you let me watch the ending of <u>Mildred Pierce</u>? Oh, and can I borrow your ankle-strap pumps?*

At the University of Iowa, Brandon aspired to be a writer and/or a graphic artist. He appeared in some amateur productions at the Norwalk Theater of Performing Arts. To earn tuition money, he modeled clothes. Regrettably, there was no physique modeling, and at least insofar as we know, no full frontal nudes.

Many of his fellow students noted his physical resemblance to Christopher Reeve, who, of course, had played Superman on the big screen in 1978. In fact, Brandon's manager submitted his name as a candidate for the role because of his amazing resemblance to Reeve.

The year 1999 found Brandon wandering the streets of New York City, making women's hearts flutter and gay eyes do a fantasy dance with his chiseled features and broad, boyish grin. Standing six feet, three inches tall also made him a standout in a city with millions of short

people. While in the Big Apple, he made contacts with agents and other showbiz people, but not much came of it. Reportedly, he got a lot of propositions, however. Finding no work, he decided to tempt fate in California.

In Los Angeles, along with thousands of other candidates, he pursued acting roles, eventually being cast as an extra in Christina Aguilera's music video "What a Girl Wants."

Then along came a major part that same year in an episode of ABC-TV's soon-to-die *Odd Man Out*. A director also cast Brandon as Wade in the TV film, *Undressed*. We deeply regret that Brandon didn't take the title of this four-episode night-time soap literally.

Playing a hot, sexy college student, Brandon appeared in 2001 on a WB's *Gilmore Girls* episode, "Concert Interruptus." He was eventually cast, beginning in May of 2001, for an 11-month gig as Seth Anderson on the soap opera, *One Life to Live*, thereby securing what had been, till then, his longest-lasting acting role. Guest roles followed on NBCs *Will & Grace*. As a means of making ends meet, Brandon worked as a bartender at Lucky Strike Lanes, a popular bowling alley in Hollywood. He and his sister shared an apartment together.

The handsome, clean-cut actor—known as B.J. to his friends—attracted attention in Los Angeles, especially when he turned up in 2003 at a Hollywood Halloween party dressed as Clark Kent. His shirt was open to reveal the Superman "S" underneath. A year later (2004) he attended another Halloween costume party, but came as Batman.

Long before Warner Brothers decided to cast Brandon as Superman, many other actors with far lesser bodies were considered—namely Brendan Fraser (one of the few candidates with a body to match the S-Man mystique), Nicolas Cage, Josh Hartnett, Paul Walker, James Marsden, even Demi's toy boy, Ashton Kutcher.

Things changed the moment Bryan Singer signed on as director: He demanded that an unknown be cast in the role of Superman.

By that time, Brandon had turned a ripe 25. Singer watched one of Brandon's videotaped auditions, pronouncing it the "embodiment of our collective memory of Superman." He defined Brandon's Midwestern looks as a "combination of vulnerability and confidence," and noted his resemblance to both Christopher Reeve and the comic book hero.

On August 13, 2004, Singer came face to face with Brandon and that very day cast him as Superman. But for some reason, he waited until October to inform the actor of his good fortune.

Once the director's decision was announced, Brandon became "an overnight celebrity," and immediately went to work beefing himself up for the role. To prepare for the role of Superman, Brandon did workouts that began at 4am, "I did rope yoga, a mix of Pilates and yoga. It's all about core training so that I could be flexible on the wires used to make me fly. I also began lifting heavy weights. I had to change my diet. No more beer when we started shooting in Sydney. No junk food." He sighs. "A lot of vegetables and quite a bit of protein." At the peak of his fitness, he had gained 22 pounds of pure muscle, putting him at a flying weight of 215 pounds.

Filming on *Superman Returns* began in Australia in early 2005 and the film went into world-wide release on June 26, 2006. It is now available, of course, on DVD.

During the shooting of the film, there was much Internet speculation that Kevin Spacey would fall for his handsome co-star. "The idea that the *American Beauty* star may be a homosexual first arose after *Esquire* printed a controversial story insinuating such in 1997," wrote journalist Elise McIntosh. "Since then, a number of tabloids have traced that assumption, trying to 'Out' Kevin once and for all. In response to the allegations, Kevin has repeatedly stated, 'My sexuality should not matter.' The Oscar winner needs to learn that the statement itself is bringing more attention to the matter."

Despite his origins in the cornfields of Iowa, Brandon is hipper than that guy from Krypton. If you ask him, he'll sing Woody Herman's "Caledonia" for you or talk about Dizzy Gillespie.

In August of 2006, Brandon confirmed that he was engaged to his long-time girlfriend, Courtney Ford. His publicist, Kacey Spies, claimed, "They are very happy." Hell, yes. What red-blooded man or woman wouldn't be happy with the prospect of a nightly face-off with "The Bulge?"

Brandon told *People* that "Ford is my personal kryptonite. She brings me to my knees."

[*Brandon, por favor: Please explain more fully to your fans what you meant by that?*]

Since then, Brandon and Courtney have made a 15-minute short thriller entitled *Denial*, directed and written by Joel Kelly. Brandon plays a man who doesn't see that his relationship with his live-in girlfriend is falling apart as she reaches out to him to get things back to where they used to be at the beginning of their romance.

You can also catch Brandon in a brief cameo in *Karla*, directed in 2006 by Joel Bender. It depicts a notorious Canada-based crime case in which a man and his wife kidnapped, sexually abused, and murdered three young girls. Many outraged Canadians called for a boycott of this movie.

The real-life killers were Paul Bernardo and Karla Homolka; Bernardo is still serving a life sentence, whereas Homolka was released in 2006 after serving 12 years.

Just to protect themselves, and just in case the movie-going public falls absolutely, insanely in love with Routh's interpretation of the Man of Steel, WB lawyers have already signed Brandon and his Bulge as the key players in two potential sequels.

The first of these has been announced as *Superman: The Man of Steel,* to be directed once again by Singer, for a possible release in 2009. Other cast members have not been confirmed.

One blogger, calling himself "Hotpants," posted this comment: "At least if Brandon Routh never works on another major film again, he can sleep well at night knowing porn is always a viable option—that is *Super Hung Man* or *Superman XXX*. What about *Cock Steel* or *Superman vs. Assbeads of Kryptonite*?"

So what does Brandon Routh, a lifetime Superman fan, have to say about all this girly gush over him in blue tights and the "S" on his chest?

He graciously replies, "Christopher Reeve is still my Superman!"

"I'm Not Gay," Brandon Proclaims.

In Sydney for a promotional tour, Brandon Routh, the handsome actor who plays superhero Superman, proclaimed that he is not gay. He denied all rumors circulating about him. He also issued an astonishing denial that Superman is not gay either, when all along we thought he was.

Many members of the press claimed that Brandon was "too pretty" for the part of Superman, and that his portrayal was "less macho" than that of Christopher Reeve or George Reeves.

"Even though I am not gay, people will have that discussion as much as they want," Brandon said. "It's a topic for people to talk about. You find whatever message you want. Everybody is going to interpret the film differently."

"I'm sure I will do another one," Brandon said, meaning a sequel to *Superman Returns*. "There is really no doubt. I want to know what is going to happen next as much as everyone else."

Reporters in Sydney forgot to ask him if in the sequel he's going to ditch Lois Lane and take up with another hunk like himself.

"There's always been a hint of Jesus (and Moses) to the character of Superman, from the omnipotence of his father to a costume that, with its swaths of red and blue, evokes the colors worn by the Virgin Mary in numerous Renaissance paintings. It's a hint that proves impossible not to take. Intentionally or not, the Jesus angle also helps deflect speculation about how straight Superman flies. Given how securely Lois remains out of the romantic picture in *Superman Returns*, now saddled with both a kid and a fiancé (James Marsden), it's not a surprise that some have speculated that Superman is gay. The speculation speaks more to our social panic than anything in the film, which, much like the overwhelming majority of American action movies produced since the 1980s, mostly involves what academics call homo-social relations. In other words, when it comes to Hollywood, boys will be boys and play with their toys, whether they're sleeping with one another or not, leaving women to weep, worry and wait to be rescued."

Manohla Dargis
The New York Times

"Director Singer, working again with writers Michael Dougherty and Dan Harris, has devised a beautifully crafted, emotionally resonant and heavily nostalgic Man of Steel guaranteed to appeal to several generations of Superman fans. From the 1978 movie, Singer recycles the fabled John Williams theme (ably supplemented by John Ottman, the new movie's composer and ace editor).

Lou Lumenick
New York Post

"The only semi-disappointment in the cast is Bosworth. First off, she seems too young to have been working for the newspaper for more than five years and to plausibly have had her kid for the same length of time. More significantly, she comes off as flinty and cold for too long, denying Lois a beating heart beneath the brusquely professional m.o. You never get a strong sense of the woman inside the news hound with an unrivaled inside connection to the most famous man in the world."

Todd McCarthy
Variety

"The greatest casualties are the performances: Routh, channeling Christopher Reeve in looks and vocal tics, only makes the late star seem a master of nuance, while Bosworth—unsuccessfully brunette—has all the fizz of a warm can of Blue Crush."

Time Out New York

"In Bryan Singer's film, Superman is played by Brandon Routh, who appears to be under instructions to deliver his finest impersonation of Christopher Reeve. Also present are Lois Lane (Kate Bosworth), who has gained a child but lost much of her zip and wit, and Lex Luthor (Kevin Spacey), whose plans to hatch a new landmass made of crystal seem unwieldy even by his standards. Nevertheless, comic-book fans will gorge themselves on the set pieces and on the now familiar sight of Spacey playing the devil—silken of voice, bare of morals, and infinitely bored."

Anthony Lane
The New Yorker

SUPER STUD FACES A SHRINKING

Page Six of the *New York Post* said it all—"It's a bird, it's a plane—it's superbulge!" The gossip page broke the news that Brandon Routh is supposedly giving the suits at Warner Brothers fits because of his prodigious package of masculinity. The 26-year-old beefcake's extra large endowment is said to be so distracting through his skin-tight costume that producers had to shrink the onscreen depiction of his genitals during post-production.

And that's exactly what they did, or so it was alleged. Although still impressive, only a reduced version of Brandon's bulge was shown, not the rumored $10\frac{1}{2}$ inches.

The well-endowed actor was just too much for even the big screen, much less for showing on TV sets in its DVD release. The word went out from Warner Friars: "Shrink his package with digital effects." Like most gay men, we're rather blasé about digital enlargements of this and that, but we're absolutely horrified by the idea of shrinkage.

Costume designer Louise Mingenbach said, "There was more discussion about Superman's package than anything else on the set. Was it too big? Was it big enough? Was it too pointy? Too round? It was somebody's job for about a month just working on codpieces. It was crazy." Her final verdict was that Warners should absolutely not retain the original size of the package. "Ten-year-olds will be seeing this movie." Apparently, Warners did not want these little boys to develop inferiority complexes as a result of too much visual exposure to Brandon Routh's basket.

It's comforting to know that Superman's schlong will be kid-safe. Had it been "too pointy," toy safety gurus might have had to issue a warning sticker with Superman dolls. "If it was too pointy, it might punch out a kid's eye," said a toy merchandiser.

One gay wardrobe designer at WB was quoted as saying: "If Routh's prick is somewhat larger than is sartorially convenient, any wardrobe wrangler could solve the problem with little more than a roll of duct-tape and some elbow grease. If given the job, I would work for nothing just to get into Routh's underwear."

One assistant on wardrobe said sarcastically, "It would have been easier if Routh had taken that cucumber out of his underwear."

Parker Posey, who plays the villain's dog-friendly girlfriend, said, "Poor Brandon. He's got everybody touching him all the time. He's lying on his stomach and he's got five people coming up and pulling his underwear down, sticking their hands up the butt of his suit."

Brandon said he was "pretty OK with myself and with my space. I don't have special issues with people getting too close to my bubble. And I wasn't even in the room when there was discussion about my codpiece," Brandon said. "Frankly, I don't really understand the uproar over it, though technically I guess you could file it under 'Good News.' It's better to have good news spread about the film than bad news. To be honest, my codpiece was a lot like a football player's protection for that special area. That's pretty much what it is except softer, because unlike a football player, I didn't have to worry about getting hit."

"The first time I wore the suit was really kind of nerve-wracking because there were a lot of people watching me and I hadn't worked out for the film yet," Brandon said. "I kind of would have liked to have done it alone in my own room. About 10 people were all kind of watching and taking notes. I never got to read those notes. Everybody seemed interested in only one part of my anatomy: How was I hung?"

Brandon claimed that the first time he put on his Superman costume, he found it "very confining. But once you get past that—which is sometimes hard—it's also very empowering. First time I put it on, I felt . . . stronger. Like a different level of who I am. It makes playing the character much easier."

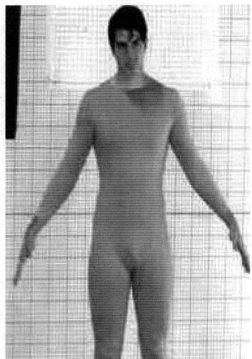

GQ entered the controversy with an open letter to Superman. "Sweet cape! Awesome boots. Excellent tights—and, hey, nice circumcision. Man, we haven't seen Spandex that tight since Brian Boitano glided to a gold metal at Calgary. By now everyone's heard of Superman's Super Package. Seriously, you could call this one *Superman: Boogie Nights*. You need a hit, Superman. You haven't had a film since Reagan's last term. It's time for a comeback, Superman. Embrace the modern world. Ain't no telephone booths in the 21st century. You're going to need a new place to change. Good luck, Superman. We still believe in Truth, Justice, and whatever the last thing was. P.S. Seriously, man, is that thing real? Tommy Lee wants to know."

Richard Johnson in the *New York Post* provocatively printed that "Routh's overstuffed basket must be steaming up the camera lens of openly gay, boy-crazy director Bryan Singer. The horny helmer—who reportedly pushed for Routh over the studio choice, Jim Caviezel—has a history of frisky behavior with hunky young actors."

It wouldn't be America if there weren't dissenting opinions about Superman's big bulge. The website, **www.defamer.com**,("L.A. IS THE WORLD'S CULTURAL CAPITAL. THIS IS THE GOSSIP RAG IT DESERVES.") posted a picture (see above) of Brandon in a tight-fitting body piece, showing a close-up of his cock and balls without underwear. His prick is clearly visible for all the world to judge.

As stated by the website: "[There's a] DVD bonus feature in which [Routh] is wearing a skin-tight, leave-no-nut-to-the-imagination leotard, [which has] magnified the critical area for your bulge-scrutinizing convenience. And while Mr. Routh has nothing to be ashamed of, it's certainly nothing close to the elephantine sex-organ-goiter the press initially made it out to be. Perhaps it's a SuperGrower. And who doesn't love a SuperGrower more than any other?"

Also on **defamer.com,** someone who identified him/herself as a "Generation X Eurotrash Jetsetter Club Member" voiced the following steely opinion. "What's with the artificially phallused male characters this year? Who in Hollywood really thinks that the box office is going to go up because people hear that random, not very attractive actors (*à la* Brandon Routh and Daniel Craig) have big dicks? Especially when there's ample evidence that such rumors aren't even true. Jesus, people, cast Jason Priestley if a big dick is really that important to you."

Another blogger on the same site chimed in with, "Nothing super to see here!"

Even though a debate over Brandon's dick still continues, a fan of this guide wrote in: "Brandon Routh, 4¹/₂ inches or 10¹/₂ inches, you're welcome to take off that cape and those blue briefs, put them under my bed, and crawl in any time you want!"

SUPERMAN—Gay or Straight?

Almost since their inception, comic books have contained a certain amount of gay imagery. In the 1950s, a congressional probe into the homoerotic content of comics was launched, and an organization was created to "regulate content." The fear was that homo-erotic content in comics would turn American boys into screaming, flaming drag queens. So much for Enlightenment during the 1950s.

Even today, like a divided America itself, the jury of public opinion is undecided about Superman. And whereas young straight boys deny and have always denied that Superman is or was ever gay, young men hiding in the closets of America during the 1940s and 50s always knew that Superman was gay and in the closet like themselves, claiming him as one of their own.

The Advocate, in its May 23, 2006 edition, added fuel to the debate about gay Superman with a cover shot of a gorgeous Brandon Routh and a "second coming" headline—HOW GAY IS SUPERMAN? A subhead asserted, "FROM THE MAN OF STEEL TO THE X-MEN, SUMMER MOVIES FLAUNT A BOLD QUEER SPIRIT."

The same magazine made some additional claims as well. Within a feature entitled MCKELLEN VS. SPACEY, *The Advocate's* then-Arts and Entertainment editor, Alonso Duralde, said, "Superman's efforts to avoid intimacy, much less matrimony, with Ms. Lane probably rang true with a lot of young gay readers back in the Eisenhower era."

In reponse to this and to the rivers of Internet speculation about Superman being gay, Super-helmer Bryan Singer issued a strong denial, insisting that the caped hero and Man of Steel is and always has been

"*If you were a little boy in search of an idealized masculine imagery—or a little girl starved for images of strong, powerful women—comic books were often where you got your fill.*"

as straight as an arrow. "Superman is probably the most heterosexual character in any movie I've ever made," Singer said. "I don't think he's ever been gay."

[Really, Bryan, why did you ever say such a thing?]

Singer, in making this statement, seems to have feared that (homophobic) mainstream audiences would avoid, or even boycott, a movie that even inferred that an American icon might be bent.

One executive at Warner Brothers, preferring to remain anonymous, said, "It's like this. Young men are our targeted audience. They don't want a girly man (a term coined by Arnold Schwarzenegger) playing Superman. They want a Man of Steel, even if the character of Superman is 68 years old. This concept of a gay Superman can hurt us at the box office."

Trenton Straube, editor-in-chief of the *New York Blade*, wrote: "The appeal of Superman works on a lot of levels," he said. "On the surface," he's very attractive, but on a deeper level he has a secret identity that he didn't choose to have, and a lot of people can relate to that identity. Although I'm sure it doesn't hurt that he's wearing tight-fitting clothes and you can see his muscles."

Of course, in Brandon's case, you can see more than muscles.

Bryan Singer

Straube also noted that, "If you can be in denial about someone in your family being gay, certainly you can deny Superman being gay. With the Senate vote on gay marriage," Straube continued, "homosexuality is a hot topic. If this were coming six years ago, I don't know that it would have had the same response."

"Superman is a very attractive man, always has been," wrote Paul Schindler, editor-in-chief of New York City's weekly *Gay City News*. "He has a certain virility and an ambisexual appeal. Any time characters are cast as attractive to both men and women, there is a gay appeal. Hollywood loves to play with the gay angle. Even actors who deny connection to the gay world are happy to be cast with a homoerotic appeal."

We know that to be true in many, many cases with the possible exception of the couch-jumping and very heterosexual Tom Cruise, who goes bat-shit whenever someone infers that he might be gay.

Superman, in a view held by thousands of homosexuals, is a gay icon. He is forced to live a double life with his super-self in the closet. The day he finally comes out of the closet, long lines will form in the competition for who will become his new boyfriend.

Rich Johnston, author of the "Lying in the Gutters" column for www.**ComicBook Resources.com**, made this claim: "I'm told that Bryan Singer has a particular theme in mind regarding the film. He's wanting to give the world a new, young gay role model and is looking to employ either an openly gay or a closeted gay who'll Come Out to the public as part of the movie's publicity campaign. Superman itself can also be seen as an allegory for closeted homosexuality."

In the evangelical red states, some devotees of Superman see him as Jesus, a hero sent to Earth by his father (we guess that makes Marlon Brando God) to serve mankind and save the world from Evil. Superman's return to Earth, at least in some Bible Belt states, is likened to the eventual return of Jesus one day as described in the Book of Revelation. If they wish to find it, movie-goers will see Christian imagery in *Superman Returns*. At one point in the film, Superman sustains a stab wound evocative of the spear jabbed into Christ's side by a Roman soldier. In yet another scene, Brandon poses with his arms outstretched as if crucified.

Although we recognize the appeal of some of these Jesus comparisons, we're not sure they're valid. Jerry Siegel and Joe Shuster introduced the character of Superman in 1938 in a comic book. Both men were Jews. They were said to have been inspired by the Old Testament story of Moses and the supernatural golem character from Jewish folklore. The director, Singer, is also Jewish. He claimed that the origin of the story is very much the story of Moses—not Jesus.

"Just like Jesus, in some ways Superman transcends parities and politics and cannot be co-opted to serve the narrow interests of others," said Craig Detweiler, who directs the film studies program at Fuller Theological Seminary in Pasadena.

Rabbi Simcha Weinstein, who wrote the just-published book, *Up, Up and Oy Vey!* (Leviathan Press), concluded that the Man of Steel was really a Yeshiva boy. "Only a Jew would think of a name like Clark Kent," said the Brooklyn rabbi. "He's the bumbling, nebbish, Jewish stereotype. He's Woody Allen. Can't get the girl. Can't get the job—at the same time, he has this tremendous heritage he can't express." And, most scandalous accusation of all, beneath Superman's form-fitting tights, according to Weinstein, "there lurks a circumcision."

Special Feature:
Batman & Robin:
Two Other Queens in Tights

In 1954 when Frederick Wertham wrote *Seduction of the Innocent*, he really upset homophobic America by asserting that Batman and Robin "represent the wish dream of two homosexuals living together." When not roaming the streets of Gotham City, wearing tights and capes, they spend a lot of time at the gym in tank tops and shortie short shorts.

Batman and Robin have long been suspected of being homosexual partners, with Robin the bottom, the older Batman topping him.

Special Feature: Batwoman Flies Out of Cave a Dyke

Batwoman has reappeared and been welcomed back with global press coverage, having made her comeback in DC Comics' 52 series during the summer of 2006. Batwoman—a.k.a. socialite Kathy Kane—has been around since the mid '50s.

The last time she was the centerpiece of a DC title was back in 1979. This time she's an Out lesbian with a detective ex-girlfriend. Even her fabulous high heels are more combat-oriented. The original Batwoman wore stilettos.

Batwoman in her resurrection appears as a 5-foot 10-inch superheroine with flowing red hair, knee-high red boots with spiked heels, and form-fitting black latex. Opinions of the new Batwoman range from outrage to approval, others accepting the transformation in ways more tongue-in-cheek.

"This is not just about having a gay character," said Dan DiDio, vice president and executive editor at DC Comics. "We're trying for overall diversity in the DC universe. We have strong African-American, Hispanic, and Asian characters. We're trying to get a better cross-section of our readership and the world."

Just How Small is Smallville?

Before Brandon Routh, there was another Superman—or at least a Clark Kent. Teen heartthrob Tom Welling, born in 1977 in Putnam Valley, West Point, New York, was a former fashion model before becoming famous playing Clark Kent on the TV series, *Smallville,* beginning in 2001 and continuing for (at the time of this writing) six consecutive seasons.

The series tells the story of a young Clark struggling to find his place in the world as he learns to harness his alien powers for good and deals with the typical troubles of teen life. After a nationwide search, Welling was offered the role in *Smallville,* but turned it down twice before finally accepting. After the series, he was named as one of *People* magazine's "Breakthrough Stars of 2001."

Despite rumors to the contrary, Welling was not considered as a potential candidate for the Man of Steel in *Superman Returns.*

There has been no nationwide speculation over Welling's bulge or as some gays refer to it, "lunch box."

How does Welling's bulge compare to Brandon's? Inquiring minds want to know. The only "sighting" we could find posted on the web came from a gay student who attended Okemos (Michigan) High School with Welling in 1995. It is not clear from his posting if he saw Welling's package in the locker room after he'd played a baseball game or at a urinal. Referring to himself as "Bad Boy," he wrote: "I've certainly seen bigger but no one would turn Tom down if he flashed it in a gay bar."

We have nothing to add to that, but we manage to confirm one crucial measurement for Tom: He wears a fourteen-inch shoe.

Need we say more?

Does Flash Gordon Have a Big Head?

In the June (1975) issue of *Playgirl*, horny young women and gay men (an alleged 25% of that magazine's readership) opened the issue to the centerfold and gasped. There in all his glory was a big, strapping former. U.S. Marine going by the unlikely name of "Andrew Cooper III." As suspected by some readers, the name turned out to be an alias created by the editors to suggest a man of wealth.

Under a different name, Mr. Cooper III went on to carve out a successful career for himself in Hollywood. He is one of the very few *Playgirl* models to succeed in movies. The *Playgirl* centerfold with the big dick made his first film appearance opposite Bo Derek in 1979 in the romance comedy *10*. By that time Andrew Cooper III had changed his name to Sam J. Jones, the "J" being bogus, as he wanted to avoid confusion with other actors named Sam Jones. His real name is Samuel Gerald Jones, and he was born on August 12, 1954.

His big break came when helmer Mike Hodges cast him as Flash Gordon in the action/comedy/sci-fi adventure in 1980. Even though he'd had a different billing, gay men immediately recognized Sam Jones as the *Playgirl* centerfold. This discovery was greeted with headlines around America. Some critics falsely claimed that this full frontal exposure stalled his career. Actually the real culprit was the critical and commercial failure (at the time) of the movie, *Flash Gordon,* itself.

Sam was so well hung he could have carved out a career in XXX-rated films. But instead he chose television and low-budget action films, notably in the role of Chris Rorchek in the TV series *Code Red* (1981-82). Among his better flicks are the romantic comedy *My Chauffeur* (1986) and *Jane and the Lost City*, a 1987 film based on a popular British comic strip.

As a goodwill ambassador, Sam travels extensively throughout Asia, Europe, and America, making speeches, personal appearances, and showing up for charity fundraisers. He has received numerous civic and humanitarian awards during his lifetime, including "Citizen of the Year," presented by the California State Senate.

But in spite of his charitable endeavors, many size queens of a certain age still hang that *Playgirl* centerfold in their bathrooms. You've heard of mushroom clouds. Call Sam "the mushroom head."

The Queering of the Comics

Forget lavender--things are beginning to look downright purple.
Batwoman has Outed herself as a dyke, and Out writer Allan Heinberg
recently relaunched a decidedly omnisexual version of Wonder Woman.
Princess Diana (no, not that one) of the Amazon warrior tribe first appeared
in All Star Comics in December, 1941, the year the Japanese attacked Pearl
Harbor. She was as "beautiful as Aphrodite, wise as Athena, swifter than
Mercury, and stronger than Hercules."

Almost instantly she became an underground icon for lesbians all over
America as an empowered independent female character. The character
was brought to the small screen as part of a popular, and endlessly campy,
TV series that starred Lynda Carter from 1975 to 1979.

Heinberg and artist Terry Dodson relaunched Wonder Woman in the
summer of 2006 as part of Marvel Comics *Young Avengers* series. It's
notable for its treatment of the relationship between two gay teenagers,
Wiccan and Hulking.

Tim Fish's *Something Fishy This Way Comes*, another comic series, is filled
with campy, quirky humor. Fish's past work includes the self-published bittersweet gay romance series, *Cavalcade of Boys*.

Ellen Forney, within *I Love Led Zeppelin* (Fantagraphics Publishing, 2006),
pulls together 13 years of cartoons and stories which include advice on "How
to Smoke Pot and Stay Out of Jail," and "How to be a Fabulous Fag Hag."
each populated with drug users, call girls, militia men, exotic dancers, and
high school dorks. Forney created the series through collaborations with
comedian Margaret Cho and novelist Kristin Gore (a.k.a. Al's daughter).
Forney spends her free time as a wrestler in an all-female wrestling league
called the "Pin Down Girls."

Another recent example of how comics have come Out and Queer is Abby Denson's *Tough Love:
High School Confidential*, a compilation which has been described as "a well-crafted soap opera with a
fable-like charm." Compiled into a single volume based on a successful comic series from the 90s, it tells
the story of Brian, a newcomer to his suburban high school, and his budding romance with Chris, a classmate. Denson confronts issues of adolescent homosexuality with a self-conscious sincerity. Naturally,
you expect such scenes as jocks at school assaulting Brian.

Alison Bechdel's *Fun Home: A Family Tragicomic* is a graphic memoir that documents the author's
childhood experiences and coming-of-age as a lesbian. Her lead character lives with her closeted gay
father, who is an English teacher (which presumably allows him access to teenage boys) and owner of
the local funeral parlor. *The New York Times Sunday Book Review* referred to it
as "a pioneering work, pushing two genres (comics and memoir) in multiple
new directions." Bechdel is otherwise best known for her comic strip, *Dykes To
Watch Out For*.

In a similar vein, Paige Braddock's *Jane's World*, proclaims itself as a
comic strip, "for all those gals out there who are just trying to figure life out,
where female cartoon characters are free to be goofy, flat-chested and self-
absorbed."

In 2007, five of Eric Shanower's graphic novels were re-published within a
single large volume entitled *Adventures in Oz*. Shanower's work incorporates
characters and concepts from the Oz books he'd read as a child, while adding
new characters and storylines in the same spirit of the originals, but with a contemporary interpretation of the adolescent trauma sometimes associated with
"Coming of Age."

32

"Most of our pictures have little, if any, real substance. Our fear of what the censors will do keeps us from portraying life the way it really is. We wind up with a lot of empty fairy tales that do not have much relation to anyone."
Samuel Goldwyn, 1938

Part Two:

Full-Length Feature Films A to Z

"All my life, I've spent time with gay men. Montgomery Clift, Jimmy Dean, Rock Hudson. There is no gay agenda. It's a human agenda"
Elizabeth Taylor

*"**The Celluloid Closet** is a profound account of how the movies have consciously and consistently denigrated homosexuals. Written by Vito Russo, it's militant and marvellous, and must be read by anyone who goes to the movies, and that's just about everyone."*
Arthur Bell, in *The Hollywood Reporter*

"That dikey bitch"
Margaret Sullavan, referring to Katharine Hepburn

AGNES AND HIS BROTHERS

(AGNES UND SEINE BRÜDER)

A Trio of German Siblings Compete for Most Fucked-Up

First released in Germany in 2004, this drama was both directed and written by Oskar Roehler. Some German fans hailed it as "the best German movie in decades!" But most American critics were highly skeptical.

It did not generate massive box office during its limited U.S. release, one theater reporting a weekend gross of $86 in August of 2006. Yet the film did rather well on the festival circuit, opening everywhere from Venice to Rio de Janeiro. As might be expected, the movie did much better in the Fatherland, and helmer Roehler won Best Screenplay at the Bavarian Film Awards in Munich.

What's it all about? Roehler juggles the tale of three brothers—one of them now transgendered—who try to escape from both the real and perceived traumas of their childhood. The film moves adeptly along between drama and farce, with the drama winning out.

Sex-starved Hans-Jörg, played by *Munich*'s Moritz Bleibtreu, one of the brothers, is convinced that the neuroses of his family come from repressed memories of their horrible father (Vadim Glowna) molesting Agnes as a child. With his long, shaggy mane, Glowna, an affluent hermit, suggests a "near-catatonic acid casualty of the 1960s," to one reviewer.

Hans-Jörg plays an introverted sex addict, working as a librarian. The therapy-addled, Peeping Tom turned porn actor is on intimate acquaintance with his right hand. He keeps a mannequin in his apartment for stimulation at night, but during the day slips into the bathroom where he jerks off spying on women through a peephole whose view extends into the next stall.

His older brother, Werner (Herbert Knaup) has his act a bit more together, but not by much. A boorish, deluded Green Party politico, he lives in a mansion in the suburbs. Only problem is, his beautiful wife, Signa (Katja Riemann), hates him. She seems more sexually interested in their son, Ralf (Tom Schilling), whom she likes to massage. Ralf sets up surveillance cameras to catch dear old dad taking a dump on the floor of his office.

Riemann, playing Katja, evokes Annette Bening, and is one of the most talented of the cast. Her *Rosenstrasse* brought her the Best Actress Award in Venice in 2005. Bleibtreu and Knaup have worked together before in *Run Lola Run*.

Last but not least is Martin Weiss in the title role of Agnes, a gentle fragile dancer, a lonely male-to-female trannie, whose transgendered status is inseparable from her tragic aura. Teetering on high heels, she is the most sympathetic of the brothers. When her loutish, blue-collar boyfriend, Rudi (Oliver Korittke), kicks her out, she's befriended by a kooky barfly, Roxy, played by Margit Carstensen, a refugee from Fassbinder films. She should feel right at home here since *Agnes* was so heavily influenced by Fassbinder. Helmer Roehler explores his familiar themes of sexual obsession and inadequacy, as he did in such previous films as *Suck My Dick*.

Weiss is not as well known as the rest of this family, but she brings a delicacy to her scenes, appearing as fragile as an eggshell.

In spite of the best efforts, this satire never lifts off. The movie is an indictment of middle class angst and a Sartre-like journey into existential darkness, yet filled with a certain buffoonish satire. Perhaps it's not soup yet, but the film can be especially engaging in a serio-comedic sense.

But is it Dr. Freud or Dr. Phil?

Above left and bottom right: Martin Weiss as Agnes

"Sometimes perverse and darkly funny, sometimes wistful and yearningly romantic, writer-director Oskar Roehler's tale of a dysfunctional German family gives us both a touching personal saga and a sharply critical portrait of contemporary Germany and its social/political problems. It's a slick, ambitious movie that doesn't always nail all the many moods and themes it's after."
Wilmington Tribune

"Unspooling like a Freudian wet dream, complete with anal fixation, Oedipal conflicts, possible child molestation, and a transsexual title character, *Agnes and His Brothers* reps a Teutonic version of *American Beauty* with added dysfunctionality."
Variety

"The three messed-up adult children spawned by one perverse SOB of a father in this German family drama ought to get together with the damaged brood from *The Celebration* and share pan-European miseries. Roehler spends all his energy on cataloging 'outrageous' behavior and none on giving the transgressions any meaning."
Entertainment Weekly

"The title's pointedly incorrect pronoun is typical of the film's obtuse childishness. Painfully literal/ironic soundtrack choices add to the general unpleasantness, and the nods to Fassbinder's great *In a Year of 13 Moons* only emphasize what this scattershot satire most decidedly is not."
Village Voice

"The film tips its hat to Fassbinder, nods in its title to Visconti, and borrows its loud, solid-colored décor from Almodóvar. The resolutions don't wash, but the movie is occasionally entertaining in a schizophrenic way—like a family reunion that's gotten out of hand."
Time Out New York

"It isn't until the very end that *Agnes and His Brothers* begins to resolve itself in the most unsatisfying way. Beneath the accumulated resentment, contempt and alienation, it seems that love will hold things together. This unearned sentimentality undermines the satire and leaves you simply baffled. Might its message be that the secret of happiness in modern Germany lies in proper toilet training? If so, let's hear a round of applause for clean diapers."
Stephen Holden
The New York Times

ALL-STAR: THE FILMS OF TODD VEROW

Cult Hero of the Underground Film World Compiles a Series of His Independent Flicks on DVD

You'll either love or hate the controversial Maine-born filmmaker, Todd Verow. Born on November 11, 1966—"a day that will live in infamy," according to his critics—Verow has been called the Spielberg of film's new digital age and in some cases, the posterboy of New York City's underground cinema. He's been called a lot of other things as well, but we'd prefer not to print them.

Verow burst onto the filmmaking scene in 1995 with the release of his first feature film, *Frisk*, a notorious 88-minute interpretation of Dennis Cooper's novel with the same name. Under Verow's direction, *Frisk* became a first-person narrative of the exploits of a gay serial killer configured into a deeply disturbing drama about violence. Set into a context of erotic sado-masochism, it exposed the sexual appetites of a young man to whom killing and eating his victims becomes the ultimate thrill.

After the completion of *Frisk*, Verow established his own production company, Bangor Films, which was the corporate entity which subsequently produced most of his other films

All-Star is a DVD containing 13 queer short films and videos directed by Verow. They share a common thread of raw sex and shredded emotions, and as a plus for men who love dick, most of them contain a degree of porn, including in some cases at least one cum shot. *Frisk*, incidentally, is not included in the *All-Star* collection.

Some film aficionados adore Verow's work; others, including many who voted for George W. Bush, find it utterly repellent. Here follows a rundown on the individual films which collectively comprise *All-Star*.

Superstar Make-Up Tips shows drag star "Philly," as played by Eric Sapp, who demonstrates how to achieve that "bruised mutilated look." Philly appears again in:

Fetal tries on all her shoes in a high camp romp designed as a masturbatory aid for foot fetishists. The drag queen does yet another star turn in the short film:

All Star is the short film from which this video collection takes its name. As part of its plot, Philly wanders into a straight crowd at Boston's Fenway Park and endures the stares.

Nob Hill Stylish and hardcore, and loaded with images from an all-male strip show, *Nob Hill* was shot at the notorious Nob Hill Cinema in San Francisco, where strippers tantalize gays with their dicks. *Nob Hill* employs unused super-8 footage which was originally shot during the filming of *Frisk*.

Fluff Sharing several aspects in common with *Nob Hill*, Fluff was also shot at the above-noted San Francisco cinema house, revealing more of the strippers.

Built for Endurance Starring Frankie (Frisk) Payne, this film was based on what became the original screen treatment for *Frisk*. It is perhaps the best of the shorts, giving new meaning to "carving turkey."

Eat Me casts Verow's superstars eating bananas, revealing their talent for the real thing.

Amen depicts anatomically correct dolls having sex with condoms.

Thigh High is actually an extended music video for "SugarBitch's" tune, "Toys."

The Flesh Is Willing tells the story of a bisexual heroine destined for the big time—or at least a better dress.

Operator is a radical reworking of gay French author Jean Cocteau's film *The Human Voice*, a drama that unfolds through one woman's monologue. It was originally filmed in 1966 in Sweden, and focused on a then-aging Ingrid Bergman playing a middle-aged woman who, thanks to a recently ended love affair, is on the verge of a nervous breakdown. *Operator* features actress Susan Becker, who stars as a *femme fatale* working in a fiber optics plant. *Operator* is a pay-for-play melodrama set in a hi-tech landscape in which Verow suggests that with an equivalent sense of ease, you can call either your grandmother or what Verow refers to as "your silicone mistress." And with the same sense of *insouciance,* on a moment's noice, you can launch missiles, thereby wiping out entire nations. One reviewer suggested that you need to be on acid to truly appreciate this film.

The Death of Dottie Love. When this flick was released in 1990, one critic said it was as if "Maya Deren had sex with Luis Buñuel and gave birth to this film." In the 10-minute short, "a flamer," Charlie, is brutally murdered in Bangor. A mysterious prostitute arrives in town to avenge his death. Calling herself Dottie, she launches her grisly revenge, first seducing then drowning Charlie's assailants one by one in her hotel room's bathtub.

V Is for Violet. The final flick within this collection, with a play time of only 15 minutes, this is the story of two teens: a male hustler and an actress named Violet. Originally released in 1989, it has been labeled as both "Orwellian and Warholian—yet as American as a TV dinner." Violet is an actress wandering through her career in this kaleidoscope of color, sex, and American pop culture. Also in the film, a young man tries to make it in New York City but ends up hustling.

 WHAT THE CRITICS SAID

"In Todd Verow's horribly, hauntingly candy-colored films and videotapes, beauty like Verow's camerawork exists in a state of divine agitation. The filmmaker's frenetic and corrosively low-rent visions of the American verities, raw sex and shredded emotion, portray glamour as a kind of drug-induced condition. Gender assignments collapse, narrative logic disintegrates and memory dissolves in a frenzied spin-art spew of teased hair and tangled psychodrama, baubles, bangles and bulging briefs."
San Francisco Bay Guardian

"Embracing feature production on portable digital equipment, Verow has become a missionary for a fast and cheap aesthetic that has created remarkably moving character-based stories."
Filmmaker Magazine

ALPHA DOG
Homophobic Morons Smoking Weed and Shitting on the Carpets

Within a film chock-full of *Sturm und Drang*, we get to see Justin Timberlake take off his shirt, revealing that he was heavily tattooed for the role of Frankie, a drug dealer with the dubious real-life honor of becoming the youngest man ever placed on the FBI's Most Wanted list. Although we've seen far greater chests and even better-looking boys, we admit that no one would turn down Timberlake if he solicited them in a gay bar. Although this depiction of rich boys gone wild received massive condemnation, Timberlake emerged unscathed—in fact, in review after review, he won praise, proving that he can do more than assist Janet Jackson in her wardrobe malfunction.

Time Out New York pronounced Nick Cassavetes' "cruddy" *Alpha Dog* the worst movie of the year. The magazine had a point, at least for gay men. *Alpha Dog* contains pathetic dialogue such as this: "I fuck bitches. You're a homo." How many guys have said that to us over the years? More than one, no doubt. Don't be surprised at such dialogue, though. The sybaritic, monosyllabic, adolescent Angelenos in *Alpha Dog* are each portrayed as homophobic morons.

The film is based on a true crime story from 2000. Jesse James Hollywood (that was his real name) was a 20-year-old marijuana kingpin in Los Angeles, a teeny Tony Montana. He ordered the kidnapping and later the murder of his half-brother, Nicholas Markowitz, because he owed him $1,200 for a dope debt and refused to pay. Young Markowitz was kidnapped while walking near his San Fernando Valley home. Although the kid partied with his captors at first, Hollywood eventually realized the severity of the crime and ordered his henchmen to get rid of the captive. He was shot multiple times and left to rot in a national forest with sweeping views over the Pacific.

After the murder, Hollywood fled to Brazil where he was apprehended in 2004. He is currently in jail awaiting a trial on a charge of murder. Since then, four others have been arrested, tried, and sentenced for the death of the Valley teenager.

The cold-blooded execution of the 15-year-old victim was called "a prank gone wrong." Hollywood's attorneys tried to stop release of the film, because its director, Nick Cassavetes, had been granted access to the prosecutors' files.

As noted above, alleged murderer Hollywood (or Jesse James if you will) was the youngest person to land on the FBI's Most Wanted List. In the movie, his persona becomes "Johnny Truelove," the character portrayed by baby-faced Emile Hirsch, an egomaniacal pot dealer with ties to organized crime and the cocky son of the character played by Bruce Willis. Willis supplies his son with drugs that Johnny sells to spoiled Valley girls and their hip-hopped-up boyfriends. Although a fine young actor in many ways, Hirsch doesn't seem up to the role as ringleader of an amoral gang.

Johnny's father, as played by Bruce Willis, is one of the few actors in the film born before the presidency of Ronald Reagan. Willis looks rather bored as the paunchy papa. All that we remember about his performance is a series of bad hair plugs. Harry Dean Stanton appears as Johnny's grandfather—and one potty mouth he is. Alas, Johnny's role models aren't exactly A-list.

Ben Foster of *Six Feet Under* plays a scary skinhead druggie with a tweaked-out ferocity. "You could almost see him shooting flames from his eyes," in the words of one critic. In the film, Foster, as Jake Mazursky, delivers a chilling line, "I will take you down to hell with me." To borrow a term from Harlem, this trouble-making junkie "disrespects" Johnny by shitting on his carpet and refusing to pay him the $1,200 he owes him for a drug deal. Jake quickly becomes Enemy No. 1 on Johnny's hit list. En route to get the meth-addled Jake, Johnny's henchmen encounter Jake's younger brother, Zack (Anton Velchin).

After being kidnapped, Zack is turned over to Johnny's chief henchman, Frankie, as portrayed by Timberlake, his swaggering sidekick clad in a tank-top to show off his tats. The kid, Zach, is not only young but very impressionable and eager to escape from his protective stepmother, Olivia, as played by one of our all-time favorites, the gay friendly Sharon Stone. Zack forms *Alpha Dog*'s emotional center.

At first Zack seems happy to escape from his stepmom and from his fed-up dad, Butch, as played by David Thornton. While under Frankie's tender care, the henchman introduces the wide-eyed and rather beautiful boy to wild parties, wilder girls, and lots of drugs. The virgin boy is seduced by party girls Dominique Swain and Amanda Seyfried in a pool.

To make the movie more intriguing, we only wish that for gay viewers the screenwriter had had Frankie—that is, Justin Timberlake—take off all his clothes and rape Zack. Alas, no such gay moment.

Meanwhile, Olivia is increasingly distraught. At times hilarious, at other times pathetic, she dons a fat suit late in the film. ***Note to Cassavetes***: *In future films, please keep our beloved Sharon out of that god damn fat suit.*

Daddy Willis makes his point very clear: Even a half-hearted kidnapping is a serious crime. Realizing the mess he's created for himself, Johnny searches for a way out of his self-made trap. The way out is to murder Zack, who then won't be around to testify against him.

The inevitable climax proceeds. If you're familiar with the sensational true-life case that inspired this film, you already know that the cherubic young Zack is going to be brutally murdered.

Some viewers defined this movie's theme as a call for better parenting. If that be so, critics assumed that the parents of Los Angeles "are doped-up imbeciles wearing plasticine grins or else absentee ass-holes waving the occasional iron fist."

We overheard one young man coming out of the screening we attended, say: "It's got drugs. It's got foul language. Violence. Sexuality. Nudity. What else do you want? Great art?"

Regrettably, for gay male viewers, the nudity is more female than male.

To sum up, *Alpha Dog* is about some very rabid pups.

Anton Yelchin   Emile Hirsch   Justin Timberlake

Sharon Stone   Bruce Willis   Ben Foster

"Treading disastrously on the teenage wasteland already fetishized in a million Larry Clark movies, *Alpha Dog* scratches its balls and sniffs its own butt, cynically playing its noxious characters and storyline as rough indie cred. Even Clark's prurience toward his dead-end kids is far nobler than Cassavetes' pathetic slumming in thug life. Note to Timberlake: Keep your dick in the box; three-minute SNL sketches are far kinder to your talents than a feature-length movie."
Melissa Anderson
Time Out New York

"*Alpha Dog* may well go down as the most dispiriting film of 2006. It's a sordid depiction of a bunch of sordid people doing unbelievably sordid things. The lunkheads portrayed in this film would be funny, were the results of their vapidity not so inexorably tragic. *Alpha Dog* is like a perfect storm of teenage solipsism, a worst-case scenario in which the audience's fatalism is trumped by extreme depression. If this is the characters' world, they're welcome to it. The rest of us don't want any part."
Chris Kaltenbach

"The cretins rule in *Alpha Dog*, which has much the same entertainment value you get from watching monkeys sling scat at one another in a zoo or reading the latest issue of *Star* magazine. Of course a little of that nasty stuff may land on you, but such are the perils of voyeurism."
Manohla Dargis
The New York Times

"It's hard to know if Cassavetes is desperate to look cool, or genuinely thinks that Truelove's sexy, surly and pathetically shallow life is exciting. But the only real thrill here is the discovery of a fine actor in Timberlake."
Elizabeth Weitzman
New York Daily News

"For the most part, Cassavetes is essentially just updating *Reefer Madness*, that famously bad 1936 exploitation film, with the assumption that covering his teens with tattoos and injecting the f-word into their vocabulary 20 times a minute will get his point across. If that's the only point he wants to make, consider it done."
Todd Hill
Staten Island Advance

"Foster is the best thing in the movie. For about 40 minutes, he comes at you, at everybody. His character is an elaborately inked Aryan skinhead-junkie from a good Jewish family. (The boy next door, basically.) The guy seems like he fell out of a neo-Nazi production of *Rebel Without a Cause*, blazing through every scene with melodramatic brute force. Foster is too much by half, but he's acting in the film I'd rather watch."
Wesley Morris
Boston Globe

"Don't be fooled by the presence of some pretty-boy actors. *Alpha Dog* is a gritty, gut-wrenching and disturbing film."
USA Today

Justin Timberlake

THE FILMS OF KENNETH ANGER
(VOLUME ONE)

Sensual Surrender, Homoerotic Desire, & Devil Worship

Avid movie-goers who have never seen one of Kenneth Anger's experimental films are at least likely to have read his two picture books, *Hollywood Babylon*, with Jayne Mansfield on the cover showing her tits, and the sequel, *Hollywood Babylon II*, whose cover depicts a grossly fat Elizabeth Taylor in a purple dress. Both books detailed the most sordid scandals of Tinseltown from the dawn of movies up to the 50s. Although they provoked outrage, the books became bestsellers. Anger faced charges of "lurid exposition, wild allegations, spurious anecdotes, rumor, innuendo, and minor plagiarism." The graphic images in the books included especially ghoulish death scenes of, among others, Carole Landis, Bugsy Siegel, Thelma Todd, and Lupe Velez in her coffin. Naturally, Marilyn Monroe got in on this dance of death, and a variety of orgies, suicides, and debauchery were depicted in detail, including the Black Dahlia murder and nude photographs of pre-stardom Joan Crawford.

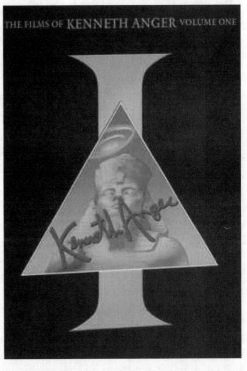

The first edition of *Hollywood Babylon* was actually published in France in 1958 and smuggled into the United States. The tell-all U.S. version didn't come out until 1974.

In addition to his publishing efforts, Kenner Anger made some very unusual films. Those who have never seen one have a rare chance to do so in Fantoma Film's 97-minute DVD release of five of his most famous shorts. The first collection does not include his celebrated *Scorpio Rising* (1963), but hopefully this daring film will be featured in a future release.

Volume One includes the much-restored 1947 *Fireworks*, the 1949 *Puce Moment*, the 1950 *Rabbit's Moon*, the 1953 *Eaux d'Artifice*, and the 1954 *Inauguration of the Pleasure Dome*.

Born in Santa Monica on February 3, 1927, Kenneth Wilbur Anglemyer (later changed to Anger)

Child star Kenneth Anger (right) in
Midsummer Night's Dream

played a child-prince in the 1935 version of *Midsummer Night's Dream*, a film that also starred another child actor, Mickey Rooney. Years later, Anger would recall that "this rite of passage scampering in spangles and plumes through Max Reinhardt's enchanted wood remains the shining moment of my childhood." Mickey went on to film glory, but Anger's career sputtered out. Before that happened, he attended the Maurice Kossloff Dancing School with another child prodigy, Shirley Temple.

Amazingly, at the age of 9, Anger made his first film, *Who's Been Rocking My Dreamboat?* He went on to become one of the pioneers of the American underground film movement—we'd call him the father of gay cinema. In the 1940s, he became known in avant-garde

Kenneth Anger, *ledermeister,* in 1964

circles in bohemian New York and California, but his gritty, often violent, and often homosexual-theme films were too strong for most American audiences. He often worked in France where he was much appreciated by another gay author and filmmaker, Jean Cocteau.

His future avant-garde films would win for Anger the appellation of "a living myth." He would greatly influence the future films of directors Francis Ford Coppola, Reiner Werner Fassbinder, Pier Paolo Pasolini, Andy Warhol and even many of the films and videos later released by MTV.

As the country's first openly gay filmmaker, Anger addressed homosexuality in an undisguised manner. He even developed a close friendship with Dr. Alfred Kinsey of the Institute for Sex Research. Anger, or so it is said, participated in Kinsey's history-making research, even allowing himself to be filmed masturbating.

Ever since the release of *Fireworks,* which he made when he was only 17, in 1947, Anger has been known as a cinematic magician and a legendary provocateur. With footage stolen from the U.S. Navy, he shot *Fireworks* during a long weekend when his parents were away from home, attending a funeral.

The first movie on this newly released collection, *Fireworks* is a homo-erotic dream within a dream. In it, Youngman experiences a series of ecstatic but also violent encounters, and is beaten up by some exceptionally homophobic sailors after he tries to pick one of them up.

One of the most memorable shots is when Anger is being beaten. His nose starts to bleed and then milk is poured over him in slow motion. But the most infamous scene in the film, and its most infamous shot, is when a sailor opens his pants and a Roman candle, symbolizing his private parts, explodes.

Running 14 minutes in tinted B&W, *Fireworks* was a rite of passage for teenage Anger, who became celebrated for his depiction of harsh graphic images of mutilation and sudden violence. Of his own film, he said, "It's a personal statement about my own feelings about violence and a certain kind of masculinity. Also a treatment of a kind of myth in America which relates to the American sailor. That's part of history now, but the sailor was a kind of sex symbol on one or another level. There was a great deal of ambivalence and hostility, latency, and fear of the image."

Cocteau praised Anger's *Fireworks* for coming "from that beautiful night from which emerge all the true works. It touches the quick of the soul and this is very rare." The great filmmaker, Maya Deren, seeing *Fireworks* for the first time in San Francisco, claimed that Anger had opened "a window on our common dreams."

In 1947, Tennessee Williams judged *Fireworks*, "the most exciting use of cinema I've seen."

The second film in Volume One, *Puce*, runs for only six minutes, but it was intended to be just a segment of a much larger film, called *Puce Women*, which was never made. The short seems to be Anger's lament of a Hollywood in decline, depicting a fading star, perhaps evocative of Norma Desmond in the 1950 *Sunset Blvd.* with Gloria Swanson. (The actual color puce, for those of us who weren't entirely sure, is a hard-to-describe tone midway between blue-violet and lavender.)

A loner, the star of *Puce* tries on one outfit after another as she rummages through 20s style clothing, the kind worn by stars of the silent screen such as Pola Negri and Theda Bara. Each dress is more vibrantly colorful than the one before. Finally, the star, as played by Yvonne Marquis, settles on an iridescent puce, "the changeable color of a lowly flea." Perhaps *Puce* was a memory film for Anger, whose grandmother worked as a wardrobe mistress for a large studio.

Puce is a harbinger of the Technicolor epiphanies of Douglas Sirk. The music, a perfect match, was added in the 1960s.

Anger later said, "*Puce Women* was my love affair with mythological Hollywood and the great goddesses of the silent screen. They were to be filmed in their homes; I was, in effect, filming ghosts."

Ironically, despite its lofty intentions, it's the least impressive of the films contained within this collection. Too bad Anger never got to make his full-length feature, perhaps because of lack of funds.

The third short is the 1950s *Rabbit's Moon*, the rarely seen original 16-minute version. As such, it strives to capture the silvery textures of a 20s nitrate film, and is tinted in the dark blue that silent movie directors used to evoke night.

Rabbit's Moon was shot in Paris where Anger attempted suicide. It's a tale about a mime called Pierrot who has an unobtainable goal, thinking he can find happiness if only he can get closer to a rabbit on the moon.

It combines elements of Japanese myth with *Commedia dell'Arte*, utilizing the classic pantomime figure of Pierrot in a chance encounter with the prankish Magic Lantern. The film also features the characters of Harlequin and Columbine. Evoking Anger's childhood memory of *A Midsummer Night's Dream*, *Rabbit's Moon* takes place in a tinselly forest.

The director, Jean-Pierre Melville, lent his Paris studio to Anger. But after a few days, Melville reclaimed his studio and the film was never completed, remaining a "lost" film for two decades until Anger rescued it, adding a Doo-wop musical score.

Rescuing his unedited footage from the Cinémethèque Française in 1970, Anger released a 16-minute version in 1971. There have been other, shorter versions of this film, but the 1971 footage is what is shown in this Volume One release.

Another great experimental filmmaker, Stan Brakhage, found the film, "Beautiful, yet beauty balanced by dreadful necessity, so that it is an emblem of the soul's experience."

The 13-minute short, *Eaux d'artifice*, was shot in 1953, the beginning of the Eisenhower era. After watching this film, Martin Scorsese claimed a renewed realization of how important music is to a movie's success. The music (Antonio Vivaldi's *The Four Seasons*) is in perfect pitch with the imagery. A baroque lady flits in and out of the Fountains of Tivoli, outside Rome, until she melts into the waters. Or, as Anger himself describes his atmospheric masterpiece—"hide and seek in a night-time labyrinth of levels, cascades, balustrades, grottoes, and ever-gushing leaping fountains until the water witch and the fountain become one."

Finally, we're treated to the 1954 *Inauguration of the Pleasure Dome*, a hallucinatory Dionysic and Eucharistic ritual with multi-layered imagery. This 38-minute film, widely regarded as Anger's masterpiece, depicts Lord Shiva inviting guests to a decadent party where they lose their inhibitions as the shadows of night deepen. For music, Czech composer Leos Janacek's *Glagolitic Mass* brilliantly captures the mood with its sinister-sounding arrangements.

Kenneth Anger

In *Pleasure Dome*, Anger appears as a magician, ingesting several substances that open "The doors of his perception to a Day-Glo psychedelia."

There's a lot going on here in this 16mm, shot at an estate in Hollywood. The "Whore of Heaven" smokes a big fat reefer, and Pan bestows the grapes of Bacchus. But Pan's cup is poisoned by Lord Shiva.

Pleasure Dome is often remembered today because of the appearance within it of the diarist and cult writer Anaïs Nin, who arrives on "wings of snow" in her role of Astarte of the Moon. She is part of this grand bacchanalian masquerade where the actors were told to "Come as your Madness."

Nin herself described her appearance, "I wore a skin-colored leotard, leopard-fur earrings glued to the tips of my naked breasts, and a leopard-fur belt around my waist. Gil Henderson painted on my bare back a vivid jungle scene. I wore eyelashes two inches long. My hair was dusted with gold powder. My head was inside a birdcage. From within the cage, through the open gate, I pulled out an endless roll of paper on which was written lines from my books. The ticker tape of the unconscious. I unwound this and handed everyone a strip with a message."

The film was inspired by one of British occultist Aleister Crowley's (1875-1947) dream rituals. Anger was very influenced by this "satan" or "beast" as his enemies called him. "The Wickedest Man in the World" is best known today for his occult writings, *The Book of the Law*, the central sacred text of the Thelema Abbey community (*For more on this, see box on next page.*)

Students of film can be glad that so much of Anger's work is still preserved. Anger's documentary about Crowley's erotic frescoes at Thelema Abbey was "lost" by the magazine, *Picture Post*, which had commissioned it. In 1949, *The Love That Whirls* was destroyed by Eastman-Kodak's developing laboratories because of the company's objections to its nude images. Many of Anger's films were abandoned because of the lack of funding, or else theft, fire, and vandalism.

And what does Kenneth Anger think of all this adulation coming so late in life?

"I've always considered movies evil; the day cinema was invented was a black day for mankind."

Diarist and cult diva Anaïs Nin
as Astarte of the Moon

Satanist iconography?

KENNETH ANGER
FIREWORKS
EAUX D'ARTIFICE • RABBIT'S MOON

mystic fire video

> The critic who forgoes the avant-garde has as much claim to serious attention as a historian who never heard of the Civil War.
>
> J. Hoberman

"Andy Warhol aside, Kenneth Anger may be the United States' best-known maker of experimental and avant-garde films. With their veil of dirt and time removed, the Anger films no longer look as angrily marginal as they once did: these are extremely handsome films, designed and photographed with a discriminating eye. The missing link between Caravaggio and Bruce Weber, Mr. Anger continues to astound and delight with imagery so luxuriant and mysterious that at times it feels almost frightening."
   Dave Kehr
   The New York Times

"Anger dispenses with traditional narrative devices, although his films definitely tell stories, using powerful esoteric images and, especially in his later works, extremely complex editing strategies that frequently feature superimposition and the inclusion of subliminal images running just a few frames. Anger bypasses our rationality and appeals directly to our subconscious mind. The structure common to his major works is that of a ritual invoking or evoking spiritual forces, normally moving from a slow build-up, resplendent with fetishistic detail, to a frenzied finale with the forces called forth running wild."
   Maximilian Le Cain

"It isn't that the visuals aren't stunning in *Inauguration of the Pleasure Dome*—they are. But this Bacchanal ode to an over-indulgent lifestyle of booze, drugs, sex, and the occult repeats its imagery to death. True, it's very calculated and beneath the surface there is something of a story here (and being as long as it is, there should be) but by the 20th or 30th time you see Pan, Hecate and the lot drinking and laughing you start becoming more and more intimate with your wrist watch. It's hard to imagine David Lynch not appreciating this film."
   Shawn McLoughlin

KENNETH ANGER, ALEISTER CROWLEY, AND THELEMA ABBEY

One of the lost films of Kenneth Anger was a documentary, filmed in 1955, on the counter-culture goings-on which had transpired 35 years previously within a utopian community known as Thelema Abbey.   Thanks to its emphasis on sun worship, mysticism, and the occult, it became the focus of moral outrage from conservative religious leaders throughout Europe during the 1920s.

Set in the hills above the medieval town of Cefalú, Sicily, it was spearheaded by British occultist Aleister Crowley and his cohort Leah Hirsig as a school and commune which, in the opinion of its detractors, celebrated "the pornographic exultation of the demonic."   Daily activities included adoration of the sun, a study of Crowley's sometimes indecipherable writings, communal observations of what contemporaries decried as black magic, and an emphasis on general domestic labor. According to Crowley, his dream involved the "Great Work" of discovering and manifesting its adherent's "True Wills."

What both the Abbey and its master actually became was the focus of rumor and hearsay, partly a result of village gossip, but mostly the product of John Bull, a British yellow journalist who aired charges of sexual orgies, animal and child sacrifices, drug use, and bestiality as regular occurences.

Crowley never admitted to any of these charges, but neither did he deny them. The accounts of one of Crowley's disciples who lived at the Abbey between 1920 and 1923 deny many of these claims.

Nonetheless, things came to a head in 1923, when Raoul Loveday, a 23-year old Oxford undergraduate, died at the abbey. His wife, Betty May, originally blamed this, in print, on his participation in one of Crowley's rituals. Later, however, she accepted a local hospital's diagnosis of acute enteric fever contracted by drinking directly from a nearby stream. (Crowley had warned the couple against drinking the water. Lawrence Sutin reports all this in his biography of Alastair Crowley.)

When May returned to London, she gave an interview to *The Sunday Express*, which included her story as part of its ongoing attacks. In the wake of this negative publicity, Crowley was famously dubbed "The Wickedest Man in the World." In 1923, thanks to these and similar rumors about activities at Thelema, Mussolini's government demanded that Crowley be deported from Italy. The Abbey was abandoned and residents, in a kind of moral cleansing prompted by local officials and church leaders, whitewashed over Crowley's murals.

The dilapidated villa still stands today, but in a state of near-ruin. "Abbey of Thelema" is associated today with witchcraft covens and Satanist rituals. It's also the name of a fan club for controversial rock star Marilyn Manson, who included the line "We're gonna ride to the Abbey of Thelema, to the Abbey of Thelema..." in one of his songs. Likewise, experimental musicians Coil refer to the abbey's murals within the lyrics to their song, "The Sea Priestess," on their album, Astral Disaster.

Alas, Kenneth Anger's documentary on Thelema Abbey has been lost as part of circumstances which remain mysterious. A depiction of one of the murals within the Abbey, with its caption, however, is depicted on the right. It's incendiary stuff even by today's standards. Its caption reads, "Stab your demoniac smile to my brain! Soak me in cognac, cunt and cocaine..."

ANONYMOUS
Sexual Addiction Taking Over a Life

Todd Verow is becoming an increasingly famous name in the world of underground films. Once again, as in so many other films, he is both the writer and helmer. Verow also produced the film and plays a character named Todd on screen.

This original psychological portrait, 82 minutes long, is provocative in its violent and frequently degrading "anonymous" sexual encounters with nameless strangers. Todd is a Manhattanite involved in a long-term relationship but also fatally attracted to sex in toilets, which he prowls frequently in search of adventure and dick.

Eventually—and inevitably—his boyfriend, John (Dustin Schell), catches him *in flagrante* in the stalls of a men's room. He beats him up and leaves him lying half naked in a pool of blood. When Todd gets home, he finds that John has changed the locks on the door. Homeless, Todd moves into his office where his compulsion for anonymous sex becomes increasingly obsessive. Todd is the night manager of a movie theater but his supervisors notice his increasing indiscretions and neglect of the popcorn concession. In one extended sequence Todd strips off his clothing in his office, prancing around in his

jockstrap, a scene that caused sighs of pleasure from gay guys watching *Anonymous* at the San Francisco International Lesbian & Gay Film Festival.

In the unlikely event you grow bored with Todd's package, the plot turns a corner. Arriving is an IRS official come to "audit" Todd. An unlikely choice for such a part, Craig Chester, is cast as the IRS agent. Chester, of course, is familiar to fans of queer cinema. Todd finds an unusual means of settling his back tax bill.

     # WHAT THE CRITICS SAID:

"The real love story here may be between Todd the exhibitionist and Mr. Verow the voyeur, peeping in on his character's activities. They look to have a long and happy future together."
Dave Kehr
The New York Times

"Sordid beatings, joyless sex, and a sullen synth score create the air of a home-brewed 60s sexploitation-noir flick, or a pre-Stonewall pulp homosexual novel, complete with narrative clichés and the occasional bit of ugly beauty."
Ed Halter
Village Voice

Official Selection - Berlin International Film Festival 2004 - Panorama

ANONYMOUS

BANGORFILMS presents a motion picture by VEROW
"ANONYMOUS" starring TODD VEROW   DUSTIN SCHELL   SOPHIA LAMAR
CRAIG CHESTER   SHAWN DURR   LEE KOHLER   and   PHILLY
original score by JIM DWYER
associate producer and director of photography ELLIOTT KENNERSON
executive producer JIM DWYER edited by FRANCES COLLINS
written, produced and directed by VEROW
www.bangorfilms.com

ART SCHOOL CONFIDENTIAL

Portrait of an Artist as a Young Man

This black comedy about artistic pretension is not really a gay film, even though it attracted a lot of G&L viewers because of its subject matter and underlying homosexual themes.

Any film with John Malkovich and Angelica Huston, if only in minor roles, can't be entirely bad. Malkovich's performance as a drawing instructor is the most insightful portrait. Ironically, he played two roles back to back in 2006 in which he had a taste for fresh young men—both *Art School Confidential* where he was cast as a blowhard art instructor and in *Color Me Kubrick* in which he impersonated Stanley Kubrick to score free drinks and snare young actors.

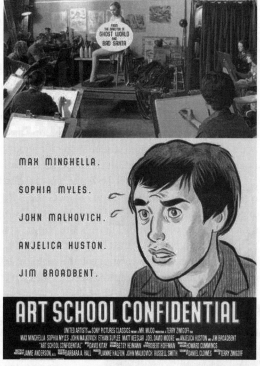

When David Edelstein of *New York* magazine asked Malkovich what it was like to play two characters "who lie their asses off to get into the pants of younger men," his answer was typically enigmatic Malkovich: "Well, again, I think all of that stuff is very normal. More and more, it seems that identity is just a question of what works for the next fifteen minutes."

That's telling them, ol' boy!

The movie is based on a screenplay by the underground comic auteur, Daniel Clowes, who teams once again with the blues-loving helmer Terry Zwigoff. Before *Art School*, they achieved great success with the near perfect *Ghost World* in 2001, where they so brilliantly used adolescent misanthropy as an object for satire.

The star of the film is Max Minghella, playing a young artist, Jerome Platz. The name Jerome evokes an alienated refugee from a J.D. Salinger story. Escaping to New York, Max as Jerome enrolls in an art school that goes by a fictional name although we suspect that it's really the Pratt Institute in Brooklyn. Screenwriter Clowes was once a student there. In his new school, Max learns how the art world really works, and he also gets hip that he must adapt his artistic vision to the reality that confronts him.

Boy Max, playing the schleppy teen and hapless hero, is actually the son of director Anthony Minghella who brought us *The Talented Mr. Ripley* in which we first saw Jude Law frontally nude long before pictures of his cock were flashed across the Internet in a full monty. The elder Minghella also directed *Cold Mountain*.

As an emerging star, Max has dark brows, a pouty, very kissable mouth, and big sad eyes, a definite turn-on to men of certain tastes.

Max as Jerome enrolls in this school inhabited by a gaggle of geeks, lunatics, and *faux* poseurs. The pretty boy's ambition could hardly be called minor. He wants to become the greatest artist of all time, following in the footsteps of his role model, Picasso.

Instead of boy-meeting-boy at the art school, he falls for Audrey, a nude model played by Sophia Myles. The snarky pansexual, Myles, known for her leading role in the 2006 version of *Tristan & Isolde*, becomes the object of Max's dreams at this fictional Strathmore Institute. He hopes to win her love with his talent and unique artistic vision.

The always reliable Angelica Huston (her father would be proud) oozes poise as she plays a world-weary professor, Sophie, The jaded woman defends the art of Dead White Males, sensibly observing that when they did their best work "they weren't dead."

Her performance is topped only by that of Malkovitch himself, cast as the married, bisexual, and narcissistic "painter of triangles" who can't get a show.

Malkovitch, as the snakish teacher, does give his students some great advice. "If you want to make money, go to banking school or website school. Only 1 of 100 of you will make a living in your chosen field."

The only actor in the film capable of competing with Malkovitch and Huston is Jim Broadbent, a fetid failure in a tenement slum. He's very effective playing a booze-sodden artist, as he festers in his cynicism, anger, and despair with much help from Slivovitz.

One of Max's roommates is the queeny but still closeted fashion design major, Nick Swardson.

The film reveals what we already knew—that much artistic hoopla is for minor achievements. In this case the child-like drawings of an undercover cop earn praise not merited. He's played by hunky Matt Keeslar, who looks like a narc and paints like Grandma Moses.

When his rickety plot screeches for oil, the director calls in a serial killer menacing the campus. Some of the characters fall under suspicion, and, of course, the students become paranoid. The plot of a serial killer on a strangulation rampage seems rather contrived.

Sadly, as he pursues his love and his art, our Candide-like hero, the kissable-lipped Max, devolves from his high-minded aspirations to become a bottom feeder like the rest of the students. The film no longer becomes the *Portrait of an Artist as a Young Man*, as hoped for, but *Portrait of a Young Scumbag*, in the words of one critic. There is the suggestion that everybody's got the makings of a phony in him (or her)—just waiting to crawl out and accept a grant.

Several harsh reviews suggested that there has never been a film shot about the art world that's as much an eyesore as this coming-of-age oddity. Yet *Art School* has its admirers.

Anjelica Huston   Nick Swardson   Jim Broadbent

John Malkovich and Max Minghella   Minghella and Sophia Myles

"Filmmaker Terry Zwigoff and underground-comic auteur Daniel Clowes's last collaboration, 2001's teenage alienation dramedy *Ghost World*, was a match made in outsider heaven. Setting their second joint project in the hothouse environs of an art school makes for ripe, hilarious jabs at college-aged Artforum fatuousness. The result, though, is more like a promising sketch rather than a truly absorbing portrait."
   Stephen Garrett
   Time Out New York

"With an *Animal House*-ish deportment, *Art School* likely will entertain a sophomoric audience and etch some winning college kid figures, but art house audiences will be disappointed by its paint-by-numbers storytelling."
   Duane Bryge
   The Hollywood Reporter

"There are two movies vying to occupy the same space here: a teen comedy about artistic pretension and academic double standards, and a darker, nastier movie about a serial killer. They share Zwigoff's trademark misanthropy, but it doesn't delight as it did in the perversely sweet *Bad Santa*. Now it just feels mean."
   Jami Bernard
   New York Daily News

"*Art School Confidential* is a dull and dyspeptic exercise in self-pity and hostility. A movie about art does not need to be pretty, but it should at least look like something. *Art School Confidential* is indifferent to the niceties of framing, lighting and narrative rhythm, as muddled and hectic as a student art project pulled off in a single, desperate, caffeine-fueled all nighter."
   A.O. Scott
   The New York Times

"Hugely funny moments for a sharp, satirical look at the Gonzo world of art!"
   Richard Dormant
   Giant Magazine

"Gay stereotypes, a cast full of hotties, graphic death scenes, a clichéd through-the-glass prison kiss, and the tried-and-true simplicity of a boy meets/gets girl plot. The film fails to transition from spoof to true-crime tale and never truly succeeds at either."
   Justin Ocean

"The chief element making *Art School* hang together is Minghella in his first lead role. Both disaffected and touchingly open to experience, his brooding, expressive face depicts a physically unprepossessing, flawed young man torn uneasily between the magnetic and repellant duality of a bogus world."
   David Rooney
   Variety

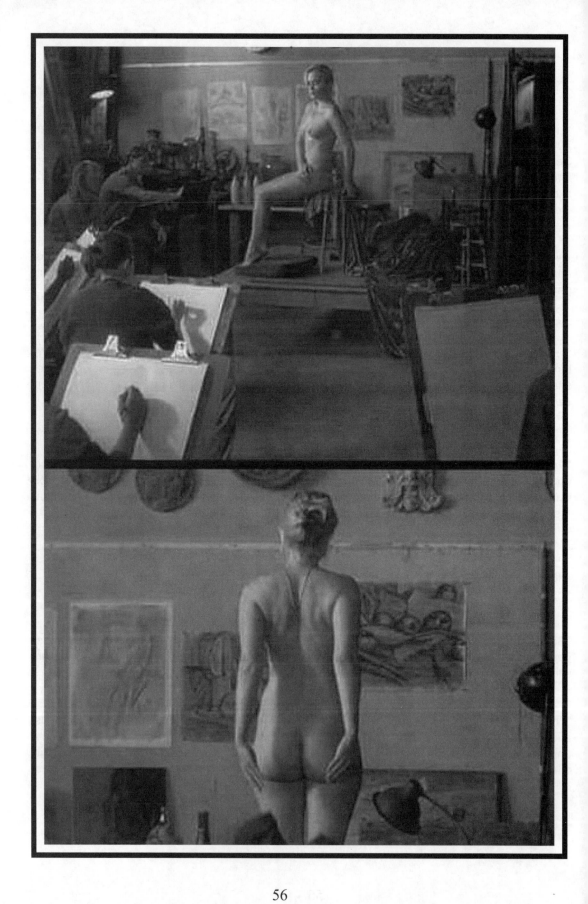

ASK THE DUST

A Moody Valentine to Depression Era L.A.

We had to wait 30 years before *Ask the Dust*, the autobiographical cult novel by John Fante, made it to the screen. It was an ultimate disappointment, but gay men, at least in New York and Los Angeles, flocked to see it. Why? We can only speculate that these men fell in love with Colin Farrell's 10½" dick in his porno flick seen on their computers and were tantalized by word of his nude scenes with the film's co-star Salma Hayek, who plays the flirty Mexican waitress, Camilla.

Hayek and Farrell appear nude right by the ocean, with the waves pounding, but it's so dark you see almost nothing. Better stick to watching that porno flick, where you see everything Farrell has to offer—and that's saying a lot.

Robert Towne directed the film and also wrote the screenplay. Towne was the screenwriter of *Chinatown* and the director of *Personal Best*. Although Johnny Depp had been slated to star, Towne finally cast Farrell as Arturo Bandini, a first-generation Italian hoping to land a writing career and a blue-eyed blonde in his arms. And although Towne didn't treat us to scenes of Farrell's dick, he does allow his star to appear in an undershirt for many of the scenes, allowing us to see his magnificent Irish torso.

Farrell plays a timid, sexually inexperienced writer famished for fame and forced to live on California oranges until his big break comes. Colin Farrell playing someone sexually inexperienced? Not bloody likely.

Towne's greatest success is not with his stars, but in his resurrection of the seedy jumble of the long-gone Bunker Hill neighborhood of Depression-era Los Angeles. The film is only brilliant when it evokes this bygone era we've seen in so many movies on the late show. Actually to find a Bunker Hill look-alike today, Towne had to fly his crew to Cape Town, South Africa.

Arturo (Farrell) meets Mexican beauty Camilla (Hayek) when she's waiting tables at a beer joint. Their attraction is immediate, but expressed with overtones of cruelty. Although each is dreaming of hooking up with an American blond (or blonde), they gravitate to each other, even though he's an Italian American and she's a *Mexicana*—or "spick," as the script stresses repeatedly. The film eventually veers into *Love Story* country.

Actually the only pitch-perfect work is done by Donald Sutherland, who plays Arturo's dissolute neighbor, "Hellfrick." Eileen Atkins, in a nuanced cameo as the landlady, expresses her distaste for Mexicans and Jews, as did dozens of other landladies of that long-ago era.

The 70-year-old Dame Eileen plays Mrs. Hargraves. During the shoot, she made world headlines when she boasted that she rejected Farrell's oft-repeated requests for casual sex. Atkins claimed that the studly Irish lothario spent nearly three hours begging her for her pussy. She said she turned him down because he was 42 years her junior. Rejected, Farrell suggested that the reason he was turned down was because Atkins feared her body "isn't as good as it was when you were young." Atkins countered that "My body is still the same weight, but it's all distributed in a different way."

Guess who produced this movie? The very heterosexual Tom Cruise.

Above and left:
Colin Farrell & Selma Hayak

Urban Decay: Downtown LA site that
inspired John Fante's original novel

WHAT THE CRITICS SAID

"Towne inexplicably softens the story's noir edge, lapsing into melodrama and hammering at his themes instead of delving deeper into his characters."
Sheri Linden
Hollywood Reporter

"Thirty years of gestation have produced a film of great beauty with unfulfilled promise—a disappointment, but with much to recommend and be glad about."
Kevin Crust
Los Angeles Times

"*Ask the Dust* is the ghost of a cult novel; it can't bring itself to life."
Richard Corliss
Time

"There's a lot to be said—really there is—for Salma Hayek and Colin Farrell romping nude in the waves of *Ask the Dust*. If you've seek Hayek in her Oscar gown, or Farrell's lusty, tender sex tape making the rounds on the Internet, you know what I'm saying. It's when they're *clothed* that problems arise in this atmospheric but awkward drama."
Jami Bernard
New York Daily News

"Farrell and Hayek are two beautiful people with absolutely no chemistry. Even when they're lying in bed together, they're so far apart that they might as well be in different movies."
John Pigliore
Premiere

"Farrell's performance possesses a touch too many mannerisms on loan from Tyrone Power and Clark Gable; you can almost hear the gears turning in his brain each time he cocks his head or raises an eyebrow in homage."
Robert Wilonsky
Dallas Observer

Billie Burke and Judy Garland in *The Wizard of Oz* (1939)

BASIC INSTINCT 2
Stone as an Older *Femme* Is as *Fatale* as Ever

We appreciate the gay-friendly Sharon Stone and were rooting for her success in this sequel to the 1992 hit, *Basic Instinct*, in which she starred with Michael Douglas. Many of her admirers had warned her that *Basic Instinct 2*, in which she reprises the role of the murderous Catherine Tramell, wasn't a good idea. And significantly, when he was offered the co-starring part in the sequel opposite Ms. Stone, Michael Douglas himself fled to the border.

We knew that things were going wrong after the first 15 minutes. The audience howled in the wrong places. The writers, the husband-and-wife team of Leora Barish and Henry Bean, will absolutely never rival Shakespeare with the quality of their writing. Sample dialogue: "Not even Oedipus saw his mother coming." "Would you like me to come in your mouth?" These screenwriters evoke Jacqueline Susann with a little help from Jeffrey Dahmer.

Yet another non-winning line is delivered when David Thewlis, playing a police detective, says: "Even the truth is a lie with her!" Although their scripted dialogue was weak, the writing team seemed to like their cinematic sex kinky, and accessorized the onscreen activities with garrotes, handcuffs, and chains.

SHARON STONE   DAVID MORRISSEY
BASIC INSTINCT 2

The preview audience did not remain silent during the show. Two uncharitable young men in front of us mocked Sharon's so-called implants, asserting that in a full frontal nude scene her bosom appeared lopsided.

Whereas the original 1992 hit was directed by Paul Verhoeven, the less successful sequel was directed by Michael Canton-Jones, who captured none of the original sleek wit or craziness. In the sequel, Sharon once again assumes the role of Catherine Tramell, a mass market crime novelist whose prose style seems inspired by the heat of her sexual energy.

In the sequel, Sharon had a tough act to follow—namely herself when she made the original at the voluptuous age of 34. When paired with Michael Douglas, she turned out a blockbuster.

The sequel, however, bombed when it opened in the spring of 2006. It sunk like a stone—forgive the pun. Seeing the sequel made us remember, with renewed respect, the original, even though the '92 version ignited the fury of gay and lesbian groups thanks to its lethal depiction of bisexuals. If there's anyone around who didn't see it—or who wasn't born at the time—they'll get another chance. Lionsgate has released a new and improved "Ultimate Edition" of the first version of *Basic Instinct* which includes a lot of extra footage. The DVD version even includes (a kind of teaser, if you will) a behind-the-scenes docu that insists it was only Sharon Stone's inner thighs that were depicted in the original version's infamous interrogation scene. If that's so, then who is the owner of that big, hairy vagina that flashed subliminally across the screen at the time?

The '92 film provided a cinematic articulation of one illogical yet popular definition of lesbianism: "Something *hawt* girls do just to frustrate and titillate men."

The sequel screenwriters were no match for Joe Eszterhas' original trashy dialogue. One character, Gus, says to Michael Douglas: "She got that *magna cum laude* pussy on her that done fried up your brain." Douglas says to Roxy, Catherine Tramell's lezzie lover, "Let me ask you something Rox. Man to man. I think she's the fuck of the century. What do you think?"

Unless a great Norma Desmond-style, *Sunset Blvd.* role emerges in Sharon's future, history will probably define her greatest screen role as her original version of *Basic Instinct*. It was the kind of part —an ice pick-wielding, chain-smoking, psychosexual, coke-snorting *femme fatale* with a big pussy—that can make or break an aspirant actress. Her part was referred to as "the ultimate spread-em if you got 'em breakout role."

Actually the best part of *Basic Instinct 2* is its opening. Racing through dirty old London whose cubist aspects appear to have been emphasized, Sharon is being masturbated by her *hunk du jour* who drools over her from his position in the passenger seat. The role is played by an ex-footballer, Stan Collymore, who could have had a career in gay porn if he fancied. During the peak of Sharon's orgasm, the car careens out of control and roars off the embankment into the murky Thames. The stud dies, a regrettable loss. But did he drown? Or was the soccer dude already dead before he hit the water? Had some substance already paralyzed his lungs? The death of the athlete prompts a police investigation.

The plot thickens as Sharon is confronted with her co-star, British actor David Morrissey who interprets the role of Dr. Michael Glass, a psychiatrist assigned by Scotland Yard to evaluate her mental state. Inevitably, he's headed for a mind-fuck from Sharon as he is lured into her seductive web. In this crime/drama/mystery/thriller, Morrissey plays his role like a cold fish shrink, no match for Sharon. As the film progresses, it becomes clear that this is one Glass bound to shatter. Several reviewers compared Morrissey to a "Liam Neeson *manqué*." At least his office is positioned within London's most phallus-shaped skyscraper.

In marked contrast to the original version, the sequel subdues any sense of Sharon's bisexuality, except for some Sapphic voodoo that she unleashes upon her co-star, Charlotte Rampling, one of our all-time favorite actresses. Citing, with irony, the "heterosexualization" of Sharon's character in the sequel, one reviewer referred to Sharon's character as FOR MEN ONLY. Of course, Sharon makes discomforting inroads on Morrissey's ex-wife, played by Indira Varma. And, of course, there's the requisite three-way coupling with Morrissey and French actress Anne Caillon. That scene alone prompted the MPAA ratings board to insist on an NC-17 rating.

Although dead bodies pile up in this flick, there is not as much sex as might have been anticipated. That prudery isn't Sharon's fault. In an interview, she asserted, "I wanted a lot of sex in it. I was coming from a really kinky place. I saw a rough cut of the film, and I wanted more nudity and more edgy verbal things. I was like, where's all that crazy stuff I did? What are we toning it down for? Let's face it: this is going to be my last hurrah doing something like this and isn't *Basic Instinct 2* supposed to be even baser still?"

As a result of this film, Sharon endured several bruising personal attacks from critics, some of whom ungallantly criticized her middle-aged body, which looked great to us. As *The Philadelphia Inquirer* put it, "*Basic Instinct 2* is supposed to help Stone show it's possible for a woman to be sexy in her late 40s. But it's Rampling—who is 60—who comes off as the more provocative and alluring. Stone's purring, snarling bedroom kink is embarrassing."

In spite of the attacks on her age, Stone has few qualms about baring all. Despite her status as a middle-aged survivor, she said, "I wanted to do the nudity in a way that's quite brazen. I wanted Catherine Tramell to be quite masculine, like a man in a steam room, and I wanted the audience to have a moment where they realize she's naked and then realize that she's a forty-something woman and naked, because

Morrissey and Stone *in flagrente*

we're not used to seeing that in movies. We're used to seeing Sean Connery appearing in love scenes with an actress who could be his granddaughter."

So, exactly what is good about this movie? It contains frequent nudity, depiction of orgies and graphic sexual encounters, constant profanity, and even violence (most of which is committed off-camera). In other words, all of our favorite things. A line delivered in the film by an actor playing a detective from Scotland Yard sums up this cinematic disaster: "She's not worth it!"

"*Basic Instinct 2* is double trouble—the femme is to die for, the film is to die from."
The Globe and Mail (Toronto)

"Morrissey gives a stiff, awkward performance, while Stone moves dangerously close to over-playing the *femme fatale*. There is little if any intrigue in the story or the characters. Even the murders don't even seem to matter much."
The Hollywood Reporter

"The laughs to be had in this deliciously awful sequel are all unintentional. A hummer for film buffs, but a ball for fans of the misbegotten."
Peter Travers
Rolling Stone

"What we may very well be looking for here is another *Showgirls*, a drag camp-fest for the Baby Jane crowd, fabulous fodder for future cabaret acts and a pleasure probably best enjoyed in a crowd—preferably a vocal one. Dead serious and stone idiotic. The only basic instinct in evidence here is desperation."
Carina Chocano
Los Angeles Times

"Ironically, the demographic that protested in 1992 might be among the few opening weekend loyalists this time around—lesbians, gays, and others once incensed by the original *Basic Instinct* bi-sex-ploitation—are now likely to queue up in anticipation of a stereotype-riddled, all-out campest. *BI-2*s faltering nerve and energy won't turn that trick, however."
Dennis Harvey
Variety

"Stone has hardened into a sort of Teutonic vamp-goddess—a cackling, stone-eyed cross between Brigitte Nielsen and Joan Crawford."
Mike Russell
The Oregonian

"*Basic Instinct 2* isn't bad, exactly, but it lacks the entertaining vulgarity of the first film; it's *Basic Instinct* redone with more 'class' and less thrust. *Basic Instinct 2* mostly takes the fun out of kink."
Owen Gleiberman
Entertainment Weekly

"Nothing compares to the fate that awaited Ms. Stone simply by growing older—older at least in Hollywood years. Now 48, the actress retains the same lucid gaze and whippet-thin body, but in this film her face looks strangely inert, and she seems deeply ill at ease. Ms. Stone has famously denied having plastic surgery, and maybe that's true, but, man, does she look weird here. To judge by the unflattering lighting and camera angles, Mr. Caton-Jones had no particular love for his star. He wasn't about to save her from herself."
Manohla Dargis
The New York Times

Sharon Stone, reprising her role of crime novelist
Catherine Tramell, presumably researching another novel....

BEAUTIFUL DAUGHTERS
"Vagina Monologues" as Performed by Trannies

Just when you thought the world had run out of ideas for reality shows, along comes *Beautiful Daughters*, either the most misnamed film of the year or the most sensitively subtle. Directed by Josh Aronson and Ariel Orr Jordan, the hour-long film explores the collaborative venture behind a transgendered version of *The Vagina Monologues*.

In the film we experience Eve Ensler, author of "Vagina," conducting meetings with a widely varied group of male-to-female trannies. Her goal is to cast her specially rewritten play. First aired on the Logo channel, the docu reveals the process by which the transgendered women's stories are transformed into dramatic theater, in much the same way that Michael Bennett got those chorus boys and girls to reveal their private behind-the-scenes life for his *A Chorus Line* in the 1970s.

The credited cast lists Calpernia Addams, Lynn Conway, Verba Deo, Andrea James, Valerie Spencer, Leslie Townsend, and Asia Vitale. Of the cast, Calpernia Addams is clearly the drama queen. Her own real-life drama formed the basis for the 2003 *Soldier's Girl*, a marvelous film that was one of the great trannie stories, one that should have had a wider audience.

Calpernia starred in that film with the very handsome Troy Garity, who is the son of Jane Fonda and Tom Hayden. Garity's parents gave him the name of his paternal grandmother for the sake of anonymity. In 1998 *People* magazine named him as one of its "50 Most Beautiful People."

There are a lot of trannie documentaries being shown out there today, but this is one of the more compelling.

Verba Deo   Lyn Conway   Leslie Townsend   Asia Vitale   Valerie Spencer

 WHAT THE CRITICS SAID

"The cast represents a wide spectrum from a professor emeritus of computer science, to a pioneer in 'transitioning,' to a stunning ex-stripper/escort-turned-real-estate-agent who has hidden her male past and sees opening night as her coming-out party. As they rehearse, the play's original transcript and performers' unique experiences begin to be an affirmation of reconstitute femininity."

Ronnie Scheib
Variety

V is for WHAT?

V-Day, which is loosely affiliated with the production of *Beautiful Daughters* and *The Vagina Monologues,* is a non-profit corporation that distributes funds to grassroots, national, and international organizations and programs that work to stop violence against women and girls. It's also a grassroots organization that's prominent in the battle for heightened sensitivity for the needs and priorities of transgendered persons. According to its founders, The "V" in V-Day stands for VICTORY, VALENTINE AND VAGINA.

V-Day grew out of the dialogues associated with the conception and production of the Obie-Award-winning *Vagina Monologues.* Jointly, the play and the movement it's based on celebrate women's sexuality and strength, and expose the ongoing violations that women endure on a day-to-day basis throughout the world.

With a highly flexible text that can be adapted to between three and twelve performers depending on the setting and the venue, *The Vagina Monologues* are based on Eve Ensler's interviews with more than 200 women. It articulates many women's deepest fantasies and fears, ensuring that no one who's exposed to it it will ever look at a woman's body, or think of sex, in quite the same way again. *Beautiful Daughters* is a creatively filmed adaptation of *Vagina Monologues*, one specifically focusing on the experiences of male-to-female transgendered persons.

According to *Time Magazine*, "Eve Ensler can soar to Rabelesian heights or move us with quiet compassion." According to actress Glenn Close, "Eve Ensler is a force of nature, a woman alive with passion and conviction. You don't just hook up with Eve. You become part of her crusade. There's a core of us who are Eve's army."

.
"I am not sure why I was chosen," Eve Ensler writes in her introduction to *The Vagina Monologues*. "I didn't, for example, have girlhood fantasies about becoming "vagina lady" (which I am often called, sometimes loudly across a crowded shoe store.) I could not have imagined that I would one day be talking about vaginas on talk shows in places like Athens, Greece, chanting the word vagina with four thousand women in Baltimore, or having thirty-two public orgasms a night. These things were not in my plans. In this sense, I don't think I had much to do with *The Vagina Monologues*. It possessed me."

Eve Ensler lives today in New York City with her partner, Ariel Jordan, who co-produced and co-directed *Beautiful Daughters* with Josh Aronson.

(left) Eve Ensler, author of *Vagina Monologues;*
(center) Actresses Calpernia Addams and Andrea James;
(right) Producers and directors Josh Aronson and Ariel Jordan, with Calpernia Addams.

The Believers

What is This Outrage? Transgendered Persons Singing Gospel?

If they ever went to see it, right-wing Christians would surely stage protests over this intriguing docu. The film follows the nation's first all-transgender gospel choir as its individual members raise their voices to praise God, and as part of the process, lift their own feelings of self-love and dignity.

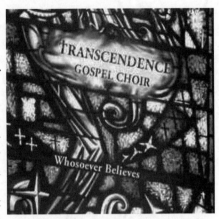

The choir's award-winning CD

Filmed over a three-year period in San Francisco, *The Believers* traces the choir's shaky origins as its members train their transitioning voices and fight over wardrobe. Director Todd Holland focuses on 15 core members of the choir as they learn to sing. Their intimate, personal stories are relayed in ways that evoke *A Chorus Line* on Broadway.

The Transcendence Gospel Choir homepage summed it up rather nicely. "We endeavor to demonstrate that the preconceived notion of a bi-polar, heterosexual, hetero-gendered 'natural order' is not reflected in the nature of God or the ministry of Jesus Christ. In this way we will challenge intolerance and hatred, transcend boundaries and restore hope to our communities."

At docu's end, the film had moved heartwarmingly through a depiction of the choir's tribulations into a polished account of an award-winning choir and a close knit family.

The Transcendence Gospel Choir has presented major performances across the country, and in 2004 the choir won an Outmusic Award for its album, *Whosoever Believes*. Although the choir stresses its interdemoninational roots, it's loosely affiliated with the United Church of Christ.

 WHAT THE CRITICS SAID

"At the heart of the dilemma is a struggle for acceptance within two worlds historically at odds with one another. As one of the film's subjects eloquently says, 'I'm living in a window. I get to see both sides.' *The Believers* is a unique story of determination and perseverance and an important look at the intricacy and diversity of spirituality and the LGBT community."
Justin Kolling

"Personalities sketched, from a male-to-female former crack addict and convict to a one-time radical lesbian turned computer-programmer dude, are incredibly diverse, even beyond the sphere of gender-identity complexities. Pic skims over interpersonal problems within choir, keeping the focus on their rousing performances."
Dennis Harvey
Variety

"Gay men are not my preference. People have their likes and dislikes. But I don't suck dick."

Mark Whalberg, 1993

"I did a movie with John Wayne and was very surprised to find out he had small feet and wore lifts and a corset. Hollywood is seldom what it seems."

Rock Hudson

BEYOND CONCEPTION: MEN HAVING BABIES

Sperm Twin-Pack Meets Donated Eggs

The joys of pregnancy

Johnny Symons' docu is about baby fever—in this case two male lovers who, of course, can't have children biologically and who opt for technology instead. They are obviously fed up with the adoption process, which, in fact, is illegal in such states as Florida, thanks in no small part to former orange juice warbler, Anita Bryant. The precursor and virtual companion to this docu is Symons' previous film *Daddy & Papa*, released in 2002.

Based in San Francisco, Bruce Gilpin and Paul Moreno turn to a lesbian couple to be their surrogates. Jennifer and Jenna Franet (same last name) who are also based in San Francisco, already have two children of their own from Jennifer's former hetero marriage. But whereas Jennifer Franet will actually carry the pregnancy to term, the actual eggs for the pregnancy were donated by a young woman known as "Jade," and subsequently inserted into Jennifer's uterus.

The movie explores the doubts that the two men have about their choice of the Franets as "birth partners." And there are even some doubts expressed about the suitability of those eggs donated by Jade: Although she's bright and alluring, Jade has a troubled family history of breast cancer.

As seen through Syman's unflinching lens, the plot quickly gets even more complicated. While Jennifer is carrying to term a child who's the product of either Bruce or Paul's sperm and Jade's egg, Jenna Franet is trying for her own conception as a means of adding to the the Franet's already existing family. "A child of our own," so to speak.

A 65-minute edition of the film was aired in the summer of 2006 on the Discovery Health Channel, but for those interested in the subject, it's better to see Symons' longer version.

A provocative question was asked at a Florida film festival: "The future is certainly all about children, but this film begs the question, 'What is the future of the family?'"

 WHAT THE CRITICS SAID

"Oh brave new rainbow-colored world! Just when you thought you knew everything there was to know about getting in the family way, here's another twist. Gay men on a mission, feisty lesbians with opinions, lots of money, donated eggs, sperm, *uteri* (or is it uteruses?), surrogate contracts. And let's not forget romance. Just make sure they're separate from the actual act of conception."
15th Annual Florida Film Festival

"*Beyond Conception* humanizes the topic of gay couples' arranging for a child, a subject that is often treated impersonally in the media. The high price of such technology is never mentioned: Pic is thus stronger at the beat-by-beat account of this single birth rather than in addressing the larger topics it naturally raises."
Robert Koehler
Variety

 SUPERMAN CHRISTOPER REEVE PLAYED GAY CHARACTERS ON-STAGE IN *THE FIFTH OF JULY*, AND ON-SCREEN IN *DEATHTRAP*. AS FOR A NUDE APPEARANCE......

"I might have gone the nude route if I hadn't done Superman, which is a role model... But if I ever did do nudity, I certainly wouldn't stand in front of the cameras and wave!"

WILLIAM HURT PERFORMED NUDE IN HIS SCREEN DEBUT, *ALTERED STATES*, AND LATER, IN *BODY HEAT*. HE ALSO APPEARED IN FULL DRESS-DOWN DRAG, LOOKING ADORABLE, WE MIGHT ADD, IN *KISS OF THE SPIDER WOMAN*.

"Nudity is an assignment, like learning several pages of script. No more no less...I will never agree to being used as a sex symbol. But if I'm nude and it's attractive to someone in the audience, what could be more natural? What's the big deal?"

A BIGGER SPLASH

New DVD Presents What Was Originally Banned for Its In-Your-Face Queer Imagery

At long last in DVD, this formerly banned semi-docu from 1971 is now available for our viewing pleasure, depicting a lot of hot dudes from the 70s. Seemingly anticipating reality TV, it traces the life of the legendary painter David Hockney, presenting a sexy and stirring portrait of the artist.

Real people play themselves in this partly fictionalized tale of Hockney, who was noted for his color and specialization in "California subjects," centering around gay life. In his paintings, Hockey was fascinated by the swimming pools of Los Angeles—hence, the name of the film. Of course, within the film, those swimming pools are filled with handsome young men in the buff.

For three-and-a-half years (1970-1973), Hockney allowed filmmakers Jack Hazan and David Mingay to follow him around with a camera as he interacted with friends, lovers, and business associates. Reportedly, Hockney, with his white blond hair (à la Warhol) and thick black-rimmed glasses, was shocked at the final result because it penetrated his personal life as deeply as it did.

The action, such as it is, takes place during a period in which Hockney and his lover, the model, Peter Schlesinger, are breaking up. The beautiful and androgynous Schlesinger served as both Hockney's lover and muse. In the docu, Hockney is attempting to finish his last painting of Schlesinger after destroying and repainting it several times.

Most daring of all is a scene in which Schlesinger and another young man make love.

With all its flaws, this is nonetheless a very important addition to gay cinema.

 WHAT THE CRITICS SAID

"However, accurate (or not) the film may be depicting Hockney's daily life, it's undeniably a powerful time capsule—a vivid, intense depiction of the swinging London of the 60s during its last dying gasps. In a lot of ways, *A Bigger Splash* plays like *Blowup* with a lot of gay sex. The film's abundant full frontal male nudity and frank depictions of homosexual sex inevitably limit its appeal to a straight—particularly straight male—audience. At the same time, it's unfortunate that *A Bigger Splash* has to be confined to such rigid pigeon-holing—it's an intriguing take on the creation of art and the artistic temperament."
Judge Jesse Ataide

"The final result is a film where the scenes simply do not come together to tell any kind of rational or comprehensible story. One major problem is that the people featured in the film are not identified or explained. A friend? A lover? A fellow artist? Or maybe just the artist's tailor."
DVD Talk Review

Nick's Pool, by David Hockney

David Hockney (born 1937)

THE BLACK DAHLIA
Tangled Plot Ensnares This Lurid Film Noir

Originally Sharon Stone was going to appear in Brian De Palma's *The Black Dahlia*, an adaptation of James Ellroy's novel about the most notorious unsolved murder in California history. But halfway into the book, she ran to the border. "Too dark!" she fumed.

Others followed suit until Scarlett Johansson signed on, as did Josh Hartnett and Hilary Swank.

In 1947, starlet Elizabeth Short, who became known as "The Black Dahlia," was found chopped up and disembow-eled. The case has never been solved. The naked corpse was discovered dumped in a South Central lot, her blood drained, her legs splayed, and her face carved into a jack-o'-lantern grin. The press soon dubbed her "The Black Dahlia" because of her dark hair and matching wardrobe.

Over the years she's entered Hollywood mythology, and this movie adds to her legend. At one point Orson Welles was among the celebrity suspects, even Franchot Tone, the bisexual actor once married to another bisexual, Joan Crawford.

The movie isn't so much about the Dahlia but about the posthumous spell she cast on two cops, Bucky Bleichert (Josh Hartnett at his laconic best) and Lee Blanchard (Aaron Eckhart). Both men play ex-prizefighters. Lee introduces Bucky to his girlfriend, Kay (Scarlett Johansson), a lush-lipped blond dish.

Johansson plays dress-up like a mini-Lana Turner, which she, of course, could never be. No one did *femme fatale* like Lana. During the making of this film, Hartnett and Johansson were red-hot lovers off screen but merely gorgeous stiffs on screen.

Our favorite scene is when Bucky (or Hartnett) wanders into La-La Lesbian Land at a swanky sup-per club where k.d. lang sings "Love for Sale." Several dozen lesbian chorines gather in a mock orgy for-mation on a grand staircase. Here Bucky pursues another "Black Dahlia," played by a glamorous Hilary Swank, who delivers the most dynamite performance in the film. However, some critics attacked her bisexual role, saying she was miscast as a mysterious *femme fatale*. "Sexy isn't Swank's strong suit," wrote Walter Scott in *Parade* magazine. He claimed that movie-goers want her to play tomboys as in *Million Dollar Baby* (2005).

We totally disagree. We adored Swank when she took off her boxing gloves and played a sexy vamp. In the film she comes from a wealthy but freaky L.A. family.

Swank, playing an heiress with a taste for the low life, seduces Bucky. Dressed like a post-mortem Dahlia, she's got plenty of sex appeal. It is Hartnett who can't get a hard-on in this flicker. There is absolutely no heat between the two of them.

Swank introduces Hartnett to her family, the wacko Linscotts. Her father (John Kavanagh) is a self-made real estate millionaire and a megalomaniac. But the unhinged pill addict of a mother, Fiona Shaw, is something out of *Sunset Blvd*. She steals the show as the crazy rich bitch matriarch. Her demented histrionics are fun to watch, more campy than revelatory.

There are some intriguing things in *The Black Dahlia*—it was good to see the wonderful cinematog-rapher Vilmos Zsigmond working in full command of his talent on a big picture after several years pur-suing marginal projects. Much of the film was shot in Bulgaria but you'd never know that.

As Bucky plunges deeper into Hollywood's heart of darkness, the film grows murky. It was never too clear to begin with.

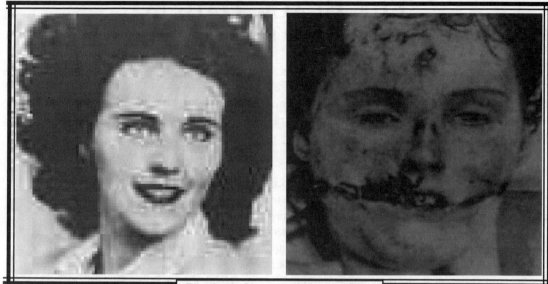

Elizabeth Short, before and after

 WHAT THE CRITICS SAID

"Steeped in sexual pathology, replete with mutilation, fetishes, and porn, Ellroy's Dahlia scenario would seem to be De Palma's meat. The movie, however, is anything but overheated and largely impersonal. The exposition is sluggish. For all the posh dollies, high angles, and Venetian blind criss-cross patterns, *The Black Dahlia* rarely achieves the rhapsodic (let alone the delirious)."
J. Hoberman
Village Voice

"This overripe period detail, doused in thick, glowing amber (is this a movie or a pancake?) has a kitsch waxworks quality to it, complete with the kind of hard-boiled 40s-era voiceover that no doubt made Edward G. Robinson a very popular party guest. The brief glimpses we do get of Dahlia herself, both as a gruesome corpse in police photos and as a sad lost girl in myriad screen tests, are the most compelling thing about the movie. But even she gets lost in the teeming swarm of morally compromised and terminally obsessive characters, each burdened with a Byzantine past and hulls full of florid baggage."
Carina Chocano

"Only Ms. Swank, who puts some Katharine Hepburn into her voice and just as much conviction into the rest of her performance, delivers the goods. Her character, a rich brat out of Raymond Chandler by way of Mr. Ellroy (think *The Big Sleep*, but creepier) lives with her whack-job family in one of those mansions that serves as a tomb for its inhabitants and a monument to their ambitions. Mr. De Palma obviously enjoys hanging out with this decadent brood, whose demons read as symptomatic of the city it calls home and whose pathologies prove nattily entertaining."
Manohla Dargis
The New York Times

"Hilary Swank is Madeleine Linscott, a randy rich woman who looks a bit like Short, slept with her once, and—after her death—takes to dressing like her while prowling lesbian bars. Scarlett Johansson is an ex-hooker given more loving close-ups than Garbo got in *Camille*. The convoluted plot would be exhausting if it were believable. It isn't."

Jack Mathews
New York Daily News

"Eckhart gives such an excellent account of himself that the movie suffers when he's off the screen. The wooden Hartnett (who is apparently contractually obligated to take off his shirt in every movie) and the bland Johansson (who wears 40s clothes well in an underwritten role) confirm their reputation as two of the most overhyped actors of their generation."

Lou Lumenick
New York Post

"In classic noir fashion, a smoky haze seems to suffuse much of the atmosphere. Unfortunately a narrative haze obscures much of the story. *The Black Dahlia* moves beyond pulp and takes a nosedive into the realm of pap."

Claudia Puig
USA Today

Mia Kirshner

Hilary Swank

Josh Hartnett

Aaron Eckhart

Scarlett Johansson

Elizabeth Short's dismembered body, as dumped in a vacant lot in South-Central Los Angeles in 1947. The crime remains unsolved.

BLADES OF GLORY

Ice Queens

Will Ferrell as a figure skater—that's a bit much. He uses his flab to droll effect, as he teams with a male partner, Jimmy MacElroy (played by Jon Heder of *Napoleon Dynamite*). In the film, Heder's character is a blond-haired girly man who's supposed to be straight. If you believe that, then you believe that Liberace was straight and that George Bush eats cheese imported from the moon.

In this comedy where machismo goes hand in hand with homosexual panic, Ferrell plays a slob, Chazz Michael Michaels, a sex-obsessed galoot. When he sees a female fan, he likes to grab his crotch, and hopefully he has more to grab than either Madonna or Michael Jackson.

The weak plot has the rivals breaking out in a fist fight in front of their stadium fans, which ends in their lifetime disbarment in the singles competition. The directors, Will Speck and Josh Gordon, have a certain brilliance in sending up TV blowhards and celebrity athletes, although you might say both those elements are easy targets. The directors are the creators of those GEICO cavemen commercials. That may not be a recommendation for the movie, however.

Along comes coach, Craig T. Nelson, who finds a loophole in the skating commission's rules. Barred from competing solo, there is nothing in the rule book that says Ferrell and his femme partner can't compete as a male duo.

As a skating promoter, Darren MacElroy (William Fichtner) is marvelously unctuous. He adopts child prodigy Jimmy and raises him to perform in one of the most effeminate acts on ice. At the end of his performance, Jimmy releases a white dove and at one point he impersonates a peacock. He's also not opposed to wearing pink in case gays don't get the message.

The villains of the piece are Will Arnett and Amy Poehler as Stranz and Fairchild Van Waldenberg, an incestuous brother-and-sister pair whose characters evoke a pill-popping Marilyn Monroe and her lover, JFK, on ice. Their kissing scene is okay. In real life, they're not really siblings, but a married couple.

Appearing in cameos are skating legends Brian Boitano, Nancy Kerrigan, Peggy Fleming, and Dorothy Hamill.

"Hey, you guys, figure skating—it's girly! We know this because the men have powder blue outfits, stuffed animals, reflective jumpsuits, a tattoo centered above the butt, Farrah Fawcett hair, sequins, a polar bear rug, poetry, fringe, 'a couple of diaper bags I made for Faith Hill,' a pink sash, a *Breakfast at Tiffany's* poster, a shiny silver scarf, homoerotic skating routines (crotch to face, crotch to butt, crotch to crotch, crotch to crotch again, a cranberry-colored stole, a 'Kristi Yamaguchi' lifetime achievement award, headbands, a hankering for cosmetics, and a $12,000 hairbrush with which 'I brush my hair 100 times.' Ferrell is supposed to be a butch rocker, but the script can't resist throwing a lot of girly and gay stuff his way. You might be offended because the movie's anti-gay, but what's really unforgivable is that it's anti-funny."
Kyle Smith
New York Post

"The notion of a male figure-skating team in which one member is a chest-beating, fire-breathing Lothario and the other a persnickety, virginal girly-man cries out for the kind of easy, gay-baiting jokes that mars comedies like *Wild Hogs*."
Stephen Holden
The New York Times

"The one drawback is that the implicit movie-long gag, about how ridiculous it is to watch men dance with each other, may strike some auds as one long, unspoken but obvious gay joke—and they wouldn't be far off."
John Anderson
Variety

"Never mind the opening weekend grosses; a few more of these cash-ins, and Ferrell may find himself on thin you-know-what."
David Fear
Time Out New York

"The idea is better than the movie: The adventures on and off the ice, and the endless flow of innuendo (lots of crotch jokes and winking allusions to homosexuality), signify humor without actually being funny."
Richard Brody
The New Yorker

"There's a hetero romance between emotionally abused ingénues: Jimmy and a radiantly pretty Jenna Fischer as the sister of a conniving brother-sister skating team. But that's window dressing. Better are the scenes in which each man learns to overcome his revulsion to being touched by another dude. The climatic ice dance—to Queen's immortal theme from *Flash Gordon* ('Flash! Ah-ahhh! Savior of the universe!')—might be the apotheosis of man-boy love. Platonic, of course."
David Edelstein
New York Magazine

THE BLOSSOMING OF MAXIMO OLIVEROS
(ANG PAGDADALAGA NI MAXIMO OLIVEROS)

Remember the First Time You Fell in Love?

A buoyant and endearing film, this Filipino movie is groundbreaking in that it presents a 12-year-old queer pre-teen without trepidation or compromise. Nathan Lopez plays a girly little boy, Maxi, a kid growing up on the seedy side of Manila.

He dotes on his father and two brothers but falls for a handsome and older police officer, Victor (JR Valentin). The film is directed with charm, clarity, and insight by Auraeus Solito, who worked from a perceptive script by Michiko Yamamoto. A colorful, exotic portrait of sexual awakening is presented. The young teenage boy has a desire for cross-dressing, and his family earns their living with petty thefts.

There are hints of eroticism between Maxi and the rookie cop who takes him under his wing, and there are near-romantic encounters at times, although the helmer keeps it platonic.

Maxi's family consists of Paca (Soliman Cruz), who loves Maxi, as do his older brothers, Boy (Neil Ryan Sese) and Bogs (Ping Medina). Maxi cooks for "the men in his life," and also mends their clothes. He provides, in fact, the glue that binds the family together, since the mother is dead.

Maxi, wearing lipstick, walks the shantytown back alleys of Manila in a kind of hip-swiveling fabulousness, as if these dark alleys were pageant catwalks.

Stick around for the final scene, a heartfelt tribute to Carol Reed's 1949 masterpiece, *The Third Man.*

This film comes as a wake-up call—dare we suggest mini-Renaissance?—in the country's long dormant cinema.

Nathan Lopez as Maximo, and JR Valentin

"*The Blossoming of Maximo Oliveros* is a unique coming-of-age film, for Maxi is such an intriguing mix of the streetwise and the innocent, self-aware yet emotionally vulnerable. Solito's ability to inspire such a daring, unself-conscious portrayal from Lopez is no less than astonishing. The film's graceful, richly hued cinematography and its beguiling score contribute crucially toward the making of a distinctive and outstanding achievement."

Kevin Thomas
Los Angeles Times

"The film has charmed audiences with its refreshingly blasé handling of homosexuality, its amiable actors, and its delicacy of milieu. Credit, above all, the talented Mr. Lopez, whose effortless charisma buoys the movie even when it goes heavy with contrivance."

Nathan Lee
The New York Times

"Maxi's attraction to Victor is presented with an honesty few American directors could muster. But the film doesn't achieve the dramatic tension its deadly finale requires."

Tom Beer
Time Out New York

"It's hard to tell the boys from the girls in *Blossoming*. Biologically, Maxi is a boy. At heart, he's a girl. He looks like one, walks like one, dresses like one, and thinks like one."

V.A. Musetto
New York Post

"Forget *Brokeback Mountain*. It didn't deserve an Oscar anyway. Anyone fooled by Ang Lee's Heath Ledger/Jake Gyllenhaal film should rush to see *The Blossoming of Maximo Oliveros*. It offers the real thing—progress."

Armond White
New York Press

"Auraeus Solito's feature debut confronts the taboo of pre-teen sexuality with a startling mix of openness and sensitivity. No less than precocious Maxi, the film is alarming, endearing, and utterly unflappable."

Dennis Lim
Village Voice

We congratulate this film's director,
AURAEUS SOLITO
for his designation as runner-up for
BLOOD MOON'S BEST DIRECTOR AWARD
for his work in
The Blossoming of Maximo Oliveros

THE BOOK OF DANIEL

Pill-popping Priest with Family Issues Talks Directly to Jesus.

It seemed as if NBC within this TV series wanted to add some spice to their nightly line-up and provoke the ire of the religious right as a means of getting more viewers to tune in. The ill-fated series starred the handsome Aidan Quinn as a Vicodin-addicted Episcopal priest who talks to Jesus and has a gay Republican son (Christian Campbell). That's not all. His sister-in-law is bisexual.

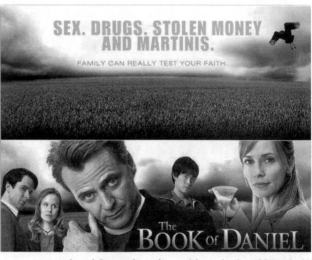

The anti-gay American Family Association denounced the dramedy, but its own creator, out Jack Kenny, seemed none too alarmed. The association in particular objected to the "unconventional" white-robed and bearded Jesus who spoke to Daniel. Kenny responded, "Isn't that the most conventional Jesus there is—white robed and bearded?"

In an interview with *The Advocate*, Kenny was asked: "The Episcopal Church is facing a schism over homosexuality. Will the show address that?"

He responded, "I'm hoping down the line that Peter (Daniel's gay son) will want to get married and have his father perform the ceremony."

Daniel's troubles go way beyond having a gay son. His wife, Judith (Susanna Thompson), loves her early-day martinis. Their 16-year-old daughter Grace (Alison Pill) sells pot. They also have an adopted son, Adam (Ivan Shaw), who is Chinese, opening the door for all manner of ethnic jokes. This Chinese son is busted for banging a rich parishioner's daughter.

There's a subplot as well—a brother-in-law stole the rich parishioner's money before being murdered by his lesbian girlfriend who is seducing the murdered man's wife.

Garrett Dillahunt plays Jesus Christ as a slow, dull "buddy parent," who has no insights, no healing abilities, and, in the words of one critic, "just passively nags Daniel to quit" his bad habits.

Ellen Burstyn delivers as Bishop Congreve. She isn't above sampling from Daniel's pill chest.

The helmer links the Catholic church to the Mafia. The church is represented by a priest played by noted heavy Dan Hedaya. One of these Mafioso types confesses to Daniel that he's gay.

The victim, as played by Mia Kirschner, is a wannabe starlet with a taste for men in uniform and a couple of credits in porn flicks.

Regrettably the series was canceled after only four episodes. Of course, pressure from conservative Christian groups might have been the reason. But we suspect that the real reason is that no TV viewer watched the series.

Heartthrob Aidan Quinn as an Episcopal priest with his personal Jesus

WHAT THE CRITICS SAID

"Unfortunately for viewers, the clips don't add up to anything more than soapy froth and, well, it's no great feat to pull a stem-winder on religious groups these days."
Tim Goodman
San Francisco Chronicle

"There's an underlying message in all this—namely, that everyone, the reverend included, is human and struggling to do right, however crazy and mixed up they might be."
Brian Lowry
Variety

"If you're gay or anti-religion and want to see a bunch of religious straw men knocked down repeatedly, this will be an excellent addition to your *Will & Grace* collection."
Don Houston
DVD Talk Review

BORAT: Cultural Learnings of America for Make Benefit Glorious Nation of Kazakhstan

How Many Lawsuits Have Been Filed Relating to This Movie?

Before the release of *Borat*, directed by Larry Charles, Sacha Baron Cohen, its star, was famous for his HBO series *Da Ali G Show*. In it, the comedian's alter-egos interviewed ignorant people and humiliated them for our pleasure. He continues that theme in *Borat*, this time with a cultural vengeance against redneck America.

In the scenario, Borat plays a clueless Kazakhstan TV reporter coming to America to find the bosom of Pamela Anderson, even if those tits aren't completely real. Anderson gamely plays herself. It was rumored that she was not in on the joke and was horrified at what was happening to her once the action started.

The release of the film created a boom in little-known Kazakhstan, where tourists suddenly wanted to see if you could really purchase a local bride for 15 gallons of pesticide. Americans, often baby boomers, flocked to the country, anticipating views of locals drinking horse urine. Potential travelers got an early taste of the culture of Kazakhstan when they learned that booking hotels online did not necessarily mean that the hotel actually existed. The country was even promoting its beautiful women in tourist brochures. These women looked a lot lovelier than Borat's wife in the film.

Borat flies to New York with his obese producer, Azamat Bagatov (Ken Davitian), on a vaguely defined trip to interview locals about American customs.

For gay audiences Borat is a riot, especially when he joins a gay parade and goes back to the hotel room not knowing that he's being entertained by queers. Later Borat asks a stranger, "Are you telling me that the man who tried to put a rubber fist into my anus was a homosexual?"

Borat kisses men on the lips, and even shares sexually provocative photographs of an underage male relative. At one point he meets up with a Bible Belt redneck, telling him that gays are hanged in his country. The homophobic moron responds, "We're trying to do the same here."

But nothing is more provocative than Borat's nude public brawl with the rotund monster, Azamat. They end up in positions that even the *Kama Sutra* hadn't envisioned.

Cohen was saddened by all the lawsuits filed against his film in which he pokes fun at stereotypes. Many "actors" who appear in the film as themselves have filed a string of lawsuits objecting to how they were depicted and claiming they were misled by filmmakers.

For example, Cindy Streit, the owner of Etiquette Training Service in Birmingham, Alabama, was one who sued. Streit said she arranged a sit-down dinner party with some of her friends. Clips of the dinner were included in the film, in which she "toilet trains" Borat. He later appears at table holding a plastic bag of shit which he dangles in front of her uptight guests.

Kazakhstan also threatened legal action. But Cohen defended *Borat*, claiming, "I think the joke is on people who can believe that the Kazakhstan that I describe can exist—who believes that there's a country where homosexuals wear blue hats and women live in cages?"

If it means anything to you, *Borat* was banned in Russia, but not because of any porn content; rather out of fear of upsetting the country's neighbor, Kazakhstan, which used to be part of the Soviet Union.

Not just Russia, but almost everybody was offended by the movie, especially those innocents who were set up by Cohen to appear in his satire. "They wind up confused and stammering, often unmasked as boorish, bigoted or, at the very least, not so bright," wrote Bob Townsend in the *Atlanta Journal-Constitution*.

Born in London, and a lot more sophisticated in real life than the character he portrays, the actor stands tall at 6'3". He gets away with his anti-Semitism perhaps because he is Jewish himself.

Many homosexuals laughed along with Borat, even when the jokes were on them. Other gays felt that Cohen was sending up homosexuality, and some critics accused him of being homophobic. We doubt that he is. If he is, he does it in such a delightful spirit that gays should forgive him. He's really on "our"

side. We love the way he makes macho men uncomfortable by the blatant homosexuality he displays on screen.

It has been announced that Cohen has been signed by Universal for $43 million to appear in the guise of a gay Austrian fashion designer named Bruno.

Incidentally, Sacha Baron Cohen in real life is not gay, although he should be. What is this guy thinking in his refusal to turn homo? He'd be a natural, especially since he seemed to fill out his "sling-shot" bikini rather well.

Sacha Baron Cohen is Borat

 WHAT THE CRITICS SAID

"Eyes wide, face fixed in an avid grin, Sacha Baron Cohen's ersatz Kazakh TV reporter, the ineffably oafish Borat Sagdiyev, goes looking for America. It's a documentary of sorts. The road trip—he's afraid to fly "in case the Jews repeated their attack of 9-11"—takes him from New York to Los Angeles (where he hopes to bag Pamela Anderson) by way of Mississippi, and well beyond the boundaries of taste. In the most spectacular example, Borat's bedroom tussle with his heavyset Kazakh producer (Ken Davitian) caught masturbating with a picture of Pamela, escalates into a naked chase down the hotel elevator, through the lobby, and into a banquet of the local mortgage brokers' association."

J. Hoberman
Village Voice

"The joke begins with an apparently never-washed gray suit badly offset by brown shoes, which the performer accents with a small Afro and a kind of mustache usually now seen only in 1970s pornography, leather bars, and trend articles. Think Harry Reems, circa 1972, but by way of the Urals. Married or widowed, and he appears to be both, Borat loves women, including his sister, the 'No. 4 prostitute' in Kazakhstan, with whom he shares lusty face time in the film's opener. He's a misogynist (a woman's place is in the cage), which tends to go unnoticed because he's also casually anti-Semitic. That Mr. Baron Cohen plays the character's anti-Semitism for laughs is his most radical gambit."

Manohla Dargis
The New York Times

"Sacha Baron Cohen's comedy is all about letting Joe American hang himself while Cohen slyly offers the rope. Homophobes, racists, classists, and generally unaware schmoes all share their shining, if slightly manipulated moment, in Cohen's cross-country romp."

Instinct

BOWSER MAKES A MOVIE

Porn for Geniuses, Loan Sharks, and Bandit Nuns.

Much to the chagrin of his straight-laced parents, Bowser (Nick Louis) pursues his dream of making his own adult movie.

After Bowser's father proudly proclaims that the mortgage on the family home is totally paid, Bowser disguises himself as his father and re-mortgages as a means of financing his film.

That's not all. He overhears a conversation among the top brass of the company, "For Geniuses Corporation," where the president, Mr. Belami (Mathew Goldman), is voicing his discontent regarding slow sales of their books. With tons of chutzpah, Bowser storms into the meeting, hyping his book, *Porn for Geniuses*, which he claims will make a fortune. But that's just a book, right? Where's the movie?

Helmut Schwantz Sauger (Peter Marinelli), the watchdog the president has assigned to Bowser's new task, has his own sleazy agenda. He invests in the X-rated DVD which will be produced concurrently with Bowser's book.

Using the money he raised from the refinancing of his parents' house, Bowser first loses the money to a nun riding on the famed

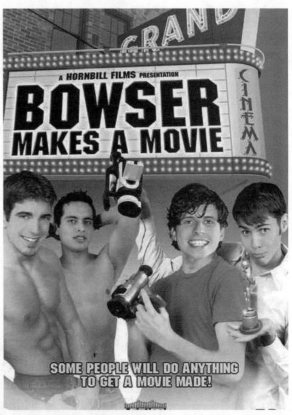

Chicago El Train. Hoping to save the day, his buddy, Adam (Kevin Viol), borrows money from dangerous mob loan sharks. When the loan isn't repaid, the mob pursues Bowser's parents, who have no idea their son has mortgaged their home.

With trouble brewing on all fronts, Bowser wonders if his cinematic dream will ever come true.

"Some of the most rough-hewn men I have known or know of have been homosexual, while certain men that gave a delicate impression were dyed-in-the-wool heterosexuals. But I won't name names if somebody is living, or if they requested me not to name them before passing on. The problem with the homosexuals, it's with the way they're treated. Inwardly, I think most men are jealous of them and their freedom."

David Niven, 1980

"I'm a supporter of gay rights. And not a closet supporter either. From the time I was a kid, I have never been able to understand attacks upon the gay community. There are so many qualities that make up a human being... by the time I get through with all the things that I really admire about people, what they do with their private parts is probably so low on the list that it is irrelevant."

Paul Newman

Anita Bryant, Miss Oklahoma, 1958

BOY I AM

No Room for Transphobia

Running only 60 minutes, this docu, produced and directed by Samantha Feder and Julie Hollar, is one of the first to seriously tackle the subject of transgender surgery. Feder is sometimes billed as "Sam Feder." *Boy I Am* was voted the Best Documentary Feature at the Seattle Gay & Lesbian Film Festival. The film features FTMs in various stages of "transition." Lesbians also appear, questioning whether transitioning from female-to-male is congruent with feminist principles.

This is not your usual tranny movie. It follows a trio of female-to-male trans as they undergo surgery and hormone therapy. Norrie, Keegan, and Nicco are all in their 20s, facing a completely new and altogether frightening transgender chapter of their lives. Norrie, an African-American, is especially concerned about the pressures and after-effects of turning into a man.

 WHAT THE CRITICS SAID

"*Boy I Am* juxtaposes powerful portraits with a number of articulate women who raise questions and voice doubts that many are thinking about but don't say aloud. The interviews with Judith ("Jack") Halberstam talking about gender are worth the ticket price alone."
Erica Marcus
San Francisco Bay Times

"The filmmakers effectively use their tiny DV cameras to make their subjects feel comfortable opening up, and directly address the problems lesbians have with women determined to become men."
Robert Koehler
Variety

"At birth we are given a body, and, from that point on, we are constructing our identity."
Blade

"I didn't think with my brain but another part of my body when it came to women. The young Kirk was too interested in sexual pursuits. That took a lot of time. I was in an environment with incredibly beautiful women - Rita Hayworth, Lana Turner, Ava Gardner. I was surrounded by beauty, so I was like a kid in a candy store, not knowing which one to reach for. You grow out of that state. But I still love to look at beautiful women. You never grow out of recognizing that a woman looks sexy."

-Kirk Douglas, at the age of 90

"What a dump!"

BOYS LIFE 5

Four Short Israeli Films on a Single DVD

In *Boys Life 5*, we're presented with four short films – some, of course, far better than the others. *Time Off* is the longest film in this series with 20 speaking parts alone. It was an early work of Israeli director Eytan Fox, and it is obvious how this pioneering effort led to his longer and more successful film, *Yossi & Jagger*.

In *Time Off*, Fox builds sexual tension between a foot soldier and his domineering lieutenant. Yonatan, the young soldier, is impressively acted by Hanoch Reim, who is beginning to realize

that he's gay and attracted to a handsome young unit commander, beautifully acted by Gil Frank. A scene with Yonatan in the men's room of a city park is played most effectively, Reim a study of unfulfilled lust.

Fishbelly White is a heartbreaking story of a farm boy who befriends an older teenager. Sean Abbey wrote that "the languid pace at which this story unfolds lets the viewer invest deeply in the characters, which makes the young boy's act of self-preservation in the end both justified and horrifying."

Late Summer is the sweet and rather poignant tale of a young teenage boy who goes to live in the house of his uncle and aunt after he loses his father. Here he is befriended by his older cousin. Lustful minds might be disappointed at how this relationship develops.

The story depicted in the collection's least compelling film, *Dare*, is either a cliché or a page ripped from our own lives—potentially both. It tells the story of a geeky yet handsome gay high school student who pines for the sexy school jock. Adam Fleming stars as Ben.

 ## WHAT THE CRITICS SAID

"While breaking no new cinematic ground, *Boys Life 5* delivers what fans of the series expect—doe-eyed, full-lipped, underage pretty boys in four short films of varying quality."
Sean Abley
The Advocate

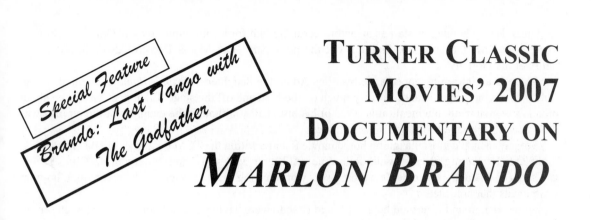
TURNER CLASSIC MOVIES' 2007 DOCUMENTARY ON *MARLON BRANDO*

Turner Docu Plays It Safe, Reconfiguring Brando Into Something Purely Hetero.

In *Vanity Fair*, an ad appeared hawking the May, 2007 TCM docu on Marlon Brando. The two-hour docu was billed with the words, "He embodied the soul of every character he portrayed, without ever sacrificing his own. He transformed audiences and redefined his art. Discover the life of a reluctant icon, as told by those who knew him best, including Robert Duvall, Jane Fonda, Edward Norton, Al Pacino, Martin Scorsese, and John Travolta."

First, let's have a little truth in advertising. These people might have met Brando but they didn't know him, as their cloying and relentlessly vanilla overview of the actor revealed. Even Brando's wives hardly knew him.

Perhaps the only person who ever really did was Wally Cox, his long-time lover, and he's gone forever, his ashes—preserved by Brando in a glass jar for many years—scattered in the desert winds along with those of Brando himself.

In spite of an impressive cast, the TCM docu offered few insights into Brando that we didn't already know. A highlight was the appearance of Laurence Olivier, claiming that Brando was a better actor than he was.

In the 1940s, Brando had a brief fling alone with Sir Larry, and another fling with both Olivier and his wife at the time, Vivien Leigh, when he was starring with her in *A Streetcar Named Desire*.

Brando was a self-admitted bisexual, and an equal opportunity seducer. At least he had the balls to admit it, unlike so many of today's stars, one of whom threatens a multi-million dollar lawsuit if someone even hints that he might not be altogether hetero.

The comments on TCM about what a great actor Brando was seemed oily and unctious. Only the appearance of Fonda in a ridiculous cowboy hat with a flag attached provided (rather silly) relief from all that mawkish praise.

Fonda claimed that Brando's mother (with whom he may have had an incestuous relationship) gave her father, Henry Fonda, his start as an actor, recruiting him for a community play in Omaha, Nebraska, where young Marlon grew up. Jane left out the juicy part—that Mama Dorothy also relieved young Henry of his virginity.

There is an intriguing appearance by Ellen Adler, the daughter of *grande dame* of Method acting, Stella Adler, who taught Brando so very much . . . both on and off the stage. Ellen goes on and on about Brando's womanizing. No mention is made of his bisexuality, although the daughter of the prophet was almost certainly aware of Brando's peccadilloes.

For gay men, the most intriguing home movie footage within the TCM docu was an odd clip, "Boys' Night Out," featuring Brando with fellow actors Kevin McCarthy and Montgomery Clift. Seeing McCarthy and Brando in women's clothing was worth having to sit through all the reverential, ho-hum testimonials that preceded it.

Some background is needed here: Clift and Brando were having a tumultuous affair. Though screwing around with Brando, Clift longed for the love of the very straight McCarthy, which was not forthcoming.

By the time Brando reunited with Clift for the 1958 filming of *The Young Lions* in Europe, all the hot sex they'd shared had faded with last year's ice cream. But Brando still felt, at least to some degree, like a protective father.

In his unauthorized 2006 biography, BRANDO UNZIPPED, author Darwin Porter (who is, incidentally, co-author of this film guide) relates a scene in Paris that was relayed to him through Brando's former best friend and henchman, Carlo Fiore:

"From a young French boy Monty had been sleeping with at the Hotel du Palais-Royale, Marlon and Fiore learned that night that Monty had gone to a gay bar on the Left Bank. It was called Tabou. Arriving at the club, Marlon and Fiore didn't spot Monty among the patrons, although Marlon attracted a lot of attention from the gay men. Fiore led Marlon to the back room where, to their horror, they discovered a nude Monty lying on a pool table. He was being fucked by a young man who wore only a leather jacket. At least ten other gay patrons of the back room had lined up to sodomize the American movie star. Much to the anger of the other gay men, Fiore and Marlon forced Monty to get off the table. They dressed him and took him in a taxi back to his hotel, where they undressed him and put him to bed."

One critic suggested that Porter's BRANDO UNZIPPED might be "a curious corrective to the whitewashing of Brando's legend by the TMC bio."

 # WHAT THE CRITICS SAID
ABOUT THE TCM DOCUMENTARY

"This film could use a skeptic, though it's eventually to be commended for refraining from bashing Brando too hard for his obvious personal failings. In the end there's something direct, simple and thorough about Brando. With the leading man gone, the film seems to come with remarkably little baggage and few strings. The same probably cannot be said about any production involving Brando when he lived."
Virginia Heffernan
The New York Times

A Disclosure Statement from the Publisher

Blood Moon Productions has a vested interest in the propagation of the Brando legacy. In 2006, two years after the actor's death from congestive heart and lung failure, we published Darwin Porter's unauthorized **Brando Unzipped (ISBN 0-9748118-2-3)**, which immediately provoked a flood of critical commentary and acclaim from both the mainstream and underground press. Shortly thereafter, the book was re-published in both Dutch and Portuguese.

In 2007, it won a Silver IPPY Award from **The Independent Publishers' Association of America**, and was nominated for "Best Biography of 2006" from the respected literary review, *Foreword Magazine*.

In March of 2006, it was serialized in a lengthy adaptation, with extensive commentary, by London's most prestigious newspaper, ***The Sunday Times***, which described it as "Lurid, raunchy, perceptive, and definitely worth reading." By the end of that same year, that same publication described the book as, "One of the best show-biz biographies of 2006."

At presstime, Darwin Porter's **Brando Unzipped** was almost sold out of its fourth printing. Laid out below is a razzmatazz description of its contents, as compiled by our advertising department.

Immediately following that is a serialization (i.e., condensation) of the book as published early in 2006 by *Womens' Weekly*, the largest-circulation English-language magazine in the Southern Hemisphere, reprinted with the appropriate permissions.

A Tell-All Biography That Had to Wait for The Godfather to Die

The mystery that always enveloped Marlon Brando (1924-2004) was unwrapped and exposed 18 months after his death in this "warts-and-all" biography, BRANDO UNZIPPED.

The greatest of all 20th-century film actors lives again in these carefully researched pages that were gathered over the decades. Biographer Darwin Porter talked or even knew many of Brando's lovers—both male and female—and many of his friends or enemies as well.

Each person had a different story to tell, often contradicting heretofore published accounts of encounters. Hostile witness or living friend, each subject added one more piece to the puzzle. The end result is a fully rounded view of this revolutionary actor who, like "lightning on legs," electrified the world in such roles as *A Streetcar Named Desire* (a Broadway play in 1947, a film in 1951); his Oscar-winning turn as Terry Malloy, the boxer who could have been a contender in *On the Waterfront* in 1954, and his electrifying comeback as Vito Corleone in *The Godfather* in 1972.

The enigma called Brando appears as a flesh-and-blood creation in this revelation-studded bio. It's all here: "The Rebel Without a Cause" who made rebellion hip. The suicide attempts of former girlfriends. Startling stories of "Sleeping With the Enemy," including bedding a stalker who turned out to be a cannibal in disguise. The ill-fated marriages, bitter divorces, and child-custody battles. A son with a murder rap. Jealous actors who wanted to seduce Brando and become him on screen.

With candor, the author reveals the ongoing disaster that Brando called "my life." The same animalistic intensity he brought to the role of Stanley Kowalski lives again in the pages of this bio. From sex symbol of the 1950s to an overweight slob who became a tabloid scandal in the 90s, Brando was one of filmdom's true originals.

Women wanted him, certain men wanted him, and Brando was willing to share his charms with a string of lovers whose addresses included both A-list boudoirs and the back streets of harbor towns between New York and the South Pacific.

BRANDO UNZIPPED chronicles a variety of love affairs, usually of short duration but played out with the same kind of intensity he brought to the screen. His affairs crossed the American plains and landed on both coasts. His lovers were as mercurial as his own personality, and included Doris Duke, the richest woman in the world, and Burt Lancaster, the actor originally offered the role of Stanley in *Streetcar*. True stories about his explosive relationships with Elizabeth Taylor and Frank Sinatra are printed for the first time, as are descriptions of an array of friendships or feuds with such unlikely figures as Charlie Chaplin and Michael Jackson.

The roles Brando lived off screen were more provocative and intriguing than those he portrayed on screen. He paraded through the bedrooms of, among others, an aging Marlene Dietrich and enjoyed one-night stands with both Grace Kelly and Jacqueline Kennedy.

His tortured relationships and love affairs with both James Dean and Montgomery Clift are explored in depth, as is the passion of Tennessee Williams, who trysted with Brando on the beach one summer night in Provincetown long before the role of Stanley existed.

At Brando's peak, his list of lovers included members of the pop or cultural elite: Leonard Bernstein, Kim Stanley (then queen of Broadway), Rita Moreno, Shelley Winters, Tyrone Power, Gloria Vanderbilt, Greta Garbo, Cary Grant, and Jean Peters (his co-star of Viva Zapata! and the mistress of Howard Hughes). Revealed for the first time are details about his neurotic, always troubling, but enduring love affair with the doomed Marilyn Monroe, as well as anecdotes about his so-called "mercy fucks," with Joan Crawford, Bette Davis, and John Gielgud.

Less stellar seductions included "almost every Japanese woman associated with the film, *Sayonara*."

One of the most poignant episodes concerns his brief but evocative affair with the psychologically troubled Vivien Leigh during their filming of *A Streetcar Named Desire*. Explored also are the legendary stars of stage and screen who pursued Brando, notably Anna Magnani and Tallulah Bankhead.

Equally moving is the long-enduring affair he maintained with Wally Cox. The TV star of Mr. Peepers posed for the controversial fellatio photograph taken in 1952 when the two men were roommates. This intimate snapshot, the subject of massive debate around the world, was published for the first time, in all its XXX-rated glory, on page 404 of BRANDO UNZIPPED!.

The most controversial charge spins around Brando's incestuous relationship with his teenaged daughter, Cheyenne. Brando later acknowledged his transgression with Cheyenne and blamed himself when she hanged herself in 1995.

Once asked to sum up his life, Brando said: "I've never been circumcised, and my noble tool has performed its duties through thick and thin without fail!"

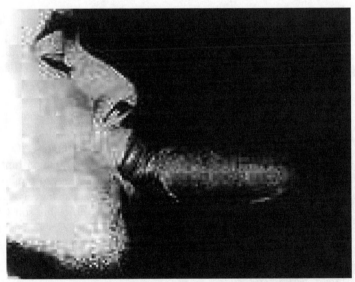

Marlon (left), with a friend, (right), snapped at a
Christmas Party in 1952. This photograph was later entered
into the official court record of Marlon's divorce
from Anna Kashfi.

HOLLYWOOD'S MOST SEDUCTIVE BAD BOY

BY KAREN MOLINE

The following condensation originally appeared in the November 2005 edition of **Women's Weekly***, the largest-circulation magazine in Australia.*

It was based on Darwin Porter's BRANDO UNZIPPED, an unauthorized biography published in 2006 by Blood Moon Productions. Blood Moon, co-incidentally, also published this film guide.

★

There has never been an actor like Marlon Brando. Impassioned, iconoclastic, imaginative, impulsive, indomitable, and, most of all, impossibly attractive. How well he knew it!

In an astonishing new biography, **Brando Unzipped**, veteran Hollywood reporter Darwin Porter paints an extraordinarily detailed portrait of Brando, particularly about his early years, that is as blunt, uncompromising and X-rated as the man himself.

"I don't think I was constructed to be monogamous," Brando once declared. "I don't think it's in the nature of any man to be monogamous. Sex is the primal force of our and every other species."

From a starving young wannabe who jumped off a train from Nebraska headlong into New York's theatre scene, the sexually charged Brando became within a few scant years one of the greatest performers ever—"lightning on legs," he was called by critics in 1947 as he strode onto the stage as Stanley

Kowalski in A Streetcar Named Desire, and changed acting forever.

For many, it is nearly impossible to remember the man decades before the tragedies of Brando's personal life overshadowed his early accomplishments. After three tempestuous marriages and countless other relationships that produced 11 children (five from his wives; three from his former maid; one adopted; two from affairs), the fiercely private Brando was shocked and grief-stricken after his son Christian killed the fiancé of his troubled daughter, Cheyenne, in 1990. He blamed himself for Cheyenne's lifelong unhappiness and never recovered from her suicide by hanging in 1995.

It is nearly impossible to explain to those who have only seen Brando as The Godfather in 1972, or as a bloated behemoth in his last films, how Brando's uninhibited carnality and skin-tight jeans shocked and astonished audiences in the late '40s and early '50s. He was the living, breathing embodiment of sexual desire in an era where movie censors forbade the word "virgin" on-screen.

No one who swooned for Brando in his early years would have dreamed that he would end his days as an obese recluse in his home in the Hollywood Hills, before dying at age 80 of congestive heart and lung failure on July 1, 2004.

While in his final days, Brando replaced his voracious appetite for sex with food, in his heyday, he wielded what he happily called his "noble tool" with deliberate impunity. Women (and a fair share of men) literally fell at his feet.

The list of his lovers was a who's who of Hollywood and society: one-night stands and brief relationships with Marlene Dietrich, Grace Kelly, Jacqueline Kennedy (who claimed, "Marlon is one of the most interesting men I've ever met"), Ingrid Bergman, Gore Vidal, Leonard Bernstein, Ursula Andress, Edith Piaf, Joan Collins, Faye Dunaway, Bianca Jagger, Kim Stanley, Veronica Lake, Hedy Lamarr, Joan Crawford, Bette Davis (her first words to him were, "I've done everything a woman can do in life, but meet Mr. Marlon Brando"), Jean Peters, Gloria Vanderbilt, Doris Duke (then the richest woman in the world), John Gielgud, Burt Lancaster (originally intended to play Stanley in Streetcar), even (allegedly) Princess Margaret, and hundreds if not thousands of other bit players, the rich and famous, as well as complete strangers.

Perhaps Brando's "noble tool" provided some measure of oblivion; perhaps he was merely a sex addict. After all he did say, "All my life I've never been interested in someone else's sex life—only my own. My noble tool has performed its duties through thick and thin without fail!"

He was only half-joking, as ever hiding his true feelings behind bluster and a blunt façade. "I put on an act sometimes, and people think I'm insensitive," he admitted. "Really, it's like a kind of armour because I'm too sensitive. If there are 200 people in a room and one of them doesn't like me, I've got to get out."

The great tragedy of his life was that Brando did doubt himself, and he never seemed to have been able to come to terms with his raw, unparalleled gift for acting, often belittling himself and suffering long bouts of debilitating depression. He was, according to Darwin Porter, suicidal after his mother, Dorothy, died of acute alcoholism in 1954. His grief was so deep he didn't bathe, or eat for weeks, veering between praising his mum and blaming her for what he considered to be the "mess" of his life.

"It's because of her that I have never been able to commit to another woman," he bitterly claimed.

"Marlon has a very, very dark side," his best friend and confidant, actor Wally Cox, once said. "Sometimes he can go for months and repress that side of him. But sometimes it comes out."

Raised by a cruel bully of a father and an alcoholic passive/aggressive mother, who doted on him and shared his bed—whether sexually or not is a matter of conjecture—it's hardly surprising that Brando was a mass of contradictions. He was nakedly (in every sense of the word) ambitious while intensely ambivalent about his profession; determined to fully reap the benefits of stardom while craving privacy; staggeringly promiscuous, yet willing to marry several of his girlfriends when they became pregnant; hostile to the press, yet deeply hurt by cutting reviews; profoundly egomaniacal yet generous and steadfast in his willingness to help the underdog in a wide variety of charities and causes; a loyal friend to his inner circle, yet stunningly disdainful if not cruel to those who fell out of favour. He was even loyal to his dreaded pet raccoon, Russell, who had an unfortunate tendency to leave a stinking mess wherever Brando dumped him.

Brando was at ease in his own skin long before even partial nudity was fashionable, and he was often quite the exhibitionist. Early in his career, he was appearing in the Jean Cocteau play, The Eagle Has Two Heads, opposite the theatre's grande dame and great eccentric, the alcoholic and equally sexually ravenous Tallulah Bankhead. By the time the play was about to preview in Boston, Tallulah and Marlon knew the play was going to be a flop, calling it "The Turkey with Two Heads." On opening night, Marlon showed his disdain for the production during one of Tallulah's long, dramatic monologues. He turned his back to the audience, spread his legs, unbuttoned his fly, and proceeded to urinate against the stage scenery. The audience could clearly see what he was doing, but Tallulah couldn't understand why they were laughing. When she found out what Marlon had done, she had him fired.

After that, Marlon was lucky his talent was so immense producers took a chance on him anyway. Still, you'd think he'd have learned his lesson—but he was too much the prankster to care. When his first film, The Men, was trounced by critics, Brando took the train back from Hollywood to New York, displaying his buttocks through the window at railway stops across America. "I made an ass of myself in The Men, so before America sees it, I wanted them to look up close and personal at the real thing."

Several years later, he took a girlfriend to a screening of The Wild One. Ever his own worst critic, he couldn't bear to watch himself. Before running out, he shouted at the audience, "Look at Marlon Brando's fat ass!"

Brando was also an equal opportunity lover. Perhaps most surprising is the casualness of his bisexuality, switching easily as he did between male and female lovers with equal ardour. Streetcar co-star and life-long friend Kim Hunter said, "Marlon told me some of his deepest, darkest secrets, including his fear of being forever a mama's boy." Marlon also told her that after a particularly intense affair with a man, he'd go crazily promiscuous: "screwing every girl who will go to bed with me—and very few of them say no."

His agent, Edith Van Cleve, explained Marlon's penchant for going after men. "Instead of being hostile to actors with whom he was competing, Marlon tried to seduce them," she said. "It was as if the act of seduction gave him the edge. Take poor Monty (Montgomery) Clift, for instance. Instead of being leery of Monty, Brando overpowered him sexually. At any rate, when I combed all of New York for Brando to tell him he was on again for the part of Stanley, he was screwing Burt Lancaster. If I had been a man, I too would have wanted to screw Burt Lancaster." "I have guilt about sleeping with men, and, almost to atone for it, I go in the opposite direction," Brando claimed. "The more the merrier. That way, I manage to convince myself I'm a bona fide heterosexual, until the queer side of me comes out again."

As well as countless casual encounters, Brando had much more complicated relationships with Rita Moreno (whom many said was the one woman he should have married and didn't); Tyrone Power (with whom he frolicked in a *ménage a trois)*; Burt Lancaster's lover Shelley Winters; playwright Tennessee Williams; and actor Montgomery Clift, his great rival. Privately, he called Clift "Princess Tiny Meat."

"Their friendship—dare I call it an affair?—was brief and intense," his acting teacher Stella Adler said. "So intense that it was destined to burn out quickly. It was rivalry that tore them apart. They were both the two young geniuses of 1940s Broadway and later the two young geniuses of Hollywood."

Years later, Brando told Clift's dearest friend, Elizabeth Taylor, "Your friend Monty and I were alike in only one regard. Both of us had desperate hopes and nursed unspeakable desires."

When Liz asked him to explain himself, Marlon said, "Both Monty and I have human hearts. But they beat in the wrong places."

Brando's heart often seemed to beat in many places at once. Elia Kazan was blunt: "During the months he appeared under my direction as Stanley Kowalski, Marlon was a "f**k machine. He became a phallic dream for both gay men and thousands of female theatre-goers. Later he would become the wet dream for millions of film fans around the world. He was, in essence, the male sex symbol of the '50s, with Marilyn Monroe wearing the crown for women."

Kazan ought to know. According to Darwin Porter, Brando had first met Marilyn Monroe at a bar in New York in 1946, when she was so strapped for cash that she was turning tricks in between modeling gigs.

"I wouldn't call her a rising starlet," Brando said, when she came to "entertain" him several years later in Hollywood. "Seems to me she spends more time on her back."

Yet they became great friends, more than occasional lovers, and confidantes, sharing the same intense drive. "I know a lot of gals arrive in Hollywood dreaming of becoming a movie star," Monroe told him. "But I have one up on them. I can dream harder than they can." They were also sexual kindred spirits, for Monroe was quite a lot more complicated and pragmatic than the vulnerable girly-girl of legend.

"A girl should use sex like a weapon," she told Brando with characteristic candour. "I think this is the only way a girl can get ahead in a town ruled by men." Over the years, she and Brando stayed in touch, often falling into bed when the urge struck. When he was filming Viva Zapata in Mexico, Monroe showed up to visit director Elia Kazan, with whom she was having an affair. When Kazan's wife unexpectedly arrived, Monroe happily took to Brando's bed, which made his own affairs with co-stars Rita Moreno and Mexican actress Movita (who later became his second wife) a tad complicated.

Kazan later told Tennessee Williams that "the most outrageous event took place," claiming that, on a lark,

Getting Napoleonic with Marilyn

Brando and Monroe slipped away and got married under assumed names. "When she was sleeping with me," Kazan claimed, "she called herself Mrs. Brando, and told me that since I was married and she was married we were committing adultery. I told her I had no problem with that!"

Brando obviously had no problem with adultery either. He flatly denied having an affair with *Streetcar* co-star Vivien Leigh in his autobiography, Songs My Mother Taught Me, claiming that her husband, Sir Laurence Olivier, was such a "nice guy." In truth, however, he had already spent some time under the covers with the bisexual Olivier, who'd been captivated after Brando's small but electrifying role onstage in Antigone. Like Monroe, Vivien Leigh was sexually uninhibited. She quite surprised Brando when she introduced herself by saying, "Her Ladyship is f**king bored with formality." Then she went on: "As you'll get to know me, and I hope you will, there is nothing respectable about me. In London, I pick up taxi drivers and f**k them. Don't be surprised—I'm just as whorish as Blanche DuBois."

Director Kazan referred to the couple as the pairing of "a gazelle with a wild boar." The jungle did become a bit overcrowded during the filming of *Streetcar*, when Brando was invited to stay with the Oliviers in their Hollywood home. He spent nights playing musical beds, even though Olivier was then having a well-known affair with the actor Danny Kaye. At one party, when Brando showed up on the arms of Leigh and Olivier, Kaye, whose hair had been dyed a bright red for a film role, saw them and flipped. He slapped Brando full in the face. Brando, who'd had no idea about Kaye's relationship with Olivier, merely said, "Like your hair colour."

Then he went back to the house and packed his bags, leaving a note for his hosts: "Dear Vivien and Larry," it read. "Thank you for your hospitality. You were both wonderful to me. But it is time to move on now, and I'm heading back to New York to resume my life. My regret is never having gotten to know either of you. But, then, I have always depended upon the kindness of strangers."

One famous stranger he soon met was Cary Grant, with whom he had a brief relationship. "Spending some time with Cary Grant has convinced me of one thing," Brando said. "Of all the possibilities for me in all the world, I don't want to be a "f**king movie star. Let me out of this cage!"

Another was the young James Dean, who approached his idol after Brando gave a talk at the Actors Studio. "I'm confused about a lot of things," the avowedly bisexual Dean told him. "Very confused. But not confused in my admiration for you." The two spent quite a lot of time together in the winter of 1951.

"A boar with a gazelle"
Marlon with Vivien Leigh

"He was completely in charge of our lovemaking," Dean reportedly said. "He told me what he wanted, and I went along for the ride." But Dean quickly became obsessed, showing up unannounced at Brando's apartment, often spending the night outside in the cold, hoping to be let in. Brando sometimes took pity on Dean—and sometimes ignored him completely before telling a mutual friend, "You'd better get your boy to a psychiatrist right away. He's an emergency case. One crazed sicko! If you only knew what he wants me to do to him."

Later, after he learned that James Dean had died, he commented: "The trouble with Jimmy is that he wanted to be me. I don't know why. Even I, myself, don't want to be me."

Despite his sexual shenanigans, the young Brando threw himself into his work, particularly during the filming of *On the Waterfront,* where his calm yet impassioned reading of the line, "I could have been a contender" has become one of the most iconic in film history. Co-star Eva Marie Saint—one of the few leading ladies who had no interest in bedding him—has fond memories of their work together. "He had a wonderful sense of humour," she said. "It was cold and I wore red flannel long-johns. When it got bitter, I'd pull up my skirt and do a can-can for him. He always loved that. When it got really cold, he'd look at me and say, 'I think it's time for the can-can.'"

Finally, Brando got a much-deserved Oscar for Best Actor in 1954 for his role in On the Waterfront. "Thank you very much," he said graciously after accepting the award. "It's much heavier than I imagined. I had something to say and I can't remember what I was going to say for the life of me. I don't think that ever in my life have so many people been so directly responsible for my being so very, very glad. It's a wonderful moment, and a rare one, and I am certainly indebted. Thank you."

Later that night, he left a star-studded party. "I've got a date with a blonde," Brando said. "And there are still those people who spread the rumour that I don't like blondes."

The blonde was Grace Kelly, that year's Best Actress Oscar- winner for *The Country Girl*, who couldn't resist Brando's charms, even though she'd been having an affair with her co-star, Bing Crosby. "What happened in Grace's suite around three o'clock that morning is still not known in exact detail, but Bing Crosby arrived for a showdown with Grace. Instead of that, he found a nude Marlon in her bed," Darwin Porter relates.

The affair was short-lived. Kelly went on to marry Prince Rainier, and Brando went on to make a string of films, many of them less than stellar. Although vowing never to wed, he nonetheless fell for the actress Anna Kashfi, an Indian-born actress whose real name was Joan O'Callaghan, marrying her in 1957 when she was pregnant with Christian. "She was probably the most beautiful woman I've ever known, but she came close to being as negative a person as I have met in my life," Brando said. "Marlon attracts women like faeces attracts flies," Kashfi retorted.

Viva Zapata co-star Movita (born Marie Casenada) became his second wife in 1960. "I know my reputation for preferring jailbait, but I often throw a mercy f**k to older women," Brando had said when he met her. "I think Movita is funny—she makes me laugh. She's also beautiful in her own kind of way, smart and very sympathetic to my problems when I lay my head on her breast at night."

That union barely lasted two years. While filming *Mutiny on the Bounty* in Tahiti, Brando fell in love with the young and lovely Tarita Teriipaia, married her in 1962, and bought a private Tahitian island, which became his retreat from the pressures of Hollywood and his own tormented, contradictory nature.

Although Brando again astonished filmgoers when *The Godfather* and *Last Tango in Paris* became blockbuster hits in 1972 and 1973 respectively, his passion for acting gradually dissipated and his eccentricities became more pronounced. After he died, his ashes were mixed with those of his best friend, Wally Cox, then scattered to the winds of the California desert. "Now we'll be united for eternity," Brando said.

Even in death, he had not wanted to be by himself. Still, the glory that was Brando in his prime will live on forever.

Two Oscar Winners,
The Academy Awards 1955:
Grace Kelly (*The Country Girl*),
Marlon (*On the Waterfront*)

Upper left, Brando with Maria Schneider in *Last Tango in Paris*
Right center, Brando backstage during a performance of *Truckline Cafe*
Lower right, Brando, lei'd in the South Pacific.
Lower left, with Rita Moreno, getting expressive.

Hall of Fame:

Alas, this book isn't big enough for a comprehensive list of who Marlon actually unzipped for, but reliable sources document some of the lucky ones as having included the following:

Wally
Cox

Vivien
Leigh

Laurence
Olivier

Monty
Clift

Doris
Duke

Rock
Hudson

Truman
Capote

Jacqueline
Kennedy

Cary
Grant

Marlene
Dietrich

James
Dean

Grace
Kelly

Rita
Moreno

Tennessee
Williams

Kim
Stanley

Shelley
Winters

Tyrone
Power

Gloria
Vanderbilt

Greta
Garbo

Leonard
Bernstein

Jean Peters

Joan
Crawford

Bette
Davis

John
Gielgud

Anna
Magnani

Tallulah
Bankhead

Ingrid
Bergman

Ursula
Andress

Edith
Piaf

Hedy
Lamarr

Veronica
Lake

Marilyn
Monroe

Burt
Lancaster

The Break-Up

Routine, Stereotype-Stuffed Sitcom With Pretensions

Expect *Scenes From a Marriage* for teenagers in this old-fashioned film that stars a fattened Vince Vaughn during the time he was screwing Jennifer Aniston in real life. Incidentally, no one ever accused Vaughn of being another Brad Pitt. But he was the man Aniston turned to when Pitt unceremoniously dumped her for Angelina Jolie.

Even though *The Break-Up* is no *Annie Hall*, it billed itself, with some degree of accuracy, as an "anti-romantic comedy." The film is directed by Peyton Reed of *Bring It On* and *Down With Love*.

Brooke Meyers (Aniston) and Gary Grobowski (Vaughn) are very different. She's an art dealer at a snooty gallery; he's a tour guide on a bus. Early in the film, we realize that this love affair is doomed because of this Mars-Is-for-Men, Venus-for-Women script. On screen, Aniston and Vaughn are as mismatched as Oscar and Felix.

Gary and Brooke meet at a Cubs game and soon are joint owners of a yuppie Chicago condo engaging in the kind of sexual combat that fueled those classic Katharine Hepburn and Spencer Tracy comedies. But Aniston and Vaughn are far removed from this famous bisexual couple, even though the script was co-authored by a guy named Jay Lavender.

We wouldn't even be reviewing this so-called straight movie in a gay and lesbian film guide except to comment on its swish supporting characters, who are positioned within it like the eccentric swishes within a 30s screwball comedy.

There's a sassy gay sidekick, Justin Long, playing Brooke's gallery co-worker. There's also John Michael Higgins playing Brooke's closeted gay brother who sings in an *a cappella* group called "The Tone Rangers." In that role, Higgins virtually steals the movie. His scenes warbling with his choral group are the film's most hilarious moments.

Gary's brother, Lupus, whom Carina Chocano of the *Los Angeles Times* referred to as "a deluded perv," is played by Cole Hauser. His other brother, Dennis (Vincent D'Onofrio, best known as the sleuth on *Law and Order: Criminal Intent*), has been dubbed "socially awkward to the point of pathology."

Some gay fans of Ann-Margret flocked to see the movie when they heard she was in it, but this former hottie is only briefly glimpsed.

After filming *The Break-Up*, tabloids blazed with the news of Aniston and Vaughn breaking up in real life. If their off-screen chemistry was as dull as their on-screen lack of chemistry, we shouldn't be surprised.

Vaughn and Aniston

John Michael Higgins (top)
and Justin Long

WHAT THE CRITICS SAID

"Audiences expecting a good time will instead be rewarded with wildly unsympathetic lead characters and uncomfortably long stretches without a laugh in sight. While they might initially be drawn in by the marketing department's promise of something a lot more entertaining, the end box office result will likely be less than amicable."
   Michael Rechtshaffen
   The Hollywood Reporter

"It's *Friends* meets *The War of the Roses*. Taking a cue from Will Ferrell and Adam Sandler, Vaughn flaunts a jelly belly and a slob wardrobe; he doesn't act in this film so much as he hangs out in it. So what's Gary's side of the story? We're meant to feel his pain when Brooke's brother, a men's chorus leader played by John Michael Higgins from *A Mighty Wind*, leads the dinner table in a campy impromptu version of 'Owner of a Lonely Heart.' But why should Gary care that his girlfriend's brother is a showboating music queen?"
   Owen Gleiberman
   Entertainment Weekly

"Near the end, a weary Brooke concedes, 'I don't know how we got here.' It's a sentiment most of the audience will doubtless share."
   Brian Lowry
   Variety

BROKEN SKY *(EL CIELO DIVIDIDO)*

Mexico's Arty Gay Soap Opera

Helmer Julian Hernández proceeds at a very slow pace indeed in this tediously long aesthetic exercise. But he had the good taste to cast a trio of handsome young actors in this love triangle played out almost in pantomime which is virtually dialogue free.

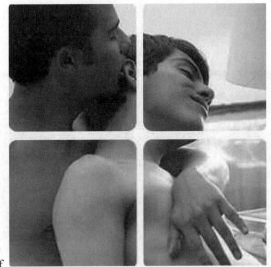

The sensitive one, Gerardo (Miguel Angel Hoppe), is in love with Jonas (Fernando Arroyo), and they seem a happy duo for the moment at their university. But Jonas is dazzled by a fleeting encounter with a stranger in a dance club (Ignacio Pereda). This breaks the heart of Gerardo who turns to Sergio (Alejandro Rojo) for love in hopes that he can mend a broken heart.

In this boring, long, and pretentious film, there are some tender moments, but not enough. Much of the so-called action is repetitious.

Some of the gay press looked far more kindly upon this epic queer romance, Gary Kramer of *Gay City* calling it "a highly stylized masterpiece and one of the sexiest films of the year."

But as one viewer so accurately put it, this is a "dance of love, rejection, pain, new love, guilt, return to old love."

That about says it.

 WHAT THE CRITICS SAID

"Auteur Julian Hernández tortures viewers as thoroughly as he does narrative and genre conventions in this punishingly long, overabstracted first-romance tale. Not even Alejandro Cantu's rapturous camerawork can make up for the whimsy-deprived pretentiousness or overall tedium."
Mark Holcomb
Time Out New York

"That's the movie—desperate grasps, huffy affronts, gulping kisses, and one juicy (if silent) sex scene, early in the film, before our senses have been deadened by boredom. Without dialogue, we don't know who the characters are, so we can't care about what they do."
Melissa Levine
Village Voice

"Movies, and our expectations of them, remain so much in thrall to outmoded conventions of the novel and theater that *Broken Sky* may seem flagrantly precious. It is no more contrived than Keats. Mr. Hernández doesn't always grab what he's reached for—his talent soars untethered by discipline—but the thrust of his effort lights up the sky."
Nathan Lee
The New York Times

EL CIELO DIVIDIDO

THE BUBBLE *(Ha Buah)*

Forbidden Love?

Helmer Eytan Fox won a lot of gay fans in America with his love story between two Israeli soldiers, *Yossi & Jagger*. With *The Bubble* he set off a firestorm in Israel and elsewhere when he made one of the lovers, Ohad Kroller, playing an Israeli man, fall in love with Yousef ("Joe") Sweid, a Palestinian. The film sparked controversy not only in Fox's native Israel but in other parts of the homophobic Middle East.

First, there was resistance at many European film festivals, which refused to screen any film from Israel because of its recent war with Lebanon. In Tel Aviv, movie goers charged that the film was "pro-Palestinian," which it really isn't, of course. As for Arab countries, exhibitors would not screen any movie from Israel anyway, especially a gay one.

The most irreverent moment of the film is when the subject of gay suicide bombers is brought up. Do they receive virgin women or virgin men when they get to heaven?

The movie is well crafted and deserves to be seen in spite of efforts to suppress it. Other films have been made about lovers who cross dangerous lines, both political or social. Take Romeo and Juliet, for instance.

Love scenes in the film are exquisite, especially the tender relationship between the two men. The acting is excellent, dialogue often witty, and Eytan Fox does it once again. We applaud him for daring to take on such a provocative subject matter.

 WHAT THE CRITICS SAID

"As with prior films, Fox's greatest strength lies in conveying genuine affection between youthful lovers and friends, which in turn lends eventual cruel twists of fate greater poignancy. Climatic events that push the central gay Israeli-Palestinian pairing toward predictable tragedy feel overcontrived and psychologically less than credible."
Dennis Harvey
Variety

BULLDOG IN THE WHITE HOUSE

Gaining No-Holds-Barred Access to the President's Bed

Has this underground film secretly been shown at the White House, depicting George W. Bush as "doe-eyed and dopey" and his Laura as a combo Lady Macbeth and faghag? Rumors have it that Karl Rove arranged just such a showing. The Bushes were allegedly outraged but don't plan to sue.

The "horny, plotting, and evil" Bush White House is seen in this daringly avant-garde adaptation of *Dangerous Liaisons*, Choderlos de Laclos's classic tale of power and deceit within France's *ancien régime*. At the Chicago Underground Film Festival in 2006, *Bulldog* won as Best Feature Film . . . and it deserved that honor.

Experimental filmmaker, Todd Verow, who burst onto the scene with *Frisk* in 1996, directed this film and cast himself as the tenacious Bulldog, a seldom-clothed, hustling power broker going from bed to bed, hoping to acquire a "hard pass" that would grant him access to the bed of our "gay president." Yes, in this outrageous spoof, the White House players are all queer—and, in the words of one festival viewer, "ensnared in incestuous webs of diabolical seductions and random hook-ups."

There is a left-wing political point of view here. But, so as not to get too preachy, Verow throws in some gay porno action, perhaps hoping to emulate the decadence associated with the aristocrats of France in the 1700s.

Karl Rove is the *grande dame* Marquise, who dallies with the hustler, Bulldog (the transposed Valmont) to throw up a road block to an alliance being brewed between Bush and a neo-Nazi religious leader as performed by Michael Burke.

 ## WHAT THE CRITICS SAID

"Cheerfully obscene...the semi-coherent narrative tracks as a burlesque revue of Bush II scandals."
The Village Voice

"You can expect cocks, spit and ass to be swapped willy-nilly, all to the detriment of democracy and ultimately for the entertainment of a gurgling Jabba-the-Rove."
New York Underground Film Festival

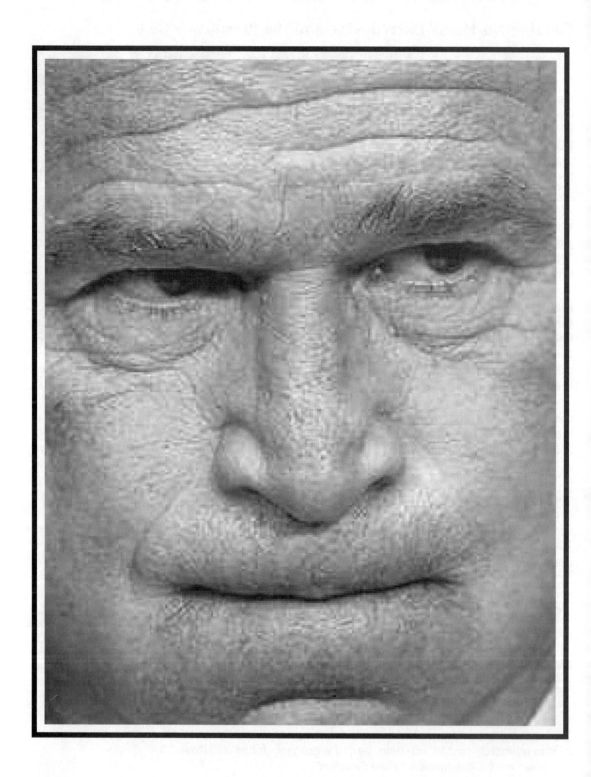

CAMP OUT

Can You Be Gay, Teenaged, and Christian at the Same Time?

The film traces the odyssey of 10 teenagers to the country's "first gay Christian Bible camp." Unlike other films of this nature, this camp doesn't try to turn its interns straight, but hopes instead to help them reconcile their sexual orientation to a faith that so often condemns them.

The skilled helmers are Larry Grimaldi and Kirk Marcolina, who so amused us with their TV series on Bravo, *Boy Meets Boy*.

For these six Midwestern boys and four girls, it's just as hard to come out as a Christian as it is to come out as gay. They're caught in the battle between religion, politics, and sexuality.

These kids are outsiders—their straight classmates ostracize them and their churches reject them. But like all teens, they yearn to feel at home, somewhere. Struggling to find a way to be true both to their spirituality and their sexual identity, these teens come to camp hoping to finally find a place of acceptance.

 WHAT THE CRITICS SAID

"From pre-interviews with select participants in bunkhouse confessionals where campers can gossip about each other, the soundbite-driven docu gives these ostracized teens, many of them virgins seeking same-sex life partners, a platform that will likely cause some Christians to reconsider their biases against homosexuals—and vice versa."
   Peter Debruge
   Variety

"The directors get some profoundly personal and even deeply philosophical portraits of the teens. They range from chubby, depressive Tim, who's fresh out of drug rehab, to Stancy, a gregarious, fuchsia-haired dyke who's loud and proud. These kids offer up rich, funny, and poignant pictures of gay youth."
   Marc Thomson
   The Bottom Line **(Palm Springs)**

"Can you be gay and Christian at the same time?"

CAMPOUT

CASINO ROYALE
Bond Redux, Retuxed & Not To Be Fucked With

Word spread quickly among horny gay men. The new James Bond, as played by British actor, Daniel Craig, was rough trade, and worth the price of admission to Casino Royale. The news on the street was that the world's sexiest spy just got sexier. Craig plays Bond as envisioned in Ian Fleming's first novel of the master spy, first published in 1953.

There's a scene in Casino Royale that was talked about from coast to coast. The reincarnated James Bond emerges from the ocean in a skin-tight and very sexy blue bathing suit looking like a raw piece of male flesh chiseled from pure granite.

He is the perfect male figure, rising from the sea. He looks lubricated, lubricious, even fuckable (but he's no doubt a top). He evokes Ursula Andress in the first James Bond movie, *Dr. No* in 1962. The mostly male audience at a screening we attended let out a little gasp of sexual anticipation as they voyeuristically took in Craig's inches, with his (in the words of one viewer), "Sisyphus shoulders and pecs so well defined they could be in Webster's."

The camera lingers long and lovingly over this buff, tanned torso. Craig goes shirtless more than any other actor playing Bond. He once confessed to the press that male nudity should be required of actors the way it is of women.

The swimwear scene wasn't in the original script. Producer Barbara Broccoli insists the moment was entirely coincidental. "Daniel had to go into the sea for a scene," she said. "But when he came out all the women on the set gasped. It wasn't intended for the scene to go that way but he made a real impact."

And so he did.

A lot of men who like other men flocked to see this hottie, a radioactive blue-eyed blond actor who'd kissed "Truman Capote" in *Infamous*. Craig, 37, had replaced suave Pierce Brosnan, a ripe old 52, beating out Colin Firth, Hugh Grant, Ewan McGregory, Hugh Jackman, Heath Ledger, and the big-dicked Colin Farrell.

In private life, there's no sign that Craig is gay. Sigh. He's been known to date model Kate Moss and even Sienna Miller, his *Layer Cake* (2004) co-star and the on/off fiancée of Jude Law.

Craig was Angelina Jolie's rival and love interest in *Lara Croft: Tomb Raider* (2001) and he appeared in *Road to Perdition* (2002) with Tom Hanks and Paul Newman. He most recently appeared in Steven Spielberg's *Munich* in 2005, followed by *Infamous* in 2006 where he was at least bisexual (perhaps gay).

You can get to see a lot more of Craig's body in *Love Is the Devil: Study for a Portrait of Francis Bacon* (1998). He played hustler George Dyer, and we got to see all of him. Craig filmed sado-masochistic love scenes with Derek Jacobi. After *Casino Royale* came out, some distributors re-released this rather boring film, subtitled: BOND, NAKED BOND.

Craig's hiring as Bond was so controversial among some fans that they threatened to boycott the movie. But after the release of *Casino Royale*, most fans agreed Craig was the best Bond since Sean Connery.

Oh, yes, the plot of *Casino Royale* if we can stop gushing over Craig: Bond's first mission involves stopping a banker from winning a casino tournament and using the prize money to fund terrorist activities.

We could skip the plot and get to the sexual content and nudity. Craig is teamed with an actor some Europeans consider far sexier, Mads Mikkelsen (see box).

It is said that sadists rented the DVD and masturbated to the scene where Mads as Le Chiffre forces Bond to strip naked and ties him to a bottomless chair where he admires his masculinity before whipping his balls with a fierce rope made with steel threads.

The heroine is Vesper Lynd (French actress Eva Green), who is the female counterpart to Bond. She's cool and calculating. Gay men would have preferred to cast Bond as queer this time. If only there weren't those millions of straight film-goers to cater to.

Other than his beating of Craig's balls, Mads steals the scene every time because of a memorable flaw. His injured eyes sometimes produce tears of blood.

Of course, there's the inevitable Judi Dench, playing the head of Britain's MI-5, giving her usually grand dame performance, and doing so exceedingly well.

| Daniel Craig | Judy Dench | Madds Mikkelsen | Eva Green |

Daniel Craig Blames Nudity on Booze

New James Bond Daniel Craig has vowed never to drink alcohol around film directors, because he often finds himself agreeing to outrageous scenes while under the influence. The 37-year-old actor, who stripped down in his 2000 movie *Some Voices*, blames a heavy boozing session with director Simon Cellan Jones for his gratuitous nudity. Craig says, "The scene was written as me running down the road stripped to the waist covered in tomato juice. But then I got drunk at Simon's and said, 'I'll do it naked!' The lesson is never get drunk with directors."

Mad About Mads
But Is He Really the Sexiest Man in the World?

Danish star Mads Mikkelsen was voted "sexiest man in the world" in 2006 in his home country of Denmark where he is big, George Clooney/Brad Pitt big. Playing arch-villain Le Chiffre in *Casino Royale*, Mads became known to millions of fans around the world. American gay men, except sadists, however, don't consider him sexier than Daniel Craig.

The forty-one-year Dane started out as a dancer. Making the rounds in Hollywood, he was seriously considered for *The Da Vinci Code* but dropped.

Will *Casino Royale* make Mads a big international star, even though he's the world's sexiest man? Not likely. Villains in Bond movies rarely become romantic leads in international movies. Even so, he's definitely on the radar screen, especially if one needs a good sadist to beat their balls with a rope.

"Whatever happens outside of Denmark is just icing on the cake for me," Mads told the press.

 WHAT THE CRITICS SAID

"*Casino Royale* relaunches the series by doing something I wouldn't have thought possible: It turns Bond into a human being again—a gruffly charming yet volatile chap who may be the swank king stud of the Western world, but who still has room for rage, fear, vulnerability, love. Daniel Craig, the superb British actor who has taken over the role, has small, wounded-looking eyes of coldest android blue, ears that stick out, and a mouth that puckers into a scowl. With his blondish hair trimmed to a thatchy bristle, Craig is handsome, and buff as hell, but not necessarily the most handsome guy around—he looks like a dyspeptic Steve McQueen. The fact that he isn't tall adds to the sense that he's always working a bit harder, that he's a badass with too much eating away at him to bother playing pretty-boy games. Craig's 007 has an itchy trigger finger, he treats M (Judi Dench) like a meddlesome aunt, and he growls at a bartender who asks if he wants his martini shaken or stirred, 'Do I look like I give a damn?'"
Owen Gleiberman
Entertainment Weekly

"Craig comes closer to the author's original conception of this exceptionally long-lived male fantasy figure that anyone since early Sean Connery."
Todd McCarthy
Variety

119

Daniel Craig

COFFEE DATE
Comic Caffeine for Sexual Confusion

Indie gay cinema takes a mincing step forward in this film about the nature of friendship, love, sexual orientation, and sociological subdivisions. Writer/director Stewart Wade took it from a 17-minute short, originally released in 2001, to a 94-minute feature film. As it gets rolling, a blind date unfolds, awkwardly, as a practical joke between a supposedly straight guy Todd (Jonathan Bray) and a gay man, Kelly (Wilson Cruz).

The perpetrator of this *brouhaha* is Todd's endlessly gauche brother, Barry, as played by Jonathan Silverman.

As a result of this encounter, Todd's life begins to spin out of control as an unexpected friendship develops between Todd and Kelly. In the aftermath, Todd's family and co-workers assume, incorrectly, that Todd is gay.

Todd and Kelly decide to take revenge on Barry by reversing the joke. After their "date," the pair saunters past Barry holding hands. Freaking out and convinced that Todd is gay, Barry calls their mother, Mrs. Muller (Oscar nominee Sally Kirkland), to break the news. She's on the next plane.

Todd denies that he's gay to his mother, who has her own opinion. After all, Todd didn't show an interest in sports when growing up, but gravitated to movies.

In a marvelous performance, Kirkland is determined to prove to her son that she loves him regardless of his sexual orientation. After an attempt to prove he's straight with a sexy young woman, Todd starts to wonder. Could his feelings for Kelly be more than he'd ever suspected? Is he, in fact, gay?

Expect camp comedy, beefcake, and a cameo performance by Deborah Gibson who immortalized

Wilson Cruz (left) and Jonathan Bray

herself as the 80s pop star, "Debbie" Gibson. This is the kind of film Hollywood used to turn out back in the days of Katharine Hepburn and Cary Grant, or later with Doris Day and Rock Hudson.

An outstanding performance is delivered by actor/comic Jason Stuart, one of America's leading openly gay comics. In an interview with *The Advocate,* he admitted that he too is looking for Mr. Right. "Oh, I think I'd be a great husband - I'm romantic. I'm funny. I'm passionate. I'm thoughtful. I have my own life and my own friends, but what I'd like to do is find a guy who can add to my life, not someone who has to be needed in my life."

121

"Pic takes the implausible position that a straight man might start to believe that his friends know something he doesn't. Stuck fence-sitting for most of the movie, Bray has a distracting tendency to bob his head and exaggerate gestures, while out-and-proud Cruz seems much more comfortable on screen. By the time Todd and Kelly sort things out, even these two love-struck movie buffs would agree their troubles don't amount to a hill of beans. Story would be easy to take more seriously if the technique weren't so unpolished."
  Peter Debruge
  Variety

"Whatever and however Todd and Kelly end up, they face challenges: It will be hard for Kelly's attraction to Todd not to turn into love. If they end up in a friendship rather than a relationship, Todd will forever face assumptions from others that he's gay when he is with Kelly. In the process, Wade challenges with humor, compassion, and a sense of absurdity the tyranny of stereotypes, gay or straight, and knee-jerk political correctness."
  Kevin Thomas
  Los Angeles Times

"An experience with a girl at work leads Todd to Kelly's bed, a half bottle of Jack Daniels and some sort of 'experience.' I would have preferred a long talk into the night on top of the covers—not under. Seducing vulnerable, drunk, straight guys isn't the best PR for gays. Guys who seek emotional, substantial relationships with other dudes aren't all metrosexual, bi, or just gay enough. They're a diverse bunch who make up half the movie-going audience."
  Anderson Jones
  FilmStew.com

"Stereotypes and *Will & Grace*-esque punch lines abound, but what the film lacks in freshness it makes up for in sweetness."
  Raven Snook
  Time Out New York

"With pitch-perfect timing and comedic demeanor, Sally Kirkland makes Mrs. Muller the mother everyone wants to hide in the closet when company comes. From the smallest mannerism to the biggest tantrum, she can't be beat."
  Debbie Lynn Elias
  Culver City Observer

"Despite a pair of affable, attractive leads—Cruz looks particularly fetching shirtless—the film's debunking of gay stereotypes is more decaf than espresso. *Coffee Date* is a passable gay date film, but nothing more."
  Instinct

COLOR ME KUBRICK
A "True-ish" Account of a Flamboyant Gay Con Man

John Malkovich delivers a hilarious performance as a flamboyantly gay fruitcake con-man who successfully impersonates director Stanley Kubrick despite scant knowledge of the helmer's work. The British film is actually based on a true event that occurred during the production of Kubrick's last film (a disaster), *Eyes Wide Shut*. If you were unfortunate enough to have seen that one, it starred the very heterosexual Tom Cruise, walking around on platform shoes, and Nicole Kidman. (That's the picture where they sued one journalist who claimed that Kubrick had to bring in a sex therapist to teach them how to play straight love.)

In full camp mode, Malkovich romps through the film as con-man Alan Conway, who as Kubrick's impersonator leads the good life at other people's expense and cons hopeful young men into taking off their pants to satisfy his libido. Most of the action takes place in London during the 90s.

Malkovich is awash in accents, mannerisms, and constant narcissistic invention—and in some ways he's never been better. It was the role he

John Malkovich is *not* Stanley Kubrick

COLOR me KUBRICK

Based on a True-ish Story.

"A sly, enormously entertaining romp." —Variety

was destined to play, insulting living actors by referring to them as "Little Tommy Cruise" or "Miss Kirk Douglas."

From the inception of the project, both the screenwriter and director were deeply familiar with the material. Helmer Brian Cook, who made his feature debut with this film, worked with the real Kubrick for some 30 years, and was assistant director on such films as *The Shining*, *Barry Lyndon*, and *Eyes Wide Shut*. The scripter, Anthony Frewin, first worked with Kubrick on *2001: A Space Odyssey*.

In a rather brilliant scene, the Kubrick posturing comes to an end when Conway meets *New York Times* theater critic Frank Rich (William Hootkins) and his wife Alex (Marisa Berenson) in a London restaurant. Rich becomes suspicious and eventually exposes Conway. The aptly named con man, Conway, died in 1998, three months before Kubrick himself went down. For Kubrickphiles, there will never be a movie this delightful.

Stanley Kubrick

"*Color Me Kubrick*, which avoids bringing in the real Kubrick, is great fun for the first 20 minutes—which include Kubrickian tracking shots and music from *2001* and *A Clockwork Orange*—but seems long at 86."
  Lou Lumenick
  New York Post

"No one savors his own weirdness like Malkovich. Under each layer of weirdness there's another layer of weirdness. Not even Charles Kaufman could really get into his head. That might be the problem here. You can't empathize with this man the way you could, to varying degrees, with the lying protagonists of *Catch Me If You Can* and *Shattered Glass*—not even to the point of vicariously enjoying his bogus celebrity."
  New York Magazine

"It's incredible to think that a flamboyant gay man who basically knew *nothing* about Stanley Kubrick or his work managed to convince so many people that he actually was the famous director. Malkovich seems to have a blast working his way through all the mad variations of Conway's Kubrick—a different Stanley for each new sucker he comes across, with increasingly outrageous accents and eccentric outfits."
  Instinct

"Malkovich's slightly fey, chameleon-like powers are perfectly utilized in the role of Conway, whose bottomless chutzpah coupled with the genuine Kubrick's absence from media glare were his greatest assets. Although Conway's wardrobe here (cooked up by costume designer Victoria Russell) ranges from total schlep to flaming queen—with nothing sober or conventional in between—Conway's marks, be they musicians, cab drivers, or trendy businessmen, are more than willing to overlook a few sartorial eccentricities. Conway's homosexuality and fondness for gay haunts translates into many of his marks being gay. But pic confirms that gullibility and wishful thinking are present in every walk of life. Still, two haughty men authoritatively discussing how Kubrick left a 'calling card' in *2001*, by making HAL an obviously homosexual computer, is a silly delight."
  Lisa Nesselson
  Variety

"The movie is a grand in-joke for fellow fetishists. It's an impressive moving wax museum, certainly, but even metatextual follies eventually need a pulse."
  David Fear
  Time Out New York

"The scam to which the movie devotes the most time involves Conway/Kubrick's promise to help establish Lee Pratt (Jim Davidson), a gold tuxedo-wearing entertainer with dyed blond hair, as a star in Las Vegas. While they lay plans to conquer America, Lee, a low-rent Liberace with an Elvis gleam in his eye, installs Conway in a luxury hotel suite on the south coast of England. The sharpest satire is reserved for the fools who swallow an act that seems transparently fake."
  Stephen Holden
  The New York Times

CONFETTI

Gay Wedding Planners Organize a Nude Wedding

Shot entirely in London as a "fictional docu" (aka a "mockumentary"), and with an improvised script, *Confetti* is a tale of three couples who compete to win a magazine contest. They vie for the title of "Most Original Wedding of the Year."

Matt and Sam (Martin Freeman and Jessica Stevenson) envision a musical ceremony à la Busby Berkeley. In their dream, leggy maids-of-honor will gyrate on a three-tier wedding cake.

Josef and his Canadian fiancée, Isabella (Stephen Mangan and Meredith MacNeill) are superb athletes and plan a Wimbledon-inspired "tennis wedding," complete with dancing ballboys, a referee for a preacher, even a sudden rainstorm.

Michael and Joanna (Robert Webb and Olivia Colman) are nudists who want to express their "I Dos" in the buff, despite the mag's objection to running pictures of "naturists."

The fun pair of *Confetti* are the dowdy, hyper-emotional gay wedding planners, played by Vincent Franklin and Jason Watkins. These fussbudgets provide marital counseling to the straight couples, tell off overbearing mothers-in-laws, and they even procure has-been English pop star Cliff Richard to make a surprise appearance.

The film stars some of the brightest lights in British comedy, including Freeman (*The Office*), Jessica Stevenson (*Bob and Rose*), and Olivia Colman (*Look Around You*).

Cast as the magazine's publisher, comic Jimmy Carr is hilarious. "I'm a bride's best friend," he proclaims, then adds with resignation—"and I'm not gay!"

Those tantalized by full frontal male or female nudity will get some here, but it's decidedly unsexy.

With all this hetero love on display, the true heroes of the piece are the gay wedding planners who are most likable—in fact, the paragon of an enduring lovable couple.

Debbie Isitt (*Nasty Neighbors*) has created an amiable mock-docu with funny moments, but scenes often fall flat.

WHAT THE CRITICS SAID

"*Confetti* marries the deadpan comedic style of *The Office* to the loopy camp of *Strictly Ballroom* while wearing its plainly sentimental heart on its sleeve. As with any improvised comedy—there was no screenplay—the jokes are hit and miss. Still, *Confetti* hurdles toward the Big Day at a jaunty clip, and the energetic cast, enduring all manner of indignities, is a delight."
   Tom Beer
   Time Out New York

"Isitt's inspiration is clearly Christopher Guest, but she doesn't seem to have his nerve; for every broadly satiric scene, another is played with oddly atonal sentiment. Still, she earns points for an anarchic spirit that's miles from the usual twee Britcoms."
   Elizabeth Weitzman
   New York Daily News

"Straight people may want to hog the institution of marriage all for themselves, but there's something almost drag queen-ish about the pomp and grandeur of most weddings. There's lots of wonderfully cruel British humor—one bride-to-be gets rhinoplasty that leaves her nose even worse than before—but the movie veers from bitter laughs to the soppiest sentimentality."
   The Advocate

"*Confetti* is in the finest tradition of English vulgarity, but has nothing whatever to say about marriage. It's a loud belch in the face of a billion-dollar wedding industry that has sprung up to service the longings of the post-feminist young for ceremonial opulence. And if nothing else, this affectionately off-the-wall confection offers exuberant confirmation of every suspicion you might ever have had that the English are charmingly eccentric. They're barking mad."
   Ella Taylor
   Village Voice

THE CONRAD BOYS

How Far Would You Go for Love?

Captivating newcomer Justin Lo makes his film debut as Charlie Conrad, a 19-year-old history buff with the weight of the world on his shoulders. In descending order, Lo is also the producer, director, editor, and writer. One reviewer suggested that he should have hired a better actor for the lead, "but then this low-budget indie would lack its vanity project *raison d'etre*."

Just when Lo, playing Charlie, a high school senior, is accepted at Columbia University, his mother suddenly dies. He is forced to postpone college to work at a local joint to support his 9-year-old sibling, Ben, whose real name is "Boo Boo" Stewart.

Strapped with new parental responsibility, Charlie yearns for freedom and romance. He gets part of his dream when he meets Jordan Rivers (Nick Bartzen), a charismatic drifter. They embark on a torrid romance. We admire Lo for treating Charlie's gayness as a non-issue; his Eurasian genes are also handled matter-of-factly.

And then the villain of the piece arrives in the form of Doug (Barry Shay), Charlie's long-lost father. He returns to town and wants to take care of Ben himself, claiming he has reformed. Caught in a struggle to keep Ben and eager to hold onto Jordan, Charlie must do some soul-searching to make the most momentous decision of his life.

 WHAT THE CRITICS SAID

"Charlie gets involved with sexy but irresponsible drifter Jordan (Nick Bartzen, persuasive in a sketchy part), whose troubled past instigates eventual silly melodramatics that nonetheless enliven tepid screenplay. While Lo's multi-hyphenate moxie is admirable, his bad bowl haircut, scant screen charisma and pedestrian dialogue suggest future projects should be more collaborative."

Dennis Harvey
Variety

"The script's insights are drawn straight from freshman-dorm late-night rap sessions—as illustrated by the meet-cute scene in which Jordan and Charlie banter over the merits of novels versus history books. The actors don't so much interact as watch one another's lips move, then mouth their dialogue when their screen partner's mouth goes still."

LA Weekly Film + TV Reviews

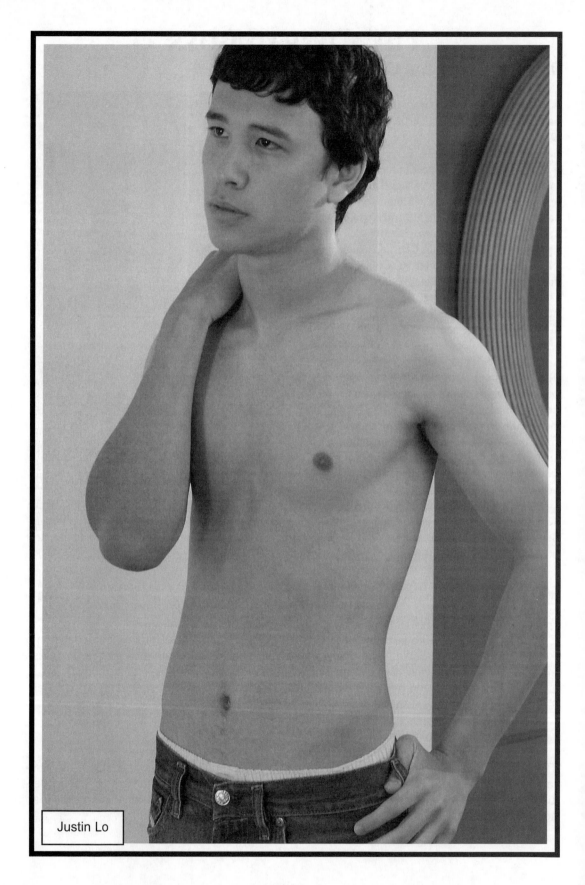

Justin Lo

Contadora Is For Lovers

An Engaging Bisexual Romp Through Paradise

This is the latest in a series of films written, produced, developed, and directed by Hollywood iconoclast, Brazilian/Panamanian Jorge Ameer, producer of several films which we've reviewed within earlier editions of this film guide. Those have included *The Singing Forest*, Ameer's ode to resurrection, mysticism, and true love that survives across the great divide of death.

Contadora Is for Lovers represents the fruition of a complicated series of negotiations whereby Ameer persuaded the tourist authorities of an unspoiled tropical paradise, the Panamanian Island of Contadora, to turn their beaches and jungles over for a film production which, presumably, brought the island's many charms to the attention of North American holiday-makers. (By anyone's standards, Ameer's persuasiveness quotient is high—the fact that local authorities agreed to the use of their island for the production of a bisexual-themed film is remarkable.)

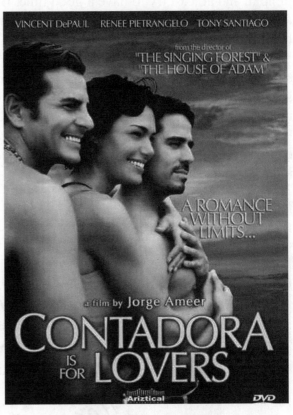

Playmates for a perfect holiday: From left to right, Vincent De Paul, Renée Pietrangelo, and Tony Santiago (a.k.a Sago)

This sun-drenched paradise provides a sensual setting for Ameer's study in the expression of and acceptance of bisexuality. Newlyweds Mike (as played by Vincent De Paul) and Helen (as played by Renée Pietrangelo) arrive on-island to celebrate their recent marriage. Into the equation steps Gabriel (as played by Tony Santiago (a.k.a. Tony Sago), the ingratiating and very humpy guest services director of the resort. they've selected. Gabriel, we learn, is not above preying upon the occasional (willing) male guest for whom palm trees, pina coladas, and feminine charms simply aren't enough.

During an all-male circumnavigation of Contadora, Mike and Gabriel do, indeed, become physically entangled, and eventually swap fluids between bouts of nude sunbathing and swatting at fire ants and mosquitoes.

As might be expected in these brouhahas, the men's growing sense of commitment to each other eventually forces a confrontation with Helen, who by now has spent a lot of time dining alone and staring at the sea. The holiday isn't completely ruined, however, and before long, everyone manages to pile into the same hammock, thereby proving that the best thing a girl can do, when it comes to a husband's philandering, is to jump in and at least try to have a good time. By the end of the film, it's virtually guaranteed that this recent gringo marriage can't continue as a closed or self-contained system ever again.

The big question Ameer's movie asks is, "Will the couple's complicated relationship survive? And if it does, will Gabriel become an ongoing part of it? Or will Mike and Helen return, alone, to their home in California, waiting for the intrusion of other, newer, sexual marauders to spice up their sex lives?

It's a thorny issue. We hope that after seeing this film, at least some couples, gay or straight, might begin a new regime of communal experimention as a means of devising some personalized solutions.

De Paul and Renée Pietrangelo

"I came across this old photo of Dietrich, dressed in manly attire. She was standing there in her glory, with Gary Cooper and Maurice Chevalier as her bookends. It's like what Oscar Wilde said, that nothing looks so innocent as an indiscretion... She had everyone, that one! The twist is, she preferred Chevalier to Cooper. See, Mo was supposedly impotent, at least with the ladies, whereas Coop the lady-killer supposedly had the longest handle in Hollywood. Our Marlene may have been promiscuous as all get out, but she wasn't fond of being penetrated. For one thing, she liked to be in control..."

-Louise Brooks

Blood Moon's Featured Actor:

VINCENT DE PAUL

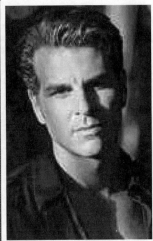

Vincent De Paul

One of the most appealing things about *Contadora Is for Lovers* is the fact that its male lead is Vincent De Paul, who combines his darkly handsome good looks with an acting talent that sometimes hits you like a shot in the heart. Like one of his heroes, John Waters, Vincent was born and reared as Vincent Zannino in Baltimore, the son of a mortuary scientist. His somewhat macabre background in Baltimore later served him well—specifically for the role he nabbed in *Hairspray,* which any aficionado knows is set in Baltimore. Later, his childhood associations with the burial business informed the character he played within a Season 2 episode of *Six Feet Under,* where he was cast as a Hollywood junkie snorting the ashes of his cremated friend.

Vincent is one of the few actor/models who began his adult life as a medical student at the prestigious Johns Hopkins University, where he studied epidemiology, biomedical ethics, and bio-statistics. When he graduated, and just before beginning his internship, he went south to the Mount Sinai Medical Center in Miami Beach.

Soonafter, and following a decisive change in his career thanks to a chance meeting with Versace, whom he met while jogging along South Beach, his dark good looks began appearing in such magazines as *GQ, Vogue, Men's Health*, and *Cosmopolitan*. Later, while juggling an increasing number of modeling assignments, Vincent nabbed a role opposite Drew Barrymore in *Riding in Cars With Boys*. playing the kind of hunkily adorable football player we all secretly wished we'd dated in high school.

Vincent is well connected in show business circles, having been a devoted friend of the late Shelley Winters and a buddy of the kind of women we all really want to know: Sally Kirkland and Dreamgirl Jennifer Hudson. He's also on a first-name familiarity with an impressive scattering of fashion and media industry leaders, including Oscar de la Renta. Then again, it never hurts to have a personal doctor on-call when you're in pain—especially if he looks and acts like Vincent.

He stands 6'1" tall, and has golden brown eyes, dark wavy hair, and an appealing sense of self-deprecation about his pre-Wilhelmina origins as Vincent Zannino. He plays soccer, badminton, and basketball, and is a master swimmer. All this staying in shape served him well for his appearance in *Contadora Is for Lovers*, where, with panache, he strips to the buff for "tropical paradise" scenes where he cavorts in the azure surf with—depending on the moment in this bisexual drama— one or another member of his rapidly self-defining *ménage à trois*.

Vincent is an optimist, with a can-do attitude that many Hollywood insiders find infectious. Our favorite of his many memorable quotes? "I believe that life is relatively cool."

Should Hollywood ever get around to bringing sloe-eyed Valentino back to the screen, post-millennium, Vincent is our choice to play the role of The Sheik.

Barbara Stanwyck: The Lesbian Thespian

COWBOY JUNCTION

Is That a Pistol in Your Jeans, or Is It Something I Did?

The best reason to see this movie involves views of the beautiful body of James Michael Bobby, who plays a young cowboy in the film. Fortunately, he's not clothed for most of the running time, though there's nothing frontal.

The work is really the statement of Gregory Christian, who not only co-stars as "The Husband," but also directed and scripted the film. He was the executive producer as well. Talk about wearing many hats.

Christian picks up Bobby in the desert and has hot sex in a car with him before bringing him home to his wife, Elyse Mirto, cast in the always thankless role of a woman married to a gay man.

Eventually, Bobby is hired as a caretaker of the property and moved into a cottage out back. When hubby goes off to work, wifey appears scantily clad in the garden, trying to turn the cowboy on to her charms. But he tells her that he's more into cowboys than cowgirls.

Nonetheless, alone in her bed she fantasizes that cowboy is seducing her. Fantasies are about all she has left, since husband has stopped fucking her and his cowboy has moved out back.

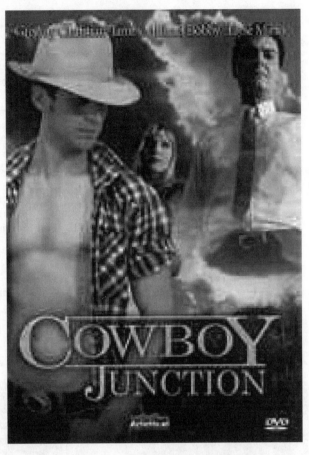

When cowboy tries to fuck husband, he protests at first that he can't take it, but later turns out to be a natural bottom. There's a subplot of a hit-and-run accident, and the cowboy suffers nightmares at the loss of his friend who was killed by a car. It doesn't take an Einstein to decipher the identity of the driver who killed cowboy's friend.

Actually, the plot doesn't matter. What gay man can take his eyes off the cowboy? He's the movie.

QUOTABLE
BLOOD MOON'S
HOLLYWOOD

"They all start as Juliets and end up as Lady Macbeths."
William Holden in *The Country Girl*

"Come on, give Mommy a big sloppy kiss."
Elizabeth Taylor in *Who's Afraid of Virginia Woolf?*

"You man, let's see your legs. No. No. No. No. New rule tonight: Every man here has got to show his legs... Come on, come on, the other one, too."

Rosalind Russell in *Picnic*

Cruel and Unusual

Transgendered Women in Men's Prisons

This unusual 66-minute docu takes an unflinching look at the lives of transgendered women in men's prisons. Shot over a period of three years, the film challenges the viewer's basic ideas about gender and justice with graphic stories, vibrant landscape portraits, and stark prison footage.

The film's creation was a labor of love by directors Reid Williams, Janet Baus, and Dan Hunt, who told the story of such transgendered

Members of a vulnerable minority: Transgendered persons in prison

women as Ashley, Linda, Anna, Yolanda, and Ophelia, each of whom was incarcerated in a men's prison anywhere between Wyoming and Florida. Denied medical and psychological treatment, and ongoing victims of rape and violence, the docu asks if the punishment for their crimes is indeed cruel and unusual.

Prison officials determine where to place inmates based on their genitalia, not their gender identity. Ophelia, for example, has lived in the prison of a man's body for all of her 46 years. She now is jailed in Virginia, having been sentenced for 67 years for bank robbery with an unloaded gun. Denied female hormone treatments, Ophelia felt she had no choice but to mutilate her genitals to force the system "to finish what I started."

Anna Connelly had been living successfully as a woman, raising her son, and working toward sexual reassignment surgery. She was on hormone therapy as prescribed by a doctor for five years before she was incarcerated. Thereafter, she was refused additional hormone treatments and placed into solitary confinement, which contributed to her later attempts at suicide.

Ashley, an inmate in Arkansas, said, "A lot of times I wake up, and I look around at my surroundings—and I see all these men. And I think, what am I doing here?"

Once a person begins estrogen treatment, their body stops producing hormones, which is akin to denying a woman hormones after a hysterectomy. Coupled with the psychological effects of returning facial hair and losing breasts, transsexuality in prison becomes an untenable situation.

Social scientists and filmmakers
Dan Hunt, Janet Baus, and Reid Williams

WHAT THE CRITICS SAID

"Masterful editing packs compelling punches of brutal realities of life behind bars."
Kate X. Messer
Austin Chronicle

"Four stars! 100% worth a look."
Eric Snider

"*Cruel and Unusual* is a remarkable and essential work. At a time when torture has haltingly become part of the national conversation, and when all Americans need to be thinking seriously about the violence in our systems of punishment and detention, *Cruel and Unusual* draws emotionally devastating attention to victims of violence who are persecuted for their stubborn visibility within the penal system—but remain invisible to an indifferent world outside."
Scott Long

"Groundbreaking! At times graceful, at times unflinching. *Cruel and Unusual* is haunting, urgent and intense."
M.J. Herrup

"This moving and thoughtful documentary raises awareness about the abuse, isolation, and poor medical care faced by transgender prisoners. We hope that the film's insight will be a springboard for new policies that adequately protect this vulnerable community."
Elizabeth Alexander

136

The Da Vinci Code
Out Gay Actor Steals This Controversial Film

By now nearly everyone on the planet—or so it seems—has read Dan Brown's novel, *The Da Vinci Code*. Millions have already seen Ron Howard's movie version starring Tom Hanks in the lackluster role of Dr. Robert Langdon.

For readers of this G&L film guide, the news for those yet to see it on DVD is that out actor, Ian McKellen, as Sir Leigh Teabing, is the best thing in the movie.

In fact, the wonderful McKellen is the only one to get it right in this God awful picture. One critic noted that McKellen's name of "Sir Leigh Teabing" was a sodomite moniker if there ever was one. McKellen plays the role extra-fruity, and we loved that. At least we woke up when he came on the screen.

David Edelstein, in a review in *New York Magazine* headlined "Oh, Jesus," attacked the director Ron Howard for "desecrating" *The Da Vinci Code*. "If there's anything to be learned from this dud, it's that when you adapt an explosive property like *The Da Vinci Code*, playing it safe isn't safe: either swallow hard and make the damnable thing or give it to someone with more guts and/or less to lose. Here is a saga whose premises bombard the very foundations of Western religion. But on screen, there seems to be absolutely nothing at stake."

That's telling 'em David.

We also applaud Maitland McDonagh's comment in *TV Guide*: "Only McKellan seems to understand the profound silliness of the film in which he finds himself, and he camps it up accordingly."

What about the usually reliable Tom Hanks? It's his worst performance . . . ever!

Of the mysteries concealed within Brown's novel, the main one is did Jesus have a girlfriend and did they have a daughter whose descendants live today? Is Opus Dei, the ultra-conservative Catholic sect, that horrible? Massive protests followed both the novel and the picture. But maybe it wasn't to be taken as a scholarly Biblical world. One authority on the Bible dismissed it as a "great plane read" instead of a seriously ecclesiastical expose to challenge the very foundations of Christianity.

The movie is often lifeless and doesn't have the melodrama of the novel. Ron Howard always likes to play it safe, and in this bomb he's tried to smooth over the issues that sparked debate - questions about the divinity of Jesus Christ, for example. The movie is also bogged down in too much exposition and too much blah-blah.

True to form, Howard avoids the novel's graphic depiction of a sex rite. Our advise. Except to witness the performance of McKellen, it's better to read the pulpy page-turner in its original incarnation.

Ian McKellen: England's Stateliest Homo

In the summer of 2006, at London's gay pride festival, the largest in Europe, McKellen topped the *Pink List* as Britain's most influential homosexual. Pop legend Sir Elton John came in second on the annual list documenting gay men and women who are leaders in fields ranging from the arts and media to politics and business.

McKellen, who played Gandolf in *The Lord of the Rings* film trilogy, was 67 at the time. "There can be few actors who manage to produce such extraordinary variety and quality while connecting with so many people," *The Independent* proclaimed in London. "He is our number one."

Oscar-winner McKellen not only made the Da Vinci movie, but reprised his role as Magneto, a villainous mutant who uses his ability to control metals to take on his heroic fellow freaks of nature in *X-Men: The Last Stand*, the third film in the franchise.

Audrey Tautou with Sir Ian McKellen

Of course, he was never better than when he appeared in the 1998 *Gods and Monsters*, in which he succeeded in getting hunky Brandon Fraser to strip naked for him.

An outspoken gay-rights activist since declaring his homosexuality in the late 1980s, McKellen likens fear of mutants in *X-Men* with societal homophobia.

As regards his role as Magneto, he told The Associated Press: "We've got to peddle the lie that we're all the same so we all buy the same products. That's why they don't like openly gay people on TV. We upset the view that we're all the same. What is Magneto going to say about that? Well, what everybody should say. Not on your life! There are people who think you can cure homosexuality. Scientologists will tell you they can cure you. That they can CURE you! But the truth is, 'We ARE the cure!' And when I realized that, Magneto suddenly became an easy part to play."

WHAT THE CRITICS SAID

"Hobbling around on two canes, growling at his manservant, Remy (Jean-Yves Berteloot), Teabing is twinkly and avuncular one moment, barking mad the next. Sir Ian, rattling on about Italian paintings and medieval statues, seems to be having the time of his life, and his high spirits serve as something of a rebuke to the filmmakers, who should be having and providing a lot more fun. Teabling, who strolls out of English detective fiction by way of a Tintin comic, is a marvelously absurd creature, and Sir Ian, in the best tradition of British actors slumming and hamming through American movies, gives a performance in which high conviction is indistinguishable from high camp."

A.O. Scott
The New York Times

"The juice that made Brown a magnate doesn't begin to flow until Ian McKellen, as an eccentric academic on a Grail quest, shows up with his capable jowls packed with exposition."

Michael Atkinson
Village Voice

"Temporary relief comes, an hour in, with the arrival of Ian McKellen as Sir Leigh Teabing, an immensely wealthy Holy Grail fanatic to whom it falls to explain, in unavoidably fascinating monologues, the alternate history the story advances. It is Teabing's thesis that the early church, beginning with the Emperor Constantine, suppressed the feminine aspects of religion both stemming from pagan times as well as from the prominent role in spreading the faith he insists was played by Mary Magdalene, a role underlined by a close look at Da Vinci's celebrated *The Last Supper*. More than that, however, Teabing insists that Mary Magdalene, far from being a prostitute, was actually Jesus' wife and that they had a daughter whose bloodline has persisted. McKellen seems to relish every moment and line, which can scarcely be said of the other thesps."

Todd McCarthy
Variety

We congratulate

Sᴉʀ Iᴀɴ McKᴇʟʟᴇɴ
for his designation as winner of
***Bʟᴏᴏᴅ Mᴏᴏɴ's Bᴇsᴛ Sᴜᴘᴘᴏʀᴛɪɴɢ Aᴄᴛᴏʀ
Aᴡᴀʀᴅ (2007)***
for his work in
The Da Vinci Code

Dante's Cove

Possessed and Undressed; Melrose Place Meets Dark Shadows

Do you really want to know the tangled plot of this TV series? One reviewer suggested that you watch *Dante's Cove* only to see the hot, sexy "alternative people" and that you should turn off the sound and skip all those trivial scenes—"you know, the ones about the plot. Just stick to all that naked passion." Frankly, we think this is good advice.

The series is gay soft-core porn, with some real hotties appearing shirtless (or with even less) in sexy sweat. It's a campy soap. Helmer Sam Irvin put the boys through their romantic and very hot sex scenes.

Oh, yes, that plot: In the 19th century, Ambrosius Vallin (William Gregory Lee) is out for revenge against a coven of witches known as the "Tresum." He woos one of the bitches, Grace (Tracy Scoggins), hoping to marry her and learn the secret of the coven's power.

But she catches her groom *in flagrante* with her butler. Naturally, the butler has got to die. But she has other plans for Vallin. He's imprisoned in the dungeon beneath her home where he'll be trapped in the body of an old man. He won't be free until a Prince Charming comes along to kiss him.

Switch to the present where we find lovers Kevin (Gregory Michael) and Toby (Charlie David) having problems in their relationship. Even so, Kevin, after trouble with his family, travels to Dante's Cove (read that Key West) where Toby is a bartender.

Complications spew forth as Kevin and Toby find themselves being used as pawns in a deadly game

of revenge between Ambrosius and Grace (yes, the witch is still around after all these years). Now that Kevin has kissed that old fart, Ambrosius, he's developed the hots for his liberator.

We won't go on and on with this plot, which suggests that "some loves will haunt you forever." Instead of the storyline, we were much more intrigued with those scenes of boys getting it on together and wearing next to nothing. But there is also girl-on-girl action too—just not so much.

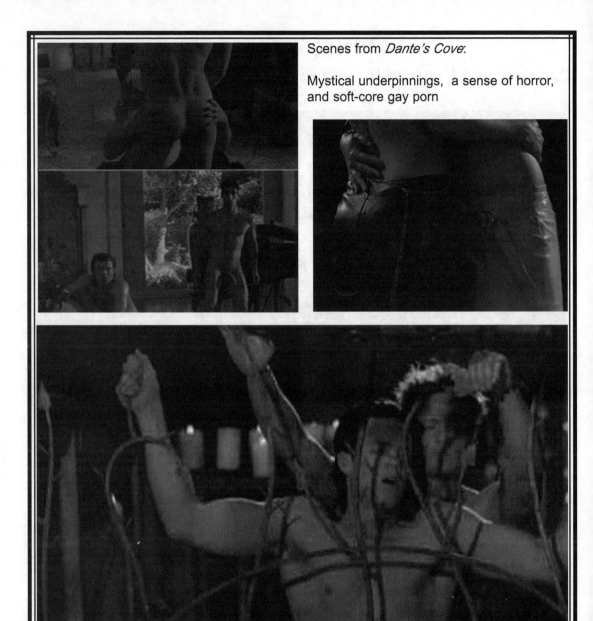

Scenes from *Dante's Cove*:

Mystical underpinnings, a sense of horror, and soft-core gay porn

 WHAT THE CRITICS SAID

"The series, packed-to-the-abs with heartbreaking gorgeous men and women, all powerfully queer and seemingly ensorcelled toward prenatural arousal, tends to dance around the horror . . . so as not to interfere with all that sexual tension or sex. As Baphomet as my witness, the series' mystical underpinnings are of an exclusively Tantric variety."
  Keith J. Olexa

DELIVER US FROM EVIL

Child Sex Abuse Within the Catholic Church

Father Oliver O'Grady, now living in quiet retirement in Ireland, was an equal opportunity seducer. He went for both little boys and little girls, including within his roster of conquests a nine-month-old female infant. The Rev. O'Grady is pretty creepy. He was defrocked and later imprisoned before he was deported to his native Ireland after serving seven years in jail. In his 60s, he now roams free.

In this docu, director Amy Berg paints a portrait of a preying—and betraying—man. O'Grady himself appears in the film, his face showing no signs of shame even as he admits to the awful acts he perpetrated.

O'Grady himself is a twinkly eyed Irish priest straight out of Central Casting. But during his reign of terror, the priest raped and sodomized hundreds of boys and girls across California.

At one point it is revealed that he seduced an older mother in order to get to her teenage son for sex. It is also revealed—not surprisingly—that O'Grady himself was also abused by a priest when he was a boy.

"People gotta understand," moans Bob Jyono, a parent of one of the abuse victims, "he's not a pedophile, he's a rapist!"

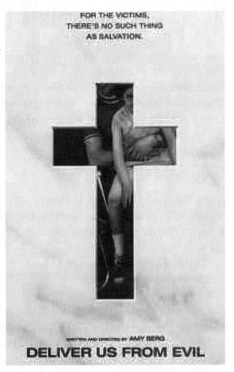

Indicted is the Catholic Church which shunted the pedophile priest from one central California parish to another, ignoring oft-repeated accusations against him. In each of his new parishes, he continued to abuse children until forced to move on again.

The docu intercuts interviews with the defrocked priest and also shows some of his grown and deeply bitter victims.

One of the most shocking elements of the docu is watching court testimony of some of O'Grady's superiors in the Catholic Church. One such official has the temerity to make a distinction between abusing little girls and little boys. The first act, or so it was said, was one of "curiosity," the second act—that is, raping young boys—"was far worse in that it *may* constitute homosexuality."

Between *The Da Vinci Code* and *Deliver Us From Evil*, the Vatican is having a bad year at the movies. The picture is harsh and damning of the Catholic leadership, especially Los Angeles-based Cardinal Roger Mahony, who declined to be interviewed. Mahony oversaw O'Grady's stewardship at various West Coast parishes in the 70s and 80s and faced charges that the Church operated "like the Mafia."

What is O'Grady's take on all this. "I merely wanted to cuddle the children because I loved them."

This is one of the year's best documentaries, even though it's a bit hard to watch.

Father Oliver O'Grady (left) and Director Amy Berg (right)

143

"The brilliance of *Deliver Us From Evil*—what makes the film a revelation and not just a rehash of headlines—is the way that Berg portrays a kind of terrifying psychological chain, linking the abuse, the obscene entitlement experienced by a man like O'Grady, and the squirmy arrogance of the Catholic authorities who, in effect, hid his crimes, giving allowance to child rape because they believed their mission to be above sin."
Owen Gleiberman
Entertainment Weekly

"When Berg photographs O'Grady strolling through Dublin in close proximity to children, he is a figure as frightening as Hannibal Lecter and the father in *Capturing the Friedmans* put together. As for Cardinal Mahoney, he comes off as a combination of Michael Corleone and Richard Nixon."
Carrie Rickey
Philadelphia Inquirer

"*Deliver Us From Evil* is so horrifying it makes *Texas Chainsaw Massacre* look like a walk in the park. Filmmaker Amy Berg has made an indelible film on a disturbing yet riveting topic. She deftly avoids sensationalism with deliberate pacing and heartbreaking interviews with victims and their emotionally shattered, guilt-ridden parents."
Claudia Puig
USA Today

"Berg has crafted not merely a work of moral outrage but one of ideas, with historians, theologians, and therapists offering insights into the politics, economics, and psychology of an institution that forbids practicing homosexuals from taking communion but allows practicing child molesters to administer it."
Sheri Linden
Hollywood Reporter

"Celibacy, currently fingered as the chief culprit in priestly abuse, is neither here nor there in 'Father Ollie's' case, for he freely admits with that naughty boy smile of his that nothing in the adult body turns him on as much as the smooth flesh of a tot in a swimsuit."
Ella Taylor
Village Voice

"I don't know what kind of vetting procedure a would-be priest goes through, if any, but from everything O'Grady has done—and from the repulsive hint of nostalgia on his face when he recalls his crimes—it seems likely that the simplest personality disorder test would have washed this nut out."
Jack Mathews
New York Daily News

DESERT HEARTS

Called the Best Lezzie Film Ever Made

Wolfe Video has released a new two-disc Collector's Edition of the lesbian classic *Desert Hearts*, filmed in 1985. Packed with bonus features, the new DVD feature includes never-before-seen bonus footage from that now-famous woman/woman love scene.

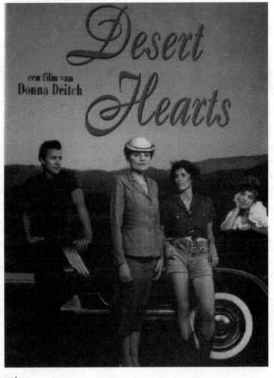

This release heralds the launch of the new Wolfe vintage collection, aiming to reintroduce classic queer imagery to today's audiences. A whole new generation has come into adulthood since some of these classics were first released.

Based on a novel by Jane Rule, and directed by Donna Deitch, *Desert Hearts* is set in 1950s Nevada. Professor Vivian Bell (Helen Shaver) arrives to get a divorce. At the time of casting, Shaver was an underrated Canadian actress of cool elegance. Arriving in Reno by train, she meets Cay Rivvers (Patricia Charbonneau), an unabashed lesbian who falls in love with Vivian at first sight.

The third star of the film is Frances Parker (Audra Lindley), a no-nonsense older woman who runs the guest ranch where divorcees-in-the-making wait out their Nevada residency requirements.

Eventually Vivian and Cay perform what became a notorious sex scene, although this is not a soft porn movie. Back in the Reagan era, it caused a lot of steam and a lot of comments. The emotions released by the developing intimacy of the relationship of the two women, and Vivian's insecurities about her feelings toward Cay, are played out against a backdrop of rocky landscapes and country and western songs, including those of Patsy Cline.

This was one of the first films to portray lesbians in a normal, positive manner. No vampires. No slashers.

Helen Shaver (left), and Patricia Charbonneau (right)

145

WHAT THE CRITICS SAID

"The chemistry between these two women is amazing and it shows on film. Their intense stares, awkward fumblings, and deep passion make even the worst of dialogues shine. In fact, the chemistry is much stronger than the dialogue and carries the film along. The movie is sometimes boring and tends to drag on much longer than it should but the physical intensity that oozes from the film certainly makes up for it."
   www.opinions.com

"I might have enjoyed *Desert Hearts* more if it had been more subtle and observant about the two women. It might have been a better movie if it had been about discovery instead of seduction. The screenplay by Natalie Cooper would have benefited from an overhaul (there are times when the actresses are stuck there on the screen, reciting lines that are awkwardly literal and designed only to further or explain the plot). And yet *Desert Hearts* has undeniable power, and the power comes, I think, from the chemistry between Shaver and Charbonneau."
   Roger Ebert

Charbonneau and Shaver

THE DEVIL WEARS PRADA

The Gayest Mainstream Movie of the Year

As the Queen of all she surveys, Meryl Streep proves once again that she's incomparable. Within this fashion world fantasy, she plays the terrifying editor, Miranda Priestly, who bears a strong resemblance to Anna Wintour. As the cruel empress of the magazine *Runway*, Streep is a real *tour de force* as the fearsome editrix.

With a crested gray mane and laser glare, Streep as Miranda wears the world's chicest wardrobe, one dazzling outfit after another. With her modulated stealth missile sarcasm, she is a monster...but what a glorious monster. She plays the role as Oscar material.

The movie is based on the best-selling *roman à clef* drivel, inspired by Lauren Weisberger's stint

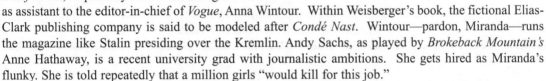

as assistant to the editor-in-chief of *Vogue*, Anna Wintour. Within Weisberger's book, the fictional Elias-Clark publishing company is said to be modeled after *Condé Nast*. Wintour—pardon, Miranda—runs the magazine like Stalin presiding over the Kremlin. Andy Sachs, as played by *Brokeback Mountain's* Anne Hathaway, is a recent university grad with journalistic ambitions. She gets hired as Miranda's flunky. She is told repeatedly that a million girls "would kill for this job."

Andy settles uneasily into her new job and her 15-minute lunches, performing tasks that rival the Twelve Labors of Hercules, obtaining a pre-pub copy of the newest Harry Potter novel and getting her boss a flight out of Miami in the middle of a hurricane.

In contrast to Miranda, Andy is likable, but as one critic noted, "There's something about her that gives off the unmistakable scent of a doofus. Hers is a bovine complacency."

Patricia Field, the visionary lesbian behind *Sex and the City*'s glam couture, brought her fashion-savvy eye to the well-dressed screen adaptation. In an interview with *The Advocate*, Field commented on being an out lesbian in the fashion industry. "I don't feel a rub about my sexuality. I don't consider myself a woman or a man professionally. Half the creative industry is gay, so if anything, I would almost say it's a plus."

Prada exerted an enormous appeal on gay men. It was estimated that some 20% of the opening audiences in Los Angeles and New York were gay. "And for gay male filmgoers, there's the Meryl factor," said Michael Jensen, editor of *afterElton.com*, an MTV-owned pop culture site for gay and bisexual men. "She's been an icon forever, because gay men admire strong actresses like her. And you can't underestimate the pull of seeing the New York fashion world."

There's also the appeal of Devil's gay character, Stanley Tucci, who plays a witty, deeply embittered art director. "He's not a stereotype, and in fact represents a nice trend toward meaningful gay roles that have appeared since *Brokeback Mountain*," Jensen said.

Abraham Walker of Washington, DC, said, "There's definitely a buzz in the gay community. Tucci played the role appropriately bitchy, but he also tries to help Hathaway out. He's the *confidante* we all can relate to."

Directed by David Frankel and written by Aline Brosh McKenna (with uncredited revisions by the likes of Paul Rudnick), *The Devil Wears Prada* has a grand supporting cast. In addition to Stanley Tucci, it includes Miranda's newly promoted British first assistant, Emily is played by the scene-stealing Emily Blunt. Even the minor characters, including an amicably grungy boyfriend (Adrian Grenier), always the unshaven beast, perform admirably in this film.

Left to right: Meryl Streep, Anne Hathaway, Emily Blunt, Adrian Grenier, and Stanley Tucci.

 WHAT THE CRITICS SAID

"The subculture at *Runway* may be venal and heartless, but it's also consensual. (In a great bit of casting, the editorial lackeys at *Runway* are played by famous fashion models, including Gisele Bündchen as Miranda's former first assistant, recently promoted.) And the fact that the movie understands the game makes everyone look a little better. The defining characteristic of *Runway*, after all, is not shallowness but cut-throat ambition and virulent aestheticism metasta-sized out of control. Miranda may be a harpy, but she's also cunning, ruthless, disciplined and not always wrong."
  Carina Chocano
  Los Angeles Times

"The best performance comes from Stanley Tucci as the *Runway* art director. Tucci presents a homosexual man without a trace of cartoon—shrewd, skilled, and weathered without being worn. It is a well-judged and accomplished piece of work."
  Stanley Kauffmann
  The New Republic

"The whole thing is still more of a pop culture sow's ear than a Fendi purse, with the laugh-out-loud spangly bits more likely the detail work of uncredited funny fellows like Paul Rudnick than the sensibility of credited screenwriter Aline Brosh McKenna (*Laws of Attraction*). Blameless Andy is first too pure for the Priestly cult, then seduced, then pure again at the end, only with a better wardrobe. Whatever, sister—it's Streep who pops our flashbulbs."
  Lisa Schwarzbaum
  Entertainment Weekly

DIRTY LAUNDRY

Black Southern Mama Copes with Gay Son

Written and directed by Maurice Jamal, this is the story of a prodigal son. A magazine writer, Sheldon (Rockmond Dunbar) is living an ideal life until one day there is a knock on his door. Opening it, he discovers his traditional southern family on the other side, whose members he hasn't seen in a decade or so.

Once Loretta Devine as Evelyn barges in, the picture is hers, as she delivers a brilliant interpretation of a Georgia mom coming to terms with her disaffected gay son. Evelyn shocks him with the news that he has a 10-year-old boy named Gabriel (Aaron Grady Shaw). His family knows their offspring as Sheldon, but he insists that he be called "Patrick."

The picture flashes back to reveal Sheldon's life in the big city. We learn he has a boyfriend, Ryan (Joey Costello). Later Sheldon is fired from the magazine. When mama, back in the south, asks him to come home, he agrees to it but lies to his b.f., claiming he's visiting relatives in France.

 WHAT THE CRITICS SAID

"Jamal (who also plays Sheldon's bitter, blue-collar brother) does all he can to milk social comedy out of the clash between opposites inside African American culture, but his efforts tend to produce broad stereotypes rather than deeply felt comic creations. As Evelyn's floridly self-centered sister, Lettuce, Jenifer Lewis plays every moment like she's working the back row of seats. Devine, by contrast, feels Evelyn's entire range of emotions, from shock and surprise to eventual acceptance, and with a masterful sense of how to make even the corniest lines work to her advantage. Dunbar as Patrick/Sheldon is forced into the unenviable position of reacting much of the time but has a few nice asides with his young son."
   Robert Koehler
   Variety

Rockmond Dunbar

THE ADVOCATE: Tell me about Warren Beatty. How big is his dick?

MADONNA: I haven't measured it, but it's a perfectly wonderful size.

THE ADVOCATE: Does he have a gay bone in his body?

MADONNA: I would think so. Yeah, God only knows how many times Tennessee Williams tried to pick him up. He was a great beauty, and he still is a very handsome man, but I mean just drop-dead gorgeous. I don't know that he's ever slept with a man. He's certainly not homophobic. I asked him once, "Would you ever sleep with a man?", and he said he was sorry that he hadn't but that now because of AIDS he felt it was an unsafe thing to start experimenting with.

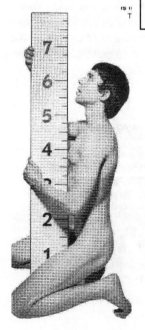

THE DL CHRONICLES

Men on the Down Low

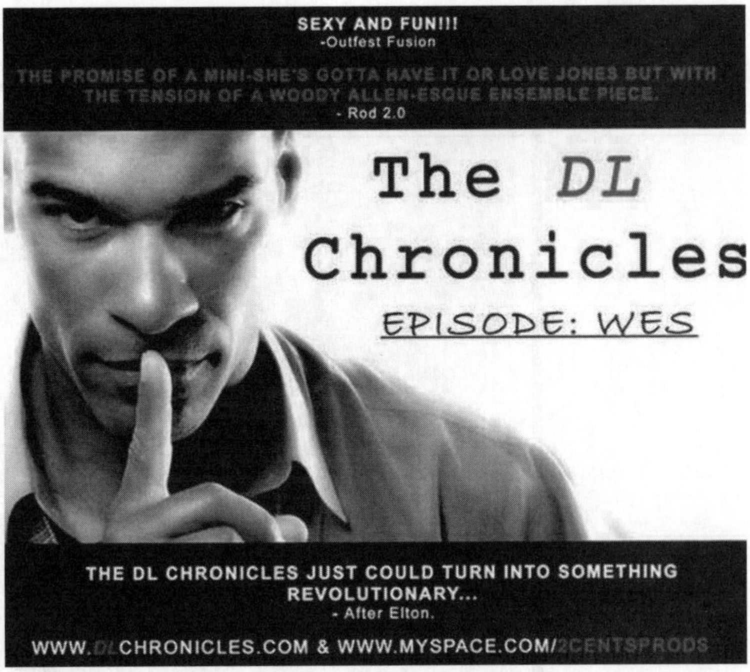

Focusing on men who lead double lives, this is a sexy, independent anthology of short films by indie directors Quincy LeNear and Deondray Gossett. It tells the story of sexually duplicitous men of color with secret lifestyles. This provocative and intriguing world of sexual discovery, denial, betrayal, love, and loss is called "The Down Low."

"Down Low" African-American men, for appearance's sake, are outwardly straight but secretly they engage in sex with men. They date women, have children, and often marry in an effort to appear heterosexual to the public. Deeply closeted, they do not identify as either gay or bisexual. They refuse to hang out in a gay community or pursue the queer lifestyle.

Our favorite episode within this anthology is the story of Wes Thomas (brilliantly performed by Darren Schnase). Its protagonist is a successful real estate broker married to the beautiful Sarah (Jessica Beshir). But he's unhappy because of his closeted attraction to men. When Wes' sexy brother-in-law comes to stay with the couple for a while, the inevitable happens.

Wes is only human and falls for the forbidden fruit in a sexy scene. When Wes wakes up alone the next morning, we are treated to a glorious shot of his naked ass as he lies in the bed.

Jessica Beshir comes on as a sultry blend of Salma Hayek and Dorothy Dandridge. She was born in Mexico City to a Mexican mother and an Ethiopian father. Darren Schnase hails from Down Under. He relocated in the U.S. in 2004 and has appeared in a number of independent film projects. We hope that he gets top roles as the first leading man of color from the Outback, and that he'll eventually join the ranks of fellow Aussie thespians who include Russell Crowe, Jew- and homo-hating Mel Gibson, and Heath Ledger.

Another episode, *Robert*, is a romantic dramedy that introduces us to the character of Robert Hall as portrayed by TV star, Terrell Tilford of *Guiding Light*. He plays a closeted talent agent who falls for a hot health food store manager 20 years his junior. What Robert fails to share is that there is a special woman in his life. When his new lover grows suspicious about his many secrets, a game of cat and mouse ensues within this humorous love triangle, with a surprising twist of events.

Gay black men in film are most often played as flamboyant drag queens; it's good to see them depicted here as sexy, masculine men who avoid the effeminate stereotype.

151

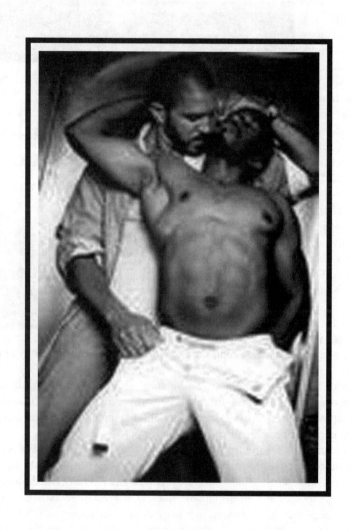

DRIVING LESSONS

Harry Potter's Sidekick Survives a Matriarchal Maelstrom

Rupert Grint (best known for his portrayal of red-haired Ron Weasley from the *Harry Potter* series) plays 17-year-old Ben, who is about to discover life. An adolescent poet in suburban London, Ben is forced to live in a household with his Bible-thumping mum (Laura Linney) and to portray a eucalyptus tree in her Sunday school play. He endures his mother's "charity work" when she takes in a cross-dressing lunatic, "Mr. Fincham," as played

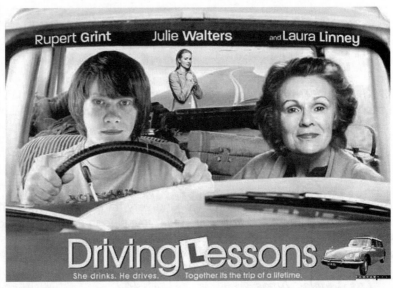

by Jim Norton, who, we learn, recently ran over his wife. The wide-eyed old fart develops an obsession for wearing Laura's dresses and gowns.

To help with household expenses, Rupert answers an ad from an over-the-hill but "legendary" actress, Evie (Julie Walters). The film is directed by Jeremy Brock (co-writer of *The Last King of Scotland*), and is to some degree autobiographical. The helmer once worked for Dame Peggy Ashcroft.

As usual, Walters is quite brilliant as the Auntie Mame-ish actress, playing her as a free-spirited and near-desiccated dipso. In the film she wants Ben to drive her to the Edinburgh festival where she is slated to perform. Along the way they form a liberating bond with each other.

Mostly Dame Evie, as she calls herself, is known to fans because of a trashy daytime soap opera called "The Shipping Magnates." The fictional soap was said to be "big on the gay scene."

Ms. Walters, of course, established her scene-chewing credentials in *Educating Rita*, but, as noted by some critics, she's not quite up there in the category of (Dame) Maggie Smith, Joan Plowright, and Judi Dench.

The dramatic core of the film is the struggle for Ben's soul waged between his holier-than-thou mother and Evie who veers between imperiousness and wild eccentricity, and is often found face down on the floor. Drunk.

For Rupert Grint, born in England in 1988, *Driving Lessons* is a chance for the carrot top to escape from Daniel Radcliffe's shadow.

WHAT THE CRITICS SAID

"There are problems among the film's charms, including a nearly incomprehensible final act and a score peppered with grating Christian pop tunes. But Grint and especially Walters—who's by turns hilarious and terrifying—provide a tender, elusive gravity that's underscored by cinematographer David Katznelson's Conrad Hallesque compositions."
Mark Holcomb
Time Out New York

"Everybody in *Driving Lessons* is working very hard to show how affecting and touching their movie can be. Indeed, the collective effort invested in this ragged mongrel of a coming-of-age story may con even the most jaded moviegoer into thinking there's something profound being put forth."
Gene Seymour
Los Angeles Times

"The screwball aging diva genre isn't the only formula guiding this stubbornly old-fashioned movie. *Driving Lessons* belongs to the silly feel-good mode of *The Full Monty, Calendar Girls, Billy Elliot, Kinky Boots,* and dozens of other celebrations of Britons defying convention to become 'free,' whatever that means. Since any connections between *Driving Lessons* and the real world are tangential at best, it's a faux liberation: the easiest kind."
Stephen Holden
The New York Times

"The sentiment's a bit thick sometimes, but Walters remains sharp, and is sure to inspire drag queens everywhere."
Luke Y. Thompson
Village Voice

"The trip [to Edinburgh] turns disastrous for Evie and revelatory for Ben, who is seduced by a twenty-something local lass (Michelle Duncan). From here, *Driving Lessons* settles into formulaic ruts before a bizarre and fitfully delirious collision of the secular and Christian, real life and the stage. But it's too little too late on what has been a decidedly middle-of-the-road journey."
Sheri Linden
Hollywood Reporter

EATING OUT 2: SLOPPY SECONDS

As Silly and Tedious as the 2005 Original

Directed and co-scripted by Philip J. Bartell, this film is a bit funnier and faster paced than the original version from 2005—but not much. In the original, Kyle (Jim Verraros) convinced his straight roommate to pretend to be gay to get the girl. In the sequel, Kyle pretends to be straight to land Troy (Marco Dapper), the new kid on the block who also just happens to be a nude model in an art class. Dapper's a bona fide hottie who would be welcome to drop trou for most gay men.

Troy supposedly is hetero, but Kyle and fag hags Gwen (Emily Brooke Hands) and slutty Tiffani (Rebekah Kochan) aren't convinced. To scope out Troy, Kyle escorts him to a "go straight" session that makes for some satirical targets.

Kyle's ex-boyfriend, Marc (Brett Chukerman) is horrified at Kyle pretending to be straight to nab Troy. He decides to pursue the sexually confused Troy with his own tactic—being his own Out gay self. Who will win Troy in the feel reel? In this boy-eat-boy rat race, the stakes get raised and sexual boundaries are obliterated. The answer is surprising.

John Waters' longtime cohort, Mink Stole, provides sass as Verraros' earthy mother.

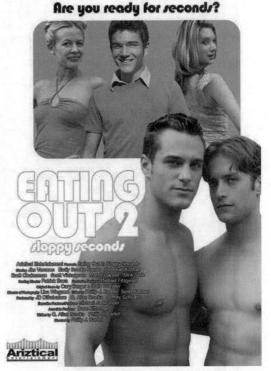

 WHAT THE CRITICS SAID

"The horny gay and straight young folks from *Eating Out* continue to crack wise and snuff out partners in *Eating Out 2: Sloppy Seconds*—and the filmmaking continues to be just as sloppy. Sequel is no more than a cheapo campy goof, but this edition does contain a higher quota of laugh lines and an unsubtle message that efforts to make gay youth 'go straight' are destined to fail."
   Robert Koehler
   Variety

"As before, the fun is somewhat capped by the absurdly stilted acting and daytime-soap-quality DVD, but the nonstop sub-Araki glibbage is plenty peppy and so is Rebekah Kochan's ding-a-ling Tiffani."
   Rob Nelson
   Village Voice

Marco Dapper

EDMOND

Is It *American Psycho* or *Dr. Jekyll & Mr. Hyde?*

For fans of writer David Mamet, William Macy, who's known for his work in *Fargo,* is brilliant as the angry white man, Edmond Burke. Mamet, who has a cult following, wrote the screenplay from an off-Broadway play originally presented in the "Morning in America" Reagan era.

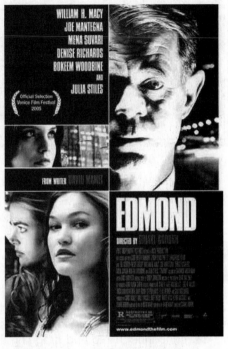

Helmer Stuart Gordon brings this drama/thriller to the screen with a knife-like plunge into the gut. The story is far too bleak for those faint of heart.

The foul language and raging machismo long associated with Mamet are here, but also some insight as to how a decent white man can be plunged into a horrifying urban hell, which is what makes this film so compelling.

In the early 1980s, Mamet, ignoring political correctness, attacked women, gays, and especially blacks. He was called a "spit-in-your-face playwright," and his incendiary language still exists in this sleazy film.

Want a line that's pure vintage Mamet?

"Don't fuck with me, you coon."

Don't get Al Sharpton on the phone, but the "N word" is frequently used.

Edmond's descent into hell begins along New York's 8th Avenue, a world of hookers, pimps, and peep shows. That scene is largely gone post-millennium, and *Edmond* has somewhat the allure of a period piece.

"You are not where you belong," says a fortune teller to Edmond in one of the opening scenes. Beset with inner demons, Edmond is about to plummet into a free fall.

After the tarot reading, Edmond arrives home to tell his wife (Rebecca Pidgeon) that he's leaving. As regards everything associated with their marriage, he just walks out the door.

At a bar, a stranger (Joe Mantegna) convinces him that what he needs is sex. His visits to everything from a strip club to a massage parlor fail because he is too stingy to pay the piper . . . that is, hooker.

Edmond plunges into the world of the homicidally berserk, taking on a leering, gold-toothed pimp who lies to him and even a young waitress and aspiring actress (Julia Stiles).

It isn't long before Edmond is thrown into prison where he becomes a sex slave to his hulking black cellmate (Bokeem Woodbine). Through degradation and disgrace, Edmond reaches a personal transcendence.

Mamet is stalking big game in *Edmond*—God, fate, man, sex, and death.

During filming of this low-budget film, Macy thought he was being tricked when prop managers on the set of *Edmond* appeared to lose the key to his handcuffs after the filming of a particularly embarrassing nude scene. The actor was left standing wearing nothing but a "sock" to cover his genitals during a prison scene. He said, "They marched me down this long hallway . . . I'm buck naked. I'm manacled behind my back and my feet are manacled. I do the scene four times and the property guy comes up and says, 'OK, we got it.' He says to the actor, who is playing the cop, 'Gimme the key,' who says, 'I don't have the key.' There's no key. They've lost the key. I'm buck naked . . . I said, 'Oh, that's really funny, you've lost the key.' The prop guy said, 'No, it isn't funny, this is really serious.' (Eventually) they found the key. I tell ya, low-budget is not for sissies."

William H. Macy (left) and Bokeem Woodbine

 WHAT THE CRITICS SAID

"But while *Edmond* might arouse suspicions that we are being played for suckers, the movie is no scam. On the contrary, it suggests a scheme by Mr. Mamet to trick himself into confronting his cowering inner wimp and dragging this poor sniveling creature into the spotlight for a public exorcism. You may love *Edmond* or hate it, but you will never forget it."
Stephen Holden
The New York Times

"The film version betrays its allegorical poses and clumsy satirical riffs on middle-class mores as something a sheltered college sophomore might pen rather than a major American playwright. William H. Macy makes a game try in the cartoonish role of a businessman free-falling through an urban hell. For one of the few times in his film career, he fails, but it really isn't his fault. As conceived by Mamet, the title character, despite living in New York, was born yesterday."
Kirk Honeycutt
Hollywood Reporter

"The character of Edmond reveals that beneath his bewildered blue eyes is a furnace of racism and misogyny, and not much respect for gay men, either."
Kyle Smith
New York Post

"Depressing, disgusting, and dated, *Edmond* is worth seeing to experience America's best-known serious playwright at his most gruesomely undiluted."
The New Yorker

ELLEN: THE COMPLETE SEASON 4

Features the Legendary Coming Out "Puppy Episode"

Lucille Ball didn't do it. Rosanne didn't do it. But Ellen DeGeneres did. She made media history when, for the first time as a central character in a situation comedy, she came out of the closet and announced that she was a lesbian.

The widely seen "Puppy Episode" has been configured into subsections Part 1 and Part 2. The episodes deal both movingly and comically with the anxiety the DeGeneres character felt as Ellen Morgan when she had to come out not only to parents and friends, but to the world.

When Ellen came out on her show in April of 1997, the ABC affiliate in Birmingham refused to air the landmark episode. Some of the show's sponsors, including Chrysler, withdrew their advertisements.

In 1999 Ellen intended to marry her girlfriend of the moment, Anne Heche, if Vermont's plans to legalize gay marriages had gone through. By August of 2000, she had split with Heche.

Ellen was at first reluctant to do a love scene with Sharon Stone in the 2002 TV drama *If These Walls Could Talk*. But Heche, still her girlfriend at the time, was directing this particular segment of the film and encouraged her to do it. Ellen eventually went for it.

One of the best features of this DVD is the appearance of famous faces in cameos or co-starring roles, especially Oprah Winfrey (also the victim of lesbian rumors herself) as Ellen's therapist. Bonnie Raitt, Gina Gerson, and k.d. lang also appear. Laura Dern plays a lesbian who aids Ellen in her coming to terms with "the truth." There's even a sight gag when Ellen literally steps out of a closet.

Of course, by now most of America knows that Ellen (the character in the series) is a neurotic, 30-something bookstore employee. She's got annoying and overbearing parents, Lois and Harold, but good friends, including Adam, the insecure photographer, and the coffee shop guy Joe Farrell. The outgoing redhead Paige (Joely Fisher) is being romanced by cousin Spence (Jeremy Piven).

The episodes also deal with Ellen's agonizing decision to sell her bookstore so she can purchase a home. She does just that, remaining on as manager and working for her new boss (Bruce Campbell), who decorates her former office with hunting trophies à la Hemingway.

 WHAT THE CRITICS SAID

"I must say Ellen's 4th season was probably one of her best, because her coming out as a lead gay character was groundbreaking! I just loved the way she poked fun with the gay innuendo during most of the episodes that led to her actually coming 'out.' The fourth season also included a lot of really funny episodes involving her parents' separation, Joe's sugarmama Florence Henderson, and Ellen going to the rock and roll fantasy camp starring Aaron Neville and Bonnie Raitt. I'm so looking forward to the release of the fifth and final season."
Tamra J. Gibson

Pottymouths

"I remember Tallulah [Bankhead] telling of going into a public ladies' room and discovering there was no toilet tissue. She looked underneath the booth and said to the lady in the next stall. 'I beg your pardon, do you happen to have any toilet tissue in there?' The lady said no. So Tallulah said, 'Well, then, dahling, do you have two fives for a ten?'"

Ethel Merman

"Mama [Judy Garland] and I were someplace like Lake Tahoe and went into the ladies' room. There was an old lady drunk there, and she said, 'Oh Judy, you're terrific. You've got to always remember the rainbow.' When Mama went into one of the stalls, the lady knocked on the door and said, 'Judy, never forget the rainbow.' Later on, she went up to Mama and went on and on again about her not forgetting the rainbow. Finally, Mama turned and said, 'How can I forget the rainbow? I've got rainbows up my ass!'"

Liza Minnelli

END OF THE SPEAR

Love the Message, Hate the Messenger

The casting of gay activist Chad Allen in *End of the Spear* set off an uproar among the Christian Right. This is a new Christian-made movie telling the real-life story of a son who makes peace with an Amazon tribe who killed his missionary father. Apparently, the movie producers didn't know Allen was a gay activist when they cast the film. Obviously they don't read *The Advocate* where Allen outed himself on the cover in August of 2001.

In the film Allen appears in a dual role, both as the slain missionary and later as his grown son. *The Spear* tells the story of five American missionaries who were slaughtered by members of a remote Ecuadorian tribe while trying to establish contact with them in 1956. It also has a redemptive twist, showing the tribe's subsequent conversion to a "less self-destructive lifestyle."

Not only is Allen a gay activist, he's a former drug-using teen heartthrob and lapsed Roman Catholic. The movie producers were horrified at the controversy over the casting of Allen, as they were hoping for a *Passion of the Christ* type turnout.

"The story is one of the most well-known mission stories of the past century," said Jason Janz, a Colorado minister who sparked the controversy on his blog. "It was bad judgment to cast one of Hollywood's most gay activists in the lead. The casting of Allen was like Madonna playing the Virgin Mary." Amazingly the very homophobic Jerry Falwell, months before his death, did not agree and actually encouraged his congregation to see *End of the Spear*.

Left and right: Chad Allen

The film's director and co-scripter, Jim Hanon, said, "It's a disappointment," referring to the schizophrenic response from the Christian Right. "Especially because the message of the story is that you should reach out in love to people you disagree with."

Hanon refused to apologize for the casting of Allen as demanded by the Rev. Janz. "If we make films according to what the Bible says is true, it's incumbent upon us to live that. We disagree with Chad about his homosexuality but we love him and worked with him—and we feel that's a Biblical position."

WHAT THE CRITICS SAID

"Coy crypto-Christian claptrap masquerading as feel-good ethnography, *End of the Spear* is a part missionaries-in-peril potboiler (*sans* pot) and part Bush-era evangelical screed. It's the kind of oversweet cinematic Kool-Aid they used to force-feed us in Sunday school, a dramatic retooling of *Beyond the Gates of Splendor*, a documentary also directed by Jim Hanon that was marketed to churches."
   Mark Holcomb
   Village Voice

"Pastors protesting the casting of Allen claim they're worried about what will happen when their children rush home from the movies, Google Chad Allen's name, and discover that he's a 'gay activist.' ('Gay activist is a term evangelicals apply to any homosexual who isn't a gay doormat.) They needn't be too concerned. Straight boys who have unsupervised access to the Internet aren't Googling the names of middle-aged male actors gay or straight—not when Paris Hilton's sex tapes are still out there. Frankly, I can't help but be perplexed by the criticisms of Mr. Allen from the Christian Right. After all, isn't playing straight what evangelicals have been urging gay men to do?"
   Dan Savage
   The New York Times

EROTIKUS: A HISTORY OF THE GAY MOVIE

A Closer Look at a Classic: AKA: A Definitive Take on Gay Porn

Many young readers are searching for this 1973 movie that in 90 minutes surveys the history of gay porn from the nudie/not-quite-nudies of early filmdom to the "money shot"-filled feature-length releases that introduced such "stars" as Casey Donovan (Cal Culver) with his 8½ inch dick. We even get to see clips of Monte Hansen whose nude pictures used to adorn the bathroom walls of many a gay man. He was one of the first and most successful nude models of the 1970s, and he never had a problem being photographed with a hard-on (or never had any trouble raising one). His thick sausage is shown in archival footage.

Fred Halsted (1941-89) is the narrator. What gay man coming of age in the 70s doesn't remember the films of Halsted, including *LA Plays Itself/Sex Garage* (1972)? A scene in *Sex Garage* got a New York City movie theater raided. Halsted himself appeared in this one.

He also brought us *A Night at Halsted's* (1980), often considered a classic, especially its Plexiglas glory-hole scene. Halsted in *Erotikus* not only narrates but jerks off in one scene. The movie also highlights the first cum shot shown (no pun intended) in public release (i.e., not as a scene within a secret "blue movie").

Halsted was not only a great porn director, he was often a star in his own features. He started out as a gardener for Vincent Price. When not watering the roses, he treated the campy gay actor to some jizz. Halsted claimed that Price once extracted three loads out of him without ever coming up for air.

The porn helmer hired blond and skinny models of the California surfer type. "My type," he said.

Halsted's lover was Joey Yale, who appeared in some of his films. Halsted recalled that he first met Yale in front of a Hollywood leather bar in 1969. The kid was too young to go inside. "He was the cutest blond I'd ever seen, and I decided I had to get into his pants. There was no sense in going into the bar and getting drunk. So I took him home and fucked him, and we've been doin' it ever since."

The word "twinkie" was coined to describe Yale.

Halsted, who also directed the notorious *El Paso Wrecking Corp.* in 1978, committed suicide at Dana Point, California, on May 9, 1989. He overdosed on sleeping pills after the death of Joey Yale. Halsted wrote a suicide note: "I had a good life. I've had looks, a body, money, success, and artistic triumphs. I've had the love of my life. I see no reason to go on."

The director of *Erotikus*, Tom DeSimone, is no stranger to gay porn, and is credited with having produced the first so-called "homosexual feature film," *The Collection*, with sync dialogue, an original soundtrack, and a plot that went beyond the basic collection of sex scenes. It told the story of a madman who kidnaps young guys and keeps them captive to satisfy his personal sex trips.

If you can locate *Erotikus*, try to get the longer version—not the 54-minute quickie, the latter of which is marred with a big chunk of missing scenes. Apparently, the video distributor thought some of the longer clips boring and was worried about other scenes that relied heavily on pop music that perhaps would raise copyright issues and some legal hassles.

Incidentally, DeSimone also directed several campy horror movies in the 70s and 80s, including *Chatterbox*. This "sexy comedy" starred the famous actor, Rip Torn, and was the story of a woman with a singing. . . ahem, female body part. The songs were co-written by Neil Sedaka. We're not making this up!

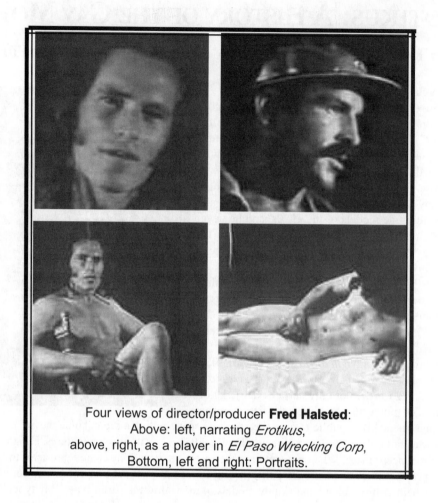

Four views of director/producer **Fred Halsted**:
Above: left, narrating *Erotikus*,
above, right, as a player in *El Paso Wrecking Corp*,
Bottom, left and right: Portraits.

 WHAT THE CRITICS SAID

"Halsted was one of a small cadre of innovators in the early days of the hardcore gay features. Many of the others, such as Wakefield Poole, were based in New York, but Halsted brought an 'L.A. Malaise' sensibility to the mix, documenting the peculiar torpor of life in the Big Orange through a series of rough (in every sense) S&M porn features. *L.A. Plays Itself* was celebrated or vilified as perhaps the earliest film to show fist-fucking. Halsted's sex is sweaty and desperate, set against images of cruelty and destruction both in the bedrooms, bathhouses, and casual sex spaces where it occurs and in the grim, trashy world looming just outside."
  Gary Morris

EYE ON THE GUY:
ALAN B. STONE & THE AGE OF BEEFCAKE

Gay Male Erotic Photos Back in the 50s and 60s

Alan B. Stone was a business-man who lived life in Montreal as a quiet suburbanite. But his hobby was the homoerotic pin-up of scantily clad, beefy men, many wearing only underwear covering their crotches.

Alan B. Stone produced thou-sands of images of men, ranging from Montreal bodybuilders to Pacific fishermen, from rodeo cow-boys to the workers who built Expo '67. He inhabited a distinct gay sub-culture back in the days when homo-sexuality was illegal. This docu explores the little-known world of "physique photography," as it was called, a scene that paved the way for gay liberation. From his Montreal basement, he ran an inter-national mail order business in male pin-ups, catering to the inner desires of closeted gays throughout North America.

Most of Stone's beefcake pin-ups models, or so it is believed, were straight, which seemed to add to their allure among purchasers of the erotica, in other words, a peek at for-bidden territory.

In the film, former models recall the heyday of Stone's studio. Stone traveled far and wide, and his photographic legacy provides a rich document of the Canadian West in the 1960s. Wherever he traveled, his eye was always on the guy.

For 48 minutes, Philip Lewis and Jean-François Monette re-create this long-gone world through vin-tage footage, old pictures, and interviews. Stone's pictures were published in muscle magazines which in time gave way to the openly gay porn magazines that began to circulate in the late 60s and early 70s.

Stone's work came to light in the mid-1980s when Thomas Waugh, a film studies professor at Concordia University in Montreal, discovered them. "I was struck by how ingenious much of Stone's photography was," recalled Waugh. "It created this sanitized yet prurient image of the male body. The pouches the men were wearing, the coy nods to homosexuality—it was all very clever, and was a prod-uct of the repression of the time."

In a word, this docu is archive-appropriate eye candy.

"*Eye on the Guy* remains a crucial bit of lost history reclaimed, a valiant effort by filmmakers to bring Stone's legacy some much-needed attention."
Matthew Hays

APPLAUSE FOR ARCHIVISTS

Thomas Waugh's documentation of differing venues of presentation of the male nude encompass far more than the nudes celebrated within the above-noted film. In 1997, he authored a seminal reference book entitled *Gay Male Eroticism in Photography and Film from Their Beginnings to Stonewall.* (ISBN: 0-231-09998-3) Cloth-bound, imposing, and academic, and with 488 pages and 377 photographs, it was reviewed by the usually straight-laced and relatively reticent *Library Journal* as follows: "In this vast and valuable study, Waugh has accumulated the most comprehensive study of gay erotic film and photography that will probably ever be undertaken."

Blood Moon would like to formally thank the archivists associated with this and with equivalent projects, past and future, for their work, their commitment, and their passion.

ALAN B. STONE, COURTESY LES ARCHIVES GAIES DU QUÉBEC

ARCHIVES GAIES DU QUÉBEC
mémoire de notre communauté

Above, right. Alan B. Stone, photographer and preservationist

FABULOUS! THE STORY OF QUEER CINEMA

Out of the Closet and Onto the Screen

Helmers Lisa Ades and Lesli Klainberg painted in broad brush strokes when they surveyed the history of gay and lesbian cinema, the love that dared not speak its name in early films. But any docu that attempts to do that in 82 minutes is destined to be broad. Even so, we were rather startled not to see the seminal film, *The Boys in the Band*, surveyed. Also missing from the lineup are such classics as Tom Hanks in *Philadelphia*. What about *Jeffrey*? Left out was *TransAmerica*, *Midnight in the Garden of Good and Evil*, *In and Out*, *Compulsion*, *Party Monster*, and even *My Own Private Idaho*. We also didn't see mention of the classic, *The Children's Hour*, by bisexual playwright Lillian Hellman.

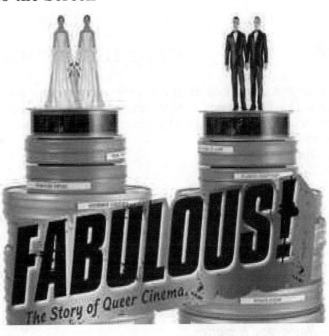

Much of the cast is predictable. We just knew John Waters would turn up, and we got our wish that Ang Lee, the director of *Brokeback Mountain*, would make some comments. Gossip maven Michael Musto can always get a laugh just by showing up. John Cameron Mitchell, the creator and star of *Hedwig and the Angry Inch*, appears, as does *Queer as Folk*'s Peter Paige as well as Don Roos who directed *The Opposite of Sex*.

For those coming to the subject for the first time, this is an entertaining lesson in gay history. For the old sailors on the deck of gay cinema, it's everything we've mopped up before. Where the docu succeeds is in showing how G&L cinema came into its own after long struggles, with men playing sissies on screen and lesbians serial killers or vampires.

The film clips alone are worth the price of admission, and the gay glitterati "talking heads" give valuable opinions. It's entirely appropriate that the filmmakers in such a short time start with Kenneth Anger's *Fireworks*. Fortunately, for those who haven't had a chance to see Anger's pioneering films, Fantoma has re-released them. See *The Films of Kenneth Anger* (Volume One) in this edition for more on this legendary provocateur who authored the infamous *Hollywood Babylon* (the book, not the movie).

The directors trace gay cinema up to *Brokeback Mountain*. The boy-meets-boy stories are better represented than fine lesbian cinema, although we do get a preview of *Personal Best*, *Go Fish*, *Desert Hearts*, and even *DEBS*. Transsexuals get short-changed in this breezy, fast-moving docu.

The last part of the film deals with the somewhat bland TV series, *Will & Grace*. It also delves into the irony of straight actors who win awards playing gay, lesbian, or transgendered characters. Critic B. Ruby Rich is the chief spokesperson for New Queer Cinema, and included in the film is a brief version of his analysis of the controversy over the National Endowment for the Arts support of Todd Haynes' *Poison* or Tom Kaslin's *Swoon*. Pictures such as these worked Pat Robinson into a lather.

As much as we enjoyed *Fabulous*, we hope that viewers will also obtain copies of Vito Russo's pioneering *The Celluloid Closet*, which unlike *Fabulous!*, sparked major debates in Hollywood about the nature of how gays and lesbians were portrayed in films, particularly in the pre-Stonewall era.

WHAT THE CRITICS SAID

"It's an interesting look at gay cinema history and provides a good thumbnail sketch of the genre. Don't expect any in-depth analysis of anything, but it's nice to hear the thoughts of pop culture pundits as they look at the lavender screen and contemplate how it has morphed since its inception."
   Judge Brett Cullum
   DVD Verdict

"Queer images in the cinema have been around since the film's origination, but we may not have known how to recognize images so much out of the mainstream for so long. It has been a long struggle for legitimacy; that is, to be accepted as a viable subject matter and mode of expression. As a subculture (and hopefully a subculture no more), gay and lesbian cinema has a longevity that this docu makes quite evident through great footage and even better research and writing."
   Marilyn Moss
   Hollywood Reporter

"Where the *Celluloid Closet* focused more on the behind-the-screen stories of gay talent and the hidden homosexual subtexts in Hollywood's golden years, *Fabulous!* celebrates the films featuring unequivocally gay characters or those made by Out directors on homosexual themes."
   Leslie Felperin
   Variety

"Essential viewing for the uninitiated. *Fabulous!* seamlessly tracks the parallel courses on which queer films and gay liberation sprinted."
   The Advocate

FACTORY GIRL
Holly Golightly on the Road to Hell

Sex, nudity, foul language, and drugs, it's all that you would expect in this semi-fictionalized account of the rise and fall of Andy Warhol's ill-fated 60s muse, Edie Sedgwick.

As if you didn't know, Edie Sedgwick (1943-71) was that leggy 60s heiress who became a *Vogue* "youth-quaker" and fleeting superstar for Andy Warhol. She led a tragic, supernova life that ended in California when her husband, Michael Post, woke up on the morning of November 16, 1971, to find Edie lying dead next to him.

Ever since 1966, her star had gone into eclipse, never to shine again. At moments of desperation in the late 60s, she stole art and antiques from her grandmother's apartment to fund her drug habit, which eventually led to her death.

The film traces her odyssey from Radcliffe to the streets of New York where she wanted to become the next Holly Golightly.

When Andy met Edie, life imitated art.

Although she appears rather innocent at the beginning of this film, she was actually a fag hag in Boston before meeting fame slut Andy Warhol in New York.

Since the pop artist was gay, there was no romance between them, but for months they appeared everywhere together, perhaps becoming one of New York's most famous couples of the 60s. Edie became the Queen of Underground Art and Fashion. If F. Scott Fitzgerald had lived, he might have romantically included her among his "The Beautiful and the Damned."

As director of this unforgiving movie, George Hickenlooper tells the same old story that movies have told since the beginning of the 20th century. Innocent girl—pretty, of course—hits town and slips into a decadent lifestyle, only to pay for the wages of her "sins." In Edie's case, those sins carried a very high price tag.

The helmer relies heavily on the performance of Sienna Miller as Edie and English actor Guy Pearce as Warhol, to pull off this movie. They can't save the film but it is not for lack of trying. Pearce brilliantly portrays Warhol as physically repulsive—"an almost soulless puppet master clueless in his cruelties," as one columnist put it. The Cambridge-born actor is the best Warhol to date. Yes, better than David Bowie, Cripsin Glover, Jared Harris, and Sean Gregory Sullivan.

Pearce is one busy actor. Many gay men saw him for the first time in *The Adventures of Priscilla, Queen of the Desert* (1994). His latest starring role is *Death Defying Acts*, based on the life of Harry Houdini.

Warhol in real life was like one of those creatures that can mate with itself—in other words, the ideal narcissist. Pearce cuts into this character with a sharpened knife and the skill of a brain surgeon. When he's "used up" someone—in this case the vulnerable Edie—he tosses the person aside like a box of stale pizza—the kind that might have been delivered to The Factory several days before.

A writer with the improbable name of "Captain Mauzner" penned this problematic biopic, just as he did another problem film, *Wonderland*, centered around the life of porn star John Holmes (13½").

Edie's would-be rescuer appears as "The Musician," played stiffly by the good-looking but bland Hayden Christensen. We know that this folk singer is a representation of the real-life Bob Dylan, but that

Dylan is never specifically named because of the folk singer's threatened lawsuit. Dylan's lawyers claimed that their client never had an affair with Edie. In real life, the exact nature of the Sedgwick/Dylan involvement (or lack thereof) may never be known. The answer is blowin' in the wind.

Like Eve Harrington replacing Margo Channing, Edie sees "the new girl" at The Factory. She's Ingrid Superstar, who burst onto the scene in 1966 as *Hedy, the Shoplifter*, obviously inspired by the late Hedy Lamarr. Her fate wasn't any better than Edie's. On December 7, 1986, she disappeared and is presumed dead, although her body has never been found.

Like Edie herself, actress Sienna Miller is no stranger to scandal. Her on-and-off relationship with dashing Jude Law made her an overnight celebrity. Following reports that he had a fling with the nanny of his three children, Sienna broke off their engagement. She learned Law's secret. But we know a secret about her. She dips her French fries into chocolate milkshakes.

After the Law scandal, Miller was reinstated in the role of Edie. She'd originally been given the part but the producers decided she was not famous enough. But after the headlines that trumpeted the subject of Jude Law's infidelity, Miller was deemed a big enough name to carry the role. In other words, she'd become A-list famous. "If you're in the papers for virtually any reason, you've made the grade and American producers want you," said one commentator.

Sienna made her own headlines after the release of *Factory Girl*. She revealed that she takes drugs because "they're fun." But she upset the good people of that sweet city, Pittsburgh, when she called it "Shitsburgh." The remark was doubly insulting because of Warhol's links to Pittsburgh.

She later claimed that her rants were the result of suffering from a form of Tourette's syndrome, which, of course, is a neurological disorder associated with the exclamation of derogatory or obscene remarks. What's Mel Gibson's excuse?

One-time Warhol acolyte and rock god Lou Reed told the press his opinion of *Factory Girl* even before filming ended. "They're all a bunch of whores," referring to helmer Hickenlooper and his cast. Reed claimed that he read the script. "It's one of the most disgusting, foul things I've seen by any illiterate retard in a long time. There's no limit to how low some people will go to write something to make money." Allegedly, Reed at one point was asked to be part of the project but the rocker gave the film a fuck-you.

 # WHAT THE CRITICS SAID

"*Factory Girl* burns brightly and then snuffs herself out. It's a peculiar movie, frantic and useless, with a hyperactive camera that gives us no more than fleeting impressions of Edie ecstatic at parties, Edie strung out on drugs, Edie lying mostly naked on a bed, with her skin blotchy from injections. Whatever shrewdness or charm Sedgwick possessed that caused people to believe that she was a revolutionary figure in New York night life, it doesn't come through in this movie."
The New Yorker

"Perhaps any biopic on as inimitable a figure as Edie Sedgwick would have been doomed to fail. There's a particular disconnect when Hollywood tries to 'do' the Warhol scene, going all the way back to 1969s *Midnight Cowboy*."
Melissa Anderson
New York Magazine

"*Factory Girl* is the sort of compulsively enjoyable bad movie that Andy himself would have loved. And he might even have perversely enjoyed being portrayed therein as an ultra-unattractive creep, a shallow villain with a talent only for exploitation."
Liz Smith

"Sienna Miller is unnervingly vulnerable as Edie Sedgwick, the classic actress/model/whatever and idle heiress ('My grandfather invented the elevator') who in 1965 New York decided to make a career out of being famous."
    Kyle Smith
    New York Post

"The world through which Sedgwick blazed and burned out was one that lived and died by the camera. It existed to be seen and drooled over. But God help you if you actually lived it. In the movie's hostile portrayal of Warhol, the pop art giant comes across as an emotional vampire who loathed his own appearance and used Sedgwick as a vicarious mirror, then turned his back when she became troublesome. In this simplistic tug-of-war, Mr. Dylan is the God of authenticity and inner truth and Warhol the Devil of superficiality and glitter, but you wouldn't know it from the ludicrous mumbo-jumbo muttered by the Dylan character."
    Stephen Holden
    The New York Times

Sienna Miller and Edie Sedgwick

Guy Pearce and Andy Warhol

Edie Sedgwick ("the girl with the tights") and Andy Warhol in NYC circa 1975

Hayden Christensen and Bob Dylan

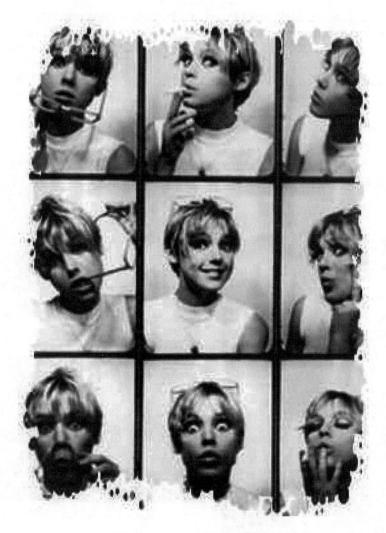

Warhol's Factory Girl: Edie Sedgwick

THE FALL OF '55

Boise Witch Hunt and Hysterical Gay Paranoia

In the fall of 1955, now notorious in the history of Idaho, the citizens of Boise were overcome with mass hysteria aimed at gay people. As Halloween approached, they were told that there was a giant sex ring preying on their local teenage boys—perhaps their own son.

No such ring existed, but a witch hunt was launched. Before it was over, 16 men had been convicted and dozens more intimidated. The men were charged with sex crimes, including accusations of having relations with other consenting adults. One family fled to Mexico; others left town never to return.

With *Time* magazine and other media fanning the flames, the fire spread by "The Boys of Boise" swept across the nation. There were calls for a "morals drive" to rid the country of "undesirables."

Even with homophobes still sitting in the White House, this 81-minute docu from journalist Seth Randal shows how far we've come since the Eisenhower era.

Scars of that post-McCarthy witch hunt remain unhealed in the Boise of today, as descendants express their bitterness over what happened.

The docu was five years in the making, and the production team visited actual locations for their shoot. Excerpted letters to the prison warden by traumatized relatives evoke "the almost unbearable pain" of that time. Regrettably, so many of the principals are long gone, and for interviews Randal had to rely on second-hand sources in many cases.

As an example of media coverage, one headline from a 1955 issue of *Holiday* read: MALE PERVERT RING SEDUCES 1,000 BOYS.

In reviewing the case in 1967, CBS News broadcast a saner sentiment. "The people of Boise tried to 'stamp out' homosexuality. They discovered it couldn't be done. In the learning process, everybody suffered."

What is missing from the film is a first-hand interview with any of the gay old-timers who lived in Boise during the 50s, and who were directly affected by the events described in the film. Had there been one available, he or she could have told us firsthand what it was like to be a homosexual at the time of the Salem—read that Boise—witch trials.

 ## WHAT THE CRITICS SAID

"*The Fall of '55* would seem hopelessly old-fashioned with its corny newspaper headlined, TV exposé-style narration, if it were not for its generous samplings of media quotations from 1955 and revelatory news reel footage, some of it sensational. Randal unfortunately relies on somewhat insipid interviews with both a victim's son and an instigator's son to dramatize the probe's impact."

Ronnie Scheib
Variety

POSTSCRIPT TO OUR REVIEW OF *THE FALL OF '55*
MORE ABOUT OFFICIALLY SANCTIONED GAY REPRESSION IN IDAHO

As this guidebook went to press, the newest twist on officially sanctioned homophobia in Boise emerged in the form of Idaho's Senator, Larry Craig, 62, who has carved a highly visible niche for himself within the Republican Party by developing and promoting anti-gay legislation.

In August of 2007, 52 years after the horrifying events described in the *The Fall of 55*, the Senator was caught with his pants down, literally, in a men's toilet at the Minneapolis/St. Paul airport. The agent who brought the affair into public view was an undercover vice cop, Sgt. Dave Karsnia, who arrested the Senator as part of an entrapment scam.

Craig pleaded guilty and signed a confession, fully expecting that his arrest would be ignored. Weeks later, news of Craig's hypocrisy broke worldwide in both print and TV media.

What's really going on? Vice cops entrapping gay men in toilets sounds so retro, so 1950s, so *Fall of '55*, in fact. On her web site, conservative columnist Arianna Huffington asked: "In the Age of Terror, isn't busting toe-tappers an insane use of our enforcement resources?"

This question raises a point about the Minneapolis police department. Do they specifically select police officers who would be attractive to gay men, and then ship them out to men's toilets throughout the city as a means of entrapping homosexuals?

Apparently, they do. When a photograph of the arresting officer was published, indeed, he was one hunky, albeit reprehensible number. We also suspect that local gay men have committed his photo to memory, thereby reducing Karsnia's effectiveness (at least in Minneapolis) as bait for future sting operations. Actually, we pity the poor slob and any other officer assigned to such duties. They must get awfully tired of checking out urinals and looking furtive.

We are deeply averse to entrapment procedures anywhere, and under normal circumstances, we'd show some empathy for Craig had he not spent most of his political career gay-bashing as a means of securing redneck votes for Republicans.

Because of the damage Craig and his cohorts have caused for gay rights (and as an extension, for human rights), very few gay Americans are in a mood to protect closeted anti-gay politicians. If Craig is indeed gay, we'll categorize him with those other deeply closeted and very dangerous American homophobes, J. Edgar Hoover and Joseph McCarthy, both of whom used gay-baiting/Commie-baiting as a means of developing notorious careers for themselves.

After his arrest and its subsequent publicity, Craig asserted with just a touch of hysteria *"I am not gay. I have never been gay."*

YEAH, RIGHT! Liberace said the same thing in a London court when he was suing *Confidential* for libel. At least in the aftermath of the scandal, more mainstream (heterosexual) Americans might raise a skeptical eyebrow when next they hear a demagogue railing about the dangers implicit by the presence of "gay people in our midst."

Idaho's Republican Senator,
Larry Craig

FAMILY HERO
(LE HÉROS DE LA FAMILLE)

Feather Boas, Cross-Dressers & French Inheritance Squabbles

This French drama was directed by Thierry Klifa and written by Christopher Thompson. *La Cage aux Folles* it isn't, although in some ways it is.

The plot begins to percolate when the septuagenarian, cross-dressing owner of the Blue Parrot nightclub in Nice, Gabriel Stern (Claude Brasseur), expires. Only the night before he'd asked his surrogate son Nicky Guazzini (played brilliantly by Gérard Lanvin) to lock up. All seems well until the next morning when Gabriel is discovered dead.

But instead of giving the cabaret to his Nicky, his heir apparent, Gabriel specifies in his will that *Le perroquet bleu* should be deeded to his godchildren, Nino Bensalem (Michaël Cohen) and Marianne Bensalem (Géraldine Pailhas). The news of this postmortem betrayal reaches Nino in Paris, where he works as an accountant and lives with a much younger boyfriend, Fabrice (Pierrick Lilliu). Nino immediately catches a flight to Nice, where he joins forces with his half-sister and co-heir, Marianne. Both the heirs are in their 30s, Marianne a hotshot Judith Regan-type editor of a popular women's magazine.

Into all this mess walks the co-star of the film, the still-beautiful Catherine Deneuve playing the role of Alice Mirmont, Nino's mother. The great Deneuve is quite humorous in this film, becoming less cold as she ages. In a self-mocking role, she enters the family pow-wow, in the words of one reviewer, "to the sound of thunderclaps as the electricity flickers; couples (gay and straight) embrace as fireworks explode over the Nice waterfront. Deneuve as the mother is the free spirit in this dour, grief-stricken crowd. Nino at one point examines her face, asking, "You've had some work done, haven't you?"

Other cast members include the pulpy Emmanuelle Béart (Léa O'Connor), who delivers comic lines while being poured into seductive gowns. On stage she'll deliver warbling torch songs in English.

On learning that they own the cabaret, the godchildren aren't very interested, but the devoted Nicky is devastated. Hoping to inherit the joint, he is broke and rather washed up, a suitably pained magician who's nearly out of tricks despite his brave gallows humor. Meanwhile, Nicky maintains ongoing discussions with the ever-present spirit of the recently deceased Gabriel.

All the feather boas, the magicians with hats, and the topless women with their lovely breasts will be put out of work if the godchildren sell the Blue Parrot. All the factions seem at war with each other in spite of Gabriel's wish for them to reconcile.

As the picture develops, we learn that the Blue Parrot represents a lot more than just a cabaret.

 WHAT THE CRITICS SAID

"So, if you like French cinema, French actors, or if you like *films chorale* (I don't know how to say it in English—a movie in which there is no protagonist, or more exactly in which everybody is), *Le Héros de la Famille* has been made for you."
   ElasticSword

"A star vehicle with spacious seating for eight *dramatis personae*, *Family Hero* centers on wounded souls forced to interact when the owner of a venerable Nice cabaret dies. Sophomore feature by former film journo Klifa (*I've Been Waiting So Long*, 2004), again co-scripting with Christopher Thompson (*Avenue Montaigne*), is full to bursting with unsuspected allegiances and long-awaited missing pieces of multiple puzzles. Script's artistry lies in how it manages to arrive at a hopeful conclusion after so much *Sturm und Drang*."
   Lisa Nesselson
   Variety

FAT GIRLS

Misfit Gay Male Teen: 'We're All Fat Girls'

Homophile viewers of both *Napoleon Dynamite* and *American Pie* might enjoy this original offbeat comedy feature, even though it hardly strives for nuance. The jokes are hit-and-miss, with enough hits to make it worth viewing.

In the movie's opening voiceover, budding writer/director/actor Ash Christian stakes out his premise: "You don't have to be fat to be a fat girl. You don't even have to be a girl. It's a state of mind. And whenever you're in a fellow fat girl's presence, you know it right away. It's almost like an unspoken club no one really talks about."

In a nutshell, this is another coming-of-age drama set in a dipstick Texas town. It zeroes in on a coterie of Texas teens (both gay and straight) who, for different reasons, are condemned as "outcasts" by their redneck peers.

Christian is skilled as an actor and promising as a director. Wisely he cast two great supporting roles—his best friend, fat girl, 300-pound Sabrina (played by newcomer Ashley Fink), and Sabrina's BF, Rudy (Robin de Jesus of the recent indie hit film, *Camp*).

Like The Three Musketeers, the outcast trio of misfits band together to overcome their mistreatment. To make for more character development, each of the three carries baggage. Rodney (Christian) is the gay son of fundamentalist Christians; Rudy, a Cuban refugee adopted by black parents, and Sabrina, the overweight daughter of two lesbian moms.

Gay actor Christian actually grew up in Texas where he claims that "someone is being harassed or beaten up every day because they're gay," in an interview with *The Advocate*. "I've always sort of felt like a fat girl on the inside, someone who didn't really fit in." After settling into California, Christian landed roles on TV shows, including *Boston Public* and *Cold Case* while pursuing his dream of filming *Fat Girls*.

The film is about the triumph of the nerds, as Rodney learns to accept the "fat girl" within himself and to discover and even celebrate his own inner beauty. This inner beauty means coming to terms with his gayness.

As the plot thickens, Rodney develops a relationship with a handsome British classmate, Joey (Joe Flaten). It develops to the point where they will attend the school prom as each other's "dates."

Left, Actor/director Ash Christian; *right,* Ashley Fink

There's also a subplot here in the relationship between Rodney and his theater teacher, Seymour Cox (played by Jonathan Caouette of the award-winning docu *Tarnation*). This gay iconic figure beautifully fulfills the role of the platonic, supportive high school teacher. Some twists of plot bring student and teacher into a closer form of "bondage" as the film moves to its climax.

Ash Christian with producer Michele Levy (center) and Ashley Fink (right)

 WHAT THE CRITICS SAID

"Ash Christian's self-penned and starring debut gets points for high school authenticity (not surprising since he was 21 when he made it), but grows too fond of its handful of jokes. It's briefly funny that his character's fundamentalist mom only allows Bible-themed food, but he should cut the cord somewhere between 'angel food cake' and 'holy hamburgers.' *Fat Girls*, for the movie's purposes, are rejects of any size or shape, although Christian throws in an actual fat girl just to drive the point home. The director ably captures the disaffection of growing up gay amid the freak show of suburban Texas, but he neglects to give his characters anything they're not alienated from."
Philadelphia City Paper

"Placing the crass high school surrealist humor of *Strangers With Candy* in the familiar frame of a gay-teenage-misfit's coming-out saga, producer-writer-director-star Ash Christian's *Fat Girls* wins no points for delicacy. Still, it does score some laughs."
Dennis Harvey
Variety

"With his true "fat girl" friend (the very funny and crass Ashley Fink) and Cuban refugee sidekick (Robin de Jesus), Christian sets off on a series of misadventures, some quite funny, some crassly derivative, and eventually bonds with his teacher, Jonathan Caouette, who at night impersonates Liza Minnelli in a wonderful performance that fans of Caouette's marvel, *Tarnation*, must see."
New York Magazine

"It is the drama surrounding Rodney's asking and taking his dream date to the prom that makes up most of *Fat Girls* story which culminates in a classic, ultimate 'high school prom' scene (think *Grease*—only geeky and gay).
Fake Gay News

THE FAVOR

Argentinean Farce in Pursuit of Sperm

This 90-minute Argentine film, released in that country as *El Favor*, was both produced and directed by Pablo Sofovich, who hired Martin Greco as scripter. It is broad Argentinean farce that in some ways evokes Spike Lee's *She Hate Me*. It searches for comedy within the context of lesbians needing a male to supply sperm so they can have a kid.

Rather good actors, Javiar Lombardo and Bernarda Pages, are the feuding but loving brother and sister. She wants him to impregnate her girlfriend, as played by Victoria Onetto.

There is some funny business along the way as the two lesbians—unknown to each other—add enough Viagra to an unsuspecting victim's drink to raise a double hard-on in a horse. Onetto plays a role that Sharon Stone could have handled in the American version, donning one "I'm-a-slut" outfit after another in a failed attempt to appear sexy. Marilyn Monroe she ain't.

 ## WHAT THE CRITICS SAID

"The affectionate brother and sister add unexpected depth to the frenetic slapstick, but cannot redeem Onetto's unfunny perf as a trying-too-hard sexpot. Bits of business between siblings develop a shared history and three-dimensionality. By contrast, gags fueling pic's sex-themed plot turn flat and repetitive."
Ronnie Scheib
Variety

"She slept with every male star at MGM except Lassie."

Bette Davis, referring to Joan Crawford

FIFTEEN ('15')

Teenage Boys Surviving on the Seedy Streets of Singapore

Still in his 20s, Royston Tan has been hailed as the most promising young filmmaker in uptight Singapore, where authorities might arrest you and paddle your bare ass for throwing a candy wrapper on the sidewalk. Known for his distinctive knack for cinematic narrative, original directorial style, and an innate ability to connect with his audience, he has collected more than 26 international and local film awards for his work.

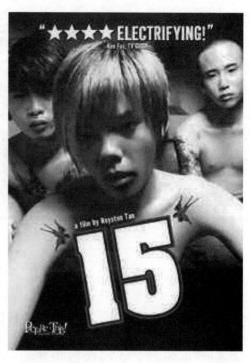

Tan's first full-length feature is *'15'*, which he extended from his award-winning short of the same title.

The movie charts the misadventures of teenage boys on the fringe of Singaporean society, a real street kids' drama that exposes the gritty side of modern-day Singapore—the kind of raw reality that travel brochures never show you.

The scrappy suburban existence of five boys is portrayed in a progression of disturbing sequences that bit by bit reconstruct the psychological and ad-hoc family dynamics of the teen rebels. Tan masterfully explores this counter-culture adolescent world whose inhabitants are addicted to video clip and videogame aesthetics. The fragmented narrative and visual style throttles the viewer's senses.

The boys in the film form a tight but complicated bond among themselves. It's a brotherhood whose code allows the shedding of blood, perhaps, but never tears. Skipping school, taking drugs, rehearsing gang raps, piercing and ritual cuttings of their bodies— this is pure drama.

Tan is very attentive to the underlying intimacy of the boys' shared suffering and the need each one eventually shows to be close to someone, even in a late-night embrace out of sight of the others.

The movie manages to depict some of the best traits of human nature—patience, caring, forgiveness, loyalty, and a willingness to be vulnerable to one another. In the end, *'15'* emerges as a brave and unique depiction of young lives pitted against a hostile world and often giving back better than the world deserves.

Tan has a talented sense of visuals and impressive technical competence. He jolts the complacency of his audience with images so brutal that they sometimes hurt.

'15' was shot guerilla style, with line producer Fong Cheng being told to "beg, borrow or steal" whatever was not included in the film's budget. No professional actors were used: Each of the "stars" was recruited from the back streets of Singapore.

Trouble began when the draconian censors of Singapore saw the finished cut. The actors, director, and producer were hauled in for questioning because of the criminal activity depicted on screen. There were concerns that the lyrics of the rap songs contained names of real gangs, and that the "public order would be threatened." In the end the movie was approved, but with 20 cuts. It was given an R rating, meaning it would have limited theatrical release, no video release, and no TV releases. But those rules apply only to Singapore.

In the DVD release, the film is as uncut as Arnold Schwarzenegger's penis. In the United States, for information about access to this DVD, call [tel] 888/604-8301.

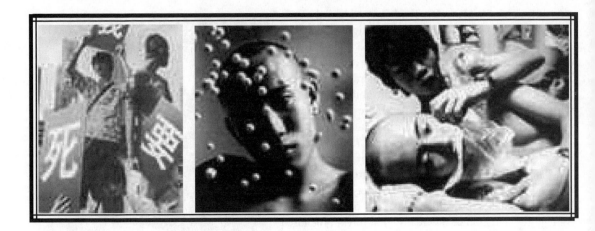

 WHAT THE CRITICS SAID

"Look at the other crap that's been churned out from Singapore and compare them to this film. It's like comparing a mule's diarrhea chunks to a little diamond. This film is the first to truly show some of Singapore's seedy underbelly—something the forces that be pretend does not exist."
   Garry Johal of Singapore

"Directing real-life street kids, Tan abruptly shifts focus from one character to another, as if mimicking their impatience and short attention span, and like Godard he playfully subverts his own material by having actors address the camera directly, spouting cultural and political asides. Tan is unstintingly graphic in chronicling the messy details of the boys' lives."
   The Chicago Reader

"The best film to come out of Singapore in years."
   Time Magazine

Filthy Gorgeous: The Trannyshack Story

Glammy Queens at the San Francisco Drag Show

If you don't live in San Francisco and don't attend the famous drag show every Tuesday at Trannyshack, you might not completely enjoy this 90-minute docu. The helmer, Sean Mullens, makes his feature film debut in this bizarre piece of entertainment.

Spotlighted are such queens as Peaches Christ, Glamamore, Rusty Hips, Princess Kennedy, and Precious Moments. As one of these ladies—we forgot which one—told us one night at Trannyshack, "I'm God damn gorgeous and you'd better write that or I'll rip off your left ball!"

There are also audience shots of the likes of David Bowie or Papa Roach spliced with plainsclothes interviews with the queens themselves. Without their flamboyant drag, they come off as completely different characters.

 WHAT THE CRITICS SAID

"You know you're at a gay and lesbian film festival when a glammy queen pulls an American flag out of her ass while lip-syncing 'The Star Spangled Banner' and not a single person boos. Sean Mullens' debut doc about San Francisco's infamous Tuesday night cabaret is all lip-liner, hairspray and bags of cocaine—the foundations upon which their country was built. Self-congratulatory and skin-deep, *Filthy Gorgeous* has earned its seat in the pantheon of glittery drag documentaries, despite its inability to wipe away the eyelash glue."
Ashlea Halpern

FOR THE BIBLE TELLS ME SO

Filmmaker Tosses a Grenade at Religious Zealots

Daniel G. Karslake both co-authored and directed this 95-minute docu exploring the "intersection" between religion and homosexuality in the U.S. and how the religious right has used its interpretation of the Bible to stigmatize the gay community.

Regrettably, it's preaching to the choir, since G&L people are the most likely candidates to screen this movie. Such noted churchy homophobes as orange juicy Anita Bryant, the "sinning" Rev. Jimmy Swaggart, and that ferocious crocodile of the right, James Dobson of the Focus on the Family group, aren't likely to see it.

The film deals with a hot-button issue, and Karslake isn't afraid to press that button. It's ambitious and daring, attacking the traditional Christian stance against homosexuality, offering other interpretations of the very few verses in the Bible that specifically deal with the subject.

Providing reinterpretations are such ecclesiastical heavyweights as Archbishop Desmond Tutu and Gene Robinson, the first openly gay bishop to be consecrated by the Episcopalians. That heroic act on their part set off a firestorm which is still threatening to split that church.

Robinson relates the coming-out story he delivered years previously to his parents. Other heavyweights weighing in are former Rep. Dick Gephardt, wife Jane, and daughter Chrissy. Presented also is Mary Lou Wallner, who became a cultural warrior against homophobia following the suicide of her lesbian daughter. Missing is Dick Cheney's daughter.

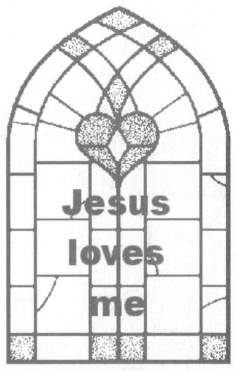

 WHAT THE CRITICS SAID

"With great conviction, Tutu and others repeatedly point to Jesus' teachings of love and inclusion as the standard by which the church must regard the gay community—a standard certainly not upheld by the legacy of hate crimes, fire-and-brimstone sermons and condemnations perpetrated in the name of God, as recapped in extensive archival footage."
Justin Chang
Variety

Co-author & director Daniel Karslake

"In my movie *Querelle*, Brad Davis plays a sailor. He wears pants so tight you know what religion he *isn't*."

Director Rainer Werner Fassbinder

FRIENDS OF GOD:
A ROAD TRIP WITH ALEXANDRA PELOSI

A Pelosi Films Human Crocs in Red-State America

Alexandra Pelosi's mother is the most powerful woman in U.S. history—yes, even more so than Hillary Clinton. Daughter Alexandra Pelosi decided to go on a road trip to film some of America's gay-bashing religious nuts, including the disgraced pastor, Ted Haggard, who had that hustler problem.

Her film highlights "The Big Three" flashpoint points of controversy in contemporary American politics: Evolution, Abortion, and Homosexuality. But it does so much more, hitting the Holy Land Experience Theme Park in Orlando, a drive-through church, a visit with "Cruisers (of cars) for Christ," and even a stopover with the Christian Wrestling Federation (we're not making that up).

The God-fearing wrestlers pummel each other in a ring surrounded by cheering crowds of young children, including prepubescent girls screaming for God to "invade" their bodies. They appear to be sexually

Women We Love:
Filmmaker Alexandra Pelosi with her mother, Senate Majority Leader Nancy Pelosi

turned on by the wrestlers, which seems to suggest they are eager to lose their cherries. Please, say this impression isn't true.

Alexandra is no stranger to docus, having made *Journal With George*, which captured a kinder, sillier side of then first-time presidential candidate George W. Bush. The new director won an Emmy for her job. In that film, Dubya utters his now famous line: "I like a good baloney sandwich."

For *Friends of God*, Alexandra rambled through 16 states in a rental car. She meets these "Christlers," who place scripture in truck-stop menus and put huge crosses alongside state highways.

The film has a voyeur factor—maybe better called "The Mom Factor." Here is the daughter of a woman who is more hated by the Christian Right than Hillary herself. Nancy Pelosi was a figure vilified by conservative Christians during the midterm elections as the leader of the supposed ultra-liberal San Francisco gay rights agenda.

A former producer for NBC News, Alexandra, in her docu, is not an attack dog, and she's learned to distinguish those old dragons of hate—the late, lardy Falwell, the increasingly wacko Pat Robertson, and that vicious scorpion, the very, very anti-gay James Dobson—from some younger evangelicals.

"Young evangelicals tell you that these men don't speak for them," Alexandra noted. "Rick Warren, Joel Osteen, the younger versions—they care about the poor. They care about the environment. Just because these old scolds say, 'This is what 80 million people believe, doesn't mean it's true.'"

"I was blown away by how organized they were politically," Alexandra said. "They don't just believe in something. They actually go to meetings. I get annoyed now when people say critical things about evangelicals, because, I say, 'When was the last time you got off your couch to defend anything you believe in?'"

The docu examines the practices, politics, and beliefs of fundamentalist evangelical Christians, no friends of the gay and lesbian community. Of course, they air their tired old themes, claiming that evolution is a myth, homosexuality immoral, and abortion murder. They utter these myths with the same hysteria that Joseph Goebbels spoke for the Third Reich.

Naturally, there are clips of those "one-man, one-woman" sermons delivered every Sunday morning on TV.

Filmed months before he died, the Rev. Jerry Falwell is shown in his pulpit in Lynchburg, Virginia, advising, with nuanced rhetoric, his congregation to vote only for conservatives on the ballot, especially those who abhor abortion and homosexuals. So much for the separation of tax-exempt church and the state. When homophobic Falwell found out who Alexandra was, he kicked her out of his office.

Unlike her reception from Falwell, she was warmly received by Ted Haggard, then president of the 30-million-member National Association of Evangelicals. After the filming, trouble lay ahead for this hypocrite when he was forced out of his position when revelations broke that he'd used crystal meth and spent time with a male hustler.

Filmed before his appreciation of man-on-man action became public knowledge, Haggard astonishingly says, on-camera, that "Christians have the best sex lives." He then proceeds to interview two men in what one critic called "squirm-inducing detail" about their sex with their wives. Haggard bows out of the docu with a brief lecture about "sexual purity and the responsibility of pastors to live a pure life." Actually we were taken aback by Haggard's voice. It sounded like a faggy Paul Lynde after a weekend bender.

The Christians in this film, almost in every case, know "the truth" and don't want to hear any other opinions, especially from homosexuals. Much of the rhetoric in this movie sounds like the sort of bile you'd hear from Saddam Hussein—before the hangman got him, of course. Just what are some of fundamentalist Christian children being taught? Here's a dilly. Did you know that dinosaurs not only coexisted with humans but actually worked for them as beasts of burden? We want the movie rights to that one.

Okay, the show's named *Friends of God*. What's our blunt, tagline opinion? We don't think God on her throne wants most of this motley crew from the Dark Ages as her drinking buddies.

 # WHAT THE CRITICS SAID

"*Friends of God* is a safari film for liberals to gawk at the Evangelical natives. This is not to say that the documentary is unfair: Pelosi makes a genuine effort to understand what motivates these god-minded fellow countrymen and, in the process, gives Evangelicals the chance to see themselves as others see them."
   Rebecca Cusey
   National Review Online

"We really do have two different countries within our borders. There's a group of people who as far as they're concerned, live in an American theocracy. They don't give a rat's ass about tolerance, pluralism, the constitution, or live and let live. As one spokesman put it, 'If you don't believe in Jesus Christ, you are a loser.' Central to the film is the recently disgraced Ted Haggard. He smugly rants on and on about how happy Christians are, and how they have the best sex! I'm sure he never suspected we would ever find out he was talking about his meth-fueled man-shagging. Equally revealing was that he questioned two other men about their sex lives—pointedly asking 'if their women came every time,' to which they replied—'everytime!' Did anyone think to ask the women?"
   Black Sun Journal

"*Friends of God* succeeds at getting past the tension one might expect in a film that has the daughter of the most prominent pro-choice, pro-gay rights politician in America examining an anti-choice, anti-gay rights culture. By using the quirkiness of Roadside America as her visual language, Pelosi finds a commonality that is absent from much of the discussion of born-again Christians."
   Erik Moe

FUCK

The Movie That Dare Not Speak Its Name

Who would have ever believed that the star of *April Love* in 1958, Pat Boone, Mr. Goodie Two-Shoes of the white bucks, would end up appearing in a 93-minute docu called FUCK made in 2005? But here he is, although no longer the exceedingly wholesome and whitewashed non-threatening pop star that he used to be.

Like many singers of his generations, Boone tried to parlay his chart success into movie fame, failing along the way. But in Steve Anderson's FUCK, the "Love Letters in the Sand" singer stages his Last Hurrah.

The veteran crooner is still as pure as the new fallen snow. He has found an inspired way to get around Richard Nixon's favorite expletive. Every time he has the need to say, "Oh, Fuck!," he says, "Oh, Boone!" instead. Isn't that adorable? Ice-T jokingly contends that the Boone-word could actually catch on. We, however, disagree, feeling that George Carlin will not have to amend his "Seven Dirty Words" in the near future.

Our vice president, Dick Cheney, still prefers the not-so-*bon mot* "mother of all curse words," at least when Senator Patrick Leahy enters the chamber.

To counter-balance Boone's blandness, Anderson uses that ugly porn star, Ron Jeremy and his 9½ inch dick, as a member of the cast. That cast also includes various talking heads, including news commentators, celebrities, politicians, and linguists. To spice up the film, movie, video, and audio clips are used, including original Bill Plympton animations. As such, the F-word turns out to be remarkably resilient in this docu.

Joining the cast are such august figures as Bill Maher, Ben Bradlee, Sam Donaldson, Judith "Miss Manners" Martin, porn star Tera Patrick, plus a particularly ripe Billy Connolly and the late Hunter S. Thompson in one of his last interviews.

Also appearing are such standard bearers of morality as Janet Jackson and Eddie Murphy, their appearances based on archive footage. Tit-exposing Justin Timberlake also appears as himself.

The docu does explode a myth or two, particularly the most popular one, about the origin of the word fuck. If you can believe Anderson, it was never an acronym "For Unlawful Carnal Knowledge," at least according to some experts. Nor was it an acronym for "Fornication Under Consent of the King."

So where did the word come from? Its origins, if we believe the linguists, are unknown. All we know is that the very use of the word *fuck* can drive uptight people into spasms of righteous indignation. Two people getting worked up about the use of the word are Robert Peters, of Morality in Media, and right-wing watch dog, Michael Medved. The talk show host, Dennis Prager, characterizes the fight over the word's usage as central to civilization's "battle to preserve itself." Our reaction to that opinion? "Get a life, gal!"

Public figures have even been arrested for use of the word. Lenny Bruce was arrested twice and convicted for his refusal to stop saying *fuck* publicly.

The word *fuck* is invoked about 800 times in this docu, and the first Hollywood studio film to use the word was *M*A*S*H* in 1970. In *Scarface* the word appears 182 times, and in *Jay and Silent Bob Strike Back*, 228 times. But in the HBO series, *Deadwood*, it is uttered 861 times. On a personal aside, we think no movie actress ever said it better than Miss Elizabeth Taylor herself.

"From Scots national poet Robert Burns, to American comedian Lenny Bruce; from Country Joe McDonald's *Give-Me-an-F* cheer at Woodstock to *South Park: Bigger, Longer and Uncut*, the offensive word that provides the title for Steven Anderson's penetrating documentary/social critique has either enriched or infected Western culture to the point that we're either drowning in a 'floodtide of filth' or blessed with the best verbal relief valve ever devised by man."
  John Anderson
  Variety

"Although its premise could easily make for a dire, dim-witted snarkfest, Steve Anderson's exegesis of the word fuck as a linguistic and cultural phenomenon makes for a thoughtful and even challenging doc. Profanity's role in the culture wars is given a sophisticated airing. Trenchant blowhards on both sides of the issue hold forth."
  Mark Holcomb
  Time Out New York

"Is this evidence of cultural decline? It's hard to think of a short answer that wouldn't be made more vivid by the insertion of the forbidden word. So skip it. No, not the movie. What, are you kidding me? No way. Go. Help yourself."
  A.O. Scott
  The New York Times

"The film is so ultimately repetitive, un-enlightening and lacking in substance, Drew Carey seems bored by the end when he asks, 'When are guys going to make the c'nt documentary?'"
  Scott Warren
  Premiere

"Although marquee placement could be tricky without a well-placed asterisk or two, FUCK makes perfect, undeniably timely sense with the right distributor. And down the road, given the theme of freedom of speech in the present political climate, it could form a dream triple bill with *Inside Deep Throat* and *The Aristocrats*."
  Michael Rechtshaffen
  Hollywood Reporter

Pat Boone in the 1950s
"Oh Fuck, Oh Boone!"

FUNNY KINDA GUY

A Musical Odyssey of Simon de Voil from Female to Male

This 83-minute docu from the UK traces the saga of singer and songwriter Simon de Voil who changed his gender from female to male. Although he finally achieved his long-sought masculinity, he sacrificed the elegantly trained quality of his singing voice, the result of extended hormone treatment.

Directed by Travis Reeves, *Funny Kinda Guy* is very slow moving, although de Voil himself is charming.

All his life, de Voil apparently knew he was in the wrong skin, preferring to be a "transman" to a butch lesbian. The docu is very realistic, even depicting de Voil giving himself his first shot of testosterone.

The happy ending shows the blue-haired lead in a Tranniboy T-shirt becoming all man and dancing in the rain with his bride-to-be.

 WHAT THE CRITICS SAID

"*Funny Kinda Guy* is not a likely title for a documentary about a transgendered singer-songwriter who, while gaining his true identity as a man, must sacrifice his voice to hormone treatment. Yet Scotland's Simon de Voil is so charismatic and good-natured, the title quickly grabs and never lets go."
Jim Norrena
San Francisco LGBT Film Festival

"A strong sense of compassion towards a clever and sitty guy struggling to come to terms with his own masculinity... *Funny Kinda Guy* scores by simply telling it straight."
Isla Leaver-Yap
The List

"A standout at the Melbourne Queer Film Festival is *Funny Kinda Guy*, a painful journey taken by transgendered singer-songwriter Simon de Voil's transition from male to female."
Lesa Beel

"*Funny Kinda Guy* explores travels from Scotland to Australia through transgender protagonist Simon. The main character, Simon, actually fails in love with an Australian girl from Brisbane. "
Megan Carrigy

"I found out Carole [Lombard] wasn't a natural blonde. We're in her dressing room, talking. She starts undressing. I didn't know what to do... She's talking away and mixing peroxide and some other liquid in a bowl. With a piece of cotton she beings to apply the liquid to dye the hair around her honeypot. She glanced up and saw my alarmed look, and smiled. 'Relax, Georgie, I'm just making my collar and cuffs match.'"

George Raft *(Some Like it Hot)*

193

GARBO: THE SIGNATURE COLLECTION

Renewed Notoriety for a Dragon of the Silent Screen

Although film star Greta Garbo (1905-1990) frequently wanted to be alone, you can now keep company with her on DVD, thanks to the recent re-release by Warner Home Video of ten of her best films. The boxed set includes a full-length documentary by helmer and film historian Kevin Brownlow, with narration by Julie Christie. Also included on the boxed set are interviews with friends and associates, once-obscure outclips, some of them in German, and cinematic extras which collectively illuminate Garbo the legend and Greta the person.

Seventy years after the original release of her films, and more than a century after her birth in Stockholm, we at Blood Moon remain unabashed and unapologetic fans. The pages that follow, through individual descriptions of the films within the re-digitalized release, attempt to celebrate Garbo's enigmatic luminosity.

She was the most alluring actress of the 1920s and 30s, and the movies in this collection were the ones that catapulted her to international movie stardom. In some uncanny way, Garbo's grip on our imagination remains as potent today as it was back in 1927 when she brought rapture to the world in *The Flesh and the Devil*.

The new 10-film boxed set from Warner Brothers includes seven of her best sound films, and three of her best silent films. The films with sound include her first talkie, *Anna Christie* (1930) and *Queen Christina* (1933), about the Swedish bisexual monarch who escapes her royal duties by masquerading as a boy. Among the silent films included within the collection is *Flesh and the Devil* (1927) with John Gilbert. In each of her silents, she was cast in vamp roles rather than in the more dignified roles of her talkies. The prints for all these are as pristine as the ravages of time and the current state of restoration technology will allow.

A few of the discs have generous extras—*Camille*, for example, offers a bizarre 1921 modern dress version of *Camille* with the lesbian actress, Nazimova (Nancy Reagan's godmother) sporting Afro-like hair and a young Rudolph Valentino (gay as a goose) pretending to be her admirer.

"If you want to see what screen glamour used to be, and what originally 'stars,' were, this is the example of all time," wrote critic Pauline Kael.

The off-screen lovers of the bisexual actress were almost as legendary as Garbo herself: Joseph P. Kennedy, Cecil Beaton (although he was mostly gay), John Gilbert, Louise Brooks, Mercedes de Acosta, Dolores Del Rio, Beatrice Lillie, Leopold Stokowsky, Robert Taylor (though he mostly preferred men), and Salka Viertel, the lesbian actress and writer. Also among them was Carson McCullers, the emotionally fragile author of *Member of the Wedding*.

Garbo also conducted a secret affair with another movie legend, Katharine Hepburn, thanks partly to George Cukor, who played Cupid. Before that, during the early 1920s in Berlin, Garbo had an affair with Marlene Dietrich, although later, during the 1930s in Hollywood, Garbo pretended she had never heard of Dietrich.

Apparently, she wasn't a great sex partner. Author Eric Marie Remarque said: "Garbo is lousy in bed. So is Marlene in the missionary position. But she gives great blow-jobs."

Garbo once said, "I have tried everything at various times in my life, but my body and my thoughts were never satisfied."

ICONOGRAPHY AS ART
OR "EVERYBODY LOVES A DAME"

Self-portrait, circa 1996, in the style of Greta Garbo, by Yasumasa Morimura, Japanese artist and social commentator.

Morimura is the Asian art world's most famous drag queen. Addressing issues of cultural and sexual appropriation, he explores the concept of image, consumption, sexual identity, and desire: Where, in Garbo's exalted sense of passion and neurotic reclusivity, is the line between eccentricity and paranoia? Could Brigitte Bardot be as innocently flirtatious if she had angular Japanese features? And would Marilyn Monroe be as sexy if she were Japanese--and a man?

According to his press agent, "In his photos Morimura plays the role of an Asian *agent provocateur,* infiltrating Western collective consciousness, becoming the icons most lusted after, and in the process, making us look at them even more closely."

WHAT THE CRITICS SAID ABOUT
GARBO: THE SIGNATURE COLLECTION

"The documentary, helmed by Kevin Brownlow and narrated by Julie Christie, digs most fruitfully into Garbo's guarded private life. Stock footage and new interviews with surviving family and friends paint a woman who thrived out of the spotlight she famously shunned. Garbo biographer Barry Paris focuses on her affair with that film's co-star, John Gilbert, and tells juicy anecdotes through the fascinating lens of the Hollywood studio system. A collection of film historians dissects each silent as an example of how the entertainment industry used to run, and the result plays like an outstanding day at film school. Customers who bite and buy the boxed set will own a package that does justice to a legend."
 Mark Blankenship
 Variety

THE TEMPTRESS (1926)

Unexpressed Desire—Vamp as Camp

In the 1926 silent, *The Temptress*, the bisexual Garbo played opposite the mostly homosexual Antonio Moreno in this melodrama of jealousy and degradation. Reverberations of Stoker's vampirism were audible in a toast "to the temptress, who asks for nothing, but takes everything a man can give . . . and more!"

Garbo's lover and mentor, Mauritz Stiller, was originally hired to direct his protégée. On the first day of shooting, Stiller clashed with the Latin heartthrob and Garbo's leading man, Moreno. First, Stiller wanted Moreno to shave off his mustache. Next he wanted Moreno to wear larger shoes to make Garbo's feet look smaller.

Morale on the set went downhill from that day foreward. MGM fired Stiller after only 10 days, and in protest, Garbo wanted to walk off the picture. But at Stiller's urging, she stayed on to the bitter end, although she detested Moreno and found playing love scenes with him "disgusting."

Fred Niblo, who had "saved" MGM's *Ben Hur* the year before, was called in to direct, but Garbo found him "less than inspiring. He seems to think I'm a horse in his damn chariot race."

The film takes place in Paris and Argentina. The Paris scenes are most effective, the scenes in Argentina less so. Garbo plays Elena, the Marquess of Torre Blanca. At a masked ball in Paris, she meets Manuel Robledo (Moreno), a handsome young Argentine architect, who becomes enthralled with her even though she's married to dilettante Marc MacDermott, playing the Marquis. He doesn't mind "lending" his wife to a banker.

Learning she is married, Manuel returns to his native Argentina where he is constructing a dam. Elena follows him there.

The most dramatic scene in the film—sadists will take delight—takes place in Argentina. The villain of the piece, the rather ridiculous Roy D'Arcy, is challenged to a bola fight—call it a whip duel. As Manos Duras, D'Arcy has been harassing Elena, and Manuel sets out to defend her honor.

The whip duel is long and vicious, both men suffering cuts and lashes on their naked chests. Of course, thug D'Arcy is vanquished. At the end of the duel, Elena virtually licks the blood from her hero's chest, a bit kinky for the easily shocked audiences of 1926.

D'Arcy added to the gayness of the cast. He was a boyfriend of Ramon Novarro, Hollywood most notorious homosexual of the late 20s.

Our favorite lines in the silent:

MORENO: *Men have died and killed and been destroyed for you.*
ELENA: *Not for me, but for my body. Not for my happiness, but theirs.*

As a Latin man, Moreno's character is seeking the Madonna, and he definitely wants a virgin. That the Marquess is not. As one viewer expressed it, "he wants retroactive rights to her body as well as universal rights to her soul."

Predictably, Garbo's Elena will fall on bad days. In some ways she foreshadows Tennessee Williams' doomed Blanche DuBois in *A Streetcar Named Desire*. In the final reel she's back in Paris sitting in a café, half out of her mind and diseased, pursuing a trade that is called "the oldest profession."

That was the sad ending. MGM also filmed an alternative "happy" ending, and exhibitors were given a choice.

The film is worth watching, as the seeds of Garbo's future greatness are planted here. In spite of the title and promotion, the heavy-breathing Garbo is not exactly the devil's daughter. She's somewhat passive as she stands about looking supremely gorgeous, as silly, infatuated, lovesick men throw their hearts away like discarding a pit from an overripe plum. Lionel Barrymore, a closeted gay in real life, is driven to jealous murder at the mere sight of Elena.

One reviewer noted that Garbo wanders through *The Temptress* "like a world traveler without a passport, renting her body out to many men but pledging her love to only one. To her, sex is a pleasant timekiller, marriage a nonbinding contract, but love is a sacred vow."

Garbo, in her second film in America, was only nineteen when she vamped her way through Blasco-Ibáñez's soapy melodrama. Being Garbo, she appears far more worldly and sophisticated than any teenager we've known. Even so, this is hardly vintage Garbo of the incandescent soul. Many of her gestures seem painted on like Pinocchio's smile. When she rolls her eyes back and forth, it is almost mechanical, like something you'd expect from Betty Boop.

Not all critics of the time agreed with this assessment. Even at such an early stage, Garbo had already begun to weave her magic spell.

Dorothy Herzog of the *New York Mirror* wrote as if she were in love with Garbo. "Greta Garbo vitalizes the name part of this picture. She *is* The Temptress. Her tall, swaying figure moves Cleopatra-ishly from delirious Paris to the virile Argentina. Her alluring mouth and volcanic, slumberous eyes entice men to such passion that friendships collapse."

Garbo and Moreno were an uneasy couple. During *The Temptress* they had many fights, and playing a love scene was most difficult. Fred Niblo always claimed he knew the reason for their feud. One afternoon, when tension between Garbo and Moreno reached a breaking point, he allegedly said, "You're not the only one John Gilbert fucks." Moreno also "bottomed" for some of the leading lights of the silent screen, including "the great lover," Valentino.

La Dame aux Caméllias

FLESH AND THE DEVIL (1927)

Garbo's Homoerotic Love Triangle

In a 113-minute silent made in 1927, MGM teamed Garbo (as Felicitas) with her off-screen lover, John Gilbert, cast as Leo von Harden. The third member of this love triangle was Lars Hanson, playing the role of Ulrich von Eltz.

Leo and Ulrich were the good, virtuous couple (not only best pals, but perhaps boyhood lovers), and Felicitas is the evil interloper. Helmer Clarence Brown tries to handle this dynamic duo of Garbo & Gilbert. They fall in love at a military ball (there was always a ball in these films). The plot thickens almost immediately. Felicitas neglects to tell Leo she is married to a no-count count, Count von Rhaden (Marc MacDermott).

The two men fight a duel and the count is killed. Leo is ordered to Africa for five years. He asks Ulrich to take care of the widowed Felicitas.

Unaware of her affair with Leo, Ulrich in time marries Felicitas. After three years, Leo gets a pardon, returning home hoping to reclaim Felicitas. Back in Austria, he learns that his lady love has married his best friend, Ulrich.

Leo tries to avoid Felicitas but "The Flesh" is too weak to resist "The Devil." He returns as a lover, creating a deadly triangle involving his childhood friend.

The pace of the soapy melodrama quickens, as Felicitas, not wanting Leo killed, runs across an ice-packed river but falls through and drowns. Leo wounds Ulrich in the duel, but nurses him back to health. The two become bosom buddies once again, and, at least in the eyes of gay fans, "lovers for life," although this movie hardly spells out that possibility.

Clarence Brown has Gilbert as Leo simultaneously carrying on two very different love affairs—and two very different kinds of love in this flicker. He's in love with both Ulrich and Felicitas. The two loves seemingly can't coexist.

Brown himself was well aware of the homoerotic nature of the material. At one point he asked, "How do you have the woman die and the two men embrace without making them look like a couple of fairies?"

MYSTERIOUS LADY (1928)

Passion as a Form of Tragic Depression

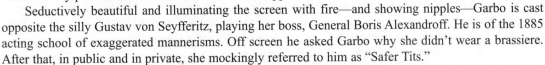

Refusing to wear a brassiere, and showing her tits, Garbo in her ninth film, *The Mysterious Lady* (1928), played Tania, a secret agent (pre-Mata Hari), who shoots her spymaster in order to save her enemy lover. The Swede hadn't yet met up with rugged Clark Gable, so she is stuck with a leading man, the stoically blond Conrad Nagel. He is one of the less fondly remembered male stars of the silent era.

Garbo provides all the passion in this film thanks to her portrayal of Tania Fedorova, a "dream princess of eternity— the knockout of the ages," in the words of a *Life* critic who got carried away with the character's temptress charms. Fred Niblo was called back to direct this woman who could convey passion even in scenes in which she appears alone.

Seductively beautiful and illuminating the screen with fire—and showing nipples—Garbo is cast opposite the silly Gustav von Seyfferitz, playing her boss, General Boris Alexandroff. He is of the 1885 acting school of exaggerated mannerisms. Off screen he asked Garbo why she didn't wear a brassiere. After that, in public and in private, she mockingly referred to him as "Safer Tits."

In a nutshell, the plot starts spinning with Nagel as the Austrian captain, Karl von Raden, attending the opera (but, of course) one night. There, he meets Tania (Garbo), who is swept away with love at first sight. The captain has to deliver some important military secrets to Berlin. Before boarding his train, he learns she's a Russian spy. She comes to see him aboard that train, admitting that she set up their rendezvous just to meet him. However, she claims that she truly has fallen for him big time. He rebuffs her coldly, and she steals his plans. That leads to his court martial and imprisonment. His influential uncle is able to provide him with one last chance to clear his name.

The captain flees to Russia where he learns that Tania really does love him. To show her devotion, she double crosses Von Seyfferitz. When her boss learns of her deception, she is forced to shoot him. To trick his bodyguards, she deceptively plays a love scene with him when he's already dead. Somewhat unrealistically (but that's the magic of Garbo), she and Captain Karl (Nagel) flee from Russia to Austria to clear his name and to start a new life as lovers.

 WHAT THE CRITICS SAID

"This Garbo girl seems to develop just a little more of that intangible 'it' with each picture, and the love scenes between her and Nagel are what might be termed burning. There are love scenes by the score, many of which are in close-ups, with the famous La Garbo kiss given full sway as well as full camera focus."
New York Morning Telegraph

"Miss Garbo takes to a close-up like no other star in Hollywood. She overcomes the handicap of an atrocious wardrobe, big feet, and widening hips with a facility of expression and charm which still keep her in a class by herself."
Betty Colfax
New York Evening Graphic

Garbo Talks—"The Voice That Shook the World!"

In 1930 it seemed that half the world wanted to know if Garbo, unlike so many of her contemporaries, could master the new medium of sound. For $570,000, an astonishing amount of money back then, MGM acquired Eugene O'Neill's *Anna Christie*, and Garbo would face a career-wrecking instrument, the microphone, playing the role of an immigrant whore with a Swedish accent.

Garbo had delayed her talkie debut until the microphones were more sensitive and mobile.

Directed once again by Clarence Brown, Garbo, dressed in the five-and-dime garb of a prostitute, slouches into a riverfront bar, collapses into a chair, and says to the bartender, "*Gif me a visky, ginger ale on the side, and don't be stingy, baby.*" The world was mesmerized by her voice. It was unlike any that movie fans had heard before. Many reviews (see below) focused only on her voice, almost avoiding commenting on the film itself.

In the plot, an old salt of the sea, Chris Christofferson (George F. Marion), awaits the arrival of his grown daughter, Anna, whom he sent at five years old to live with relatives in Minnesota. He is unaware that she's been making her living in nature's oldest profession, and that much of her spirit has been extinguished. Anna needs rest and a place to stay, so Chris moves Marthy (Marie Dressler) off his barge.

Anna falls in love with a young sailor, the deeply closeted gay character actor, Charles Bickford, playing Matt Burke, but dreads to reveal to him the truth about her past. Even though both her father and her new beau are deluded about her background, Anna cannot quite bring herself to allow them to remain in the dark about her secret life. Yes, there's a lot of soapy melodrama here; this is not one of O'Neill's great plays.

O'Neill told critic Richard Watts that he was not going to see the film because he heard that "Garbo was bad." Garbo herself preferred the German language version where she appears in Caligari make-up and is obviously more at ease speaking German than English. After seeing the English version, she told helmer Brown: "Isn't it terrible? Who ever saw a Swedish woman act that silly?"

Garbo's role, Clarence Brown's direction, and William Daniels' cinematography all earned Oscar noms. The picture made a star of the lesbian character actress, Marie Dressler, in the role of the wise old wharf rat. Garbo greatly admired Dressler's acting, but spent a great deal of her off-camera time trying to fend off the amorous advances of this lovable old broad with her cartoon bulldog face.

 WHAT THE CRITICS SAID

"Somehow, on the screen, picture and voice don't jell. It's not the occasional mispronunciations (on the order of 'the yudge told me to get a yob"), it's that Garbo's acting is pitched at the wrong level. Her Anna is a travesty of despair, and the gestures of our primal ballerina are often jerkily grandiose, as if the death throes of Pavlova's dying swan has given way to rigor mortis."
Richard Corliss

"Her voice is revealed in a deep, husky, throaty contralto that possesses every bit of that fabulous poetic glamour that has made this distant Swedish lady the outstanding actress of the motion picture world."
Richard Watts Jr.
New York Herald Tribune

One of History's Greatest Vamps

In 1931, MGM released Garbo's 15th film, a highly fictionalized biography of the notorious Javanese-Dutch spy who worked during World War I for the German Secret Service. This wasn't one of Garbo's best films, although her headgear was the most striking she ever wore.

Directed by George Fitzmaurice, *Mata Hari* remains Garbo's campiest film. She appears, for example, in everything from a Friar Tuck skullcap to a sequined *loche* helmet, compliments of the very gay Adrian.

It's true that the real Mata Hari died before a firing squad in 1917, but the rest of the events depicted in the scenario are largely apocryphal. In the film, Garbo discovers true love in the arms of one of her victims.

The Swede was very familiar with playing the role of the beautiful spider baiting the fly. It was even suggested that she could have done the role in her sleep.

In a famous "Letter to Garbo" in the 1932 edition of *Theatre Arts Monthly*, Mary Canfield wrote: "You merely walked through it, like some superior and unperturbed mannequin."

In the film, Garbo's power as a seductress was publicly hailed as a force more potent than that of the Virgin Mary. Although it was probably a brilliant piece of press and PR, it generated censorship problems in England, thereby adding to her screen allure.

Evenutally, Hollywood's most notorious homosexual, Ramon Novarro, was eventually selected as Garbo's leading man. Later, he would die violently at the hands of two brothers, both hustlers out to rob him in his home.

Garbo's love scenes with Novarro, playing the role of a brave Russian lieutenant, were not convincing. He doesn't exactly wince by having to take a seductive woman in his arms, but it's obvious she's not a member of the gender he'd like to be romancing. One of his real life former lovers, one of whom was Rudolph Valentino, would have been more to his liking.

Except for Clark Gable, with whom Garbo appeared in *Susan Lenox: Her Fall and Rise*, many of Garbo's leading men were just too fey for her strong screen presence.

A noteworthy exception to this rule is *Mata Hari,*where Garbo is backed up by strong supporting older actors. They included Lewis Stone, cast as Andriani, who sends her on her spy mission, and Lionel Barrymore, who plays her lover in the film. Barrymore's character, in exchange for her sexual favors (which he presumably cannot resist), passes on strategic military secrets.

During the making of this film, Novarro hinted to the press that he'd fallen madly in love with Garbo. Total bullshit, of course. Actually, at the time, Garbo was spending most nights in the arms of screenwriter Mercedes de Acosta, the most famous and influential lesbian muse of her era. And when she wasn't with Garbo, that Spanish beauty, social commentator, and memoirist was fucking Marlene Dietrich.

 WHAT THE CRITICS SAID

"As the German spy, Mata Hari, who wrecked men's lives to gain information, Garbo has the best role of her career and sets a standard which is almost untouchable."
  Screen Book

"That mysterious actress, Greta Garbo, gives another flawless performance."
  Mordaunt Hall
  The New York Times

Rooms for Garbo, Crawford, the Barrymores & Beery

It's certainly old fashionied—after all, it was made in 1932—but Vicki Baum's bestseller is an excuse to bring together some of the great stars of the 30s, notably Garbo as Grusinskaya; John Barrymore as Baron Felix von Geigern; Joan Crawford as Flaemmchen; Wallace Beery as Preysing, and Lionel Barrymore as Otto Kringelein. Even Lewis Stone and Jean Hersholt check in, all under the direction of gay helmer Edmund Goulding. Along with Irving Thalberg, Paul Bern of the small dick and Jean Harlow-infamy produced this flick with costumes by the very gay Adrian.

Berlin's plushest hotel is the setting where "People come, people go." There are a lot of subplots here—for example, Baron von Geigern is broke and trying to steal dancer Grusinskaya's pearls but ends up stealing her heart instead. Sure, it's pure soapy corn, but because of all these MGM legends, it's fun to watch. Regrettably, there are no scenes of Garbo and "Mommie Dearest" in the same frame. Nonetheless, Crawford was irked by Garbo's insistence on top billing and took her revenge by loudly playing Marlene Dietrich records in her dressing room.

Garbo wanted John Gilbert to play her lover but at the time, he had been designated as "box office poison." At first Garbo turned down the role because she believed that at 26 she was "too old" to play a prima ballerina.

But when Louis B. Mayer saw the final cut, he ordered more extra scenes shot with Garbo, fearing that Crawford (whom he never liked) would steal the picture.

The quote, "I want to be alone," spoken by Garbo in the movie, was listed at #30 in the AFI List of Top 100 Quotes from American films. *Grand Hotel* won the Best Picture Oscar, but it was not nominated for any other Academy Awards.

 ## WHAT THE CRITICS SAID

"Garbo dominates the picture entirely, making the other players merely competent performers."
John Mosher
The New Yorker

"That face full of wanton joy when she is happy. That face full of fear when she waits for her beloved in vain. Unforgettable! Thank you, Greta Garbo."
Vicki Baum
Modern Screen

"*Grand Hotel* is only worth seeing as a drum-beating exhibition of stars—each and all of them miscast."
Critic Sydney Carroll
Picture Play

In the 1933 release of MGM's Queen Christina, the homely bisexual Swedish monarch was transformed into the stunning incarnation of Garbo photographed in close-up at her most beautiful.

Once again she was teamed with her former lover, John Gilbert, after having found that she had no chemistry on screen with her first choice, another bisexual, Laurence Olivier. Nils Asther and Franchot Tone—even Clark Gable—had also been considered for the role which finally went to Gilbert. His Groucho Marx mustache did little to re-establish his career in the talkies, and this prestigious film did not halt his ignominious slide into oblivion. Within three years after the film was shot, the alcoholic Gilbert was dead.

Garbo felt some identity with the Swedish queen who inherited the throne in 1632 at the age of six upon the death of her warrior-father, King Gustavus II Adolphus. "I looked like a boy when I was born," Garbo once said. Christina herself was born with a body entirely covered by hair. Midwives attending the birth thought she was a boy, and as Christina matured, she developed a deep, loud voice.

Today it is believed that Christina was a pseudo-hermaphrodite—a person born with the external sex traits of one gender, but the internal reproductive organs of the other. Imitating Christina, Garbo appears in men's boots and dresses as a cavalier to disguise her sex. Both Christina and Garbo were attracted to beautiful women.

MGM was subtle (subtle?) in dealing with the Swedish queen's lesbianism, giving her lines such "I shall die a bachelor." What about this winning observation? "I think marriage is an altogether shocking thing. How is it possible to think of a man sleeping in the same room?"

The scene in which actress Barbara Barondess as Elsa, the sluttish servant girl, ran her hands up and down Garbo's legs ended up on the cutting-room floor. Barondess had great embarrassment filming the scene. "I don't want to be making love to her 35 times—she's liable to like it," she told the director. However, in the final version, a lesbian kiss was kept in.

One of the most famous scenes in all filmdom was the closing shot of Garbo's face at the prow of the ship. Director Rouben Mamoulian told his star "to think of nothing. Avoid blinking if you can, so that you're nothing but a beautiful mask. I want your face to be a blank sheet of paper. The writing will be supplied by every member of the audience."

WHAT THE CRITICS SAID

"One of the best scenes discloses Garbo, traveling as a man, and stopping at a wayside inn, there to be placed in the same room with a nobleman from Spain (Gilbert) because all other rooms are occupied. (No reason to censor and every reason to try.)
Walter Ramsey
Modern Screen

"The magnificent Garbo, enchanting as ever, is still enveloped in unfathomable mystery."
Photoplay

#8 of 10: ANNA KARENINA **(1935)**
Trapped in a Xanadu of White Russian Bric-a-Brac

In this 1935 release, Garbo was once again directed by Clarence Brown. He told her that in the title role, she'd be appearing opposite Fredric March, who had signed to play Vronsky in this adaptation of the Tolstoy classic.

Garbo already knew that he was notorious for attempting to seduce his leading ladies. As a counter-offensive, she wore garlic under her clothes and purposely developed bad breath as a means of staving off his advances.

In that she succeeded. Film-goers were left pondering why her Anna would even remotely be drawn to March's stiff, colorless count. One critic noted that to his love scenes March brought the sort of sappy conviction you might expect from Merv Griffin singing "Summertime."

On the other hand, Basil Rathbone is effective as her cold, unforgiving husband, and Freddie Bartholomew is quite fine as their son. Eleven-year-old Bartholomew was a foot fetishist, and liked to suck the toes of men or women. Garbo turned down his request for a private toe-sucking.

Brown lined up an impressive cast, including the very pretty Maureen O'Sullivan, who played Kitty, and Gyles Isham, who portrayed Levin. Other players included Reginald Owen, Reginald Denny, May Robson, and Phoebe Foster. Constance Collier, "the great dyke of the Western world," was cast in the uncredited role of Countess Lidia. When not on set, Collier was offering comfort to the bisexual actress, Katharine Hepburn.

Look carefully and you'll spot future movie star Dennis O'Keefe in an uncredited part as "Best Man."

Anna Karenina was Garbo's 23rd film and a remake of *Love*, in which she'd costarred with her on-again/off-again lover John Gilbert.

Originally, producer David O. Selznick didn't want Garbo to do another period drama. He urged the screenplay, *Dark Victory*, upon her, but she turned him down. And how fortunate that was for Bette Davis that Garbo rejected what became one of Davis' most memorable roles.

After shooting *Anna Karenina*, Garbo returned to her native Sweden. "Bette Davis can have George Brent," she said. Brent had been pestering Garbo to marry him.

In Stockholm she was seen on several occasions dancing the rumba with Noel Coward. The naïve press reported that a Coward/Garbo engagement announcement was imminent. Unknown to much of the media at the time, Coward was sucking off handsome blond Viking gods after he had escorted Garbo back to her hotel suite.

 WHAT THE CRITICS SAID

"Greta Garbo, after several years of miscasting, is back at last in her own particular province of glamour and heartbreak, of tragic lovely ladies and handsome ruthless men. Garbo's haunting beauty is what you will remember of *Anna Karenina*."
Eileen Creelman
New York Sun

"This is a weak and dull picture, yet the persuasive genius of Garbo raises it into a class of art."
Photoplay

204

CAMILLE (1936)

Transcendent Passion of a Dying Courtesan in Love; Garbo's Finest Role

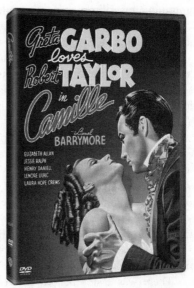

Not surprisingly, MGM teamed two of its most beautiful stars—both bisexuals—Robert Taylor and Garbo, in the 1936 version of that heart-wrencher, *Camille*. Again not surprisingly, Garbo was cast as a courtesan. She was far more convincing as an elegant courtesan than in a hooker role.

Garbo was under the skilled baton of George Cukor, the most notorious homosexual director in Hollywood.

Some reviewers impishly asked: Guess which is the pretty one? Taylor or Garbo?

Garbo was at the peak of her beauty, but so was Taylor. When not seducing Garbo on screen, he was getting regularly plowed by other beautiful men, including Errol Flynn, Tyrone Power, and Howard Hughes. In the case of Power, it was a problem—two bottoms doth not a top make.

Camille originally opened in Paris on February 2, 1852, Dumas having based the character on Marguerite, a woman with whom he'd had an affair for 11 months. She died at the age of 23. In 1936 *Camille* inspired Milton Benjamin to write a hit song called "I'll Love Like Robert Taylor, Be My Greta Garbo."

Our favorite line in the film is when Garbo asks Taylor: "You who are so young—where can you have learned all you know about women like me?"

Nearly everyone who's eaten a clam knows the story, and we won't bore you with too much repetition. As the courtesan Marguerite, Garbo falls deeply in love with Armand. One ad billed this film as "the gay *demi-monde* of Paris. (*Demi-monde*, in case you didn't know, and you probably do, translates roughly as "a jaded, decadent, stylish, and world-weary community of loose sexual morals.")

Garbo, as Marguerite Gautier, brightens her wit with champagne and seems to lead an enchanted life when Armand falls for her. Even when she descends into poverty with a terminal illness, she discovers he has not lost his love for her. It's no wonder that Giuseppe Verdi adapted the original novel by Alexandre Dumas *fils, La Dame aux caméllias,* for his opera *La Traviata*. What suffering, what tragedy, what undying love…

The screenplay was mostly scripted by Zoë Akins, with help from Francis Marion and James Hilton.

One of the most eccentric figures in 1930s Hollywood, Akins was small and fat and lived with a female companion, actress Jobyna Howland. Before Howland, Akins had been in love with Ethel Barrymore, but the grand old lady of the theater wasn't in love with "the toad," as she called her.

Akins also developed a crush on Garbo, who responded by telling her that she "had to give all my love to Armand Duval," a reference to the screen role played by Taylor. And that she did, earning as a result her third Oscar nomination. The Oscar for Best Actress seemed to forever elude the luminous Swede. Lesser talent always won instead.

For our money, Garbo's death scene, where Camille collapses into a tubercular swoon, remains the finest and most touching in cinema history. One can just feel her tentative hold on life as she keeps herself alive to see her beloved once again.

With the single exception of Robert Taylor, the cast was superb. It included Laura Hope Crewes. If you don't remember her name, surely you will recall her campy, sexually repressed hysteria as Aunt Pittypat ("The Yankees are coming!") in *Gone With The Wind*.

Maureen O'Sullivan also appears sweet and virginal, the way Louis B. Mayer liked them before he devoured them.

Richard Corliss brilliantly summed up Taylor's role, referring to him as "impossibly gorgeous." "Robert Taylor is usually ridiculed for playing Armand as a musical/comedy Romeo with a glistening, protruding lower lip, a crooner's smile, and a mellow, acting-school baritone," Corliss wrote. "This criticism underrates the actor and overrates the role. If he sometimes suggests a choirboy lost in a bawdy house, it's because he's too intensely romantic to have a worldly sense of humor."

In his appraisal of Taylor the actor, Cukor was later rather charitable to the man Garbo herself had described as "so beautiful—and so dumb." Cukor claimed that Robert Taylor made an "extremely good Armand," but he could have been pissed off at him. Throughout the filming, Taylor repeatedly turned down Cukor's urgent plea to allow him to suck Taylor's cock. "I give the greatest head in Hollywood," Cukor claimed.

Other than Garbo's, the finest performance is delivered by Henry Daniell playing the Baron de Varville, Marguerite's lame-duck lover. Of the many cinematic villains of Hollywood during the 1930s, he was the most suave. We can only speculate how John Barrymore would have been in the role for which he was originally scheduled. The baron is a man "whose lips have been locked in sarcasm for so long that he cannot unpurse them even to kiss his mistress."

The gay actor, Lionel Barrymore, overacts in one of his worst performances. Amazingly, Cukor didn't catch his onscreen blooper when he referred to Marguerite Gautier as "Margaret."

Adrian had another gay romp with Garbo's costumes, taking her from virginal white at the beginning to Grim Reaper black in her final scenes.

There was a side benefit derived from Garbo's work with Cukor. After filming was completed, Garbo asked to be taken to Katharine Hepburn's luxurious new home on Angelo Drive above Benedict Canyon in Los Angeles. Garbo was amused that Cukor had previously directed Hepburn when she was cast as a boy in *Sylvia Scarlett*. "I, too, want you to direct me as a boy one day," Garbo told Cukor.

"When Kate hauled Garbo upstairs to show off her new bedroom, I decided it was time for me to go," Cukor later told a group of his gay pals at a Hollywood party.

 WHAT THE CRITICS SAID

"Greta Garbo's performance is in the finest tradition: eloquent, tragic, yet restrained. She is as incomparable in the role as legend tells us that Bernhardt was. Through the perfect artistry of her portrayal, a hackneyed theme is made new again, poignantly sad, hauntingly lovely."
Frank S. Nugent
The New York Times

"The incomparable Greta Garbo has returned to the screen in a breathtakingly beautiful and superbly modulated portrayal of Camille. As the tragic Dumas heroine, she floods a romantic museum piece with glamour and artistry, making it a haunting and moving photoplay by the sheer magic of her acting."
Howard Barnes
New York Herald Tribune

NINOTCHKA (1939)

At the Twilight of Her Career, Garbo Laughs

As Garbo neared the end of her far-too-short career, she had one more good movie in her before oblivion. She played *Ninotchka* in this highly enjoyable comedy/romance opposite Melvyn Douglas as Leon in 1939, the year of *Gone With The Wind*. William Powell, homo-hating Robert Montgomery, and the stately queer himself, Cary Grant, were all considered as possible leading men for Garbo.

When *Ninotchka* was released, headlines across America proclaimed GARBO LAUGHS, as she'd long ago learned to talk.

Garbo was lucky to have the great Ernst Lubitsch as her director. He was known for his light touch with comedy. But when it became time for her to actually laugh, he said that "she disliked playing the scene in front of all the extras." Rumor had it that her laugh was dubbed, but Lubitsch insisted until his death that it was not.

In spite of that laugh, Douglas later said that Garbo "didn't have an ounce of humor in her."

Frank Nugent of *The New York Times* found Garbo "gay, impertinent, and malicious, playing deadpan comedy with the assurance of a Buster Keaton."

There's a plot here. Buljanoff (Felix Bressart); Iranoff (Sig Ruman), and Kopalski (Alexander Granach) have been sent by the communist Soviet government to Paris to sell the Imperial jewels of the recently deposed Romanoffs as a means of raising money for farm machinery. But the soft capitalist life has begun to tempt them.

Ninotchka is sent directly from the Kremlin to see what's going wrong. In Paris, she not only meets a new boyfriend, Leon (Douglas), but conflicts with the Grand Duchess Swana (Ina Claire), who owned the gems before she was forced to flee from Russia's Bolshevik Revolution. As a bit of fun casting, Bela Lugosi plays Commissar Razinin, the communist party official who sends Ninotchka to Paris.

Ina Claire and Garbo were rivals both on and off the screen. Claire was the widow of Garbo's old flame, squeaky voiced John Gilbert.

"Do you want to be alone, Comrade?" one of the comic commissars asks Garbo.

"No!" she replied.

It's the anti-myth in monosyllable.

Mercedes de Acosta, one of the more illustrious of Garbo's lesbian lovers, later said that *Ninotchka* was "the first gay picture Garbo had ever done." Maybe de Acosta meant something different from really, really gay.

Why, you might ask, was Lubitsch suddenly available to direct *Ninotchka?* He had recently been booted from the set of *The Women*, starring Norma Shearer and Joan Crawford, who hated each other. Lubitsch had been unexpectedly replaced with gay director George Cukor, who was known for his artistry in directing glamorous women. Ironically, Cukor himself had became available only because Clark Gable, during the simultaneous filming of *Gone With the Wind,* had refused to be directed "by a faggot" in his portrayal of Rhett Butler. Gable didn't like to be reminded of his own personal experience in Hollywood at the beginning of his career during the silent screen era, when he hustled rich men for money, usually scoring payment from them. Those early business arrangements, as well as graphic descriptions of his small, uncut dick, would return frequently to haunt Gable the rest of his life.

Ninotchka earned for Garbo her fourth and last Academy Award nomination. But on Oscar Night, Vivien Leigh snapped up the Best Actress Award for *Gone With the Wind*.

Cukor threw a party, inviting Garbo, Leigh, and her boyfriend, Laurence Olivier. Garbo and Olivier disappeared for a long time. Noting their tryst, Leigh said to the gossipy Cukor: "I hope poor Larry knows what to do. He doesn't know what to do with me, but fortunately Leslie (Leslie Howard, who played her love interest, Ashley, in *Gone With The Wind*) knows exactly what target to hit."

Unknown to Garbo at the time she made *Ninotchka*, although still a young woman in her 30s, she was only months from retirement. Regrettably, in 1941, she went on to trash her reputation by appearing in *Two Faced Women*, a disaster also directed by Cukor. The film co-starred Melvyn Douglas once again.

Time magazine summed it up: "An absurd vehicle for Greta Garbo. Its embarrassing effect is not unlike seeing Sarah Bernhardt swatted with a bladder. It is almost as shocking as seeing your mother drunk."

After that, Garbo disappeared from the screen never to return in spite of repeated offers, living as a semi-reclusive and rather dour eccentric in Stockholm and New York City.

 # WHAT THE CRITICS SAID

"To see Garbo playing a grim comrade who deviates from party doctrine on a mission to Paris, turns square briefly, and then goes overboard for romance, one would suppose that she had devoted her whole career to antic make-believe."
Howard Barnes
New York Herald Tribune

GAY HOLLYWOOD

Being Gay in Hollywood Can Still be a Drag

One actor in this 88-minute docu proclaims that Los Angeles is the gayest city in the world. So, thank God, we can skip all that anti-gay bigotry stuff that would have arisen had it been shot in a redneck town like Crawford, Texas, or Washington, Georgia. LA may be gay, and two men can indeed walk hand in hand, at least in West Hollywood, but being Out in Tinseltown isn't a guarantee of success. That's why at least ten A-list male movie stars still live in the closet, two at least famously so in spite of *South Park* urging them to come out of that closet.

In other words, if you can still get someone to stand in for you as a girlfriend or wife, it's a great career move to make outrageous straight displays of affection for that person—at least when you're on Candid Camera.

Jeremy Simmons both produced and directed this docu with a quintet of performers playing themselves.

Gay Hollywood gets moving when Dustin Lance Black voices objection to the docu, claiming that the helmer is "stacking the deck with stereotypically flamboyant gay men." His complaint against stereotypes doesn't seem completely justified except in the case of Micah McCain who steals the flick. Who can compete with him in his silly drag queen persona as "Bridgett of Madison County?"

A bit duller is Benjamin Morgan, who is a struggling writer trying to peddle scripts to bored TV execs who don't give him much encouragement, but utter stinging critiques like those delivered by Simon Cowell on *American Idol*.

Robert Laughlin is the classic example of a struggling out-of-work actor who needs to pay the rent while waiting beside a phone that never rings. Occasionally a job will emerge, perhaps as an extra in a cheapie soft-core porn video shoot.

Q. Allan Brocka has a famous uncle, the Filipino filmmaker, Lino Brocka, although this is not part of the docu. Instead we see the unknown young Brocka trying to meet his living costs by taking on such projects as directing a cheesy video. Perhaps he should drop the "Q" from his name.

Dare we suggest that *the film* about being openly gay while still trying succeed as an actor in Hollywood hasn't yet been made?

Questions and Answers with the cast of *Gay Hollywood* at Outfest

 WHAT THE CRITICS SAID

"As a promotional showcase for young showbiz talent, *Gay Hollywood* is perfectly serviceable. But as a docu purporting to explore new challenges and possibilities facing gay artists in a Hollywood more open to them than ever before, Jeremy Simmons' film is far too timid. This romp is entertaining enough in its glimpses of roller-coaster lives, but those yearning for a deeper study will be disappointed."
Robert Koehler

"High ratings is sometimes another word for 'closet.' Before *Will and Grace*, his name was Sean P. Hayes and he played a non-stereotypical gay character in the movie *Billy's Hollywood Screen Kiss*. The actor was openly gay, doing interviews. The movie did, like, ten dollars in business.

Now Sean Hayes plays a stereotypical gay on *Will and Grace* and refuses to say if he's gay. Truth in advertising is discouraged in show business."

Michael Jeter (*Evening Shade*)

GO WEST

Wartime Drama, Western Satire & Gay Love

You probably haven't seen too many movies from Bosnia-Herzegovina. Here's one that's a bit daring but awkward, telling the story of two unlikely lovers, a Muslim and a Serbian. Perhaps a master like Ernst Lubitsch could have pulled it off. But for helmer Ahmed Imamovic, the challenge was daunting.

A classical musician, Kenan (Mario Drmac), is a Muslim living with his lover, a Bosnian Serb, Milan (played by Tarik Filipovic). They live together quietly, fearing retribution from their homophobic neighbors.

When war comes in 1992, their home town of Sarajevo is under siege. Together they flee but are forced off a train by Serbian militiamen. Kenan fears he will be shot to death. To save him, Milan comes up with the improbable idea of disguising Kenan as his girlfriend. Amazingly, he manages to pass in this disguise.

Eventually the lovers reach Milan's village in Eastern Bosnia, and the protection of his father, Ljubo (played by veteran actor Rade Serbedzija). Here this "man and wife" plan to wait until they can escape to Holland. Regrettably, Milan is drafted into the army, and the situation becomes almost intolerable for Kenan.

His one companion is Ranka, a waitress in a local café who possesses dark secrets. Ranka (Mirjana Karanovic) is a sex-starved woman who discovers that Kenan is a man. She seduces him several times, and, out of jealousy, then sets out to destroy his love affair with Milan.

Ultimately, Ljubo will come to Kenan's rescue and send him off to the West.

The great actress Jeanne Moreau, an associate producer of the film, offers a strange final cameo, playing a French TV interviewer.

 WHAT THE CRITICS SAID

"It takes a major suspension of disbelief to imagine the lovers can pull the wool over everyone's eyes and continue to pass Kenan off as a bewigged 'Milena.' But in the farcical world the film has now entered, everything is possible, even a surprise wedding that Ljubo springs on the couple in the hopes of having a grandson. This clumsy back-and-forth between historical tragedy and grotesque comedy just stops working after a while. Motivation is also iffy."

Deborah Young
Variety

"How brave of Richard Chamerlain to come out as gay in his very first book... At almost seventy."

-Openly gay actress, **Alexis Arquette**

SHATTERED
LOVE
RICHARD CHAMBERLAIN

GRAY MATTERS

Lost Lezzie Struggles with Sapphic Desires

This is a romantic comedy/coming-out flick from debut director Sue Kramer. Heather Graham stars as the film's namesake, Gray, playing a winsome New Yorker living with her brother, Sam (Tom Cavanagh).

The action gets moving when Sam, after a whirlwind romance, falls for Charlie, as played by Bridget Moynahan, a sexy zoologist.

Gray's got a problem. She's not only losing her brother, to whom she's devoted her life, but she realizes she's in love with his bride-to-be, Charlie. Talk about sexual confusion.

The most memorable scene is a now infamous kiss shared between Graham and Moynahan. Graham told the press she was "really looking forward to it," although Moynahan remained "a little creeped out."

Regrettably for their lesbian fans, there was also an X-rated love scene, but the foolish director cut that out.

Graham remains best known for her role as the porn actress Rollergirl in Paul Thomas Anderson's film, *Boogie Nights*, released in 1997.

Naturally, all these young New Yorkers have a profession. Sam is an up-and-coming heart surgeon, Gray an advertising copywriter. But Charlie is a candidate for that old TV series *What's My Line?* She studies the homosexual behavior of fish at an aquarium.

The supporting players and veteran actors steal scenes from the stars.

The question we found most puzzling was this: Why is such a talented actress as Sissy Spacek, playing a flaky therapist in a downright embarrassing performance, drawn to such a silly script? The obvious answer is that roles are hard to come by once you're no longer twelve. Spacek, as the wacky shrink, conducts sessions while bowling and rock climbing.

In his role as a taxi driver, Alan Cumming is such a good sport that even after he's rejected by Gray, he dresses in drag to accompany her on her first excursion to a lesbian bar.

Just at the time of the release of the film, Moynahan made headlines by announcing that she was pregnant. The dad, according to her, is Tom Brady, the New England Patriots quarterback. She dated the handsome hunk for three years before breaking up in December of 2006.

In the limited release of this ill-conceived film, *Gray Matters* needed all the publicity it could get. One reviewer summed it up in a tagline: "Ouch! Oh, and Alan Cumming plays straight. Need I say more?"

WHAT THE CRITICS SAID

"Sue Kramer clearly wants her first film, *Gray Matters*, to remind us of 1940s screwball comedies. We get glam dance numbers, rapid-fire quips, romantic Manhattan skylines and fabulous clothes, all obviously inspired by old movies. What we don't get is the wit or warmth of those films. Instead, this exhausting romance feels more like a long-lost episode of *Three's Company*, in which Jack Tripper decides he is actually a gay."
Elizabeth Weitzman
New York Daily News

"The movie pretends to be high-end French Champagne, but is really mid-priced domestic vintage. The spirit of Carole Lombard hovers over the film. In this world Madonna never existed. Compared to *Gray Matters*, even a Nora Ephron bonbon has the weight of urban neo-realism."
Stephen Holden
The New York Times

"Heather Graham plays the title character in this badly named film, and the scene in which she shares a kiss with her brother's wife, played by the beautiful Bridget Moynahan, is pretty darn hot. Everything that follows is lukewarm at best. The movie's best moments come courtesy of supporting Alan Cumming, portraying a cabbie pining for Gray. Cumming playing a straight man?"
Staten Island Advance

"*Gray Matters* is trying so hard to be charming and screwball (not to mention politically correct) that it trips all over itself. For aficionados of gay erotica, how about a scene with giggly femmes Heather Graham and Bridget Moynahan in a bubble bath sipping champagne?"
Tom Beer
Time Out New York

"There isn't a remotely believable moment in the script here, and Kramer's leaden direction only helps strand a capable cast headed by Heather Graham in an hour and a half of virtual laugh-free tedium. Even worse, this is the kind of movie where you can deduce the entire plot, as unbelievable as it is, from the first 10 minutes."
Lou Lumenick
New York Post

"As if NYC weren't overflowing with high-femme power-dykes? Spit chai on any street corner and you'll hit one. Here, all attempts to make a cute and charming romantic comedy come off are entirely unrealistic and painfully passé."
Instinct

THE GREAT PINK SCARE

Smut-Fueled Witch Hunt Destroys the Literary Mentor of Truman Capote.

On Labor Day weekend in 1960, as part of a McCarthy-style witch-hunt against gay men, state troopers launched a raid in the little New England town of Northampton, Massachussetts. At the end of their rampage, they had hauled 15 men off to jail, three of whom were professors at the elite Smith College. The next day, newspaper headlines screamed—POLICE BREAK UP HOMOSEXUAL SMUT RING!

THE GREAT PINK SCARE

In the 1950s in America, it was more dangerous to be discovered as a homosexual than it was to be discovered as a communist. —Barry Werth, author, The Scarlet Professor

In 1960, three Smith College professors were charged with possessing and dispensing obscene literature, and convicted as felons. In the end, brilliant careers were destroyed and young lives ruined.

This story, and that of the devastating persecution that haunted these men, brings awareness to the present-day clash between an individual's right to privacy and concerns for national security.

The so-called smut was actually a stash of physique pictorials that wouldn't raise an eyebrow today—or raise anything else either.

Through vintage footage and interviews, directors Dan Miller and Tuggelin Yourgrau re-create that horrible era in a docu originally entitled *Independent Lens*. One of the faculty members arrested was Joel Dorius, who later said: "I thought sharing photos was unwise, considering the laws. But it never occurred to me that it could be fatal."

Also arrested were Ned Spofford, another Smith College faculty member, and Newton Arvin. Arvin, was labeled by the authorities as the so-called ring leader of the group. One of America's leading literary critics and a great love of Truman Capote, Arvin personally betrayed his friends in an act of cowardice. All three professors lost their positions.

The Northampton witch-hunt is re-created through archival and film commentary.

After all this scandal, Arvin became suicidal and was subsequently incarcerated in a mental hospital. He did not try to appeal his conviction, but Dorius and Spofford struggled to get the case overturned. In time their criminal records were erased but the stigma remained. All three men migrated in and out of mental hospitals for years, their once-promising academic careers destroyed. In declining health exacerbated by these issues, Arvin eventually died three years after the incident, in 1963.

If the film does nothing else, it reminds us that government does not belong in the bedrooms of consenting adults, and that we must be on guard against those who would demonize gays and lesbians.

 ## WHAT THE CRITICS SAID

"In the end, brilliant careers were destroyed and young lives ruined. The issues raised then about privacy rights and civil liberties still reverberate in American society today, more than 40 years later. In a time when *Brokeback Mountain*, a film about gay cowboys, dominated the national discussion and earned cross-over acclaim and audiences, *The Great Pink Scare* is a sobering reminder of the struggle for acceptance in both the past and present."
   The Film: PBS

A confiscated photo from Arvin's collection

IN MEMORY OF ARVIN NEWTON

During his thirty-seven years at Smith College, Newton Arvin published groundbreaking studies of Hawthorne, Whitman, Melville, and Longfellow that stand today as models of scholarship and psychological acuity. He cultivated friendships with the likes of Edmund Wilson and Lillian Hellman and became mentor to Truman Capote. A social radical and closeted homosexual, Arvin somehow managed to survive McCarthyism during the 1950s. But in September of 1960 his apartment was raided, and his cache of beefcake erotica was confiscated, plunging him into confusion and despair and provoking his panicked betrayal of several of his friends. After a stress-induced sojourn in a mental asylum, he died in 1963, the victim, according to his friends, of an irreparable sense of shame and a broken heart.

In 2002, Barry Werth, through Anchor Books, released a 353-age biography of Newton Arvin. Absorbing and well-written, **The Scarlet Professor** offers a provocative and unsettling look at Newton Arvin's life and accomplishments, and how many of them were destroyed by American moral fanaticism. It was the recipient, the year of its publication, of the coveted Stonewall Award for Non-fiction from the American Library Association.

In 1994, during a breakfast at Tiffany's in New York City, the estate of Truman Capote, as stipulated in that writer's will, announced the establishment of the Truman Capote Literary Trust. A clearly defined subdivision of that trust involved the awarding of the Annual Truman Capote Award for Literary Criticism in Memory of Newton Arvin, reflecting Capote's frequently expressed concern for the health of literary criticism in the English language. Administered by the Writers' Workshop, the $50,000 award is the world's largest annual cash prize for literary criticism.

As for Smith College, prompted partly by the publication of Werth's biography, its board of trustees recently voted to honor the victims of the 1960 Pink Scare scandal by creating the Newton Arvin Prize in American Study and the Dorius/Spofford Fund for the Study of Civil Liberty and Freedom of Expression.

THE GYMNAST

A Vertiginous, Voluptuous & Aerial Lesbian Love Story

Jane Hawkins (played by Dreya Weber) was one of America's top gymnasts, at the top of her game until a devastating injury ended her career. The injury prevented her from fulfilling her Olympic destiny.

In the film, almost 20 years have gone by while Jane has languished in obscurity, working hand-to-mouth as a massage therapist while slowly disappearing into a passionless marriage with David (David De Simone).

Secretly, she has been trying to get pregnant, although David doesn't want a child. Jane's doctor tells her that she may have waited too long to have a kid. Without her husband's financial support, she can't afford the fertility drugs that might make her pregnant.

A chance meeting with Denise (Allison Mackie), a former gymnastic teammate, provokes Jane to re-examine her life and past—to "spread my wings." On a visit to a gym, Jane is recognized by a coach and is recruited for a different kind of venture—becoming part of a Cirque Du Soleil type of aerial act.

When the ex-gymnast meets an enigmatic Korean dancer named Serena (Addie Yungmee), a sexual tension arises. Their aerial performances together become mesmerizing and beautiful—and something else as well.

Dreya Weber and Addie Yungmee

The developing relationship is not without its complications. But, of course, Jane is distressed by her lack of children, and Serena is a closeted lesbian with "coming out" problems as the adopted daughter of Jewish parents. As the stunning pair prepares to audition for their act in Vegas, the gravitational pull between the two of them becomes increasingly unavoidable.

After Denise convinces Jane that the affair with Serena is a form of denial, Jane must choose between having a child with her suddenly willing husband—or creating a completely new life for herself. This is a story of midlife liberation, coming out, and coming to terms with one's life. It's a debut feature from helmer Ned Farr, who also authored the screenplay.

 WHAT THE CRITICS SAID

"Winner of NewFest's best narrative feature award, well acted, well performed pic comes off as surprisingly engrossing despite treading familiar *Lifetime Movie*-type female empowerment territory. Helmer Farr delights in the strength and flexibility of Weber's physique, as her character's sense of self-worth incrementally manifests itself in her increasing control over her body. Indeed, the entire film unfolds in the space between physicality and sexuality, the one often sliding into the other but Farr never confounding the two."
   Ronnie Scheib
   Variety

HAIRSPRAY

There Goes the Ozone Layer

Like the original John Waters 1988 movie and the 2002 Broadway play, we return to Baltimore of 1962, which is still lingering in the 1950s. It's the heyday of hairdos, heartthrobs, hefty girls, hot dates, and hip talkers, beatniks, and hair hoppers. It's campy; it's coming of age; it's satirical, and, believe it or not, it manages to deal with civil rights.

Along with drag queen Divine in the first movie, the original cast also included Sonny Bono, Deborah Harry, Ricki Lake, Pia Zadora, and that dreadful Mink Stole. In the original, Waters appeared briefly as a psychiatrist. In the 2007 version, he passes by with a raincoat as "The Flasher."

Note to collectors of movie trivia: Waters created the role of Edna Turnblad originally for Christine Jorgensen, the famous American G.I. who became a woman after surgery in Denmark. *The Corny Collins Show* in the film was originally based on the local television station's *The Buddy Dean Show* which was aired from Baltimore for a seven-year stint (1957-1964), with some inspiration from Dick Clark's American Bandstand.

Divine, of course, became known as the Prince of Puke in Waters' *Pink Flamingos*. The homicidal heroine of that film scooped up and ate a fresh doggy turd. It was amazing that that movie found such a large audience even with its PG rating.

It is even more amazing that what began as a gay boy's wet dream, blending rock and roll with middle-class tackiness, went on to become the most successful opening of a movie musical in history when the second *Hairspray* opened in 2007. No longer appealing to subversives, tons of people, both young and old, flocked to see the latest movie version of *Hairspray*. Although it doesn't really deal with gay

Ednas left to right: Divine, Harvey Fierstein, and John Travolta

219

characters, it is perhaps the gayest musical ever made.

Generating many of the headlines is the appearance of John Travolta in drag. This role does very little to squelch those gay rumors that have spun around Travolta for years. If anything, it will start a rash of them all over again. As a drag queen, Travolta is a poor substitute for Divine, who brought a much more cutting edge to the role. In the latest version, Travolta made the role of Edna Turnblad his own. Gone are the drag queen trappings as he tries to emphasize the character's real womanhood. In doing so, he makes Edna just a little too sweet.

"I wanted her sexy," Travolta said. "I kept on sending back the fat suit, which I wore over my own body, with notes along the lines of: 'bigger breasts, bigger ass, smaller waist, smoother skin.' I didn't want the audience to see a man in there."

What is sadly missed in the film, other than that Divine creature, is Travolta's goofy cleft chin. It's his most endearing screen feature. But his face is so ballooned with latex that the cleft chin absolutely disappears. Travolta is most tender in a duet with his on-screen husband, Christopher Walken. They sing and dance, "You're Timeless to Me." Walken comes off as a musical pro, though we will always prefer him as a villain.

In his big shimmy number at the end, perhaps the greatest single moment in *Hairspray*, Travolta shakes his fat butt like a titanic Tina Turner. That boy still knows how to dance after all these years. It was back in 1978 that he made his last musical, *Grease*.

"I've missed musicals," he said. "I waited almost 30 years to do another one, and it's not because I didn't want to, it's just that I couldn't find one I wanted to do." He readily agrees that he made a mistake in turning down *Chicago*, the part going to Richard Gere.

The film is directed more or less well by Adam Shankman, whose previous films have included *The Wedding Planner, The Pacifier*, and *Cheaper by the Dozen 2*. The best number comes at the very beginning when Tracy Turnblad, as played by newcomer Nikki Blonsky, jumps out of bed and bubbles over with "Good Morning, Baltimore."

The chubby and endearing 4-foot-10 dynamo arrives at school atop a garbage truck in a witty homage to Barbra Streisand's tugboat ride in *Funny Girl*.

Tracy doesn't want to do schoolwork. She wants to dance, as does her best friend, Penny Pingleton (Amanda Bynes), always seen sucking a lollipop. They rush home from school to watch *The Corny Collins Show*, the host played by James Marsden, who does a perfect Dick Clark impersonation. His juvenile regulars—collectively dubbed the Council—are known as "the nicest kids in town."

In a brilliant performance, Michelle Pfeiffer plays the viperous, snobbish stage mother, Velma. She's also the TV station manager, promoting the career of her Sandra Dee-like "princess," blonde Amber Von Tussle (Brittany Snow). Amber's dream is to be crowned Miss Hairspray of Baltimore one more time . . . or forever.

Like Travolta, Pfeiffer hasn't sung in a musical in a long time, not since *Grease 2* early in her career. She belts out her numbers with doo-wop aplomb.

The subplot spins around the once-a-month "Negro Day," hosted by record shop owner Motormouth Maybelle (Queen Latifah) in a vanilla performance. Her son, who outshines Mom by a Baltimore mile, is Seaweed, fantastically played by the super-talented Elijah Kelley.

The dream of going on the show becomes a reality when Tracy goes to the hop that night and wins the dance competition. She defeats Amber and her big ego and wins a place on *The Corny Collins Show*.

To make Amber really pissed off, her boyfriend, the handsome hunk, Link Larkin (Zac Efron) dumps Amber for fat Tracy. He falls in love with her in spite of her weight. Much to the horror of Penny's Bible-thumping mother, Prudy (as overplayed by

Allison Janney), her daughter falls for Seaweed. Remember, this is Baltimore in 1962. The plot begins to thicken.

The movie is so clean you could take George Bush to it providing you explained the action to him. If the film has a racy moment, it's when Tracy's best friend, Penny, falls for black dancer Kelley. She claims that now that she's tasted chocolate, she's not going back. Of course, her constantly sucking on that lollipop suggests that she's a future queen of fellatio wrapping that tongue around black dick.

Of course, you know how the ending will come off even if you've not seen the previous movie or the Broadway play. Naturally, Tracy and the forces of integration will triumph over the evil Velma and Amber and their pro-segregation desires. Interracial love will win out, and fat Tracy will also triumph, grabbing Elvis from the clutches of that blonde chick.

We're not giving the film a total rave however. As David Edelstein so accurately put it, "Every number is a showstopper: pumping arms, ecstatic frugging, hyperactive editing, climax on top of climax. The songs have the same manic pitch and blur together."

With all its faults, and there are many, *Hairspray* traps you in its sheer joy and brilliantly captures the Kennedy-era mood of a young world that was still optimistic, unlike the generation growing up post-millennium.

John Travolta and Nikki Blonsky

Michelle Pfeiffer and Christopher Walken

WHAT THE CRITICS SAID

"A camp 1960s singalong drenched in pastels and swimming with pouting, preening performances—including a winning turn from Michelle Pfeiffer—*Hairspray* finds Travolta right at home in his roly poly supporting part. Tottering around in a frumpy fatsuit, his pinched lips cooing a quirky Baltimore accent, the 53-year-old reprises the part of Edna Turnblad, played by the gay icon Divine in the original film and Harvey Fierstein on Broadway, and he clearly delights in the part."

Will Lawrence
New York Post

"Michelle Pfeiffer plays Velma, the show's brittle manager and the mother of its blonde diva (Brittany Snow), and it's a marvelous turn: hysterically stylized, as if her Catwoman had joined the cast of Dynasty. Velma wants both Tracy and the coloreds off the air, and gets her chance when the girl becomes a regular at Negro platter parties ('hotbeds of moral turpitude')—overseen by a disappointingly vanilla Queen Latifah."

New York Magazine

"*Hairspray* is the best and most entertaining movie adaptation of a stage musical so far this century, and yes, I'm including the Oscar-winning *Chicago*."

Lou Lumenick

HAIR DO . . . AND HAIR DON'T

The New York Daily News has two movie reviewers: Jack Mathews, who loved *Hairspray*, and Joe Dziemanowicz, who loathed it. What follows are quotes from both men.

"*Hairspray* is a great big sloppy kiss of entertainment for audiences weary of explosions, CGI effects and sequels, sequels, sequels. At the price of a movie ticket, this roof-raising ode to the innocent last days of 60s rock 'n' roll is easily the best summer bargain on or off Broadway. To see Travolta's coquettish expressions on Edna's beachball face is funny in itself. But when the lithe dancer inside the fat suit gets it going on the dance floor—or even on the street—he becomes a hilarious, gravity-defying optical illusion. You haven't seen a more graceful dancing behemoth since the Hippo Ballet in *Fantasia*. Fortunately, Edna is not seen in a tutu."

Jack Mathews

"When Hollywood performed its extreme makeover, it spritzed out originality, magic, and humanity in this breezy, socially minded comedy about a chubby Baltimore teen who loves to dance. In the new movie musical, John Travolta plays Tracy's mother. She's not all heart—she's all fat suit. Edna is buried under so much rubber, prosthetics and makeup that she's barely human. Edna has the face of a squint-eyed puffer fish and the figure of an Aero mattress; Queen size. Inflated. Paging Sleepy's. In time, that overblown image—and the whole film musical—will fade from my mind. Unlike Broadway's *Hairspray*, which never loses its hold."

Joe Dziemanowicz

HAPPY FEET

Right-Wing Christians Condemn an Animated Film That's Part Cabaret, Part Eco-Pic

Set in Antarctica during today's era of environment upheaval, the story of this animated film follows the odyssey of young Mumble (whose voiceover is performed by Elijah Wood), a musically challenged penguin with an unusual gift who finds the heart to pursue his dream. Each penguin has a heart song, but when the other penguins discover Mumble can't sing, they think something is wrong with him and send him away.

The inspirational message behind that dynamic, as interpreted by the thousands of children and teenagers who saw it, involves being true to yourself and the identity you eventually discover. The film has another message as well: that the human race has a habit of exploiting and messing up the natural environment. But no one, especially the producers and director, George Miller, of this animated film, was prepared for the violent reaction against it from the Christian Right.

Catalyzed by the above-noted theme, Colorado-based right-wing evangelist Dr. James Dobson, ever vigilant in his war against the "radical homosexual agenda," reinforced his self-anointed role as guardian of all things moral, aided by the homosexual-hating preacher, the late, but not lamented, Jerry Falwell. Earlier, Falwell had warned us against secret gay agent Tinky Winky of the Teletubbies. Tinky Winky, in Falwell's distorted mirror, was trying to influence the sexual orientation of three-year-olds.

Dobson, in contrast, discovered a gay penguin within the (animated) cast of *Happy Feet*. He then broadcast that he had never seen the movie—"and I don't plan to see it"—but that doesn't stop this know-nothing from having a dark opinion.

During a December 11, 2006 edition of his syndicated radio program *Focus on the Family*, Dobson joined conservative commentator Michael Medved, focusing their collective ire upon *Happy Feet*. Within that broadcast, Medved insisted that *Happy Feet* contains a "subtext, as there so often is, about homosexuality." This made his learned colleague ponder aloud the possibility that the filmmakers were actually "getting at the idea that homosexuality is genetic."

Medved then continued his attack on the film in other media, posting a warning on his *townhall.com* weblog, entitled "Don't Be Misled by *Crappy Feet*." Then he asserted that *Happy Feet* is "the darkest, most disturbing feature-length animated film ever offered by a major studio."

Not only that, but the movie, as seen by Medved, contains "a bizarre anti-religious bias" and "a subtext that appears to plead for endorsement of gay identity." Medved went on to insist that whereas most of the penguins in the film aren't gay, there's one penguin within *Happy Feet* who doesn't fit in. The other penguins tell him, "You are not a real penguin," because he dances instead of sings. In response, the penguin says, "Dad, you have to accept me as I am. I can't change." Dobson and Medved went on to attack the concept of a genetic basis for homosexuality, asserting that there are some gays who have "changed their lives and have turned around their lives"—that is, become straight.

Encouraged by Dobson and Medved, the lunatic fringe of the Religious Right let loose a barrage of demented attacks on *Happy Feet*. A typical comment posted on the web read like this:

With Happy Feet, I didn't expect my conservative Christian family to be assaulted with what we all recognized as an anti-Christian screen, with open mockery of traditional Christian preaching against values and lifestyles contrary to church teachings. It was abundantly clear that Happy Feet substituted homosexuality with dancing as the 'different' lifestyle that was the unfair target of an Inquisition on ice. It was Dirty Dancing and Footloose all over again, but with the rhetoric and situation developed to make religious criticism of homosexuality counter to everything good and pleasing.

In defense of the religious community, many Christians responded with a positive interpretation of *Happy Feet*, not seeing it as part of a conspiratorial agenda threatening to destroy the world. A blogger named Lorraine, wrote:

Mumble is a male penguin who's head over heels in love with Gloria, a female penguin. If it's a homosexual agenda, it's so hidden that I can't find it. In contrast, the movie Shark Tales was an in-your-face homosexual agenda. A cross-dressing shark who wanted to be a gentle dolphin. He was blatantly gay. Mumble was just Mumble . . . a different guy who made a big difference!

Actually, the real secret of the animated characters' dance steps derived from the "Happy Feet" of dancer/choreographer Savion Glover. The virtuoso hoofer wore a penguin-body suit and, thanks to a sophisticated interface of computer software and camera imaging, he defined and brought to life the tap-dancing talent of the movie's fuzzy hero, Mumble. In the wake of Ann Miller's migration to tap-dancing Heaven, Glover has been called "without question the greatest tap-dancer alive."

Glover isn't the only star who worked on this film. For more on that, see below—"What the Critics Said."

During the course of the film, Mumble discovers that alien creatures are scooping all the fish out of the ocean. He becomes determined to right this wrong . . . to save the environment.

This makes the film, in the words of one reviewer, "as politically pointed as it is disturbing. It is a view of hell as seen through the eyes and ears of creatures we foolishly, tragically, call dumb."

That raises the big question. Who are the dumb ones? Surely not that great environmentalist, President George W. Bush. Was that Oscar-winning Al Gore we spotted slipping out of a matinee of *Happy Feet*?

 WHAT THE CRITICS SAID

"The voice of Mumble is that of Elijah Wood. On the other hand, Robin Williams gives his voice to several characters, including Ramon and Lovelace the Guru. As the Adélie penguin Lovelace, he sounds a lot like the singer Barry White, which means he's one of the few so-called black voices in a world that sounds otherwise white as deep winter. Most of the principals deliver distinctive vocal performances. Nicole Kidman recycles her baby-breathy Marilyn Monroe shtick for Mumble's mother, Norma Jean, while Hugo Weaving sticks a Scottish burr in his throat to play an elder penguin named Noah. For Mumble's father, Memphis, Hugh Jackman throws his voice into the deep dryer and comes up with something that's a little bit country, a little bit rock 'n' roll."
    Manohla Dargis
    The New York Times

THE HEART IS DECEITFUL
ABOVE ALL THINGS

Help! Why Couldn't My Mom Have Been Courtney Love?

This gritty, slice-of-life drama was based on what was later revealed as a literary fraud, the so-called autobiography" of "JT LeRoy," a character and author who never really existed. LeRoy, the male teenage hustler who supposedly endured Satanic levels of emotional, physical, and sexual abuse, is, in fact, merely the fictitious creation of a woman named Laura Albert. Ms. Albert obviously believes in Oscar Wilde's statement that "Lying, the telling of beautiful, untrue things, is the proper aim of art." Except that in Albert's case, she had nothing beautiful to say in her fraudulent kid-in-peril narrative.

During TV promotional appearances, JT LeRoy was impersonated by 25-year-old Savannah Knoop, half-sister of Albert's long-time partner, Geoffrey Knoop. For these TV appearances, Savannah adopted a persona that included a Hitchcockian getup of big shades, floppy hat, and long blonde hair. You can't make this up—that's why reality always gives novelists a hard time.

After the literary fraud was exposed, one critic said, "If you think the heart is deceitful, you should meet the author." Albert quickly became labeled as the James Frey for the hipster set. Early boosters of LeRoy included both Dennis Cooper and Dave Eggers, who predicted that LeRoy's autobiographical works would "prove to be among the most influential American books of the last 10 years." To that comment, Manohla Dargis, writing in *The New York Times*, responded, "Somewhere, probably hell, William S. Burroughs laughed."

Before the hoax of the book was exposed, stars were lured into the web of deceit. In the film, Winona Ryder appears as a social worker, Jeremy Sisto, a meth-head, Michael Pitt as "Buddy," and Marilyn Manson as a skuzzy boyfriend—yes, male.

In this episodic slice-of-low-life reality, Asia Argento, the Italian actress and filmmaker, directed, wrote, and starred in this disturbing flick that strings together lurid but unfounded tales of addict behavior. She plays Sarah, a 23-year-old doper mom who drags her young son, Jeremiah, into a drug world of one-night stands and tin-foil hits.

Her sharpest critics have claimed that this ditty of undocumented horror is actually a vanity piece for Argento. She has strung together a series of degradations almost with an uninspired 60s mentality that evokes early Warhol. Regrettably, there is little social or psychological insight here. But instead of being pieced together, *Deceitful* seems scummed together.

Argento is a household name in Italy, and this film earned her notoriety in America. *Entertainment Weekly* called her "a debauched Eurotrash starlet who oozes punk creed more than she does talent."

Born in Rome in 1975, Asia Argento is the daughter of actress Daria Nicolodi. Her father, Dario Argento, is an Italian film director, producer, and screenwriter who's known for his influence on modern horror and slasher movies. When she was a teenager, Asia was directed in her first nude scene by her father in his 1993 *Trauma*. While in Minneapolis shooting *Trauma* at the age of 16, she had two snakes and a sun tattooed on her ass.

Her performance in the 1994 *Perdiamoci di vista!* won her the David di Donatello Award. (Italy's version of the Oscar.) American audiences became familiar with her when she appeared in two movies in 1998—*New Rose Hotel* with Christopher Walken and *Monkey B* with self-admitted gay actor Rupert Everett.

Often harsh to Argento, the press also loves her because she's been called the most quotable actress in Italy. She was asked, by one reporter, "How do you want to be remembered?"

"As somebody who has done everything, but didn't know how to do anything," she bluntly answered.

To sum up her charms, at least in the view of one male admirer, "She's so big and juicy, voluptuous and silky and her heavy Italian accent is very endearing. She's frequently nude in films. She's fiery and tough. And, of course, sexy."

In *The Heart Is Deceitful Above All Things*, as noted by Owen Gleiberman, Argento is "smeared with cherry lips, peroxide hair, and a vaguely Italian croak of a voice that all blend to make her resemble Uma Thurman after a six-day bender."

Readers' comments, as posted on the *Entertainment Weekly* website, have been devastating not only about Argento, but about JT LeRoy as well. A typical response from a viewer, identified only as "Boubie," contained this comment: "I agree that Asia Argento is a worthless hag, a tired daughter of a has-been director. That being said, I'm only curious as to whether she appears naked. And wasn't JT LeRoy the fake transvestite writer who Winona Ryder lied about knowing? After a while, you begin to wonder if all these Hollywood people aren't on drugs."

In the film seven-year-old Jeremiah (Jimmy Bennett) is pulled from his foster home to lead a troubled life on the road with his wayward teenage mother, Sarah, as played by Argento.

As Sarah goes from one vile horror of a boyfriend to an even viler one, Jeremiah is repeatedly abused both physically and mentally.

Homosexuality—or rather pedophilia—often rears its head. Sarah marries one of her tricks, Emerson (Jeremy Renner). The newlyweds head to Atlantic City for their honeymoon, leaving Jeremiah locked in his room with a slice of cheese in the fridge. The groom returns alone, claiming "She run out on me," and proceeds to rape the boy without mercy.

The truck-stop hooker mom subsequently feeds her kid a diet of cold SpaghettiOs and cheese singles, perhaps meth pudding for dessert. He becomes queer bait for aspiring pedophiles who dream of his prepubescent charms. This doe-eyed creature is forced to endure belt-buckle discipline by surrogate dads as we slog through Whitetrash, USA.

In the book and in the subsequent film, Jeremiah is eventually rescued from his seducer and placed in the custody of his grandparents, both of them religious nut cases. To our shock, Peter Fonda was cast as the grandfather. Fonda as a control-freak Christian minister talks in a creepy brimstone whisper.

What is Jane's brother and Henry's son doing in a movie such as this? Henry is surely turning over in his grave—"We didn't make movies like that in my day." The grandmother is played by Ornella Muti of *Flash Gordon*.

As the years pass, young Jeremiah fades and is replaced by an older (11 year old) Jeremiah, as played interchangeably by twins, Dylan and Cole Sprouse. They are recognizable from the Disney Channel's *The Suite Life of Zack and Cody*. As one reviewer suggested, "Walt must be doing loop-de-loops in his freezer."

Eventually, the older Jeremiah is kidnapped from these pseudo-Christian horrors by his mother Sarah and her new boyfriend, Kenny (Matt Schulze). The kid is taken on the road again, where Sarah dresses him up as a girl, a most fetching Lolita, and turns him on to one of her tricks. Mother and son have a symbiotic relationship that is anything but healthy, yet it is all either of them has.

As both director and star of this flick, Argento certainly doesn't believe in sparing the audience pain—in fact, many critics found the pic unwatchable.

The performance of all three of the children she selected are scarily convincing, although she never formally broaches the subject of child prostitution, which might have been called for from the director of such a lurid tale.

However, Argento doesn't shy away from an intense depiction of child abuse and neglect, and she's strong on violence, pervasive language—with sex, sex, and more sex between drug-taking.

What is missing from this film? Those *Mommie Dearest* wire hangers.

Asia Argento with friend

Left, **Asia Argento** with the film verson of Jeremiah ("JT"), as played by **Dylan Sprouse** in Lolita drag. *Center*, Dylan's twin, **Cole Sprouse**, who also plays Jeremiah in some scenes of the film; *Right*; book agent and author **Laura Albert** (aka male hustler and abused teen "JT"), perpetrator of the original literary hoax.

"Crystal Meth is the accelerant of this cliché binge of a film. The grubby down-spiral of a meth-head (Asia Argento) who strips 'n' trips her way across Boondock, USA, *The Heart Is Deceitful Above All Things* is a grueling cinematic excretion. On and on it goes: From lover to lover, motel to motel, dead-end road to dead-end road. Like its protagonist, the film goes nowhere."
> **Duane Byrge**
> *The Hollywood Reporter*

"This is an execrable movie depicting the improbable events in the life of a young boy being intermittently raised by his crackhead, highway-hookin' mom (actress-director Asia Argento, with a face that makes Courtney Love's mug shot look glamorous), her plumb-nuts evangelical parents, and a cartoonishly incompetent West Virginia social system."
> **Jack Mathews**
> *New York Daily News*

"Empowered by what she must have thought was fact, Argento performs the script's maternal atrocities with lurid zest, all but winking at the camera when Mom puts her son to bed in an empty bathtub, then turns a loud trick just around the corner. Whatever her limitations, Argento the actor makes certain that Argento the director doesn't lack for 'action'—and that the audience doesn't lack for pain. Actually, the notion of an Italian goth queen reincarnated as a bleached-blonde, suthin-accented, scripture-quoting abuser of herself and her kid isn't nearly as punishing as Argento's fashionable refusal to tell us anything much except that hell is for children."
> **Rob Nelson**
> *The Village Voice*

"Anyone who has followed publishing news over the past six months knows that JT LeRoy is the *other* trauma-memoir fraud du jour. Maybe he wasn't spanked on national TV by Oprah Winfrey, as James Frey was, but investigative articles effectively dispelled the author's mysterious aura, revealing the supposedly teenage, male, HIV-infected survivor of childhood abuse to be a 40-year-old woman named Laura Albert who made the whole thing up. Argento throws herself into her role with hellcat abandon, unafraid to make the character unsympathetic in a larger bid for pity. Sarah, not Jeremiah, is the true focus of both Laura Albert's prose and Argento's movie. They're both slumming it in a fantasy of gutter-chic nihilism under the pretext of saving the children. You could stay home and have a better time slitting your wrists. The movie is vile beyond redemption."
> **Ty Burr**
> *Boston Globe*

"At this point, needless to say, my respect for JT LeRoy comes to life. He is just the hoax that the rage for confessional writing has been asking for. He, or she, has punched all the right buttons, telling of losers, abusers, cross-dressers, and crackpots, enabling eager readers to feel doubly validated in their response. (The announcement that James Frey, the author of the drink-sodden *A Million Little Pieces*, also had the nerve to make stuff up is great news—a little more salt on the margarita's rim.) All I need now is to hear that Dave Pelzer is, in fact, an eighty-five-year-old Frenchwoman who collects fine china, and I will be a happy man."
> **Anthony Lane**
> *The New Yorker*

HERE'S LOOKING AT YOU BOY

(SCHAU MIR IN DIE AUGEN, KLEINER)

Hit-and-Miss Docu on Gay & Lesbian Movies

The bad news first: this German film is not a worthy successor to *The Celluloid Closet* in 1995. But for lovers of gay and lesbian cinema, it's worth a look. André Schäfer wrote it, directed it, and subtitled it "a coming out of queer cinema."

The docu is a short trip down memory lane as it begins in the early 70s with "the first films to mention gays positively." Instead of a world overview, the docu concentrates mainly on Europe and the U.S. where—let's face it—most queer cinema is shot.

The usual talking heads are invoked, along with clips from selected films. Naturally, John Waters makes an appearance. He's practically become the granddaddy of gay cinema, a honor bestowed if for no other reason than he directed *Pink Flamingos* in 1972. In light of subsequent developments in the field, that's almost prehistoric.

In this documentary, we get insights from other talking heads as well, including Gus Van Sant, who at one point emerged as the candidate most likely to direct *Brokeback Mountain* with a cast that at the time looked as if it would showcase Brad Pitt and Matt Damon. He tells of his fight to preserve the shower scene between the two boys in *Elephant.*

Other big names seen in clips include Rainer Werner Fassbinder, and "big fish" such as Tilda Swinton, who played the gender-shifting title character in *Orlando,* alongside Quentin Crisp as Queen Elizabeth.

Clips also include excerpts from Stephen Frears' *My Beautiful Laundrette (*see illustration on following page) and Bill Sherwood's *Parting Glances.*

WHAT THE CRITICS SAID

"This roundup is best viewed as a quite watchable filmmaker's notebook of familiar gay titles and cheery interviews that should fulfill the goals of its consortium of small screen producers."
  Deborah Young
  Variety

André Schäfer's documentary reminds us of films we remember and films we respect

The Hidden Führer:
Debating the Enigma of Hitler's Sexuality

Adolf is Pulled Kicking & Screaming from the Closet

Homosexuals have enough problems without German historian Lothar Machtan trying to drag the closeted Führer into the bright light of gaydom. Gay men are proud to claim Michelangelo or Leonardo da Vinci as one of their own, but what about the dreaded World War II dictator who sent millions of Jews, homosexuals, and gypsies to the gas chamber?

The creators of *Party Monster* and *The Eyes of Tammy Faye*—award-winning filmmakers Fenton Bailey, Randy Barbato, and Gabriel Rotello—explore hidden areas of the Führer's private life. Their film was derived from Machtan, who in September of 2001 tossed a bombshell into the world of Hitlerian studies with the publication of his explosive book *The Hidden Hitler*. As could be predicted, it ignited a storm of worldwide controversy. After dedicating a good hunk of his life to the study of Hitler the private man, the historian (who is not gay) concluded that Hitler was a homosexual. Many Hitler-era survivors were interviewed in this film, and their testimony is alternated with some extraordinary and rarely viewed vintage images.

Before the camera, arguments pro and con about Hitler's sexuality are presented. Although Machtan makes a compelling case, there are arguments on the other side to suggest that Hitler was not a homo. The opinions expressed are often passionate.

Hitler himself said, "I cannot love any woman until I have completed my task." He also once claimed that he was "married" to Germany.

Especially effective are the encounters with Rudiger Lautman, himself a homosexual. This sociology professor once taught author Machtan himself. They engage in some challenging banter, mainly from Lautman who demands to see proof of Hitler's homosexuality, more than the author offered in his book.

Machtan builds his case by documenting that as a 16-year-old in Linz, Austria, Hitler "demanded absolute exclusivity" from his constant companion, August Kubizek. The two close companions are reunited in 1908 in Vienna, shortly after Hitler had been rejected by the Academy of Fine Arts. If only the academy had accepted him, he might have become an artist and not the world's most notorious figure.

In his 1943 memoir, published in the middle of World War II, Kubizek reported that he and Hitler were reunited with a real kiss. It's surprising that in the 1953 edition of this memoir, that kiss was downgraded to "a peck on the cheek."

The film even deals with those rumors that Rudolph Hess and Hitler were once lovers. But there is little evidence to suggest that. One of the reasons that there is so little evidence remaining is that Hitler systematically set out to obliterate all records of his past life. That Hess may have been homosexual is widely believed by many historians. In fact, many of his Nazi comrades referred to Hess as "Fräulein Anna." Ernst Röhm called him "Black Paula."

In 1924 Hitler was lamenting to friends that "My Rudi" was still locked up in prison. Upon his release, he became Hitler's constant companion. His relationship was characterized as "the most beautiful human experience" with Hitler, one of "a shared joy and sorrow, cares and hopes, hatreds and loves."

Of course, this friendship ended when Hess flew to England on an ill-fated betrayal that became one of the most infamous incidents of World War II.

There are some eyewitness accounts which suggest that Hitler paid young men for sex, and on at least one occasion was caught having sex with a soldier. Some historians dismiss these accounts as "fodder for supermarket tabloids."

In 1932, the homosexual leader of the dreaded storm troopers, Ernst Röhm, was outed in the press. This triggered his murder, along with many of his men, in "The Night of the Long Knives." Machtan claims that the massacre was prompted by Hitler's desire to bury any evidence—both human and documented—of the Führer's homosexual activities.

There's a lot of nudity in this docu, including full-frontal views of some gorgeous blond Adonis types. There are also scenes of the monumental nude statues so favored by Hitler of his "master race." One tantalizing bit of information is given. For such Herculean figures, the penises on the statues are not well endowed. At the time when these sculpted genitalia were being created, it was a widely held Nazi belief that Jews were well endowed. Therefore, the sculptors were ordered to depict Nazi cocks as tastefully modest, so there would be no suggestion that they had Jewish blood in them.

There are other revelations in the docu, including one from Gottfried, the great-grandson of Richard Wagner. He claims that Wieland Wagner was molested by Hitler. Wieland (1917-1966) was one of two sons of Siegfried Wagner and the grandson of composer Richard Wagner. In his adult role as director of the Bayreuth Festival, he is credited with ushering in a new and more modern style to Wagnerian opera. But did he really go to bed with the Führer and discover that Hitler was missing one testicle?

But what about Hitler's mistress, Eva Braun, whom he married in his final hours before each of them committed suicide?. Hitler's butler reported that he "found no evidence in the sheets" that the Hitler/Braun relationship was ever consummated. There is also evidence that she had previously attempted suicide twice before

After seeing the pros and cons of Hitler's sexuality, as presented in this film, what's a girl to think? *Sieg heil* or *sieg homo*?

 # WHAT THE CRITICS SAID

"As the power-lusting rejected painter gains power, Machtan reminds the viewer of Hitler's obsessions for youth (many clips of bare-chested 'Hitler Youth' and stills of nude body posers beef up the point) and Wagner. Over time, Hitler literally took Wagner's imagery, icons and mythology from the Bayreuth stage and used them as set dressing—from the uniforms, to 'imperial' architecture, to his own death in a 'Ring of Fire'—for his world stage."
   S. James Wegg

"Fascinating, if more than a little specious, this examination of one of history's most controversial figures leaves far more questions on the table at its conclusion than it answers. *The Hidden Führer* seems, on the surface at least, to be little more than titillating propaganda that hinges upon coincidence—however, some of the suggested research contains allegations that do give one pause. While not academically sound, it's an interesting corner of history that is successfully skimmed in this briskly paced documentary—definitely worth a rental for the curious."
   Preston Jones

"Riveting . . . compelling . . . fascinating."
   Linda Stasi
   New York Post

"Bailey and Barbato handle the complex incendiary material with skill and remarkable balance."
   Robert Koehler
   Variety

THE HISTORY BOYS

Cute Teenage Boys Pursue Sex, Sports & Higher Education

We loved Alan Bennett's play, and we also adore the way he adapted it for the screen under the direction of Nicholas Hytner. This is a warm, wonderful, beautiful film. We need more like it.

As the *Christian Science Monitor*'s Peter Rainier put it, "If the literacy of *The History Boys* is deemed uncinematic, then give me uncinema anytime."

Hytner first staged the play at London's National Theatre, then moved the same 12-member cast to Broadway.

Vibrating with exuberance and erudition, the film is set in Yorkshire in 1983, the era of Iron Lady Margaret Thatcher. It's a comedy/drama that has been called "A spirited elegy for a way of educating that is passing away."

The plot, such as it is, spins around eight boys who have been chosen for special tutoring in history to help them pass their difficult entrance exams for Oxford and Cambridge. The officious headmaster of the school (played by Clive Merrison) channels the *Zeitgeist* by hiring a young Oxford history graduate, Irwin (Stephen Campbell Moore), to teach the boys new techniques that will grab the examiners' attention. As a goal- rather than a truth-oriented teacher, his methods put him in competition with general studies teacher, Hector, as played by the Falstaffian Richard Griffiths.

Dialogues within this shrewdly acted, bittersweet film are permeated with a certain Wildean panache. The screen at times can barely contain this marvelous depiction of human intelligence. Hector, for example, tells his students: "The best moments in reading are when you come across something—a thought, a feeling, a way of looking at things, which you had thought special and particular to you. And it is as if a hand has come out—and taken yours."

The avuncular Hector steals every scene he's in. He is already well known to movie audiences, having played Uncle Vernon in the Harry Potter movies and Uncle Monty in *Withnail & I*. One critic found that he had the body of Jabba the Hun but the soul of Mr. Chips. If Hector is Mr. Chips, he's Mr. Chips with kinks.

Both teachers are gay, Hector remaining in the closet but Irwin being more forthright about his preferences. Both teachers also use all the weapons in their arsenal—wit, charisma, and, yes, even logic—to win the boys over to their way of thinking. The students are left confused as to which teacher to follow.

Irwin is a pragmatic, cynical Oxford grad, who comes to the school to polish the rough diamonds for their interviews at Oxford or Cambridge. He seems completely opposed to Hector's more liberal view of education in which he hopes to turn his boys into "well-rounded human beings."

Hector is married but has the hots for his students—and his proclivities get him in serious trouble. He likes to take his male students for rides on his motorbike and he enjoys copping feels as he does so. The very tolerant students—no child molestation lawsuits here—are well aware of his proclivities, as he's already grabbed most of their dicks. But they make light of his homosexuality. Even though they see Hector as gay and eccentric, they also recognize him for the great teacher that he is.

Frances de la Tour as Dorothy Lintott is extraordinary as the droopy, horse-faced history teacher with a baritone voice who is the wisest member of the school's academic staff. "History is a commentary on the various and continuing incapabilities of men," she says in the film. "History is women following behind with the bucket." She also delivers a sort of warning to Hector. "A grope is still a grope."

Many critics treated the homosexuality of the film in a cavalier fashion. Others, such as Lisa Schwarzbaum, of *Entertainment Weekly*, preferred to issue a mandatory PC statement: "Had *The History Boys* been an American play (rather than a Tony Award-laden import from Britain's famed National Theatre), the peccadillo that catches up with charismatic general studies teacher Mr. Hector (*Harry Potter*'s corpulent, charismatic Richard Griffiths) would more likely be pot-smoking or a thing for wearing panties on his head at home than a penchant for genially groping a teenage boy's genitals while the untraumatized student tolerates the ritual on the back of Hector's motorcycle. The frightfully eloquent British playwright Alan Bennett (*The Madness of George III*) tosses off Hector's handiwork as the minor foible of a lonely, passionate, sympathetic fellow, which I don't buy."

The History Boys sympathizes with Hector, whom Griffiths plays not as a predator but as a lonely dreamer whose ineffectual gropes are not much different from pats on the back. These whip-smart 17- and 18-year-old students not only tolerate his fumbling advances but also accept them with good humor as expressions of devotion.

We most adore Hector for broadening his students' cultural spheres by not only quoting A.E. Housman but using show tunes and dialogue from Bette Davis movies as well. None of it is terribly relevant to history but fun nonetheless.

The cast of students is memorable, even though Dominic Cooper's Dakin dominates the movie class. The cast also includes Posner (Samuel Barnett) as a gay Jewish student in love with Dakin (who isn't?). Dakin is the kind of boy that makes you want to run your fingers through his hair—and do so much, much more. Posner is a younger, nerdier version of the teacher, Irwin.

James Corden plays the overweight, clownish Timms, and the dumb jock role, Rudge, is assumed by Russell Tovey. He's dim but sporty. Scripps is played by Jamie Parker, and Andrew Knott is the badge-wearing Lockwood. Quite frankly, the ethnic minorities are barely sketched but represented by Samuel Anderson as Crowther and Sacha Dhawan as Akthar.

We agree with one wag who suggested that "only a churl would deny that this is compulsively entertaining viewing that's unafraid of treating intelligence with the respect it deserves."

If it means anything to you, Prince Charles and his wife Camilla, the Duchess of Cornwall, have given the film their seal of approval.

Actors as academics. *Left to right*:
Stephen Campbell Moore, Richard Griffiths, Frances de la Tour

"*The History Boys* is a reminder of why *Dead Poets Society* was a dishonest piece of death's-head drivel despite its posture of life-affirming, countercultural humanism. The movie showed soulless patriarchs driving tender adolescents to suicide for the crime of reading poetry aloud in the woods. It didn't have the guts to admit that along with that poetry there might be a circle jerk or two. Hector rationalizes his misbehavior by arguing that 'the transmission of knowledge is in itself an erotic act.'"
   David Edelstein
   New York Magazine

"The writing is always incisive, the wit consistently sardonic and clever. The dialogue, along with that in *The Queen*, is among the best of any film this year. But, while thought-provoking and engaging, *History Boys* has an excessively stagey quality and lacks the cinematic subtlety that would enhance its transition from stage to screen."
   Claudia Puig
   USA Today

"Both teachers [Hector and Irwin] find themselves in love with the same boy, Dakin (Dominic Cooper), who learns early on how to use his physical charms to his advantage. The story is suffused in that public British schoolboy homoeroticism emblematic of the genre, but the subject is handled in a thoughtful, non-hysterical way that you'd never see in Hollywood versions of the sacred bond between pupil and teacher."
   Carina Chocano
   Los Angeles Times

"Dominic Cooper is the straight boy you've always fantasized about. In the aftermath of Foleygate, the setup of *The History Boys* is eerily familiar. Cooper's character of Dakin exemplifies swaggering maturity. He not only serves as a model for the other students on how to handle Hector's advances with aplomb but also seduces a much younger male teacher because he can find no other way to get to him. Cooper's hot turn in *The History Boys* as a student with designs on his teacher makes us wonder: Don't some young men want to be 'molested'?"
   Sean Kennedy

"Gay U.K. playwright Alan Bennett and out director Nichols Hytner bring to the screen their Tony-winning play about a group of private-school boys and the instructor who can't keep his mitts off them. No British schoolboy drama is complete without some gay subplot, but here the gay material is especially nuanced, ambiguous, and even subversive."
   The Advocate

We congratulate

RICHARD GRIFFITHS
for his designation as Blood Moon's Runner-Up
in this year's category of

BEST SUPPORTING ACTOR
for his work in
THE HISTORY BOYS.

HOLLYWOOD DREAMS

To Live & Die (& Cry) in Los Angeles

London-born helmer and scripter, Henry Jaglom, invades the City of Angels with this offbeat film. His fans may not number in the thousands, perhaps hundreds, but he gave the world *Sitting Ducks* in 1980 and *Someone to Love* in 1987, the latter flick featuring Orson Welles.

To his repertoire, he adds his latest, *Hollywood Dreams*, featuring a red-haired newcomer, Tanna Frederick, playing a hayseed, Margie Chizek, who drops off the potato wagon from Iowa to land in La-La Land.

What a strange choice for a leading role. At times Frederick evokes Ronald Reagan Jr. in drag; at other times, she could be Chelsea Clinton's ugly sister.

Naturally, she's desperate to make it as an actress in Hollywood. Who isn't? She loves old movies from Hollywood's golden age as well as men in lingerie. Her favorite actor is Robert Williams, who died after his one big role in the 1931 *Platinum Blonde*, with sexy Jean Harlow.

In this film, Jaglom is musing over the burdens of fame and the awful price one pays for success in Hollywood. Of course, that tale has been done so many times, although Jaglom, as in all his 14 other films, provides his own improvisational style.

Margie is rescued from sleeping in her car by a kindly producer, Kaz (Zack Norman). He takes her, along with her tumbling Titian curls, to live in a lavish home with his lover, Caesar (David Proval). About to be married in a same-sex wedding, they are not the most macho of boyfriends.

In this home she meets a young actor, the rather handsome Justin Kirk playing Robin. Unlike the usual, Robin is straight but pretending to be gay to get ahead in Hollywood. In Hollywood, isn't it the other way around?—particularly for some high profile stars devoted to Scientology?

"I know six A-list actors who are gay and pretend to be straight," Robin tells Margie. "I am the only one who pretends to be gay."

In her over-the-top acting style, Frederick calls a former Jaglom *ingénue*, Karen Black. As if by magic, Black herself makes a cameo appearance in the movie, cast as a Stella Adler acting coach, Luna,

who muses with a melancholy acceptance about her former stardom. Also appearing in a cameo is the always talented Sally Kirkland, as a minister who marries the gay couple.

Also providing a cameo as a "big star" is Eric Roberts. No longer the hot stud of yesterday, the brother of Julia Roberts is aging but still good looking. He could still definitely get picked up in a gay bar.

The most sympathetic and human role is given to Margie's Aunt Bee, a terrific Melissa Leo, who pays a visit to this strange Hollywood *ménage* and immediately witnesses a lesbian kissing scene.

As for Jaglom's editing, it's loosey-goosey.

"*Hollywood Dreams* is a must for Jaglom fans. For other viewers, it will depend on how much they can take of Jaglom's improvisational style and Frederick's over-the-top, tear-filled acting. (She sobs at the drop of a Kleenex.)"
V.A. Musetto
New York Post

"Among knowledgeable moviegoers, the phrase 'a Henry Jaglom film' invokes either wary curiosity or full-blown flight reflex. Jaglom has been making his small, personal, self-funded, outrageously self-indulgent movies for so long that he bridges several eras: the New Hollywood of the late 1960s and the early 1970s, the indie boom of the mid-1980s, the corporate art-house resurgence of the late 1990s. Whether you think of him as a Left Coast Woody Allen or a poor man's Robert Altman, the guy just won't go away."
Ty Burr
Boston Globe

"It takes a special talent to play a bad actress well, and newcomer Frederick isn't experienced enough to embrace her character's insecurities honestly; instead, she pantomimes them as full-blown hysterics. A good actress embraces the ambiguity, as Naomi Watts did in *Mulholland Drive*, willfully allowing auds to wonder where performance ends and reality begins. *Hollywood Dreams* is more like Watts' less-successful bad-actress satire *Ellie Parker*, where wink-wink self-consciousness costs the character her sincerity."
Peter Debrudge
Variety

"Mostly, this is Frederick's movie, and reactions to *Hollywood Dreams* will depend largely on what one thinks of her performance. A bizarre blend of goofiness and lethal ambition, her Margie is Fanny Brice crossed with Eve Harrington. Frederick gives the party everything she has; one wishes she would give it a bit less. We're meant to find her quirks charming, not abrasive and obnoxious."
Lael Lowenstein
Los Angeles Times

HOLLYWOODLAND

Whodunit Kryptonite for Doomed Superman

One of Tinseltown's most infamous mysteries has never been unraveled, certainly not in *Hollywoodland* which marked the "comeback" of that handsome hunk, Ben Affleck, even though the movie bombed financially.

George Reeves, the actor known to millions of kids as TV's Superman in the 1950s series, died of a gunshot wound to his head on the morning of June 16, 1959. Was his death an accident, a suicide, or cold-blooded murder? The question has puzzled conspiracy buffs for decades.

With all of the principals now dead, the truth of Reeves' death is likely to remain a mystery. As for solving the case, *Hollywoodland* only muddies the already murky water.

There is enough raw material here for a gripping mystery. The Los Angeles Police Department did little to investigate the death of Reeves. None of those present at his home during "the last night" attended his funeral. His fiancée skipped town, never to return. And then there were those bisexual rumors.

Gay Hollywood, at least those born back in the 30s, used to claim Reeves as one of their own, although there wasn't a hint of this in the movie. Reeves, or so it was rumored, used to cruise Santa Monica Boulevard, picking up hustlers for quickies. Allegedly, he was arrested in his Jaguar one night— high in the Hollywood Hills—going down on a hustler. The rumor mill claimed that the cop disappeared on his motorcycle and forgot all about the incident once Reeves slipped him a fifty-dollar bill.

Reeves had made his debut appearing in the opening scene of *Gone With the Wind*, but until he donned the Superman drag for TV, his Hollywood career hadn't really gone very far. And after the Superman role dried up, Reeves at the age of forty-five seemed adrift. Superman had hopelessly typecast him.

Years after Reeves' death, and also hoping for a comeback, Ben Affleck, still looking good, campaigned for the role of potato-y George Reeves, even though it meant wearing a Superman costume.

Affleck's previous four films had flopped—*Gigli, Paycheck, Jersey Girl,* and *Surviving Christmas*. He waived his usual multimillion-dollar fee to play Reeves in a desperate bid to regain critical acclaim and box-office success. He got the part only after Hugh Jackman dropped out because of other commitments.

"Reeves had been in a car crash once, and kind of fainted," said Affleck, who read all the material he could on Reeves. "The newspapers then said 'Superman Faints at Sight of Own Blood.' People were very flip and snide about him. It was demeaning."

Although much speculation and press was generated by the bulge of Brandon Routh in his Superman tights, no one in the 50s ever mentioned or wrote about the basket of Reeves. Actually he showed no more basket than a woman in a bathing suit. Either he wasn't well hung or else he was artfully concealed.

In *Hollywoodland,* in distinct contrast, Affleck at least shows he's a man with a dick. Of course, Affleck doesn't have the body to fill out a Superman suit like Brandon Routh in *Superman Returns*. But Affleck seems amply endowed in the close-up shot of his crotch, where he wonders aloud, onscreen, if he's showing too much dick before going out to meet his kiddie fans.

Affleck doesn't exactly come off as a girly man in the film, although he wears a pinkie ring and smokes with a cigarette holder. But so did macho Reeves, who in real life had been an amateur boxer.

Hollywoodland is Allen Coulter's first attempt to direct a major feature film. He'd earned his reputation as a helmer in such TV series as *The Sopranos, Sex and the City,* and *The X-Files.*

Ironically, the actual star of the film is not Affleck but Adrien Brody, who's miscast as a Los Angeles gumshoe. Joaquin Phoenix auditioned for the role of Louis Simo, but Brody got it.

In this confused, muddled film, we follow the fictional detective Brody, as he tries to arrive at a clear solution to the enigma of the death of Hollywood's Kryptonite. He fails to deliver the goods, but does find two extra bullet holes at the scene of the crime that the police overlooked.

We did warm to the scene when Affleck meets Diane Lane (playing Toni Mannix), a showgirl turned Beverly Hills *grande dame*. Within minutes, she makes herself eager to sample Superman's blade of steel.

The real-life Toni Mannix, back in the 50s, was so hot for Reeves that she purchased a Benedict Canyon home for him—back then the price was $12,000.

Toni was the strong-willed wife of a top MGM executive, Metro "fixer" Eddie Mannix, as played by Bob Hoskins. Eddie handles his wife's affair with great style. He takes both of them out to dinner and invites his own mistress to round out the dinner party.

Lane has staked out a career, and most effectively, playing older women. The New Yorker has appeared in *Unfaithful, Under the Tuscan Sun,* and *Must Love Dogs*, a trio of movies that made the 41-year-old a symbol of fourth-decade female sexiness.

After a prolonged stint as Lane's gigolo, Affleck (alias Reeves) dumps Toni for a younger woman, a brash New York ex-showgirl named Leonore Lemmon (played by Robin Tunney).

Historically, after Reeves left Toni, his troubles began. "First the brakes go out in his Jaguar—not once, but twice," said Laurie Jacobson, author of *Dishing Hollywood: The Real Scoop on Tinseltown's Most Notorious Scandals*. He also started receiving about 20 hang-up calls a day. He notified the police of the harassment.

The ex-Superman was slated to marry Leonore but began to have doubts. Most conspiracy buffs think short-tempered Leonore killed Reeves at his home—that it was an accidental murder, not a suicide. The showgirl could have picked up the gun Reeves kept in his bedside table and fired it at him during a struggle, at least according to Reeves murder theorists.

Ben Affleck and Diane Lane

Another scenario put forth over the years is that Eddie Mannix paid off the cops to protect his wife, Toni, from interrogation and unwanted headlines about the affair she'd just concluded.

The film was originally entitled *Truth, Justice and the American Way*. But Warner Brothers threatened to sue Focus Features if it didn't change the title, which had been inspired by Superman's motto, which the studio feared might interfere with marketing rights to their own Superman franchise.

In a tagline, what does this picture tell us? It's simple. Dying in Hollywood can make you a legend.

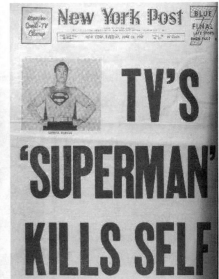

George Reeves; Newspaper headlines

Left to right: Affleck, Lane, and Brody

 WHAT THE CRITICS SAID

"Most of the time we're stuck with Brody, whose beaten basset hound act is getting tiresome. He lugs around not one but three subplots (girlfriend troubles, guilt about the ex-wife and kid, an adultery case going awry), all of which chew up lots of screen time without being interesting. Several scenes should have been cut."
Kyle Smith
New York Post

"Along with Affleck's happy change-of-pace turn, Lane impresses strongly while riding the emotional rollercoaster from self-assured seductress—she at one point acknowledges she's got seven years left to trade on her looks—to devastated woman scorned. This is not Brody's finest hour, to put it kindly."
Todd McCarthy
Variety

This page is dedicated to memories of both
GEORGE REEVES AND CHRISTOPHER REEVE

YOU WERE SUPERMEN, YOU ARE MISSED.
REST IN PEACE.

Hotel Gondolin

Sex Industry Workers Bond Together in Buenos Aires

Transvestism, prostitution, and the homosexual lifestyle as lived in Argentina come together in this Spanish-language film with English subtitles. The 52-minute docu was both written and directed by Fernando López Escriva, and the drag queen "stars" use what they call their "pussy names" such as Monica or Wanda even though their real names might be Juan or Fernando. Incidentally, they prefer to be known professionally as sex workers, and not called by the Don Imus name of 'ho."

The she-men have taken over a dilapidated hotel on the "wrong side" of Buenos Aires and painted it the world's most garish shade of purple. They live in an association where each roommate pays a monthly rental.

The motto of the girls is, "We're poor but we don't have to be homeless." Each girl has a different story to tell. One inmate, for example, says, "I don't want to be a woman, I want to be a transvestite." Others aim to go all the way surgically, whereas one girl says, "I want to get hips and a butt—the breasts can come later." Another cross-dresser claims, "Right now I want to keep my penis." One of the reasons for that is that many clients desire getting fucked by a she-male.

For most transvestites in Argentina, the only professional option for them is prostitution. The film ends with the trannies fighting politically for their civil rights and confronting difficulties with the local police.

"I was invited to a screening of Samson and Delilah, starring Victor Mature and Hedy Lamarr. Afterward, one of the studio brass asked me how I liked it. I replied, "I never like a movie where the hero's tits are bigger than the heroine's."

Groucho Marx

Photo by Baron Wilhelm von Gloeden
Taormina, Sicily. circa 1900

THE HOUSE OF ADAM

Some Secrets Can No Longer Remain Silent

Jorge Ameer, best known for earlier works which have included *The Singing Forest* and the also-reviewed *Contadora Is for Lovers*, wrote, produced, and directed this unusual crime/drama/ mystery/romance. The plot spins around Adam (Jared Cadwell), a likable gay recluse in a small town. A trio of religious fanatics murder him.

A closeted police detective (John Shaw as Anthony Ross) must find the remains of his former lover and come to terms with his own loss.

In a bit of irony, he becomes the victim of his own double-sided values, and the results, as they spin along, are both tragic and traumatic for him.

Ameer delves into the supernatural here, as Adam's spirit, which lingers between the living and the dead, remains within the cozy but isolated cabin where he lived. Only a proper burial can give closure to Adam's spirit as it haunts the cabin.

The little nest is sold to innocent newlyweds who later become terrified.

HX Magazine called the film "perfect after a long day at the beach."

 ## WHAT THE CRITICS SAID

"The filmmaker should continue with this style of filmmaking. I like it. He deals with some very heavy subject matter here but handles it in a way (dark comedic tongue in cheek) that you can't help to laugh at the absurdity of the situations some people put themselves into in real life. I applaud the filmmaker for that and look forward to seeing more of his work."
Jason McKensey

"I told my father that it's legal to discriminate against gay people on the job, that in forty states you can be fired just for being gay. He was amazed and said that's un-American."

Chastity Bono

HOW DO I LOOK?

The Question Most Often Asked in the Harlem "Ball" Community

A follow-up to the successful *Paris Is Burning*, this docu takes the voguing and fashion battle zone to the runway where various competitions showcase talents. You may remember this group from Madonna's *Vogue* video and her *Truth or Dare* docu. Wolfgang Busch is the helmer behind this ambitious project.

For those unfamiliar with the genre, the "illusion of a runway" is created at ball events that let gay, lesbian, bisexual, and transgendered people live out their fantasies and express themselves artistically. As expressed by their drag, they certainly do that—and exceedingly well. They are organized into "houses" with an elected "mother" or "father." These houses organize balls to raise money for HIV/AIDS, or whatever.

Some of the stars of the show, including Tracy Africa, Willi Ninja, or Jose Extravaganza went from these runway walks into a profession. *How Do I Look* traces 10 years of Harlem "Ball" history and features special appearances by Kevin Aviance, Out costumer Patricia Field (*The Devil Wears Prada*) and the always-unique Michael Musto. "Starring roles" include cameos by Harmonica Sunbeam (don't you love that name?). How about CoolAid Mizrahi, and Anthony Revlon?

Director Wolfgang Busch with drag entertainer Kevin Aviance

248

I Now Pronounce You Chuck & Larry

Two Straight Firefighters Get Married

Call them "The Odd Couple." Adam Sandler and Kevin James may not be your idea of marital bliss, but they do get married, although they say "I do" only to qualify for domestic partner benefits.

So as not to turn off straight audiences, director Dennis Dugan didn't dare cast two Hollywood hotties as the firefighters—that would be too much chemistry, too sexual. Imagine Ryan Phillippe with Brad Pitt in the roles. As it is, would anybody in the world—gay or straight—want to see James slipping Sandler the tongue?

We didn't look forward to attending a screening of this comedy, thinking it was another one of a series of straight-pretending-to-be gay flicks, which seem to offend gay people for the amusement of straights. In scene after scene, Chuck & Larry are often offensive with their jokes about gay men— there are even racist stereotypes—but in the end they redeem themselves. If anything, the movie contains about a half hour of footage of pro-gay apologies. Sandler even delivers a lecture that it's preferable to say "gay" instead of "faggot." By the final scenes, the film had become almost an endorsement of same-sex marriage, and an interracial one at that.

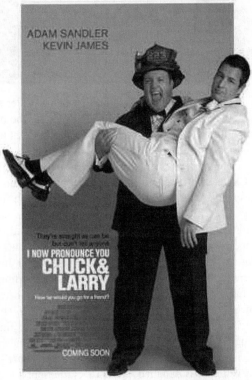

The movie opened to horrible reviews across the nation, and it is indeed flawed, but by the final reel it had won our hearts—and the country's too. Who could have predicted that such a pro-gay film asking for tolerance would have beat out the latest Harry Potter movie at the box office? But it did just that. The times, they are a'changin'.

Sandler, incidentally, has a gay family member in a long-term relationship, and reportedly was interested in filming a story that touched on discrimination faced by same-sex couples.

Larry, as played by James, has lost his wife and is still so much in love with her he can't consider remarrying. But, in the dangerous profession of firefighting, where death could come at any time, he can't provide for his two kids in the event of his death. That is, unless he remarries or enters into a domestic partnership with another man.

In one scene, Larry saves the life of Chuck, as played by the womanizing Sandler. Incidentally, in the Brooklyn firehouse's annual beefcake calendar his photograph has been designated as "Mr. February." As such, as is made clear in the script, he's got five women competing for space in his bed every night. (Okay, the script writers got carried away...) When Larry saves Chuck's life, Chuck says "I'll owe you one." Surely, he didn't expect a marriage proposal from Larry. But he reluctantly goes along with the domestic partnership agreement, partly as a means of fulfilling the favor.

After word gets around the firehouse that Larry and Chuck are gay, the inevitable laughs are set up. Take that scene in the firehouse where Chuck and Larry show up and all the firefighters conceal their genitals. Naturally, one of them accidentally drops a bar of soap.

Jessica Biel, as a bodacious legal advocate for the two men, provides eye candy. At one point, thinking Chuck is gay, she asks him to fondle her breasts by way of confirming that they are real and not sil-

icone-artificial. He has to conceal his hard-on by covering himself up with a sweatshirt.

The announcement that Larry and Chuck are gay also liberates the most fearsome looking member of the department, Ving Rhames. He too is gay. He's also black, which sets up a series of racist scenes, including when he walks nude into the shower and white men gape at his appendage. At first Rhames plays his scenes like an ax-murderer but before long he's more like a teenage girl.

The movie is directed with his usual flair for the obvious by Dugan (*The Benchwarmers*).

The worst casting in the film is when Sandler's untalented buddy, Rob Schneider, appears as a buck-toothed, near sighted Asian-Canadian pastor who marries Chuck and Larry. Apparently, Schneider is satirizing the worst casting mistake of all time - that is, the appearance of Mickey Rooney playing Japanese in *Breakfast at Tiffany's*.

Dan Aykroyd is rather effective at playing the fast-talking fire chief, who isn't fooled for one minute by Chuck and Larry pretending to be gay. He knows that beyond the posturing lurk two confirmed heterosexuals. Richard Chamberlain appears in the final reel, looking more dignified and presidential than ever. After "outing" himself in a recent memoir, he's aged gracefully.

Almost none of the nation's reviewers mentioned Larry's young gay son who dreams of being a tap dancer—a replacement for Ann Miller? He wants to star in a stage version of MGM's *Annie Get Your Gun* that originally featured Betty Hutton after Judy Garland was fired from the part. Chuck is all too aware that his "wife," Larry, has birthed a budding gay son, but Larry vainly carries on, trying to interest his son in sports before finally taking joy when his little homo dons his tap shoes. The role of the dancer is played by the very talented Cole Morgen.

Out performer Lance Bass appears in the final scenes as a band leader. His surprise appearance brought wild applause at the screening we attended.

Incidentally, the film has been deemed "safe" for conscientious viewing by a representative of the Gay & Lesbian Alliance Against Defamation, a media watchdog group.

Adam Sandler   Kevin James   Jessica Biel

"*Chuck & Larry* is the movie equivalent of a double-jointed contortionist who can walk forward with his head turned backward."
   Jack Matthews
   New York Daily News

"It's next to impossible to reconcile screen writers Alexander Payne and Jim Taylor, who excel in sharply honed, intelligent satire, with the crude laughs and nyuck-nyuck physical high jinks that characterize *Chuck & Larry*, much less the relentless barrage of idiotic jokes about gay men, most of which hinge on sex, or rather straight male fear of such sex, and involve groaning puns about backdoors and the like."
   Manohla Dargis
   The New York Times

"If Sandler and James can pretend to be a couple, and arrive at a happy ending of tolerance and inclusion, it may be time for homophobes to hang it up. At the very least, they're clearly informed in this film that they're no longer welcome in Sandler's crowd. But the question remains as to whether the image of a major sitcom star (James, of *King of Queens*) *literally* dressed as a giant fruit will be seen as helpful or hurtful to gay-marriage advocates."
   Sara Stewart
   New York Post

"Relentlessly juvenile and awash in stereotypes, *Chuck & Larry* is the kind of buddy comedy Jack Lemmon and Walter Matthau might have starred in 40 years ago, when the material would have felt less dated, if no less silly. Kevin James and Adam Sandler hardly approach that standard, and it will be slightly depressing if a barrage of schoolyard gay jokes passes for 'edgy' a quarter century after *Victor/Victoria*. Taken for what it is, pic should find its sweet spot somewhere between the easily offended and the very easily amused."
   Brian Lowry
   Variety

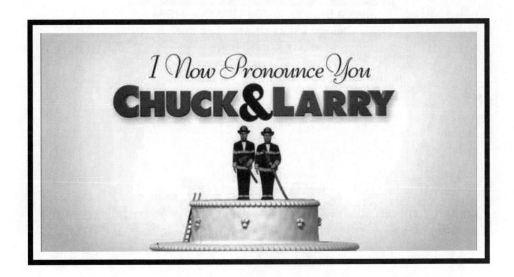

Marlon Brando, in *The Wild One* (1954)
helped establish what became
a gay iconic image.

In Her Line of Fire

Dyke Defends the Vice President

Mariel Hemingway has played a Secret Service agent twice and a lesbian three times. Here she is again playing a lesbian Rambo type whose job as a Secret Service agent is to defend the vice president when his plane goes down on a remote South American island. He is kidnapped by rebel forces and held for ransom. It's up to her and a press secretary to infiltrate the guerilla camp and save him.

The Mariel who hangs in there is tougher than Stallone, although both she and the original Rambo are a bit past their prime. Her love interest, attractive and brave, is Jill Bennett (Sharon Serrano). The preoccupation of this film is action, action, and more action. Sergeant Major Lynn Delaney (Mariel) and Jill don't have time to pick the flowers in the jungle, much less take a nude swim together.

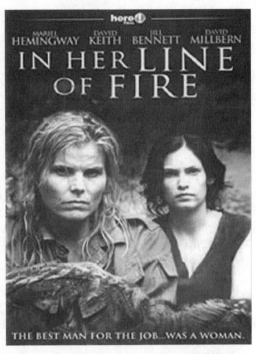

Playing Vice President Walker is David Keith, who'd get our vote over Dick Cheney. He offers the greatest advice a straight man can give to a heavily armed lesbian. "You're a marine. Act like one. Go for it!"

The guerilla force holding the veep is portrayed by the cliché-prone mercenary David Millbern.

Made at an estimated cool million, the film took in $232 over a weekend when it opened in the States on two screens.

Helmer Brian Trenchard-Smith is not big on showing lesbian lust. We love Mariel and hope she gets a better script. Why not a movie about the granddaughter of America's most famous writer who has a sister who's a druggie and suicidal and an uncle who secretly undergoes a sex change and is found nude in a Miami park? He's then tossed into the local women's prison where he (she) dies.

And make the grandfather (i.e., the famous writer) a closeted homosexual who's secretly in love with F. Scott Fitzgerald. Then introduce Gertrude Stein, who was the writer's only friend to confront him with his latent homosexuality. Pardon, we're straying too far from the granddaughter.

Mariel Hemingway and Sharon Serrano

The fledgling script could depict the heroine having her breasts enlarged for a movie role, and how she had to have the implants removed after one ruptured.

Why will Mariel live on in movie history? She was the first famous-name actress to ever appear nude on screen. The film was *Tales from the Crypt* (1989). Lesbians remember Mariel with the greatest fondness because of her 1982 role as Chris Cahill in *Personal Best*, which caused her to be inserted as a clip in *The Celluloid Closet* in 1995.

At least Mariel changed the cliché of having lesbians always portrayed as vampires from Sodom. We honor her for that.

WHAT THE CRITICS SAID

"*In Her Line of Fire*—produced to be shown on the gay cable network *Here!*—flaunts its Sapphic subplot (all five minutes of it) like a pesky contractual obligation, and otherwise plays like straight-to-video gun pornography from the heyday of Chuck Norris."
Nathan Lee
The New York Times

"With Mariel Hemingway a credible Sapphic Stallone, this passable action trash should satisfy as fun original programming for gay-targeted *Here!* cable net."
Dennis Harvey
Variety

Mariel's grandfather,
Papa Hemingway

INFAMOUS

Even Better Than"That Other Movie"

Regrettably, this undervalued film did not escape the curse of *Capote*, which won a Best Actor Oscar for Philip Seymour Hoffman. Had *Infamous* been released at the same time, it would have caused the movie, *Capote*, serious competition.

In our view, *Infamous*—and specifically the performance of British actor Toby Jones—captures the whiny-voiced little terror, Truman Capote, better than any other attempt to bring his unique essence to the stage or screen. Of course, supporting roles by Daniel Craig, Jeff Daniels, Sandra Bullock, and Gwyneth Paltrow, in a remarkable cameo as Miss Peggy Lee, helped a lot.

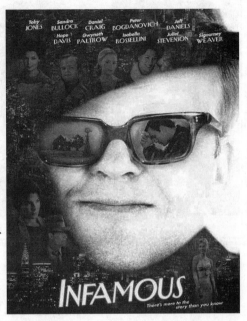

Douglas McGrath both wrote the screenplay and directed *Infamous*. It was based on a book by George Plimpton and told in oral biography style with lots of talking heads.

The story told in *Infamous* is now familiar. In Manhattan in 1959 Capote reads a newspaper story in *The New York Times* about the murder of a farm family in Holcomb, Kansas. He decides to go there with his novelist friend, Harper Lee (Sandra Bullock), the author of *To Kill a Mockingbird*, to research an article for *The New Yorker*. He would devote years of his life to the case, which became his best-selling book, *In Cold Blood*.

Along the way, he virtually fell in love with one of the killers, Perry Smith, as played by Daniel Craig (yes, James Bond). The on-screen kiss between Toby Jones and Daniel Craig—almost an attempted rape—was the hottest male/male kiss on the gay screen of 2006. Oozing menacing sexuality, Smith damn near buggers Jones as Capote.

"I never dreamed I'd kiss James Bond," quipped Jones. "Now that I've done it, I say I hope I'm just the first of many." Lee Pace was cast as the second killer, Dick Hickock, who suggested that Capote could give him a blow job if he wanted to.

After both killers were put to death, Capote got his bestseller but his life was a virtual wreck from that point on.

In *Infamous* the murders of the Clutter family are depicted with consummate skill, as are Capote's pals in Manhattan high society. Hope Davis appears as Slim Keith and Isabella Rossellini as Marella Agnelli. It's entertaining to watch Juliet Stevenson camp it up with her impersonation of Diana Vreeland. Sigourney Weaver as Babe Paley is reason enough to see this tale of the eccentric author and *bon vivant*.

These were Capote's "swans," those long-necked jet-set socialites who confided their deepest secrets to Capote. He ultimately betrayed them in excerpts from his great Proustian masterpiece, *Answered Prayers*, which was never completed.

Peter Bogdanovich plays Capote's publisher, Bennett Cerf. There is also a deliciously feline impersonation of a young Gore Vidal by Michael Panes. Jeff Daniels is in low-key but excellent form as the detective, Alvin Dewey, who leads the investigation into the murders.

The little-known actor, Toby Jones, not only bears a striking resemblance to Capote—some critics called it "a scary resemblance"—but he also had a far better script to work with. *Infamous* captures the essence of Capote's life far more than the Hoffman version did.

It is not unusual for two producers to have double vision in Hollywood—there were two movies on the tragic life of Jean Harlow for example, plus countless films starring Marilyn Monroe clones.

There was a problem with the second Capote movie, much of it associated with bad timing. Audiences just didn't want to see two films back to back about a flagrantly gay New York writer heading for Kansas to research a book about a mass murder, even if *Infamous* was better than *Capote*.

Left to right: Toby Jones, Daniel Craig, Sigourney Weaver, and Gwyneth Paltrow

WHAT THE CRITICS SAID

"And *Infamous* is better, a lot better. In every respect, it takes what *Capote* started with last fall and fleshes it out further. Even the actor playing the lead character manages things in his performance that Philip Seymour Hoffman, who won an Oscar for his effort, did not. We don't wish to take anything away from Hoffman, but we never could shake the notion that what he was doing was essentially a star turn."
   Todd Hill
   Staten Island Advance

"If there is any justice in the universe, *Infamous* will eclipse last year's obnoxious Philip Seymour Hoffman vehicle. *Infamous* is about much more than the price of fame, yet it's hard to recall another movie that understood the price of fame so wittily. The difference between *Infamous* and last year's *Capote* is the difference between feeling and sophistication."
   Armond White
   New York Press

"Jones gets everything—the gestures, the generosity, the mean streak, the bending of the ear to recitals of woe, whether across a lunch table or a prison cell. He even nails the voice, like that of a chorister caught running a racket with the incense. Not that his Capote comes off as a party piece; he is more of a puckish observer, tracing the travails in which others ensnare themselves."
   The New Yorker

We congratulate

INFAMOUS

FOR ITS RECEIPT OF TWO SEPARATE BLOOD MOON AWARDS

WINNER, BEST PICTURE (2007)
AND
WINNER, BEST ACTOR (2007)
FOR
TOBY JONES' PERFORMANCE AS TRUMAN CAPOTE.

Merit and Excellence in GLBT Films

TOBY JONES, winner of ***BLOOD MOON'S BEST ACTOR AWARD (2007)***
for his portrayal of Truman Capote.

INNOCENT

Vulnerable Asian Teen at Crossroads in Toronto

A vulnerable young teen, Eric Tang (played by Timothy Lee), follows his parents during their immigration to Canada, thereby abandoning his boyfriend in Hong Kong. Here in this new land he is forced to confront different emotional and cultural problems as he comes to terms with his gayness.

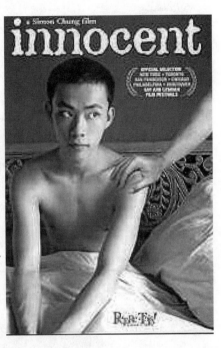

On the brink of adulthood, he struggles with his sexual identity while his nuclear family begins to experience meltdown. His father (Wilson Kam Wing Wong) lies about getting blow-jobs from young girls in the park. His mother (Jovita Adrineda) launches a restaurant business with another immigrant, an actor billed only as "Mr. Huang" in the role of "Mr. Chia."

Before long, Eric establishes sexual links in Canada, including an ongoing affair with a middle-aged Canadian "rice queen" (Larry Peloso), who functions as a sometimes protector. Despite this involvement, Eric falls for a number of other candidates, often straight guys, including his hunky cousin (Justin Penaloza). Eric also has his eye on Jim (David Yee), a rebellious classmate whose sexuality is ambiguous. His putting the move on Jim leads to Eric's banishment from the friendship. He's also ostracized by his other schoolmates.

Eric even attempts to befriend a worker (David Lieu Song Wei) in his mother's restaurant, resulting in a disillusionment so great that he runs away to New York.

In the words of one festival critic, "Although helmer Simon Chung has an appealing quiet sensibility, he never develops dramatic momentum and the film's obtuse personalities never quite gain our sympathies."

 WHAT THE CRITICS SAID

"Remarkably free of adolescent angst, Eric's gentle alienation tends to leave him open to a procession of new sensations and exotic experiences, whether wandering through the wheat fields or dancing with older men in a discothéque. Thesping is fine overall, and Chung's laid-back direction and minimal dialogue never feel forced."
  Ronnie Scheib
  Variety

"As offbeat as this tale may seem, they make it seem true-to-life, as do the scruffy suburban locations."
  Don Willmott
  Filmcritic.com

"I think it's important that [George Michael] got caught with his trousers down. I've been telling him to come out for ten years.... It's justice [the arrest in a Beverly Hills john], and while George did nothing wrong, I applaud him for finally coming out. It's long overdue for a man with $50 million in the bank."

Boy George

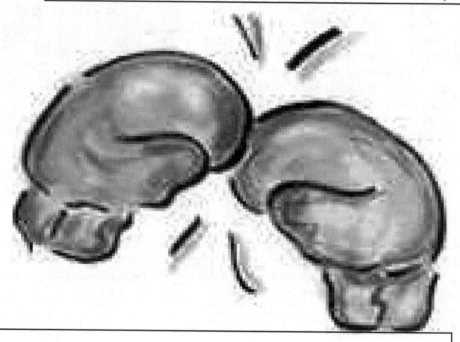

"Boy George boasts that he's never been in the closet. For starters, what use would it have been for *him* to be in the closet? The gays who can pass are the ones who do.... Besides, I remember when Culture Club was the big thing and Boy George went to the States and, just like most people who go there, he was covering up his sexuality in one interview after another."

George Michael

IRMA VAP—SHE'S BACK
(IRMA VAP—O RETORNO)

A Grotesque "Baby Jane" Parody in Bravura Drag

In Brazil, Charles Ludham's Theater of the Ridiculous smash hit, *The Mystery of Irma Vep*, set a Guinness world record for the longest running play with the same cast. But that doesn't mean it's going to lend itself to a good film. Shot in Brazil, this 80-minute movie is in Portuguese with English subtitles.

The storyline of the film, however, deviates greatly from that of the play. A Brazilian actress, Carla Camurati, directed the film. Marco Nanini and Ney Latorraca star in the film version, as they did in the play. But on stage they assumed all the roles. By far, Nanini is the scene stealer here, especially with the parody of *What Ever Happened to Baby Jane?* This actor delivers a tour de force performance, combining feminine fluttering with masculine klutziness.

You'll laugh and be delighted as Nanini as Cleide grotesquely reprises her "Sunbathing by Moonlight" kid star hit tune. Treat yourself, as the young lead, Thiago Fragoso, does, to a "zaftig middle-aged Cleide in gossamer hoops and pigtails coyly sliding down a column," in the words of one viewer.

The movie met with very mixed reviews in Brazil, most often bad. One critic called it "the worst movie I have ever seen."

 WHAT THE CRITICS SAID

"Its impact depends on the spectacle of two actors playing all the parts in the show via lightning-quick cross-dressing changes, which is irrelevant on film. Therefore, Brazilian actress-turned-director Carla Camurati opts instead for an absurdist movie about a revival of Vep encompassing off-stage shenanigans supposedly nuttier than those on stage. The result is a mixed bag."
  Ronnie Scheib
  Variety

Marco Nanini as a Charles Ludham grotesque

KEY WEST: CITY OF COLORS

The Rainbow Flag Covers the Length of Duval Street

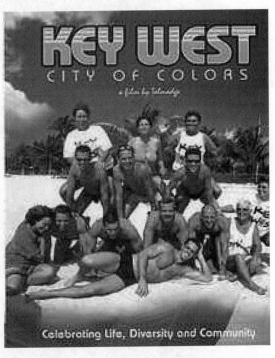

Talmadge Heyward created this 64-minute docu on the favorite resort of many gay men and lesbians. The southernmost city of the United States was for decades a gay mecca, especially during the heyday of the Navy presence in the Eisenhower era and beyond. As a gay resort, it reached its pinnacle in the 1970s—it once even had a gay mayor.

Today it attracts cruise ships and a high percentage of mainstream visitors, but the gay presence is nonetheless felt more here than in any other city south of P-Town.

The film might be of interest to members of the G&L community who have never visited. It's a fine little docu that focuses on the unraveling of a 1/ mile long Rainbow Flag along the length of Duval Street, linking the Atlantic with the Gulf of Mexico. This film was shot in 2003, marking the 25th anniversary of the creation of the flag by Gilbert Baker (call him Betsy Ross), who figures prominently into the narrative.

The docu is mainly a celebration of the little island and the people who live there. It takes a somewhat kind, sentimental view—not a hard-nosed approach.

Despite the implications of this documentary, Key West is not universally permeated with love and understanding. There is bigotry, prejudice, and stupidity here, like anywhere else. But its level of tolerance is greater than anywhere else in Florida, with the possible exception of South Beach and the Lauderdale area.

 WHAT THE CRITICS SAID

"The most important part of this documentary was seeing Gilbert Baker, the inventor of the rainbow flag. Like a reptile who lays an egg and moves on, I had only known that a veteran made the rainbow flag one day. I didn't know he was queeny and very invested in gay rights. It is great to see a middle-aged San Francisco denizen alive when so many of his peers have passed away due to the epidemic. He knew Harvey Milk personally and it was great hearing more about this gay rights leader. Baker has wide eyes and chubby cheeks, very cherubic. In his mannerisms, I did worry if he had ticks or suffered from Parkinson's disease. His interviews, especially in the outtakes, were the best part of the documentary. He is a true, old-school gay hero, like Frank Kameny, Del Martin, or Phyllis Lyons. I hope that someone is inspired by this documentary to write a biography on Gilbert Baker one of these days."
Jeffrey Mingo

Gilbert Baker, 25 years after his creation of The Rainbow Flag

THE KING AND THE CLOWN

(*WANG-UI-NAMJA*)

Gay-Themed Korean Film Tugs at Closet Door

Wang-ui-namja (its Korean name) became the highest grossing Korean film of all time, eventually earning some $70 million U.S. dollars. The movie centers on a homosexual love triangle in the royal court of Korea during the 1700s.

A young male clown is torn between his love for a fellow clown and a king on the make. The men's display of affection is tame by American standards, but taboo-shattering in Seoul.

Homosexuality wasn't removed from the list of the Korean legal system's list of "socially unacceptable acts" until 2004. As a depiction of the "love that dare not speak its name," this film was viewed as a breakthrough when it opened. Some 12 million filmgoers, or 25% of South Korea's population, bought a ticket. A local movie distributor said, "It was the equivalent of your *Brokeback Mountain*."

One of the clowns (Jang Sang) is relatively masculine-acting; the other, Gorig-gil, more *femme*. When the two men begin entertaining the court as jesters, the king becomes enamored of Gil. Naturally, Sang becomes pissed off.

The film is a groundbreaker in more ways than one. As late as 1990, or so a survey revealed, many people living in South Korea were unfamiliar with the existence of gays. One woman thought it was "impossible" physically for two men to mate. She suggested that to fornicate, one of the partners "would have to have a hole to penetrate, and only women have holes!" Another viewer said that in the future, "Because of this movie, I will now equate all pretty males as being gay. Before I did not know that a pretty boy was gay." Those viewers have a lot to learn.

Its director, Jun-ik Lee, told *The New York Times*: "This is not homosexuality as defined by the West. It's very different from *Brokeback Mountain*. In that movie, homosexuality is a fate, not a preference. Here, it's a practice."

"I always heard that Noel Coward wrote that song [*Mad About the Boy*] because of his friend Cary Grant."

Douglas Fairbanks, Jr., refuting a rumor that *he* had inspired the song.

"My favorite American lesbian!"

Clifton Webb, referring to Barbara Stanwyck.

Summer in the City

KINKY BOOTS

Drag Queens Bond with Blue-Collar Blokes

This Britcom was inspired by the true story of a traditional Englishmen's footwear factory in Northamptonshire which turned to the production of kinky boots for transvestites in order to save the ailing family business and safeguard the jobs of the local community.

HOW FAR WOULD YOU GO TO SAVE THE FAMILY BUSINESS?

The Aussie thesp, Joel Edgerton, plays the rather lackluster lead, Charlie Price. In his effort to save his old man's shoe factory, he finds an unlikely ally in "Lola," a black drag queen from London whose real name is Simon. The role is played by the charismatic black actor, Chiwetel Ejiofor, called "Chewey" by his friends and TV announcers who are afraid of mispronouncing his name.

We never knew that he could don boots made for walking after seeing him play a Nigerian doctor in the tense thriller, *Dirty Pretty Things* (2002), the calmly menacing villain in the sci-fi adventure, *Serenity* (2005), or a classical pianist in Woody Allen's *Melinda and Melinda* (2004).

Kinky Boots becomes the feel-good movie of the year when it depicts how a London drag queen finds common ground with a bunch of working stiffs in the Midlands. The parade of erotic women's boots for cross-dressers competes with the actors themselves. By the way, whoever designed those kinky boots, including the size-18 stilettos, should go into business.

Someone has to bring up the annoyance rear, and the thankless role falls to Charlie's whiney fiancée, Nicola (Jemima Rooper). When Charlie is forced to pink slip more than a dozen of the firm's faithful employees, one of them, Lauren (Sarah-Jane Potts), suggests that he start a new product line instead of just firing people. That leads Charlie south to London's Soho district to check out the footwear on a group of transvestites.

After Charlie helps the hulking drag queen, Lola, fend off attackers in a London back alley, the two form an unlikely alliance. In no time at all, Lola is showing up in Northampton where she encounters one homophobic bruiser who mistakes her for a genetic woman.

Ejiofor, who can also be viewed in Denzel Washington's *Inside Man,* clearly steals the show. He lends his husky voice to such musical numbers as the inevitable "Whatever Lola Wants."

Even straight audiences attended this movie and didn't have to worry that there would be any gay sex to offend grandpa. The issue, for example, of Lola's sexuality is barely broached. She doesn't even give Charlie his well-earned blow job.

To have developed some sexual tension between Charlie and Lola might have filled a loophole in Tom Firth's script and explained why Charlie and Lola were even in the same town together, much less working together. But, alas, it's not there.

All in all, though, helmer Julian Jarrold has come up with a cheerful, if not utterly predictable, crowd-pleaser.

You can almost predict the finish as conceived by Firth: An edgy and glittery fashion show finale in Milan, which ends with virtually everyone in Lombardy screaming for more. But the shy, mild-mannered Charlie forced to walk the catwalk is a bit much. Earlier works written by Firth, incidentally, include the not dissimilar *Calendar Girls.*

We'll go out on a limb and make a prediction for the early 21st century. The big-hearted drag queen in films will replace the whore with the heart of gold from an earlier era. The *puta* of many a film noir was often forced to die for her sins. But, as critic Stephen Holden pointed out: "The drag queen, by contrast, usually triumphs. And in the flouting of taboos, the preening cross-dresser goes her forerunner one better. Her battle cry, 'I'm more man than you'll ever be, and more woman than you'll ever get,' is meant to strike fear into the hearts of her male persecutors. But having been the life-long target of contempt and rejection, she has also developed compassion for those frightened, benighted fools."

Foot fetishists around Europe and the U.S. drooled over this movie and left theaters still slobbering at the mouth.

 WHAT THE CRITICS SAID

"*Kinky Boots*, the latest in the very long line of British comedies descended from *The Full Monty,* is an above-average entry in this niche genre, wherein groups of working-class people band together against adversity."
Lou Lumenick
New York Post

"Despite the subject matter, the script and direction are disappointingly conventional, though the performances are appealingly spirited. A charismatic Ejiofor, in particular, does what he can to put some cheeky kink into this determinedly strait-laced movie."
Elizabeth Weitzman
New York Daily News

LA VIE EN ROSE
(LA MÔME)

France's Iconic Songbird Gets a Biopic

Marion Cotillard plays "the Little Sparrow," Edith Piaf, the waiflike French songbird whose personal traumas fueled her art. Burned out at the age of 47, Piaf died in 1963, but her memory lingers on.

A bisexual, she loved men but also had affairs with women, including Marlene Dietrich, her great friend.

The helmer, Oliver Dahan, also co-wrote the script. He draws moments—the good, the bad, and the ugly—from Piaf's failures and triumphs—and weaves them into a celluloid mosaic.

If there are any souls on the planet who are not familiar with the career of Edith Piaf, she was a Gallic fusion of Judy Garland and Billie Holiday, only more so. Cotillard's portrait of the French singer is brilliant, going from famished alley cat to stooped, feeble wreck prematurely aged.

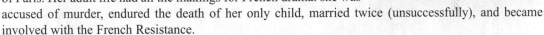

The first half hour or so focuses on Piaf's traumatic childhood when she was abandoned by her mother and lived in a bordello. She went temporarily blind and began to sing for her supper on the streets of Paris. Her adult life had all the makings for French drama: she was accused of murder, endured the death of her only child, married twice (unsuccessfully), and became involved with the French Resistance.

The biopic also stars Gérard Depardieu as Louis Leplée, the cabaret owner who discovers Piaf.

Watch for brief appearances of Caroline Sihol as Marlene Dietrich and Alban Casterman as Charles Aznavour.

Millions of people around the world were touched by the music of Piaf. Thousands will be touched by scenes in this somewhat successful film.

Edith Piaf *(left)* and Marion Cotillard playing Piaf

 WHAT THE CRITICS SAID

"Marion Cotillard's feral portrait of the French singer Edith Piaf as a captive wild animal hurling herself at the bars of her cage is the most astonishing immersion of one performer into the body and soul of another I've ever encountered in a film."
Stephen Holden
The New York Times

We congratulate

MARION COTILLARD
for her designation as winner of
BLOOD MOON'S BEST ACTRESS AWARD (2007)
for her portrayal of Edith Piaf in
LA VIE EN ROSE

LIKE A VIRGIN
(*CHEONHAJANGSA MADONNA*)
Taking Madonna's Advice: "Be What You Want to Be"

This South Korean film follows the travails of a boy who wants to be a woman. Within its country of origin, it's viewed as something of an oddball, since a few years ago gay-themed movies virtually didn't exist.

The film was both directed and scripted by Hae-jun Lee and Hae-yeong Lee, and stars Ryu Deok-hwan as Dong-gu, a tubby South Korean high school boy whose grand ambition involves having a sex-change operation.

To fund the operation, he enters a *ssireum (*also spelled *sirum*) or traditional Korean wrestling championship. Even though he is much smaller than the other sumo wrestlers, he seems to have superhuman strength.

Dong-gu is not only a great wrestler but a dancer as well. He learned his formidable dancing skills by mimicking Madonna—that's how the name of the pop star ended up in the Korean-language title of this film. Until he slowly earns their respect, his fellow wrestlers resent this girlish boy in their midst.

The boy soon develops an adolescent crush on his Japanese teacher (Tsuyoshi Kusanagi). Dong-gu believes that his teacher will love him if he becomes a woman. The Japanese teacher is so effeminate, we suspect he'd love Dong-gu more as a boy than a woman.

Oh, yes, the wrestler waiting to become a woman has a miserable home life, centering around his alcoholic father who was a former boxing champ.

 ## WHAT THE CRITICS SAID

"Ryu is a versatile, charming delight in the lead role, and manages to charm as he walks a tightrope in depicting one of South Korean cinema's trickiest characterizations in recent memory. Despite the nation's rep as a homophobic environment, Dong-gu is incredibly at ease with himself. That said, the character isn't allowed to show much interest in physical sex for a teenage boy of any persuasion. Film themes in South Korea are changing fast . . . but not that fast, it seems."
Russell Edwards
Variety

Ryu Deok-hwan imitating Material Girl...

Madonna Ciccone

THE LINE OF BEAUTY

Love, Class, and Tragedy in Britain's Tory-Dominated 80s

Helmer Saul Dibb strikes again. This time he no longer explores the gritty lower rungs of the economic ladder as he did in his sleeper debut, *Bullet Boy*. Within a mini-series originally broadcast on the BBC in three one-hour parts, he's moved up to where the rich folks—all Torys—live.

Andrew Davies adapted the plot from Alan Hollinghurst's Prize-winning novel about a young gay man, Nick Guest (played by the divinely handsome Dan Stevens), who, during the 1980s, moves into the innermost circles of wealth and power when Margaret Thatcher, the Iron Lady, ruled Britain.

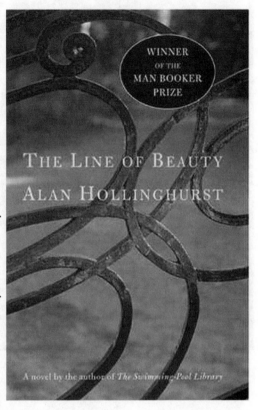

At Oxford, Nick becomes "best mates" with Toby (Oliver Coleman), the son of a rising member of Parliament, Gerald Fedden (Tim McInnerny). Is the relationship platonic? We don't know for sure. There was that certain gleam in Nick's eyes.

After graduation, Nick moves into the Fedden family's London mansion and becomes a member of their glittering world of lavish parties and summer homes on the Continent. If he has a job in this household at all, it's to befriend Toby's troubled sister, Catherine (Hayley Atwell).

But instead of maneuvering his way into Toby's pants, Nick turns to Leo (Don Gilet), a bicycle-riding socialist immigrant from Jamaica.

The film fast forwards to 1986 when Nick is still living within the Fedden family's orbit, but carrying on with a sometimes lover, Wani Ouradi (Alex Wyndham), the closeted son of a Lebanese tycoon.

As the series nears its end, scandal looms. Trouble lies ahead as an ongoing series of financial and political embarrassments burst the Tory bubble in general—and that of the Fedden clan in particular.

 WHAT THE CRITICS SAID

"As Gerald's career skyrockets toward a possible cabinet position, private matters become increasingly at risk of becoming public. While the clan privately tolerates Nick's sexuality, different standards apply to the 'gay issue' in Tory political terms."
Dennis Harvey
Variety

Gay Tories?
Left to right, Oliver Coleman, Dan Stevens, and Alex Wyndham

Margaret Thatcher,
conservative former prime minister of Britain
and spearhead of the Tory party,
at the funeral of the Queen Mother.
April, 2002

LITTLE MISS SUNSHINE
Dysfunctional Family Road Trip Comedy

Of course, an offbeat indie film with a flawless cast would have a gay character in it. In this case, it's the suicidal brother Frank (Steve Carell). Known in scholarly circles for his infinite knowledge of Marcel Proust, Frank has just lost the young grad student who was his male love, plus a MacArthur Foundation grant to a rival academic. Movie viewers know Carell for his appearances in *The 40-Year-Old Virgin* and *The Office*. In *Sunshine*, he delivers a morosely deadpan characterization, and does so brilliantly. But a gay character is not what drove gay and lesbian audiences in droves to this sleeper of the year.

It was the film's "winning" look at "losers" that drove audiences to buy tickets. The youngest player in this megahit, Olive, "Little Miss Sunshine" herself, a 9-year-old New Yorker, Abigail Breslin, may be diminutive (4-feet-1), but she towers tall as an actress without the Shirley Temple cuteness. Her performance captured the notice of producers who cast her opposite Catherine Zeta-Jones in the upcoming movie, *No Reservations*.

Giving his best performance in years, Greg Kinnear as Richard plays her dad, with Alan Arkin cast as her raunchy grandfather, who gets all the best lines.

A broken-down VW transports the dysfunctional Hoovers from their home in Albuquerque on a foolhardy trip to Redondo Beach so Olive can compete in a beauty pageant. The mother, Sheryl, is winningly played by Toni Collette. Their alienated teenage son, Dwayne (Paul Dano), is a silent Nietzsche devotee. This comedy/drama was directed by husband-and-wife team, Jonathan Dayont and Valerie Faris, from a script by Michael Arndt.

 WHAT THE CRITICS SAID

"There are probably few more obvious emblems of soulless success than a children's beauty contest. And the notion that Olive would somehow get onstage without her parents having any knowledge of the act she was preparing—or any misgivings until the last minute about the potential humiliation she's being subject to—seems implausible. But as a chaotic, cathartic bonding experience, it works, in part because the family members are so caught up in their individual frustrations and insecurities."
David Rooney
Variety

"Carell follows Richard Dreyfuss in *Poseidon* in what appears to be a new stock role: The post-suicidal gay man recently dropped by a younger lover whose sexuality has little to do with the rest of the movie. Not that I'm complaining (yet). Dreyfuss wound up an unlikely hero, and Carell comes across as the sanest person in Sunshine. If suicidal ideation somehow gives gay men more movie gravitas, bring it on."
Bruce C. Steele
The Advocate

LIZA WITH A Z

Resurrection of a 26-Year-Old Broadway Baby

When diva Liza Minnelli and Broadway legend Bob Fosse created the spectacular musical special *Liza with a Z* in 1972, they made TV history and carted home four Emmys. The film was long thought lost since the mid-80s. Now it's back in a digitally restored version that returns the old glamour of our favorite Broadway baby when she was just 26.

Today in her 60s, Liza is hardly a has-been. We prefer to call her an "always was." Okay, so she's not as great as Judy Garland. But who in the hell ever was?

Liza gave this one-woman concert at the Lyceum Theater in New York in 1972. For audiences not around in those days, the remastered 16-millimeter film reveals Liza at the very apex of her career. At least a newer generation will understand why she looms so large in both pop culture and gay iconography.

Luckily for us, Liza sings a medley from her hit *Cabaret,* the film musical that brought her an Oscar and her greatest and only plausible movie role as a romantic lead.

In the DVD we love Liza when she does her own rendition of such standards as "Bye Bye Blackbird" and "Son of a Preacher Man." Not only that, but we get music by Kander & Ebb.

Many critics viewed this new release as required viewing for the classroom of Gay 101. If you have not already become enraptured by the spell cast by Liza, this DVD might turn you into an *Ohmigodit'sLiza!* Homo.

We're still listening and watching . . . still in Liza's camp. But some post-millennium critics are a bit harsh, including *The New York Times* which suggested, "Of late, she has become a Michael Jackson-ish figure, too preposterous to function even as a nostalgia act."

That's pretty harsh. Wherever Liza appears today, we'll be there . . . and all that pizzazz.

 ## WHAT THE CRITICS SAID

"There are only a handful of female performers of her generation who have that over-the-top, knock-em-dead stage presence, but Judy Garland's daughter was neither as gifted a singer as Barbra Streisand nor as roguishly self-aware as Bette Midler. Ms. Minnelli's stardom is based on a unique confluence of talent and biography, persistence and collapse."
Alessandra Stanley
The New York Times

"Why should a budding fag of 2006 give a damn about Ms. Minnelli? There actually was a time Liza mattered. A time before she turned into the bloated self-parody of today. Put aside the image of today's loopy Liza, and see the fierce talent. There's a reason old queens gush like this."
Joel Perry
Instinct

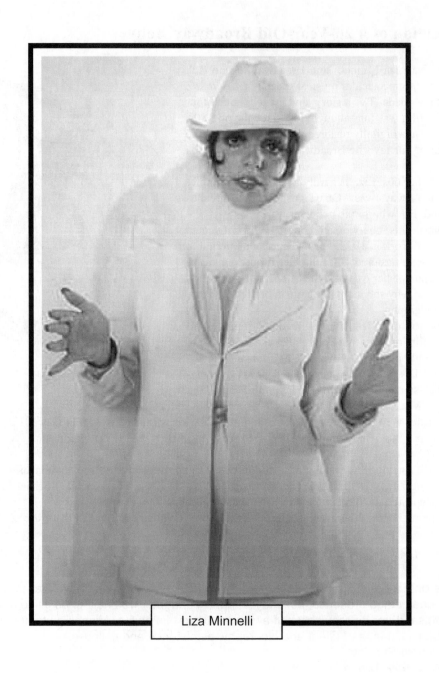

Liza Minnelli

LONG-TERM RELATIONSHIP

A Romantic Comedy About the Hard Things in Life

This is the first feature from writer/director Rob Williams, who set out to make movies that he himself would like to see. He's teamed with his partner and co-producer, Rodney Johnson.

Cast in the film are Matthew Montgomery as Glenn—a Richard Gere type—and Windham Beacham as Adam—a Brendan Fraser type. One reviewer said that you should see the film "if you've ever wanted to see Gere make love to Fraser." Montgomery's well-respected earlier work has included a lead role in the gay mystery/romance *Gone But Not Forgotten.*

Out of all the gay men in Los Angeles (and sadly, he's tested out more than a few), Glenn has finally found his soul mate—a cute Southern boy named Adam. Their relationship started, as so many great relationships have, with the personal ads ("GWM seeks LTR"). From the moment they met, it was instant attraction. Now Glenn's in love for the first time, and it feels great.

There's only one problem. Well, actually a few problems. For starters, Adam is a Republican—not the biggest turn-on for a dedicated Democrat like Glenn. But more importantly, when they finally decide to have sex, it's bad. Really bad. And they can't figure out why their everyday chemistry and compatibility don't extend to the bedroom. Are these problems big enough to be deal-breakers, or can Glenn and Adam work through their differences?

Glenn's straight friends (including married couple Mary Margaret and Andrew) encourage him to stick it out and make it work—after all, everyone's happier as part of a couple, right? Meanwhile, his gay friends (including best friend Eli and roommate Vincent) tell him to move on if he's not happy, especially where sex is concerned. Of course, Vincent has his own agenda in wanting to keep Glenn and Adam apart.

Ultimately, only Glenn and Adam can decide what it takes to sustain a long-term relationship in this classic romantic comedy that appeals to both gay and straight audiences alike.

Windham Beacham *(left)*, and Matthew Montgomery

QUOTABLE

BLOOD MOON'S

HOLLYWOOD

"Gore Vidal has never written a novel that's readable, with the exception of *Myra Breckenridge,* which you can sort of thumb your way through. His novels are unbelievably bad."

Truman Capote

"Truman Capote has made an art of lying. A minor art."

Gore Vidal

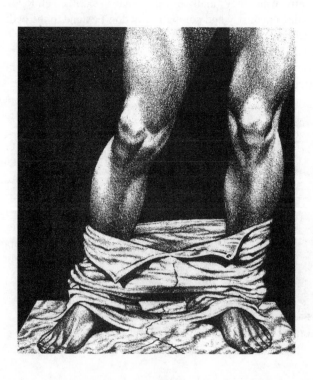

A LOVE TO HIDE
(UN AMOUR À TAIRE)

The Persecution and Deportation of Homosexuals During World War II

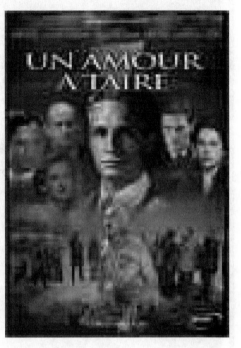

Christian Fauré, the director, gives the TV-movie treatment to a scenario set in France during World War II. It's a story about forbidden love, rivalries, pleasures, jealousies, and a subject that to many younger gay people is almost unthinkable: The legalized persecution, incarceration and execution of homosexuals.

In French with English subtitles, it stars Jérémie Renier as Jean. The actor created a stir in François Ozon's *Criminal Lovers*. Playing his lover Philippe is Bruno Todeschini.

The plot unfolds in 1942 when much of France is under German occupation. Two young gay lovers, Jean and Philippe, must keep their "third sex" relationship secret under peril of their lives.

Into the scenario falls Sara (Louise Monot), a young Jewish woman who's a former girlfriend of Jean's. While Jean and Philippe harbor Sara from the Nazis, Jean's brother, Jacques (Nicolas Gob), a black marketer, returns from prison. As everyone tries clandestinely to keep their respective secrets, Jacques' jealousy and his potential for betrayal threatens all of them.

 ## WHAT THE CRITICS SAID

"Intense, riveting, and earnest, *A Love to Hide* is a beacon of wit and sophistication in an age of too many vapid gay DVDs. The story of a Jewish girl who loses her family to the Nazis and finds sanctuary with a gay companion, the film weaves haunting authenticity with beautiful, unwavering human hope."
Randall Shulman
Instinct

"Extremely well acted, *A Love to Hide* is a worthwhile and deeply affecting film that sheds light on how various people coped during this horrible period of history."
Gary Kramer
San Francisco Bay Times

"Bad, stupid decisions made by bad-seed—if later semi-redeemed—brother Jacques gets Jean sent to a labor camp. Subsequent horrors are piled on a tad melodramatically, but polished perfs and package keep the twisty, eventually decades-spanning tale engrossing."
Dennis Harvey
Variety

Never Forget.

LOVE SICK
(LEGATURI BOLNAVICIOSE)

Lesbians from Transylvania Defy an Incestuous Brother

This film from Transylvania does not feature Count Dracula, but two romantic Romanian college students who embark on a sapphic affair. In case you care, the drama was entitled *Legaturi bolnaviciose* in Romania when it was released there by director Tudor Giurgiu.

To the world, Alex (Ioana Barbu) and Kiki (Maria Popistasu) are just good friends. They met on their first day at college and immediately fell for each other.

There's an incest theme here too, although it is handled rather matter-of-factly. Kiki and Sandu (Tudor Chirila) are sister and brother—and nighttime lovers as well. The relationship with the older brother is never completely spelled out but he acts like a jealous boyfriend with Alex—and because of the attraction of the two women for each other, has reason enough to be jealous.

 ## WHAT THE CRITICS SAID

"The two girls are polar opposites. Alex, from the countryside, is quiet and studious, eager to make her parents proud; Kiki, from Bucharest itself, is always ready to put fun (including smooching) above books. But there's a perceptible attraction between the two that comes across with very little sex shown onscreen."
Derek Elley
Variety

"The tag line for *Love Sick* is, 'It may look sick, but it's deep and it hurts.' So my big dilemma is: are they equating incest with homosexuality? Is there an underlying subtext that Kiki's relationships with Alex and Sandu are equally 'sick'?"
www.moviepie.com

Maria Popistasu

Cher in *Mermaid* (1990)

A CAMPY SATIRE ON THE AMERICAN WAY OF DEATH

Some golden films are so good, and contain such a strong dose of GLBT consciousness, that when they're re-released on DVD, we review it within this guidebook as a special feature.

That's the case with the recent re-release of this SATIRE ON RITES OF PASSAGE IN THE U.S. as interpreted by two gay Englishmen, **Evelyn Waugh**, who wrote the book, and helmer **Tony Richardson**, who directed the film way back in 1965.

For more about this, read on, all of you, *LOVED AND UNLOVED ALIKE....*

THE LOVED ONE

Helmer Tony Richardson must have had his tongue in his cheek—or somewhere—when he cast the most famous satire on the funeral business ever made. Although he employed a handful of straight actors, including Robert Morse as Dennis Barlow and Dana Andrews as Gen. Buck Brinkman, the director decided that for the majority of the players, gay's the word.

He cast John Gielgud, the grandest of England's *grande dame* homos, as Sir Francis Hinsley; gay blade Tab Hunter (who recently Outed himself in his autobiography), Roddy McDowall (Dame Elizabeth's gay pal), and most flamboyant of all, Liberace in this film. We could name several others among the cast and crew but they have never officially Outed themselves so we'll be discreet.

Margaret Leighton, also cast in the film, was not a lesbian, but she was married to Laurence Harvey, who once told Frank Sinatra, "I have this thing for black men."

Ruth Gordon and Jayne Mansfield were both cut from the original final print of the film—too bad.

Warner Home Video recently re-released this 1965 film on DVD, allowing a whole new generation of young men and women to see it in all its campy glory.

It is said that after World War II, the great English author, Evelyn Waugh, came to Hollywood to work on a movie adaptation of his novel *Brideshead Revisited*. While there, he attended a funeral at Forest Lawn Memorial Park and was outraged by the pretense and venality of the American funeral industry. He decided to satirize it in a novel, *The Loved One*. After its release, thanks to its almost surreal lampooning of the American bourgeoisie and their presuppostions, it became a cult favorite, viewed and gossiped about by thousands upon thousands of gay men and women.

Hunter was at his most fuckable when he appeared as a Whispering Glades Tour Guide, and Roddy McDowall comes off like a stately queen through his role as "D.J. Jr."

Liberace was at his most cloying and repulsive as an unctuous coffin salesman. At that time, privately, he was sending handsome young male models half of a thousand dollar bill. To retrieve the other half, these studs had to visit him and do their duty.

Jonathan Winters appears in a dual role, both as the owner of Whispering Glades and as his twin brother, who operates a graveyard for pets.

Rod Steiger manages to be revolting as the embalmer, Mr. Joyboy, "who systematically registers the state of his broken heart on the faces of the deceased." Milton Berle appears as Mr. Kenton. The comedian, who liked to dress in women's clothes, was said to have the biggest dick in Hollywood. He once whipped it out for Tom Jones to show the singer "what a man's meat really looks like."

In the film, Denis Barlow (as played by Robert Morse) arrives in Hollywood from England to arrange his expatriate uncle's burial at the Whispering Glades funeral parlor. He finds himself going to work at The Happier Hunting Ground pet's memorial home.

Terry Southern's spectacularly vulgar adaptation of Waugh's novel was tag-lined, "The motion picture with something to offend everyone." Gay author Christopher Isherwood worked on the script with Southern, inserting an orgy in the casket showroom involving Air Force brass.

The film's climax was never a part of the plotline of the book. In the celluloid version, the owner of a cemetery begins sending the cadavers committed to his care into orbit in outer space so that he'll be able to convert the graveyard into a "senior citizens' paradise."

WHAT THE CRITICS SAID

"What is offensive about it—what is hideous and gross—is the violent, undisciplined excessiveness of its morbid ribaldry. There is too much kidding around the corpses, too much clowning in the embalming room, too much nauseating juxtaposing of dead bodies and food."
Bosley Crowther
The New York Times

"Played by hugely obese actress Ayllene Gibbons, Mrs. Joyboy lies in bed most of the time and is waited upon by her son. She eagerly awaits food commercials on TV, working her jaws along with the actors, and gnaws on an entire suckling pig served up by Joyboy. She's a wailing, horrifying grotesquery worthy of a John Waters movie, and the mother/son relationship is unhealthy, to say the very least."
www.real.com

"That chrome plated butterball, Liberace, is hilariously on key as a casket salesman, peddling such optional extras as the standard-eternal or perpetual-eternal flames ('the standard only burns during visiting hours')."
TIME

Left, Liberace at his unctuous best, selling coffins in *The Loved One.*
Center, Early pinup of Tab Hunter. *Right:* Helmer Tony Richardson (1928-1991)

LOVING ANNABELLE

One Student, One Teacher, One Secret

This film was inspired by the once-notorious *Maedchen in Uniform*, a German classic released in 1931 and dealing with student-teacher love. This remake of that classic is a soft-core lesbian sexual fantasy, the work of scripter-director Katherine Brooks. It relates the story of a Catholic boarding school teacher, Simone Bradley (Diane Gaidry), who has an affair with a female student, Annabelle (Erin Kelly).

The pushy 17-year-old Annabelle pursues her teacher (a 30-something-year-old) resulting in the teacher falling for her. But after they acquiesce to their lusts, the lesbian relationship is made public—and Simone is arrested.

 ## WHAT THE CRITICS SAID

"Climatic bliss is interrupted by tragic intervention of gossips, prudes and police. Gauzy lensing, nubiles lounging in lingerie, and some high-drama moments verging on unintentional camp keep slick but silly item well removed from any semblance of real life."
   Dennis Harvey
   Variety

"The result is a disappointing, choppy, dimly lit and entirely by-the-numbers hybrid of a bad soap opera, a cheesy lesbian romance novel and any number of movies set in that clichéd hotbed of same-sex action: The all-girls' high school."
   www.moviepie.com

"*Loving Anabelle* vacillates between rosy-tinted fantasy romance, soft-core titillation, and serious drama, and it never finds a home in any of those places."
   From Johnny Web (Uncle Scoopy)

Loving Annabelle

LUNA AND THE MOON

Love Caught in the Spinning Orbit of Fate

Luna is a quiet, transgendered woman who works at a bar in Kings Cross in London. Cast as Luna is Luc Anthony, an Australian who otherwise mostly works in Shakespearean theater. But he brings the right touch to sexual ambiguity.

Luna lives in a small flat with ex-street gal, Kelly, played by Raquelle David, who has appeared on stage in real life in such dramatic roles as *Period of Adjustment* by Tennessee Williams.

In the midst of a harsh world, where men are repulsed by her and loudmouthed queens mock her, Luna is stunned one night to encounter James, a friendly and attractive man who treats her with respect and charm.

As James, Ben Dalton brings an easy-going charm to the role. He was trained in Australia's Meisner School of acting.

Full of self-doubt, Luna tests the amiable stranger's attention and in doing so places them both in danger.

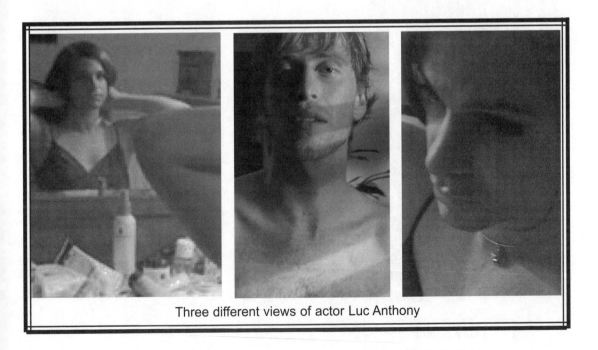

Three different views of actor Luc Anthony

289

"Mick Jagger is too old for that role, and I'd have done it better."

Boy George, who lost the drag role in the film *Bent*

"SHE is a movie star, *I* am an actress."

Bette Davis, referring to Joan Crawford

To Gay Bathhouses!

THE L-WORD, SEASON THREE

Even in an Off-Year for the Series, I'm Still Addicted

BY LISA KEETER

There's good news and bad news about Season Three of *The L-Word*. The good news includes the following: All of our favorite characters were back (some just temporarily); the show received the highest ratings of any program on Showtime; GLAAD named *The L-Word* as best TV drama; and Jenny stopped cutting herself and having circus dreams. The writing was better, guest stars were intriguing, and for the most part, were essential to the plot of each show. The characterizations of each of the women were deeper and richer than in some previous seasons. And yes, there was still plenty of sex.

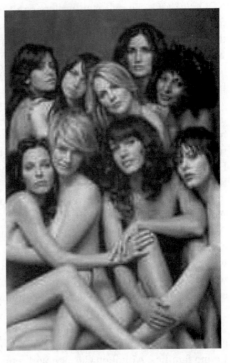

Here's the bad news: Of all of the women on the show, the character of Jenny was probably the most clinically sane. That's scary. The other (but always predictable) bad news is that once again, at the end of the season, no one is happy, and *heaven forbid*, no one sits comfortably within a monogamous lesbian relationship. Except, of course, the unlikely, but charming bi-racial couple, Kit and Angus. But the jaw-dropping, gut-wrenching, anvil-dropping bad news is that *The L-Word* producers and writers killed off a main character. Not just any main character, but one of the most beloved . . . Dana. Our professional tennis-playing, soup-chef-loving, All-American sweetheart.

Yes, we understand that *The L-Word* wanted to bring breast cancer awareness to the forefront. But what we don't understand is why an character who's essential to the show's dynamic had to be written out of the plot. Instead of shining light on how a woman can beat the disease, the producers chose the loser's way out. I realize that it unleashed a torrent of well-choreographed TV drama and brought the band of friends together. But it nonetheless left me feeling empty and angry. From the reactions of the cast and crew as conveyed within a televised special after the "death knell" episode, fans of the series weren't the only ones who were pissed off. The emotion, some of it angry, radiating outward from the cast was heartfelt and palpable. Dana's character is irreplaceable. Can the show recover from her loss? Perhaps not.

How did the series' other central characters fare in Season 3?

Bette and Tina tried to patch things up for the sake of little Angelica, but no dice. The writers succeeded in devolving them both into whiney shrews. Bette struggled with the loss of her job, and Tina returned to Hollywood to produce films at Helena's studio. For those of us who were aware of the fabulous chemistry they had shared during the first two seasons, it was painful to even watch this pair of gifted actors appear on screen together. Bette did get a chance to cozy up to Dana Delaney, who played a guest role as a hot-to-trot senator on the make for Miss Porter. But Bette turned down the offer. It also has to be noted that throughout the shooting of Season 3, actress Jennifer Beals was hiding a real-life pregnancy, a situation which for the most part was handled very discreetly.

Tina went to the dark side this year and decided to play with men again. Don't even get me started. Again, for us, it symbolized the waste of an extremely attractive actress with whom lesbians identity and care about. Ms. Chaiken, this IS a show about lesbians, remember?

Jenny, with the exception of having hooked up with Max/Moira, was actually likable this year. She even scored a book deal with a major publishing house. Good for Jenny. Even weirdos deserve happiness and success.

Perhaps Shane had the biggest transformation this year. She moved into new digs at a skate shop, WAX, and set up her hairstyling business. Shane decided to try that monogamy thing with that cute Latina hottie, Carmen. She fell off the love-and-devotion wagon once after encountering a former flame, but Carmen took her back and for a while it seemed as if they'd dance together toward the altar. But NOOOOOOO, the evil step-writers can't let that happen, right? After an encounter with her estranged father, she decides that, as Daddy's Girl, she's a philandering loser like he is and leaves Carmen alone at the altar on their wedding day. *Ouch*. Carmen and Shane's characters had hot and steamy chemistry as well. But the scriptwriters might as well throw cold water on it if it seems to be working, right?

Dana, our dear departed friend, as played by Erin Daniels, died with dignity and grace. Erin gave Emmy Award-winning performances this season and deserved better than to be written out of the series.

Alice, after a shaky start at the beginning of the season, stepped back into character as the crazy, endearing eccentric that we all love. After her breakup with Dana, she became a pill-popping, obsessive maniac. But after the soup chef (Lara) left the picture in the aftermath of Dana cutting her loose, Alice returned to Dana's side as her devoted best friend, nursing her during her fight with breast cancer. Leisha Hailey also gave Emmy-worthy performances, playing a character who deserves special kudos for her tireless devotion to her best friend.

Kit, Bette's sister and recovering alcoholic, finally finds love in the arms of her niece's nanny, Angus. Kit also employs Billie, played by Alan Cumming, to run The Planet for a short period of time. Although Billie brings his talent and, eventually, success to The Planet, his creepy, drug-laced, androgynous behavior finally brings him down. As for Kit, I'm all for letting her be happy, but last season, the writers explored her "gayer" side through a dalliance with a drag king. We all know about heterosexual relationships and how they work, and it's interesting to watch Kit explore this area of her psyche. At the end of Season 3, it looks like Kit and Angus are going to be parents. Stranger things have happened.

Carmen was a delightful breath of fresh air this season as Shane's love interest. Her fiery temper, combined with a soft, compassionate understanding of Shane's tortured soul, gave us a glimpse of an almost monogamous relationship. We also had a window into the sometimes homophobic world of Latino families. Although Carmen will return for a few episodes next season, her character will no longer be part of the mix of main characters.

Who knew Helena had a soul and a heart? In a most unexpected twist, the writers actually flushed a three-dimensional character out of the spoiled, rich socialite. Helena became friendlier and even had her heart broken by guest star Alexandra Hedison (Ellen DeGeneres' ex), who eventually slapped her with a sexual harassment lawsuit. In what promises to be a fun way to start next season, Helena's even richer mother cut off all of her money sources. Will Helena end up working at The Planet?

Moira/Max, a new character and love interest for Jenny, started off as a butch-macho alternative to the always beautiful, very femme, main characters. However, instead of just letting her be butch, for butchness' sake, the writers took Moira's character into transgender-world. Which is also fine—but can't we just enjoy the onscreen presence of a butch character without turning her into a man? Fake facial hair and testosterone flare-ups made for particularly bad acting and awkward interactions within the circle of friends. I don't really care if Max/Moira shows up at all next season. She/He didn't do a thing for me except take Jenny's place as the most annoying, irritating character in the series.

Season 4 promises that excitement will be generated by the introduction of some new characters. Oscar winner Marlee Matlin has signed on for the entire season as a fiery artist and Bette's love interest. Cybill Shepherd will also appear in most of next year's episodes as Bette's boss. Janina Gavankar also joins the cast as a promiscuous Latina who challenges Shane's grip on her territory and its harem of beauties.

Was Season 3 perfect? By no means. I was left feeling empty and disappointed by the writers' obstinate refusal to EVER let lesbians be happy. But I have too much invested in those characters who were allowed to live, and therefore I'll be there as a fan, welcoming in Season 4. There's still nothing like *The L-Word*. So until something better comes along to replace it within my lesbian fantasy world, I'll be here, patiently waiting for my friends to return.

L-Word, Season Four

Could It Possibly Be True? The L-Word Might Conclude a Season With a Happy Ending?

By Lisa Keeter

Several new characters enter the L-Word universe this year, while several notables exited. Carmen is gone, as is Lara (the Soup Chef). In their place this season are the lovely and fiery Marlee Matlin, and the surprisingly funny Cybill Shepperd. Also in for the ride is Janina Gavankar, who plays "Papi," the *über*-Shane character, who sleeps with so many women in rapid succession, that she crashes the server where Alice's hook-up chart is now online.

Season 4 picks up where the disastrous non-marriage of Shane and Carmen ended—in Canada, where everyone is picking up the pieces. Bette has taken baby Angelica and is on the lam, trying to avoid a nasty custody battle with Tina. Helena is now penniless and has no idea what to do with her life. Kit is still pregnant, but not for long. And, Shane is still trying to deal with leaving her bride at the altar, when she is forced to deal with an abandoned stepbrother, Shay, who has been left on her back porch.

We soon find out that Bette is now the dean of an art department and Cybill Shepperd, playing Dean Phyllis Kroll, is her boss. Dean Kroll, who is married with children, soon comes out of the closet and confesses to Bette that she is a lesbian. Jenny is interviewed (and receives a bad review) by *Curve* magazine, which in turn, creates the maddening character that she evolves into for the rest of the season. Helena moves in with Alice to save money and to figure out what to do to create an income source. Tina is still on the dark side with her wimpy boyfriend, trying to figure out how to get back to lesbianland. For the first part of the season, she is not accepted warmly by her former friends and remains an outsider. The annoying and ever-present Max is working for a computer firm and is passing for a man. Angus, Kit's boyfriend, thinks he's on the verge of becoming a big rock star, but his band drops him like a hot potato and he falls into a deep depression.

At a Cowgirl night at The Planet, Papi and Shane meet for the first time, and Papi puffs up to blow Shane out of the water by showing her who's queen of the mountain, but Shane is no longer a player…she's a big sister trying to raise her abandoned brother. Her heart's not in it anymore. Phyllis hooks up with Alice, who is about to show her the time of her life. Bette also eventually lets herself be involved with a student assistant who has the hots for her.

Enter Marlee Matlin, who is an artist in residence at the college where Bette and Dean Kroll work. She intentionally sabotages a meeting with an influential conservative art patron, who could help fund some of the college's projects. Fireworks ensue—a preview of things to come. Max shares the fact that he's a woman with the boss's daughter, and she freaks out, running for the hills. Shay breaks his arm and Shane is forced to model underwear for immediate cash since she has no health insurance. But she also has the fortune of meeting Paige, the mother of Shay's best friend in school. A little sparkle comes back into Shane's eyes. Jenny starts her revenge plot against the writer from *Curve* magazine by adopting a dying dog so she can take it to the writer's girlfriend who is a veterinarian. Angus decides the cure for his depression is to sleep with Angelica's other nanny, but Tina and her boyfriend are hiding behind the trees outside and find out about his indiscretions.

Alice drops Phyllis after meeting her husband and Phyllis is shattered. Jenny publishes, "Lez Girls," which is a thinly disguised chronicle of the life of her friends. It is immediately a hit, but the friends are seething after discovering that they're portrayed in such a negative way. "Lez Girls" is optioned for a movie, the rights to which Tina is forced to acquire for her film company. At a party that Phyllis throws as a fundraiser (and Helena hysterically caters), Alice meets Tasha, who is serving in the Army, and is Papi's best friend. Bette and Jodi decide to escape to the back yard and get high…and sparks continue to fly.

Papi teaches Helena and Alice how to play poker for a high stakes gambling game. Helena eventually hooks up with Catherine, who wins the poker game, and ends up prostituting herself to Catherine for the rest of the season. Tina lets news about Angus' quickie affair with the nanny slip to Kit and she finds solace in the bottle once again. Alice finds love at 4,000 feet when she takes a Black Hawk helicopter ride with Tasha.

Jodi and Bette are now getting hot under the sheets, while Phyllis is a complete wreck. They visit Phyllis and confess they are a couple and try to calm her down. Shane and Paige continue to flirt with one another. Alice and Tasha fight over their views of the war in Iraq and end up making love in the midst of the heated argument. Jenny continues to be a nut case and buries the ashes of the dog she adopted and then had put to sleep, just so she could meet the writer's girlfriend and try to seduce her. Papi decides that her next conquest should be Kit, who is drunk most of the time. But Kit passes out on the bed and Papi decides to do the right thing and tuck her in.

Shay's (and Shane's) father, the evil and charming Eric Roberts, finds out that Shane has been taking care of his son and comes to take him home. He tells Shane that she has no chance in hell to keep his son away from him and that she has a previous record. Shane falls to her knees as the car drives away with her beloved brother and her no good bastard father.

Jodi and Bette continue to play tug-a-war with each other's emotions. Jenny continues her insanity with her screenplay and trying to pick out directors. Papi continues her pursuit of Kit, still not realizing that she's an alcoholic. Angus continues his bid for her affections as well. Max's mother dies and he goes home for the funeral as a man. The girls go to the racetrack and Helena bets Alice's money on a losing horse. Bette holds a dinner party to introduce Jodi to her friends. Jodi resents her tendency to be a control freak and the relationship strains after the party. Kit turns away Papi's advances, realizing that although it feels good, she's just not gay.

Jodi decides to take a job on the East Coast and says goodbye to her students. Bette arrives to try to win back Jodi, only to find that she's left without saying goodbye. Tasha keeps having flashbacks to her best friend being killed in Iraq and then breaks the news to Alice that she has to go back to fight in two weeks.

The season's finale is a great one. Our beloved Dana, who was killed off in Season 3, makes an appearance as herself (in a ghost version, of course) to Alice, to try to convince her to make up with Tasha and not have her go off to war with their feelings unresolved. God, how I miss Dana. Papi decides to throw Tasha a going away party and of course, the gang is all there. Jenny is fired from her own movie as screenwriter and continues to wig out. Phyllis hooks up with Joyce, the hotshot lawyer from previous seasons, and they are a match made in heaven. Kate, the movie director, has feelings for Tina, who still loves Bette. In a bold move to win back Jodi's affections, Bette and Alice and Shane decide to tear down a sign that Jodi loves from an abandoned building. In one of the funniest sequences of the season, these three women take down the sign piece by piece and carry if off in a van. Jenny shows up at the party and then decides to drift off into the sea. Alice finally comes to her senses and reunites with Tasha and they spend the night on the beach in each other's arms. Meanwhile, Bette has reassembled the sign and drives it on a tractor into the field where Jodi is working on a sculpture piece. The two reunite in a passionate kiss and embrace, as Season 4 comes to a close.

Season 4 rekindled my passion for the *L-Word* series because for once, there was a promise of happiness in lesbian-land. Lesbians CAN be happy, *L-Word* creators, ok? I loved the interaction of Bette and Jodi, knowing that in real life, Marlee Matlin and Jennifer Beals are close friends. You could feel their genuine love for each other on camera. Cybill Shepperd was a pleasant surprise as Phyllis and added a light comedic touch to her role. Alice and Tasha were also an interesting couple and provided some needed diversity in an otherwise predominantly Caucasian show. Max was just irritating and I'm ready for he/she to make an exit. Had a better actress tackled this part, perhaps I wouldn't have disliked the character as much. And Jenny, well, she can float out into never-never land. Cue the *Jaws* theme song. As much as she redeemed herself last season, she fell even further down on my loathing chart this year. Papi was also an intriguing character to whom they finally gave a heart before the end of the season. Shane, that once philandering playgirl, who when called upon to become a grown-up and raise a sibling, did so with such grace and love, that it broke my heart when the boy was taken away from her.

294

MALA NOCHE
(BAD NIGHT)

Mexicano Veal Cake & the Addictive Pull of Desire

The director, Gus Van Sant, first made a name for himself with this 1985 release which has been restored. Set amid the dreary streets of rundown neighborhoods of Portland, Oregon, it tells the sad story of a liquor store clerk, Walt Curtis (Tim Streeter), who lusts for a Mexican street kid, Johnny (Doug Cooeyate), although the viewer may wonder why. You can find hotter Mexicano street kids on the corner of any big city in America.

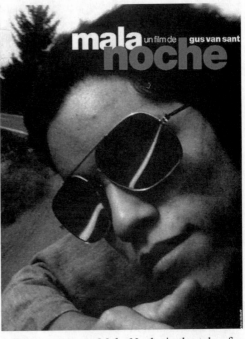

What makes this movie almost unbearable is that the street hustler is straight—not even gay for pay. Of course, he'd be gay for pay if Streeter, playing Walt, offered him $25 instead of the $15 which is all he's got for him.

In the 78 minutes he allows to tell his tale, Van Sant manages in this *film noir* to capture Twilight Zone Portland with B&W photography that is both stunning and seductive. The helmer effectively uses *chiaroscuro* to tell his tawdry tale of unrequited love. Streeter is the only brilliant performer here. Johnny is weak in his role.

Based on the Walt Curtis autobiographical novel of the same name, *Mala Noche* is the tale of an *amour fou*. In the movie, Walt in his mad love/lust, says, "I wanna show this Mexican kid that I'm gay for him." But the object of his unrequited affection speaks no English and finds Walt "strange and undesirable." In other words, he wants gringo pussy as he makes it clear several times in the film.

Johnny's friend in the movie is Roberto Pepper (Ray Monge) who, unlike Johnny, doesn't mind crashing in Walt's pad and fucking him.

Ultimately what we liked about *Mala Noche* then and now is that Van Sant refuses to treat homosexuality as something deserving of judgment. Openly gay, the helmer has dealt unflinchingly with homosexuality and other marginalized subcultures without being particularly concerned about providing positive role models.

At the screening we attended, several senior citizens, presumably straight couples, got up and walked out after the first 20 minutes.

Incidentally, the actors weren't paid to make this film, which cost only $25,000.

After *Mala Noche*, Van Sant went on to make *Drugstore Cowboy*, his 1989 film about four drug addicts who rob pharmacies to support their habit. Van Sant cast Matt Dillon as the junkie leader.

The director scored big with *My Own Private Idaho* (1991), starring River Phoenix and Keanu Reeves, playing two male hustlers. His next project, a 1994 adaptation of Tom Robbins' *Even Cowgirls Get the Blues*, was a big flop. But the helmer came back big with his 1995 *To Die For*, a black comedy that starred Nicole Kidman as a murderously ambitious weather girl. It also featured Matt Dillon as her hapless husband and Joaquin Phoenix, brother of the late River (who had died of an overdose two years previously) as her equally hapless lover.

Van Sant's mainstream breakout came in 1997 with *Good Will Hunting*, starring and written by Matt Damon and Ben Affleck. The press widely reported rumors at the time that the two handsome men were lovers, but, alas, they both ended up with women. The film won a Best Screenplay Oscar for Damon and

Affleck, plus a Best Supporting Oscar for Robin Williams. As Best Director and Best Film, Van Sant lost to James Cameron and his hugely commercial *Titanic*, which starred Leonardo DiCaprio, looking the handsomest and sexiest he's ever looked—before and since.

 WHAT THE CRITICS SAID

"Time has been extraordinarily kind to the indie legend's debut. Never mind that the new 35mm print has transformed John J. Campbell's B&W cinematography from murky into monochromatically gorgeous. Even without that upgrade, the movie's preference for the elliptical over the explicit is enduring."
Time Out New York

"*Mala Noche* is so rare and authentically personal that it feels as if it were shot through a peephole. In some ways that's the look of the film too—concentrated, partially obscured, captured on the sly. Set on the skid row streets and pay-by-the-night hotels of Portland, it's so intimate that it comes across almost as an invasion of privacy. With a few off-angle shots, Van Sant sketches out a world of barflies, transients, and rotgut drunks."
Hal Hinson
Washington Post

"*Mala Noche* sidesteps potential clichés with an attentiveness to class dynamics (even skid row has its hierarchies) and the cultural differences, poignantly underplayed, between the grunge gringo and his object of desire. Van Sant wisely lets Walt control the narrative consciousness, leaving Johnny and Roberto, sympathetic as they are, something of ciphers. The danger here is an unexamined fetishism of type (inarticulate Latino rough trade), but Van Sant finds a tactful, honest reticence in his characterization of the Mexicans and complicates Walt with an awareness of his own privilege. In light of *Elephant*, we can see *Mala Noche* as the first act of a mind interested in graphing the knowable contours of experience, the first gift from a scrupulously compassionate artist."
Nathan Lee
The Village Voice

MASAHISTA
(THE MASSEUR)

Reconciling the Role of a Dutiful Son With a Life as a Sex Worker.

A john enters the massage parlor to take his pick among the young men—often shirtless—on parade. He deals with the queenish male "madam" of the parlor, who assures him that all his boys are good looking—one "can even suck your scrotum dry."

Directed by Philipino Brillante Mendoza (who's also known as Dante Mendoza), the action takes place in Manila. The star is 20-year-old Iliac, who works in the club giving in-depth massages . . . and a whole lot more.

The film depicts the night of December 14 when Iliac's first customer for the day is a homo romance novel writer. Outside the parlor, Iliac's current girl, a bar floozy who works in Japan, asserts her sexual dominion over him.

There is family drama back home. His estranged father dies. As he makes the trip back to his home province, he is faced with the reality of decay, love, life, and survival. He must reconcile his career as a sex worker with his role as son and brother to his grieving mother and siblings.

Coco Martin as Iliac made his debut performance in *The Masseur*. The model has appeared in various TV commercials and print ads in the Phillipines. Helmer Mendoza singled him out from a "cattle call" to work in the film. Among the young male hopefuls wanting the role, Martin was viewed as a potential actor of "intensity, drive, and raw talent."

You can decide if you agree with the director.

 WHAT THE CRITICS SAID

"Brillante Mendoza's perfect combination of technique and subject reveals a sense of humanity. The story is told with honesty and integrity giving us a chance to empathise with the central character. *The Masseur* is without contrivance or conceit."
   Signis Interfaith Jury
   Brisbane International Film Festival

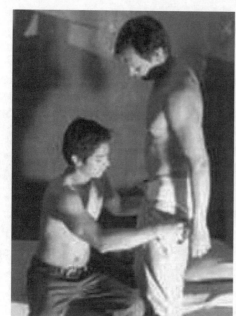

Brillante Mendoza, Director

Coco Martin

MEMOIRS OF MY NERVOUS ILLNESS

Another Gender-Bending Turn from Jefferson Mays

In 2004, actor Jefferson Mays gave a Tony-winning performance in *I Am My Own Wife,* which replicated the tribulations of Charlotte von Mahlsdorf, a German transvestite caught up in the great European dramas of the 20th century

Now, directed by Julian Hobbs, he returns again in all his glory to re-create the experiences of Daniel Paul Schreber, an esteemed German judge who, at the turn of the 20th century, composed a highly articulate written account of his own mental illness. Later, Sigmund Freud interpreted his account as a case history of homosexual paranoia and repression..

Schreber was incarcerated in a Leipzig asylum after he started to suffer various delusions, including one in which he imagines having been chosen by God to procreate a new race of men. These mental disorders were carefully charted in his journal, upon which Dominic Taylor and others fashioned this screenplay--a fictionalization of a pivotal moment in the history of psychoanalysis. The judge's lucid and intricately detailed 1903 account of his own insanity inspired both Freud and Jung.

In the asylum, Schreber is given dubious care by Dr. Emil Flechsig (Bob Cucuzza), who prescribes opium and tepid baths, and who seems deeply threatened by the possibility that his patient might be sane. The patient's pattern of rapid shifts between lucidity, violent fits, and manifestations of seductive femininity is deeply upsetting to some viewers.

Back in rouge and petticoats, Mays can even turn a straitjacket into a makeshift corset, a bed sheet into a strapless gown.

 WHAT THE CRITICS SAID

"Julian P. Hobbs directs by getting out of the way of his star's soulful eyes and considerable talent, allowing Mr. Mays to feed on the tension between the rationality of his character's grand delusion."

Jeannette Catsoulis
The New York Times

"Hobbs' inspired feature sticks close to real-life texts, retaining Schreber's disconcerting mix of Teutonic clarity and schizophrenic imaginings. Richly layered pic dramatizes a landmark doctor/patient showdown, chronicles a classic case of transgenderism, and reveals how aspects of Schreber's story prefigured Nazism. Package could lure cutting-edge arthouse auds."

Ronnie Schieb
Variety

Jefferson Mays replicates Daniel Paul Schreber's
"Case study of homosexual paranoia and repression.".

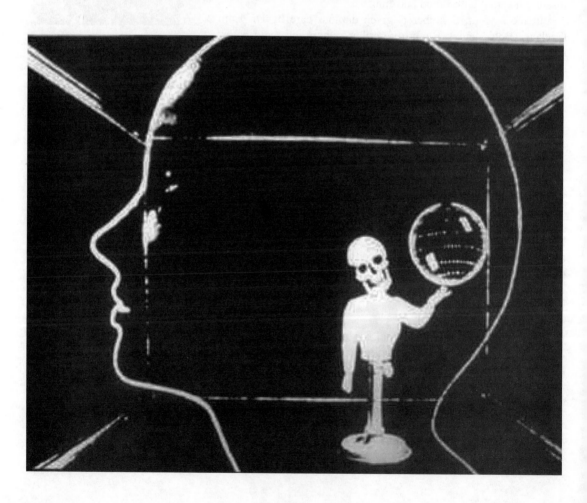

THE MEN WHO DANCED:
THE STORY OF TED SHAWN'S MALE DANCERS, 1933-1940

"On Stage, Male Dancers Should Appear Nude."

Ted Shawn (1891-1972), of course, was the father of American dance, teaching such greats as Martha Graham. He was a partner with his wife, Ruth St. Denis, in the famed Denishawn Company, founder of what has evolved into the annual Jacob's Pillow dance festival in Western Massachussetts.

Shawn brought the concept of virility to male dancing, especially through his all-male dance groups. Even though married, Shawn himself was gay, and so were many of his dancers, but they were nonetheless macho.

Helmer Ron Honsa has brought this docu to life, beginning in 1933 with the origins of the first all-male dance troupe in America.

The docu traces Shawn and his group right up to 1940, the year before the United States entered World War II. In archival footage, we get to see Shawn himself along with a notable cast of male dancers. Barton Mumaw, for example, is sexily pictured as the first soloist of the men's group. One of his most tremendously popular solos was *The French Sailor*.

Mumaw was lithe, slender, and darkly exotic, showing an impressive package in many of his tight-fitting outfits. As the stabbing warrior in *The Dyak Spear Dance*, Mumaw danced nearly nude.

By 1940, Shawn's approach to dance, even that of Mumaw, seemed dated.

Before the camera, the male dancers discuss their lives not only as dancers but as members of this daring new venture. "What's a dance troupe without a woman?" one critic of the time asked.

Most of the docu was written by Richard Philip, *Dance Magazine*'s editor-in-chief.

Shawn died at the age of 80 and was proud that he'd carved a way for American men to be accepted and respected as dancers—"not viewed as silly faggots mincing around in a ballet costume."

"The seeds sown from 1933 to 1940 are bearing fruit," he told *Dance Magazine* in 1966. He had a point—just think of the dance companies of Alvin Ailey, Paul Taylor, and Merce Cunningham.

What did the great Ruth St. Denis say about her gay husband right after she divorced him? "He should be proud of being Ted Shawn and not envious of *not* being Ruth St. Denis."

Because Shawn married St. Denis and was engaged to be married on other occasions, there was a belief among the more naïve in dance circles that he was straight.

But author Stanley Haggart, a friend of Shawn, once introduced one of the writers of this film guide to Shawn who was then aging. "I guess I was always a homosexual and didn't know it," he said. "Even in my attempts to seduce women, I always imagined some beautiful male dancer lying under me. Otherwise, I truly believe I could not have gotten an erection."

"As for male dancers," he said, "I do not prefer the effeminate. I seek the Greek ideal of bodily perfection. It is also highly desirable if a male dancer is blessed with a certain endowment to fill out his dance pouch. When they are generous in endowment, it makes them look more virile, more masculine. It was only by looking very masculine that America came to accept male dancers."

"Don't write that I was attracted to men. I was never attracted just to men. I sought out only *extremely handsome* men."

When confronted with a question about Ruth St. Denis, he was silent for a long moment. "Wife?

301

Perhaps in a legal sense. We were world famous. Our marriage brought great publicity. No. Not quite a wife. A partner, a partner in the dance. She was older. Perhaps a mother substitute."

The author asked Shawn to reveal two aspects of his long career not generally familiar to his fans. "When I staged *Pyrrhic Warriors*, I demanded that all my beautiful dancers strip completely nude behind their shields. I wanted to see their cocks and balls in movement as they danced. A man's genitals should be free. That way, the audience can enjoy all a dancer's body in movement. But, regrettably, when the dance went public, I had to put them in costume. I insisted the costumes be very tight, however, so that homosexuals in the audience could at least see the outline of genitalia."

In another memory, he said, "a lot of people don't know or remember, but in 1918 I got a call from the great Cecil B. de Mille. He wanted me for a movie where I would play a faun, who chases and catches the star of the film, Gloria Swanson. The film was *Why Change Your Wife?*" In it Shawn was dressed as a faun basking on a rock playing pipes of Pan. As a nymph, Gloria suddenly appears and he chases her. He stretches her out on a rock and squeezes grapes into her mouth. This was followed by a screen kiss of twenty-eight seconds, one of the longest ever recorded at that time.

In 1971, when Swanson was 72 and Ted 80, she visited him. Together again, and in front of a photographer, they repeated their long-ago kiss.

Shawn shocked American audiences in 1923 when he agreed to dance nude—"the Greek ideal," he noted. "It was a scene from *The Death of Adonis* where I did a cool, tasteful *plastique* (*editor's note*: a formal pose). I was reluctant to do it because my penis is not large. I always wanted a much larger penis, one that was like that on many of my other dancers. But, finally, I decided God made me the way I am, and so I decided to show off my body, small penis or not, in front of the entire world . . . or at least a very miniscule portion of that world."

Five Portraits of Ted Shawn

302

METAMORPHOSIS:
THE REMARKABLE JOURNEY OF GRANNY LEE
Johannesburg's Notorious Late-Night Revolutionary

This film, shot in South Africa, will introduce you to one of the most outrageous characters ever produced there—the notorious Granny Lee, who was also known as Granny Con, Queen Cobra, Disco Granny, and the White Queen of Africa. It's a story of illusion, occasional flashes of over-the-top glamor, satire, and struggle within the context of the racial and sexual repression of Calvinist Apartheid.

The film begins with her death at the age of 81 in a car crash and then flashes backward.

Granny was actually a South African black male (Du Plooy) who lived most of his adult life as a white woman. Although such a deception would be controversial in any society, under the repressive Apartheid of South Africa, her "deception" involved implications, some of them legal, that wouldn't necessarily have been a factor in say, the U.S. or Canada. Using one of the techniques later made famous by Michael Jackson, she lightened her natural pigmentation with creams and ointments, and otherwise barreled her way out of sticky situations with a mixture of bad-ass outrageousness and *chutzpah.*

In this 52-minute docu, Granny Lee lives again in re-enactments of her life as interpreted by actress Ruth Barter. Granny lived life on the edge, and as such, attracted a number of young male admirers--call them groupies, if you will, some of whom relate pithy anecdotes onscreen. She also openly defied the repressive Apartheid regime of the time.

Luiz DeBarros both helmed and scripted the outrageous camp of this unusual docu that includes a gruesome reconstruction of the fatal accident and even a creepy audio message which Granny Lee recorded for her own funeral.

 ## WHAT THE CRITICS SAID

"Sometimes moving and always outrageous, Granny Lee's life was obviously much more colorful than this slightly timid film."
   Rich Cline

Claudette Colbert at the time of her affairs with
Katharine Hepburn and Marlene Dietrich

MOM

Big Dreams in Little Hope, USA

This is a female buddy movie, running for only 70 minutes, and the creation of Erin Greenwell, who both helmed and scripted it. It stars Julie Goldman as Linda, Emma Bowers as Natalie, and Emily A. Burton as Kelly.

As a duo, Linda and Kelly could remake that hit TV series, *The Odd Couple*.

Market researchers Kelly and Linda are in New Hope for an annual Chili Cook-Off. When not holed up at the hostel, they make the rounds in this light, affable comedy, asking overly specific questions in customer preference surveys.

Kelly is dreaming of a coveted job as a field reporter, and laid-back Linda dreams of tattooing women in her parlor.

One of the interview subjects turns out to be an old girlfriend of Linda's. Her old flame, Natalie, is now settled down and married, but she and Linda rekindle the flame.

 ## WHAT THE CRITICS SAID

"Erin Greenwell's shoestring debut tells the story of odd couple, Kelly, an uptight market researcher, and Linda, a goofy butch cameraperson who dreams of opening a tattoo parlor. Stranded in a New Hope hostel, Kelly struggles with her identity, and Linda confronts an old fling. There are Universal lessons on friendship, love, and happiness to follow. Mom takes a while to get going, but the adventures of this offbeat duo—played with heartfelt sincerity by Emily Burton and Julie Goldman—prove that a decent script with a lotta heart can go a long way."
Termeh Mazhari

"Greenwell, in her sophomore outing, relies on little comic touches and bits of business instead of big laughs or elaborate pay-offs. Every encounter adds a touch of sociological satire or odd-ball color to the comfortable canvas, which is never mean-spirited or judgmental. Burton and Goldman amble along nicely in soft-shoe counterpoint, their routine nonchalantly synchronized to improve rhythms."
Ronnie Scheib
Variety

"The only thing that dikey bitch and I ever had in common was Billie Burke (a.k.a. Glinda, the Good Witch of the North), who supported both of us in our first pictures."

Margaret Sullavan, circa 1938,
referring to Katharine Hepburn

Kevin Aviance

MOTHER NATURE
(MATER NATURA)

Triangular Love & a Transgender Romp

This 94-minute Italian film is mildly amusing in parts. Call it a triangular love story and a serio-comic look at a transsexual hooker and her flamboyant friends.

Making a debut as a helmer, Massimo Andrei also co-scripted the project. Cast in the leading role as Desiderio, Maria Pia Calzone is a post-op hooker. But she's willing to confine her blow-jobs to just one man when she bags studmuffin Andrea (Valerio Poglia Manzillo).

Some reviewers referred to this piece of sun-tanned eye-candy as "Ulysses on horseback." Regrettably, his definition of acting involved merely removing his shirt, which is good enough for most gay men. He's got a secret, though. In addition to Desiderio, he's got a fiancée (in this case, a bio-logical, surgically unaltered woman) lusting for him as well.

Andrea can't make up his mind as to which gal he wants. Maybe he wants both of them in bed together.

To help Desiderio recover from her depression, a group of her adrenalin-pumped cross-dressers and transsexuals establish a personalized commune, counseling center, and organic farm--*Mater Natura*-- for her in the shadow of Mt. Vesuvius. The farm serves many purposes, one of which is to grow luscious produce like eggplant and zucchini with no apparent effort. Another is to serve as a center for transgen-der counseling. It's even a place where a macho man can find "the faggot that dwells within himself."

The film is not all life on the farm, however. There are some well-delivered songs, even an appear-ance by Luxuria, Italy's been-known drag performer whose talents, alas, are squandered in a trousers role.

You also get to witness far-out fashion—no *Devil Wears Prada* stuff—and plenty of queer histrion-ics amid all this trannie pageantry.

Incidentally, Sharon Stone said she always wanted to play Lana Turner on the screen, but in this romp the honor goes to Fabio Brescia.

 ## WHAT THE CRITICS SAID

"Novice helmer-scripter Massimo Andrei is over-reliant on music-vid influences, but unlike sim-ilarly themed *20 Centimeters*, allows silly subplots to get in the way of buoyant camp and seri-ous drama. Neapolitan lensing and a few good perfs help, but these girls need more to do than merely prance about."
Jay Weissberg
Variety

MATER NATURA: People have been trying to humanize the forces of Nature for thousands of years. Here's what they were crafting 25,000 years ago, long before the invention of the movie camera.

What is it?	**THE WILLENDORF VENUS**
How big is it?	4 3/8 inches tall
What's it made of?	It's carved out of oolitic limestone, a mineral not native to the site where it was discovered. It was originally painted with red ochre.
How old is it?	Estimated age: 23,000-25,000 years
Where's it from?	Discovered in 1908 in Willendorf, near Krems, in Lower Austria, it's now part of the permanent collection of the *Naturhistorisches Museum* in Vienna.
What is it?	Scholars offer at least three different interpretations:

1) It represents a Paleolithic fertility goddess *(Mater Natura)*
2) It's an idealized depiction of a woman of high status within the hunter-gatherer society that produced it
3) It's one of the earliest known examples of pornography

MR. LEATHER

Orphans, You May Find Daddy Yet

This 95-minute docu revolves around modern-day Leathermen and leather competitions, following nine contestants in a Mr. L.A. Leather Contest. It delves beneath the hide of the leather scene, revealing its manly yet (surprisingly) sweet-natured devotees—that is, in many cases.

Helmer Jason Garrett's debut feature is a journey into the leather subculture, exposing the dreams, hopes, and conceits of guys in leather, including their kinks, sense of sexual freedom, and brotherly bonding.

With all the whips, chains, chaps, harnesses, and jock straps, the contest isn't the Miss America pageant. Some S&M contestants talk of their fondness for flagellation.

 WHAT THE CRITICS SAID

"Basically, the film seems to exist to validate a marginalized minority—which is exactly what the Mr. Leather contests are doing. What's a bit peculiar is how seriously all these guys take the competition. There is no sense of irony at all here, despite an edge of campy excess that surrounds the entire event. Yes, leather is a legitimate fetish that adds to the diversity of society. But it's also just a bit of racy fun for those who find it a turn-on. So, laugh about it. Because for the rest of us it seems rather comical, really."
 Rich Cline

"I was charmed (yes, charmed) by the integrity of many of the participants. I thought some of the men being interviewed were puckishly delightful, and I'd accept a roll in the hay with two or three of them anytime. And thanks to having been fed lots of human-interest information by the filmmakers, I understood why the judges arrived at their final conclusions. What came through was the degree to which this "marginalized community" (*the filmmaker's words)* was committed to selecting pageant winners who would best, most articulately, and most authentically represent the values of the leather community to America at large. There were a lot of stylish and amusing things about this film, including some perceptive insights into some very interesting men. And the pageant was a helluvalot more fun to watch than the average beauty queen runaround. Oh, like a good gay tourist, next time I'm in Los Angeles, I'll head directly back to the Faultline. *Correctement habillé, bien sûr.* "
Leather fan **David Kindle**

THE NIGHT LISTENER

Tales of the City Author Confronts Another Literary Hoax

Even before the bogus memoirs of JT LeRoy and James Frey, Armistead Maupin in 2001 gave us the novel, *The Night Listener*. It was written during the period he was breaking up with his partner, Terry Anderson, after he was duped into a phone friendship with someone posing as an abused teenage boy.

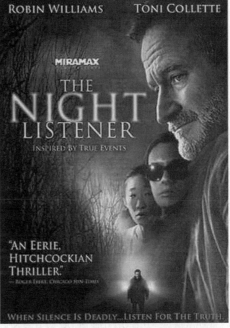

Helmer Patrick Stettner brings this story within a story to the screen. He cast Robin Williams as Gabriel Noone, a fictional name used for Maupin. In the film, Gabriel is a radio yarn-spinner in the midst of a crumbling relationship with his male lover.

In 1992, the real Maupin received a manuscript allegedly written by a 14-year-old boy, detailing the sexual abuse, including rape, he'd suffered as a child. However, he claimed that his nightmare was over as he was spirited away by a social worker.

In the film, this social worker is called Donna Logland, as played by Toni Collette. We know it's getting confusing at this point. Over time, the real Maupin developed an intense relationship, by phone, with this "boy."

In 1993 a shocking memoir was published by a so-called Tony Johnson called *A Rock and a Hard Place*. Maupin wrote a publicity blurb for it. Eight years later, in 2001, in a *New Yorker* article by Tad Friend, "Tony Johnson" was exposed as an entirely fictitious invention by his supposed adoptive mother, Vicki Johnson.

So, *The Night Listener* becomes a movie adapted from a novel that was inspired by the "memoirs" of a boy who probably never existed.

Ironically, even when Maupin first published his novel, which he chose to define as fiction, he might have suspected that Tony never actually existed. As Maupin admitted, there was even fear of a lawsuit.

"For all I knew, in the middle of the book tour, I was going to be confronted by a one-legged, one-lunged, one-testicled boy who would call me the most horrible monster that ever lived for doubting him," Maupin said.

At least during Maupin's long phone conversations with this so-called Tony, he learned a new word to describe gay men. "Dick-smoker."

At one point within *The Night Listener*, Gabriel Noone, the Maupin character as interpreted by Williams, begins to suspect that the boy doesn't exist, that he might be a character created in the mind of this "social worker."

In the movie, Bobby Cannavale takes the role of Jess, Gabriel's lover, a character based on Terry Anderson in real life. It was he who first noticed that the voice over the phone of "the boy" and "the social worker" were virtually identical.

The character of Pete (Rory Culkin) is played mostly in flashbacks and fantasy sequences, but the question remains. Does the boy really exist?

To answer that question, Gabriel journeys to the Middle West to investigate the mystery. At this point, with its dark, moody lighting, the film takes on the aura of a Hitchcock-like thriller.

Once in Wisconsin Gabriel runs into barriers. He is told that Pete (Culkin) is in an unnamed hospital battling AIDS. In Gabriel's search for Pete, an eerie Twilight Zone suspense haunts the film.

Left to right: Robin Williams, Toni Collette, and Rory Culkin

 # WHAT THE CRITICS SAID

"So this is a Chinese-box movie with puzzles lurking inside puzzles and a melodramatic over-lay that keeps one on the edge of the seat. *The Night Listener* is one of the few films that manages to be highly cerebral and a great popcorn movie simultaneously."
   Kirk Honeycutt
   Hollywood Reporter

"Mr. Williams, in one of his blessedly shtick-free performances, effectively conveys Gabriel's weary, worried stoicism, but the movie limits his character to a few easy, literal motivations. We understand that Gabriel, who nursed Jess through a period of life-threatening illness, needs someone to protect and care for, and that Pete represents a beguiling mixture of toughness and innocence, but the psychological and intellectual implications that hover over the story are lost in the spooky atmospherics and overshadowed by Ms. Collette's off-kilter showboating."
   A.O. Scott
   The New York Times

"Casting Williams in this thriller, adapted from Amistead Maupin's novel, was a bigger mistake than the actor's performance."
   Jack Mathews
   New York Daily News

"This Sundance dud is a turgid gay soap opera with a limp wrist, showcasing Robin Williams at his maudlin worst."
   Lou Lumenick
   New York Post

NOAH'S ARC

A Gay and Black Version of *Sex & the City*

Now on DVD, and running for 200 minutes, the complete first season of this glossy gay TV series was advertised as "The answer to your *Queer as Folk* withdrawal symptoms." The DVD version contains extra features, including the original pilot, deleted scenes, extended episodes, and cast comments.

The series follows the daily lives of four African-American gay men living and loving in Los Angeles: Noah (Darryl Stephens), Alex (Rodney Chester), Ricky (Christian Vincent), and Chance (Douglas Spearman).

The shows, acquired by Logo, are wonderfully sexy, with hot men and occasional moments of charm. Jensen Atwood, who played Wade in a dozen episodes, was singled out by one reviewer as "the sexiest man on TV apart from Rockmond Dunbar."

Light-hearted whimsy is mingled with serious drama. Reportedly, some networks are considering picking up the show and refilming it for a wider audience. One gay viewer lamented that if that happened, CBS or NBC might give it the *Will & Grace* treatment.

Noah believes that he has finally found true love in the shape of his new boyfriend, Wade. But he soon realizes that he, along with his best friends, must endure the everyday drama and hardships of life in the Big Orange. From new BFs to strained relationships to career misadventures, these men persevere and live their lives with a certain grace and wit, even if they have to sell a treasured car to pay the rent.

What are some of the soap opera-ish problems? Noah wants to meet some of Wade's straight friends. But he feels uncomfortable when he learns that Wade hasn't come out to them yet. When Wade's career takes a downward turn, Noah suggests they collaborate on a project. But the results are disastrous.

As *Noah's Arc* goes into his its second season, black queer visibility on TV will no doubt reach new heights.

The original title was called *Hot Chocolate*. Can you imagine that?

Jensen Atwood and Darryl Stephens

NOTES ON A SCANDAL

An Evil Lesbian Juices Up a Cat-and-Mouse Thriller

Judi Dench walks away with the picture in this story of two misguided schoolteachers. It's soapy melodrama, of course, a tale of sex, betrayal, and loneliness.

An embittered old lesbian, Barbara Covett (Dench) has the hots for her target, a young new art teacher, beautiful Sheba Hart (played by Cate Blanchett). Sheba mistakes Barbara's affections for friendship partly because she is distracted by her smoldering affair with a 15-year-old hottie, one of her students. The student is a working-class Irish youth, Steven Connolly (Andrew Simpson), whose performance blurs the line between schoolboy innocence and sexual predator.

When Barbara learns of Sheba's indiscretion, after having caught her in a compromising position with Steven, Barbara confronts Sheba rather ferociously.

Barbara is invited to Sheba's home where she meets her somewhat self-involved husband, Richard (Bill Nighy), who delivers his usually brilliant performance.

As the film progresses, Dame Dench is delicious at her delusional best, as she begins her manipulation of Sheba.

In the final scenes, Barbara sets into motion the scandal that will rock both their lives in ways they never imagined.

Richard Eyre directed this drama, illustrating that one woman's mistake is another woman's opportunity. It was scripted by Patrick Marber, who based it on a novel by Zoë Heller.

 WHAT THE CRITICS SAID

"Though every line spoken by both women is a master class in acting, the resulting film is like a plate of Chinese food: wonderfully good, yet soon after, unsatisfying."
Instinct

"Barbara may be a fright, but, as Judi Dench plays her, she's hardly a stereotype. Abrupt and formidable, she can silence a class of noisy teens with a stare and freeze the faculty-room banter with a put-down. But when we hear her read from her diary, in which her hopes of taking control of other people are mixed with girlish romantic dreams, Dench's voice slips into a yearning croon. And when Barbara's self-control collapses, Dench's facial muscles tighten, her eyes dance, her stolid carriage tilts upward in a rage."
David Denby
The New Yorker

Cate Blanchette (left) and Judi Dench

We congratulate **Dame Judi** for her designation as

Blood Moon's Best Supporting Actress (2007)

for her portrayal in
Notes on a Scandal

of a sexually and emotionally frustrated lesbian academic.

We wish her, along with anyone who might have inspired or
instructed her performance, our best wishes and respects for 2008

316

NOVEMBER SON

Gay Gore & a Lot More

The helmer and scripter of *November Son*, Jason Paul Collum, had an original dream film which was released as *October Moon* in 2004. It was the tale of a closet case who fell real big for his sexy male boss. *November Son*, more or less, could be called a sequel.

The plot, as stated by B+B Productions, gets a bit murky. See if you can follow along.

It's been nearly two years since an obsessive love destroyed not only the lives of three young men, but also those they left behind. Emily Hamilton (Judith O'Dea) tries to cope with not only the loss of her son Elliot (Jerold Howard), but also the guilt of possibly driving him down his obsessive, murderous path. Nancy (Brinke Stevens) is desperate to find the love, friendship and support of a man similar to Corin (Sean Michael Lambrecht). Maggie (Darcey Vanderhoef) desires the companionship of a best friend, someone to be her *confidante* in the same vein as Jake (Jeff Dylan Graham). And Marti (Tina Ona Paukstelis) has deteriorated into a shell of a human being, harboring a secret so deeply connected to those in Elliot's life that she has had no choice but to run from it for the last two years.

Enter Eli (Sacha Sacket) and George (Lloyd Pedersen), two men who have become a part of these women's lives, and who hold the keys to saving them from their misery . . . or perhaps creating it. The men have a shared secret about their own pasts which will force the women to confront their own fears and guilt over the events which have already destroyed them. When the truth comes out, the terror once again begins as each of the women and both men are tossed into scenario after scenario of bloodshed, torture and the ultimate hell of death, mutilation and destruction. Who is the November Son, and what secrets does his own past hold that will either leave these women saved . . . or buried six feet under?

We'll give you some trivia and leave it at that. Some characters are named George W. Bush, Dick Cheney, and Hillary Clinton. The director hired a real hot guy for a full frontal, but the dick display was nixed by a company rep. We can only dream what this scene would have looked like. The model in a white thong (instead of nude) will ignite a blaze.

"Bette Midler is more interesting when she talks than when she sings"

Helen ("I Am Woman") **Reddy**

"They arrested Helen Reddy for loitering in front of an orchestra."

Bette Midler

THE EFFETE FUSSBUDGET Franklin Pangborn
(1893-1958), Hollywood character actor known for his
skill at playing fussy, fastidious, eccentric roles usually
thinly veiled as gay stereotypes.

OPEN CAM
Serial Killer Roams Gay Sex Website

The tagline of this film was, "the Internet's not just for sex anymore." Directed and written by Robert Gaston, *Open Cam* is a comedy/drama/mystery/thriller wherein a DC-based gay sex website becomes home for a serial killer with a flair for exhibitionism.

Manny Yates (Andreau Thomas) is a rising young artist whose secret obsession involves cruising the web for possible sexual liaisons. He soon finds himself out of his clothes and into deep trouble when he witnesses a murder online. Think a 21st-century version of Alfred Hitchcock's *Rear Window*.

Hamilton (Amir Darvish), a studly detective, shows up to solve the case and, while he's at it, to top Manny. The original film featured some male nudity, including bubble butts. But the DVD bonus features have more steamy scenes, including shots of guys jerking off and erect dicks on screen. Yes, our hunky hero, Manny Yates, shows it hard.

One fan, who found Andreau Thomas the hottest man on the planet, claimed that *Open Cam* "successfully puts the Cock into Hitchcock."

 ## WHAT THE CRITICS SAID

"*Open Cam* sports some surprisingly high production values, giving all the scenes a slick and polished look that goes far in suspending disbelief. And believe me, that suspension requires some heavy lifting. Just don't spend too much time wondering why a sex hook-up site that broadcast multiple live castration murders of users would ever have traffic again... A couple plot holes aside, *Open Cam* is worth the ride... Oh, and there's a lot of sex, if you're into that."

Sean Bugg
Washington Metro Weekly

Clifton Webb: He extended helping hands to hunks like James Dean and Robert Wagner

OUT OF THE CLOSET, OFF THE SCREEN:
THE LIFE OF WILLIAM HAINES

The Man Who Fucked Clark Gable

In 1930 William Haines was America's Number One Box Office Star. But by 1935 his film career was only a memory.

This 45-minute docu of Hollywood's first openly gay star originally premiered on American Movie Classics. Haines was definitely on the A-list of stars, and a frequent guest of William Randolph Hearst and Marion Davies at their castle in San Simeon.

His best female friend was Joan Crawford, whom he called "Cranberry." But when studio chief Louis B. Mayer learned that he had a male lover and liked to suck dick and fuck sailors, plus other rough trade on the side, he was ordered to dump his lover, Jimmie Shields. Haines refused to do that, and Mayer sent him into what he thought would be oblivion.

But Haines was very resourceful and launched himself into a second career as an interior decorator. As such, he decorated the homes of some of the biggest stars in Hollywood, including Carole Lombard in her pre-Clark Gable days. (Incidentally, in a bit of Hollywood lore on the side, Haines in the late 20s once fucked the bisexual Gable.)

A heartthrob while closeted;
a pariah when Outed:
Actor and activist
William Haines (1900-1973)

"Billy Haines is one of the forgotten giants of the silent era," said Marc Juris, executive vice president of AMC. "Even though he was the number one male box office star, he did something that a lot of people wouldn't have had the courage to do."

"This is a man who sacrificed his career for the man he loved," said the executive producer of the film, Fenton Bailey. "It also takes a rare look at Hollywood's ongoing struggle with how to deal with homosexuality."

Haines, who once "roomed" in Greenwich Village with Cary Grant, often played callow, cock-sure collegians in comedy/dramas. He first came to major American attention in *Brown of Harvard* in 1926.

Amazingly, Haines became as desired as a decorator as he was as a star during his heyday. In addition to decorating for his beloved Cranberry, he also decorated the homes of Alfred and Betsy Bloomingdale, Jack Warner, and even Ronald and Nancy Reagan. Decades after his death, the furniture he designed is prized by collectors. Celebrities such as Ellen DeGeneres and Cameron Diaz own pieces.

Narrated by Stockard Channing, the film stars Christopher Lawford as the young Haines, Herb Gore as the actor's older incarnation, and Chris Allen as the younger Shields, Bob Wildman as the older one.

If you ever have a chance to see it, Fred Niblo's 1930 *Way Out West* is a wacky western with an outrageously gay lead performance from Haines, who wasn't even supposed to be playing gay. It's a screaming campy fest.

You can only admire Haines for wanting one thing even more than a screen career: A handsome young man named Jimmie Shields. Crawford called them "the happiest married couple in Hollywood." Despite their ups and downs, Haines and Shields lived together for some half a century. This docu from Randy Barbato and Fenton Bailey (*The Eyes of Tammy Faye*) brings their touching love story out of the closet.

DID YOU KNOW? William Haines was offered a role in the 1950 filming of *Sunset Blvd.* by Gloria Swanson, supposedly to play one of the has-been actors within her collection of friends ("The Waxworks"). But by then, he had been out of films for almost 15 years and was a successful interior designer, so he said no. Or perhaps he considered a role as a has-been within the industry which had rejected him just too painful.

Clockwise from lower left:
- William Haines, during his screen heyday;
- Haines with Marion Davies in 1928;
- Crawford with Haines at the Brown Derby in 1935;
- Jimmy Shields, Haines, Crawford, and her then-husband Al Steele in 1957. A year after Haines' death in 1973, after a relationship which had spanned 48 years, Shields committed suicide.

 WHAT THE CRITICS SAID

"*Out of the Closet* strains to view its subject as a rebel who lived a truly authentic life. The reality was more complex: Money, privilege and a tacit 'don't ask, don't tell' policy among A-list cronies (Reagans included) made Haines and other gay stars immune to censure, so long as their proclivities remained private. (Before his 1973 demise, he supposedly voiced disgust at the new phenomenon of out-and-proud 'gaylibbers.') His drunken, promiscuous off-screen escapades (continuing well after Shields moved in) attracted police attention more than once, a fact as likely a key to his MGM fall as the potential gay cohabitation scandal.

Decision to deploy actor Christopher Lawford as a middle-aged Haines looking back on life is more distancing than engaging. Commentators range from Christina Crawford (author of *Mommie Dearest*) to the irrelevant (later day gossip Michael Musto). Stockard Channing's narration sounds like an uninterested rush job."

Dennis Harvey
Variety

OUT OF HAND

Tragedy in a Teen Wasteland in Germany

This 92-minute German film tells the story of two 16-year-old boys, Sebastian and Paul. Bored with school and homelife, they set out on self-created adventures, stealing liquor, drinking, and bonding. A wolf-like nature deep inside each boy attracts them to each other. Gradually Sebastian falls in love with Paul, but he can't admit that to himself.

They discover a disused factory owned by Sebastian's father and turn it into a lair away from the eyes of the world. Then, on a dare, they abduct Sonja, a woman in her early 30s, and tie her up in the factory. Fear and lust rule the day. They don't really know what to do with their prisoner. They try out a number of ideas.

The deserted factory is discovered by Chris, Sonja's boyfriend. But rescue is not immediate. Chris blames her for creating this mess. He soon ends up just as helpless as Sonja.

Tensions mount as Sebastian clutches his father's gun. He loses all vestiges of self-control. A shot rings out.

The fun and games are over.

Sergej Moya, Elisabetta Rocchetti, and Ludwig Trepte

323

Sergej Moya

PAPER DOLLS
(BUBOT NIYAR)

The Lives of Transsexuals in Israel

Paper Dolls, written and directed by award-winning filmmaker Tomer Heymann, is a docu about a group of pre-op transsexual Filipino immigrants in Israel. By day they take jobs as home attendants for elderly Israelis, but by night they perform as drag entertainers in Tel Aviv nightclubs.

In this low-budget film, interviews with the ladies are mingled with their observations of daily life in a strange new country that doesn't always tolerate them with ease.

 WHAT THE CRITICS SAID

"They [the *Paper Dolls*] fit in as best they can, speaking pretty good Hebrew and ignoring the occasional stares that come their way, especially in the Orthodox neighborhoods where they work. Most have mixed feelings about their temporary home, which is a more open, less sexually repressive society than the one they left, but also one they find to be cold, materialistic, and bureaucratic. The documentary seeks to illuminate a subculture without allowing its curiosity to become exploitative or prurient."
   A.O. Scott
   The New York Times

"The director, a gay man himself, does not conceal his bias and prejudice when he introduces and interviews the main characters of his film. It is interesting and sweet witnessing how he sheds his own homophobia (tranniephobia, should we say?) and develops respect and affection towards the *Paper Dolls*."
   Rafael Solis

Paper Dolls: A documentary about pre-op Philipino transsexuals working in the Israeli health care system

THE PERVERT'S GUIDE TO CINEMA

But Who's the Pervert?

First, let's dispense with the title. This is not a film review of movies dealing with sexual perversion. As director Sophie Fiennes (sister of Ralph and Joseph) explained it, "The title is something of a McGuffin, just a way to get you into this network."

So be it. All serious cinephiles will want to take this one in, whether they are straight, gay, bi, lesbian, or anything in transition.

The director takes us on an exhilarating ride through some of the greatest movies ever made, as we explore the works of Hitchcock, Lynch, Tarkovsky, and others.

The star of the film is the bearded, rather unkempt looking Slovenian philosopher, Slavoj Zizek. Fiennes gives Zizek ample time to expound on his more extravagant theories.

To make the docu visually intriguing, Zizek turns up appearing to actually be in the sets of the movies he's discussing. We see him in a rowboat on Bodega Bay watching the invasion of Hitchcock's *The Birds*; again tiptoeing in and around rooms #771 and #773 of the former Jack Tar Hotel in San Francisco deconstructing the toilet scene in Francis Ford Coppola's *The Conversation*; in the Bates basement in *Psycho*; and perched on the corner of Dorothy's couch in David Lynch's *Blue Velvet*. Zizek applies a Freudian theory to his view of films, and you may not always buy his philosophy. Do you think, for example, that the moral of *Vertigo* is "the only good woman is a dead woman?"

 WHAT THE CRITICS SAID

"A virtuoso marriage of image and thought, *The Pervert's Guide to Cinema* is a propulsive, stream-of-consciousness sprint through the movie-projector mind of Slovenian philosopher and psychoanalyst Slavoj Zizek, who uses clean and properly framed clips from some 43 mostly high-profile films to illustrate his ideas on sexuality, subjectivity and that old standby, fantasy vs. reality."
Eddie Cockrell
Variety

"At best it is a cross-pollination of Zizek's genuine understanding of Freudian theory and his obvious admiration for the works of Hitchcock and Lynch, without being particularly enlightening on either psychology or cinematic technique. An entertaining look into Freudian theory through cinema, but ultimately a little pointless."
Kirk Miller

"Whether he is untangling the famously baffling films of David Lynch, or overturning everything you thought you knew about Hitchcock, Zizek illuminates the screen with his passion, intellect, and unfailing sense of humor. *The Pervert's Guide to Cinema* is really about what psychoanalysis can tell us about cinema."
P. Guide Ltd.

"You were very good in it, Olivia. When you weren't in a scene with me, you managed to keep the audience's attention."

Bette Davis, to de Havilland,
after a press screening of their film.

"She plays peasants, I play ladies."

Gina Lollabrigida, a fellow
Italian, referring to Sophia Loren

"The fans are so young! Their parents could hardly have been born when Bette [Davis] started out."

Olivia de Havilland, at the New York
premiere of *Hush, Hush, Sweet
Charlotte* in 1964

PIRATES OF THE CARIBBEAN
DEAD MAN'S CHEST

Johnny Depp, an Honorary Gay by Adoption, as "The Swishbuckler"

There was no doubt about it: Helmer Gore Verbinski created the purest popcorn entertainment during the summer of 2006. Now much of the world, including lots of gay men, are seeing it in DVD release.

Alas, it doesn't illuminate the secret life of Captain Jack Sparrow as much as we would have liked. But Johnny Depp spins his pirate into something very obviously gay, with a fey, kohl-eyed pranceabout. Jonathan Riggs in *Instinct* magazine wrote that, "That fine pirate booty minces about the starboard deck and works the plank like RuPaul on the runway."

Depp told *Rolling Stone* that during his interpretation for the role, he was instructed by a book called *Sodomy and the Pirate Tradition*. In it, historian B.R. Burg wrote: "What did these men, often on the high seas for years at a time, do for sexual fulfillment? Buccaneer sexuality differed widely from that of other all-male institutions such as prisons, for it existed not within a regimented structure of rules, regulations, and oppressive supervision, but rather in a society in which widespread toleration of homosexuality was the norm and conditions encouraged its practice."

As Depp himself put it: "I liked the idea of Jack being sexually ambiguous, because women were thought to be bad luck on ships. And these pirates would go out for years at a time. So, you know, there is a possibility that one thing might lead to another. You're lonely. You have an extra ration of rum. '*Cabin Boy!*'"

Depp claimed that he was partly inspired by the persona and mannerisms of Keith Richards, the Rolling Stone guitarist, as his role model, partly because pirates, in his words, "were the rock stars of their day." Co-incidentally, Richards has already signed to join the cast of the third version of *Pirates*.

Depp's other inspirations for the role included both "a touch of Michael Jackson" and the wobbly cartoon character Pepe Le Pew. One reviewer asserted that Depp drew more of his inspiration from Mary Pickford than he did from Douglas Fairbanks Sr.

Over the years Depp has won many gay friends through his interpretation of idiosyncratic characters who have included drag queens, among others. But who could have predicted that he would eventually transform himself into a mainstream Hollywood commodity as widely marketed as Mickey Mouse and Goofy? Or, as Mark Binelli said in *Rolling Stone*, Depp sold out without selling it.

Emerging from the theater after seeing this film, gay viewer Zack Snider, 27, claimed, "Johnny Depp has gotten much better-looking with age. He's gotten more European and less of a typical American macho guy. I like it best when Depp gets grimy for roles. In *The Libertine*, he was supposed to be all dirty and disgusting, but it was sort of hot instead. He was like a Victorian pervert. *Sexy.*"

Depp is one of the sexiest guys in the movies, enjoying the private nickname, "Donkey Dong." (Incidentally, gay men used to refer to Gary Cooper as "The Montana Mule.") But alas, we don't see

329

this aspect of Depp in this adventure flick. *The New York Times* quipped that this movie might have been subtitled *The Battle of the Cheekbones*: Orlando Bloom vs. Keira Knightley vs. Johnny Depp.

It's true that Orlando Bloom is sexier and handsomer than Depp, at least in *Pirates*. Many critics found the Bloom character bland, but nonetheless, he seems to appear on every list of Hollywood's "the hot, the sexy, and the beautiful." But in radical contrast to Depp's outrageously gay acting style, Bloom comes across as almost too sincere. Think Errol Flynn in the 1930s.

If you even care about the plot, which can seem contrived and a bit silly at times, it revolves around a blood debt Sparrow owes to Davy Jones (Bill Nighy), the legendary demonic fiend who commandeers a ghostly ship, *The Flying Dutchman*. To escape the fate associated with that long-ago debt, Sparrow must recover a key that will open a buried chest containing his nemesis's still-beating heart, then use that much-abused heart as a tool in the bargaining process with Davy Jones. This is obviously very far from a realistic portrait of life on the high seas.

That horrible villain, the East India Trading Company's Lord Beckett (Tom Hollander), imprisons, but then releases, Will Turner (Bloom) and Elizabeth Swann (Keira Knightley) on trumped-up charges as a means of motivating them to beat Sparrow to the coveted prize. Davy Jones emerges as genuinely repulsive. His head is that of an octopus, his face encumbered with wiggling tentacles. Regrettably, except in very young children, Davy Jones doesn't evoke horror or even pity as much as boredom.

Interspersed with ho-hum moments, expect the inevitable sword fights, tavern brawls, sea monsters, sailors returned from the Dead. and on ongoing sense of buccaneer fun and games. Also, insofar as plot devices go, expect a bit of bewildering and tepid confusion. Overall, this film provides Depp with room to perform in what one critic called "The Great Lounge Act of the Seven Seas."

Johnny Depp

Orlando Bloom

Keira Knightley

Bill Nighy as Davy Jones

WHAT THE CRITICS SAID

"Depp is less a swashbuckler than a swishbuckler as he prances and preens through the movie with a devil-may-care attitude of a hero who knows things will turn out well. He is the comic gel that holds the enterprise together. The performance is a total delight that somehow combines Bugs Bunny, Peter Pan, and Charlie Chaplin."

Kirk Honeycutt
Hollywood Reporter

"The sequel has Johnny Depp doing . . . whatever it is he's doing. His eyes rimmed like a glam rocker's, his gait a tipsy tiptoe through the tulips, his Captain Jack Sparrow would win a gonzo-effeminacy contest with Marlon Brando's Fletcher Christian—which I write with admiration and awe."

David Edelstein
New York Magazine

"Disney executives were reportedly horrified and wanted Depp to tone it down. He refused—and is laughing along with those execs, all the way to the bank. As engaging as his Sparrow is, Depp, 43, seems to have hit on some magical formula for crossover appeal that few actors can match. He's got the great looks that make women (and gay men) swoon, but straight men don't resent him as a pretty boy."

Reed Tucker
New York Post

"Depp was left with his own insouciance, and what he came up with was not so much a haze of hippiedom as the latest in a singular cinematic breed: the effeminate leading man. At the birth of the breed, unsurprisingly, lies Chaplin, with his simpers, his balletic borrowings, and his bustling, wide-kneed run. Depp, too, has his special sprint, waving his arms in a helpless sem-aphore—not like a girl, but like a schoolboy's mocking impression of a girl."

Anthony Lane
The New Yorker

POSTER BOY

What Would You Do If You Were Jesse Helms' Son?

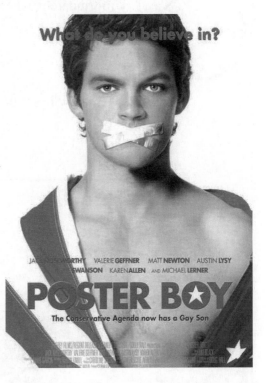

In this film, Henry Kray (as interpreted by Matt Newton) is the gay son of a North Carolina senator. (That senator's character might have been inspired by that dreaded homophobe, ex-Senator Jesse Helms, who, mercifully, retired in 2003 because of senility.)

Young Henry has a few problems: Young Republicans across the state have threatened to Out him, and other gays are keeping files on his sexual escapades. His daddy has scheduled a highly visible political rally at his college campus. Playing the role of Henry's father, the arch-conservative senator, Jack Kray, is actor Michael Lerner. The character he plays makes Joe McCarthy look like a den mother.

The senator has problems of his own. In addition to having a gay son, his fur-collared wife, played by Karen Allen, has a drinking problem. Of course, married to him she has plenty of reason to hit the sauce. Allen is quite effective as the salty, wise, and boozy Southern belle.

Just prior to daddy's arrival, his son has had hot gay sex with a jaded AIDS activist (Jack Noseworthy), who also wants to Out Henry. Or has the rabble-rouser fallen in love with our hero?

WHAT THE CRITICS SAID

"The setup is contrived, and the hunky leads ordered directly from the A&F catalog, but *Poster Boy* does manage to touch the eternally raw nerves of gays and American politics."
Tom Beer
Time Out New York

"Directed by Zak Tucker, *Poster Boy* is a muddled coming-out movie that for no good reason unfolds flashback style as Henry tells his story to a sleazy newspaper reporter. The device slows the little momentum the narrative builds. Still, Tucker's message is sometimes on target, even if his film isn't."
V.A. Musetto
New York Post

"Directed with more sincerity than skill, *Poster Boy* is a plodding indictment of extreme conservative intolerance. The screenwriters, Ryan Shiraki and Lecia Rosenthal, unfortunately, are better preachers than dramatists, juggling plot contrivances in a desperate effort to bring everyone together for the big reveal."
Jeannette Catsoulis
The New York Times

"Many actors go to Hollywood to try and become someone else. Unfortunately, Charlton Heston didn't succeed."

Talk-show host **Ricki Lake**

"Her show has too many weirdos on it for me to watch."

Charlton Heston

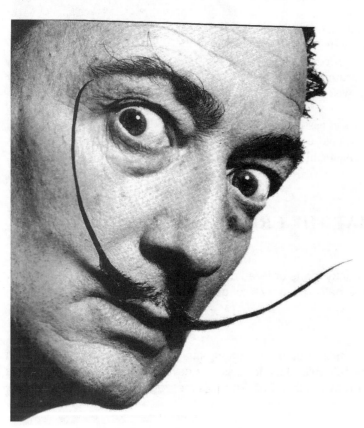

Surrealist, Salvador Dalí

PSYCHOPATHIA SEXUALIS
"Forbidden Desire" from the Case Studies of Krafft-Ebing

Young gay men in the early part of the 20th century often secured a copy of the 19th-century medical research of the Austrian psychiatrist Richard von Krafft-Ebing (1840-1902) to read "tales of deviance and forbidden desire."

In 1886 Krafft-Ebing published his famous study of sexual perversity called *Psychopathia Sexualis*. It remains well known for its coinage of the term sadism after the Marquis de Sade. He also coined the term masochism, using the name of a contemporary writer, Leopold von Sacher-Masoch, whose partially autobiographical novel, *Venus in Furs,* tells of a protagonist's desire to be whipped and enslaved by a beautiful woman.

Krafft-Ebing often called homosexuality "contrary sexual desire." He felt that the purpose of sexual desire was procreation. In his view, any form of desire that didn't have as its ultimate goal pregnancy was a "perversion." Therefore, rape, although an aberrant act, was not a perversion in his distorted view since pregnancy could result.

This docu is a multi-narrative adaptation of his notorious medico-forensic study of so-called sexual perversity. Before its release, and to get an NC-17 rating, helmer Brett Wood had to remove a shot of urination in someone's mouth. The 2-minute sequence, which included a depiction of male frontal nudity. hit the cutting room floor.

Nonetheless, there remains some strong sexual content, including not only graphic nudity but some violent and disturbing images.

Wood employs an eclectic array of devices to tell his story, even puppet theater and true-crime reality TV. Case histories were selected at random from Krafft-Ebing's files. Flashing on the screen before us are the misadventures, maladjustments, and obsessions of the "sexually inverted" of Victorian England.

The film uses such thesps as Daniel May who has a resemblance to the infamous somnambulist of *The Cabinet of Dr. Caligari.* Lisa Paulsen and Veronika Duerr grapple with the love that dare not speak its name.

  ## WHAT THE CRITICS SAID

"Bodily fluids are consumed, wealthy johns are whipped and stomped by *fin de siècle* Bettie Pages, lavender love is variously expressed and repressed. PS is as naughty as a Madonna concert, circa 1992."
Melissa Anderson
Time Out New York

Psychopathia Sexualis?

PUCCINI FOR BEGINNERS

Screwball Comedy of a Bisexual Roundelay

Writer-director Maria Maggenti won many lesbian fans with her coming-of-age drama, *The Incredibly True Adventure of Two Girls in Love*. But that was some 12 years ago.

She's back with this romantic comedy about a separated couple whose members each have affairs with the same woman.

The references to Woody Allen were rife in the reviews. Lou Lumenick in *The New York Post* suggested, "Imagine for a second if *Manhattan* centered not on Woody Allen's teenage-girl-loving character but on Meryl Streep—his lesbian ex-wife. Allen certainly hasn't managed anything remotely this funny lately." Even *The New York Times* wrote about the way this film contained "the crackle of vintage Woody Allen." It went on to say, "As any number of stilted duds can attest, applying a Philip Barry or Woody Allen sensibility to 21st century New Yorkers in their 30s is as delicate a craft as diamond cutting."

Davy Ray claimed that *Puccini for Beginners* was "better than Woody Allen's last five movies combined."

Maggenti's movie was summed up in this tagline: Girl Leaves Girl, Meets Boy and Then Meets Boy's Girl.

The plot? Reaser plays Allegra, who is on the rebound from her love affair with Samantha (Julianne Nicholson). Samantha has fled the nest to take up with Jeff (Brian Letscher).

Allegra then takes up with Philip (Justin Kirk), an assistant professor of philosophy at Columbia. This Woody Allen scenario begins to look like something from Noel Coward when Allegra meets Grace (Gretchen Mol). What Allegra doesn't know is that Grace is Philip's soon-to-be ex. Are you still with us?

The chemistry heats up between Grace and Allegra. Allegra is now "torn between two lovers," as the song goes. Reaser pulls it off beautifully and steals the picture, just as she did when she played a Norwegian mail order bride who comes to 1920s Minnesota in *Sweet Land*. She is a modern lesbian feminist writer with "commitment issues."

Of course, what Hemingway might call "the moment of truth" comes at the inevitable moment of reckoning. Also evocative of a Woody Allen film, minor characters sometimes turn to the camera and mouth off.

 WHAT THE CRITICS SAID

"The central characters are amiable sorts, and though it may just be my fantasy, you're half-hoping they'll end up in a three-way. That's better than what Maggenti has in store."
Jack Matthews
New York Daily News

"The film carries off the difficult feat of making this tiny segment of the chattering class more or less likable. Compared with these intellectually refined people, the characters in *Will & Grace* and *Sex and the City* are crude, materialistic boors."
Stephen Holden

Writer/Director Maria Maggenti

Elizabeth Reaser (left) plays Allegra;
Gretchen Mol (right) plays Grace

THE QUEEN

A Mass-Media Spin on Nobility, Frigidity, and Empire.

Dame Helen (Mirren) won the Oscar for her brilliant, deadly accurate portrayal of the cold British monarch, who's faced everything from the nude photo snapped at a distance of her heir apparent to rumors of a gay son. Other scandals have included Fergie getting her toes sucked.

Diana, though, was her worst nightmare. Of course, Tony Blair (Michael Sheen), new to office, comes off great in this film. He'd just been elected, and he knew how to hype the PR about the "people's princess," and all that. Stephen Frears hit his stride with this movie in which people stood outside the gates of Buckingham Palace baying for blue blood.

You might call *The Queen* Frears' royal flush. Prince Philip comes off as the sour, uncharitable twit he really is. He even makes anti-gay remarks, in spite of rumors, which have seen print, that he's had a gay dalliance or a few in his heyday.

The film might also have been entitled *The Great Gray Monarch versus The Great Modernizer*. It's big-time drama—in fact, a power struggle worthy of Shakespeare.

James Cromwell as the Duke of Edinburgh and Alex Jennings as the Prince of Wales capture their essences extremely well.

Our friend from long ago, Sylvia Syms, is marvelous as the dotty Queen Mother. Syms plays the Queen Mum as an irreverent hag with a taste for gin. It's not in the film, but the real Queen Mother used to call out to her staff: "Would one of you queens bring this old Queen some gin?"

Mirren in her award-winning performance displayed a potent mix of autocratic condescension and touching pathos. It's the performance of the year.

Our favorite moment in the film is when Mirren, as Queen Elizabeth, tells then golden-boy Blair that "one day, quite suddenly and without warning, the same thing [public hostility] will happen to you." She renders the perky pol speechless, and proves to be quite a prophet. We had other favorite moments as when the Queen says, "bugger it" when her jeep gets stuck or when Philip calls her by the conjugal nickname of "Cabbage."

The Queen was written by Peter Morgan, who has become a specialist in fanciful reconstruction.

The real *Elizabeth Segundo* of England formally announced that she had no plans to see Helen Mirren impersonate her in *The Queen.* Yet later, the British tabloids erupted with an exaggerated story about how Mirren "snubbed" an invitation to Buckingham Palace in the wake of having won an Oscar for her performance.

Maybe the real reason the 80-year-old monarch didn't want to see the film was that she'd have to relive what was arguably the most painful week of her 55-year reign—that is, the period in 1997 after Diana, the Princess of Wales, died tragically in a Paris car accident with her Egyptian lover, Dodi Fayed.

But gay men and some lesbians flocked in droves to see this movie. Maybe the men thought it was about another type of "Queen."

Helen Mirren and Queen Elizabeth II

 # WHAT THE CRITICS SAID

"Elizabeth no more likes Diana after death than before. When the queen does break her silence, as we know she will, it isn't because of this vexing woman. It's because Elizabeth, standing along in the Scottish countryside, Mr. Frears's camera hovering close and then moving off to take in the glorious view, has finally understood not only the implications of her past but also those of the present."

Manohla Dargis
The New York Times

"Helen Mirren needs to clear shelf space for her best-actress Academy Award. With a potent mix of autocratic condescension and touching pathos, Mirren delivers the performance of the year in a difficult role as a universally known figure – Queen Elizabeth II, amid the crisis over the death of Princess Diana. Ever-wily director Stephen Frears injects great humor and subtle historical depth to a story that plays out over just a matter of days."

The Associated Press

"Tradition and informality collide – and mutually benefit – in the deliciously written and expertly played *The Queen*. Dramatized versions of the week following the death of Princess Di, from the different vantage points of the British Royal Family and the newly elected Prime Minister Tony Blair, cheekily mixed on-the-nail perfs and docu footage into a witty and finally moving re-creation of a period that challenged both royals and pols."

Derek Elley
Variety

Director Stephen Frears

We congratulate
STEPHEN FREARS
for his designation by Blood Moon as

the Year's **BEST DIRECTOR** (2007)

based on his film
THE QUEEN

But based on her *tour de force* performance, are Helen Mirren (shown above with James Cromwell, playing Philip) and Elizabeth II still feuding?

Conrad Veidt in the first film ever to deal explicitly with homosexuality: *Anders als die Andern* (*Different from Others*, 1919)

QUEENS
(REINAS)

Not Penis Envy, Almodóvar Envy

This film is not so much about gay sons getting married but about five mothers (three of them longstanding Pedro Almodóvar muses). Now that Spain has officially sanctioned same-sex marriages, it was inevitable that some filmmaker would come out with a picture about gay marriage.

Too bad it wasn't Almodóvar himself. Instead we get helmer Manuel Gómez Pereira, who failed to pull it off in spite of a cast of some of the most talented actors in Spain.

The movie is about three gay couples and their pending nuptials. The mamas take over as their sons bicker over furnishings. Their discomfort at the upcoming communal wedding is played out by their seducing the wrong men.

Nuria (Verónica Forqué), for example, seduces her drunken future son-in-law. A successful hotelier, Magda (Carmen Maura), runs to the arms of her head chef while dealing with a strike of her employees. Reyes (Marisa Paredes), a rich actress, lusts after her gardener. She seems to ignore the fact that he (Lluís Homar) will become her new in-law after the knot is tied. Pressed into duty is yet another mother, a judge (Mercedes Sampietro), who will preside over the ceremonies.

For those who don't get off on gay weddings, there's even a dog-poop joke. Not only that, but we're treated to everything from "aggressive" bosoms to a single intimidated penis.

 WHAT THE CRITICS SAID

"Despite the rich potential of the movie's basic premise, *Queens* is frantic, shrill, and dreadfully disappointing. (And I'm a gay son of two Spaniards, mind you—good luck finding a film critic more inclined to have liked this movie.) Director Manuel Gómez Pereira and his co-writers fail to create a single character for the audience to relate to or even like. Everyone on screen is so shrill and selfish and irritating that it's impossible to give a tinker's damn about any of them."

Alonso Duralde
The Advocate

"The most remarkable thing about *Queens*, a silly but generous Spanish farce, is its unadulterated worship of middle-aged women. Not one of its five female leads will see 50 again (and two have stared down 60), yet the movie cheerfully crams them into lethal heels, cleavage-baring frocks and enough lip gloss to grease a long-distance swimmer. Thus adorned, they flirt, frolic, and have fabulously wicked sex. *Viva España!*"

Jeannette Catsoulis
The New York Times

MOMENTS IN GAY HISTORY:

"Oh no, not our Larry!" screamed the British press when news of Sir Laurence Olivier's affair with Danny Kaye was revealed. "But nobody wants to fuck Danny Kaye," Samuel Goldwyn had once said, commenting on the actor's perceived lack of sex appeal.

How wrong he was. Olivier, Shirley MacLaine, and Princess Margaret would disagree. Olivier, whose other affairs encompassed Richard Burton, Errol Flynn, Greer Garson, and Jean Simmons, abruptly dropped Kaye one day. But not until the affair, as noted publicly by Olivier's wife, Vivien Leigh, had continued for many years. Mostly, however, she was too busy with her own distractions to pay much attention.

One of her distractions involved Marlon. Both Vivien and Sir Larry had enjoyed the favors of Brando during the filming of *A Streetcar Named Desire* (1951).

Above, Danny Kaye in the lobby scene of *Up in Arms* (1944).

QUEER DUCK, THE MOVIE

A Fruity Fowl & Cult Hero in GLBT Circles

What's not to like in this raunch-loaded animated feature? The title alone won us over. We first met Queer Duck, an odd bird if there ever was one, when he appeared on the Internet as part of the *Icebox* website. The cartoon character was created by Xeth Feinberg who wrote for *The Simpsons* and now is director of the movie. *Queer Duck* shorts were shown by Showtime after the popular *Queer as Folk* on Sunday nights.

Jim J. Bullock was hired to be the voice of our favorite duck. The other voices are equally wonderful, including Jackie Hoffman as Lola Buzzard; Maurice LaMarche as Oscar Wildcat; and Tress MacNeille as Dr. Laura Schlessinger, a monster easy to hate. Kevin Michael Richardson is the voice of Openly Gator, with Bill West doing the soundtrack for Bi-Polar Bear. He sounded like Paul Lynne.

Celebrity voices, all great sports, include cameos by Tim Curry, Mark Hamill, Bruce Villanch, Andy Dick, Conan O'Brien, and David Duchovny as of all things "Tiny Jesus."

There are parody impersonations of such gay-friendly divas as Rosie O'Donnell, Liza Minnelli, Elizabeth Taylor, and Barbra Streisand, but a rather unflattering portrait of Jacko. Most of the humor seems targeted to gay males rather than a lesbian audience.

Seymour Duckstein (Queer Duck) leaves his lover, Openly Gator, when he, the duck, becomes enamored of and marries the Norma Desmondesque-Ms. Buzzard.

As with *South Park*, you're treated to musical numbers, including such tuneful interludes as "Jimmy Couldn't Master Masturbation" or "Have Sex With Animals." You even get a pastiche from the Village People's "YMCA." The black-and-white penciled *What Ever Happened to Baby Jane* remains one of our favorites.

As the writer, Mike Reiss came up with some hilarious lyrics, including a spoof of Gilbert & Sullivan's *H.M.S. Pinafore*. "I watched them sing and I watched them dance/And I watched all the bulges in the sailors' pants."

"Jokes are cruelly obvious, and often scatological, but that's the point. The whole idea is to have a gay cartoon without any reverence for convention, and in that the cast and crew succeed. The animation and jokes are both crude as hell, but like water off a duck's back it hardly keeps you from having a good time. Straight audiences will be baffled, but the more gay you are the funnier this little movie is. Have a few cosmos, and watch it with the boys. It's good old-fashioned faggoty fun, and sometimes silly is just as subversive as straight."
   Judge Brett Cullum

"Irreverent, raunchy animated feature, overflowing with throwaway gags, warped show tunes, caricatured celebrities, genial good humor and bad puns, successfully explode the Showtime series of three-minute cartoons into a 72-minute nonstop gagfest. Director/animator Xeth Feinberg's crude, flat, outrageous-looking but never stiff design creates a Rocky & Bullwinkle-like interplay between witty words and pleasingly abstract characters."
   Ronnie Scheib
   Variety

"For a gay audience, it is important to point out the humor and characterizations are also a bit dated in an old gay man way. Even the writer admitted in one of the included featurettes that the movie has the humor of a 45 year old gay man and feels more like the gay '80s than the gay world today. He freely admits that a twentysomething gay male may not connect to the jokes the same way. We agree that there are too many old-school gay references that just seem a bit out of place in the contemporary world. You feel drawn back in time to a stereotype of the gay world where Streisand, anonymous sex parties, musical numbers, bitchy flamboyant behavior, and old-school drugs like roofies and coke were all the rage. These things are really meaningless to the gay identity of most twenty and thirtysomething gay men today, but most will still at least understand the humor enough to appreciate it, although they likely won't feel the same insider emotional connection as an older gay man to Queer Duck's humor."
   Raymond So
   DVD Talk Review

QUINCEAÑERA

Ostracism & Liberation—2 Sides of the Same Spinning Coin

A real couple in private life, helmers and scripters Wash Westmoreland and Richard Glatzer brought us that gay fave, *The Fluffer*, one of the hottest indies we've seen in a long time. Their switch to more mainstream cinema came as a surprise to us when we attended a showing of *Quinceañera*.

In Mexico, *una quinceañera* is a "coming out" party announcing a girl's 15th birthday. Magdalena (Emily Rios) is looking forward to the big day. There's a problem. She's pregnant, although technically a virgin. She became pregnant by her boyfriend in a rare instance of nonpenetrative sex. She is kicked out of the house by her devoutly Catholic papa. One outcast seeks two other outcasts—in this case her cousin, Carlos (Jesse Garcia), a *cholo* (person of mixed Amerindian and Spanish descent) who has also been evicted by his family for being gay. He lives with his gentle great-uncle, Tomas (Chalo Gonzáles), a life-loving 80-plus character who hawks *champurrado* (a popular Mexican hot drink) on the street.

The setting is Echo Park in Los Angeles, a neighborhood inhabited in large part by Mexican immigrants though it's going through a gentrification.

The producers were very impressed with their hot new star, Garcia, who hails from Wyoming. "Jesse, as an actor, has so many emotional layers, and he's so ready to go places and try things," says Glatzer. "He's almost a return to that kind of 50s innocence, like Brando and Dean, where you don't need to think of what you are sexually, you just go with it."

We'd endorse that remark, although "innocence" in the case of Brando and Dean might be the wrong word.

 # WHAT THE CRITICS SAID

"*Quinceañera* exhibits such stalwart faith that its troubled characters will prevail that its underlying bleakness is largely camouflaged. The filmmakers have described *Quinceañera* as kitchen-sink realism in the tradition of British working-class dramas of the late 1950s and 60s. And it is, except that the suffocating atmosphere of despair and social stagnation of classical kitchen-sink dramas like *A Taste of Honey* (which the directors cite as an inspiration) is replaced by a spirit of hope and the optimistic portrayal of ethnic assimilation in the land of opportunity."
Stephen Holden
The New York Times

"When Carlos's new neighbors, a white gay couple whose presence is the surest sign of the neighborhood's changing face, invite him to their all-male housewarming party, you wait cringing for the moment when the wrong person will make a pass at him and he'll erupt in violence—only the moment never comes, replaced by a more intriguing twist."
Philadelphia City Paper

"Anna Nicole Smith is giving golddigging a bad name."

Romantic novelist **Barbara Cartland**

"Anna Nicole Smith gives sleaze a bad name."

Roseanne Barr

"Roseanne Barr will never see a bikini again, except from the outside."

Anna-Nicole Smith

Homophobe Mel Gibson

RENO 911! MIAMI

Don't You Love It? Cops in Bootie Shorts

Running only 84 minutes, and seemingly too long for some viewers, this freewheeling Comedy Central parody of *Cops* is one of the latest television series to come to the big screen in theaters before its race to the border for DVD release.

Of course, you get gratuitous nudity, vulgar language, and below-the-belt gags. The city of Reno didn't seem spicy enough, even though it's said to be "like *Mayberry*, except everyone's on crystal meth and prostitution's legal." Helmer Robert Ben Garant moved the action to Miami, which is a good excuse to put the hot, studly cops in bootie friendly short shorts.

A rag-tag team of Reno cops is called in to save the day after a terrorist attack disrupts a national police convention during spring break.

There are cameos by Danny DeVito, Paul Rudd, and Dwayne 'The Rock' Johnson, so the bar wasn't set very high in this heavily padded spoof.

The movie was written by Robert Ben Garant, who plays Deputy Travis Jr., and Thomas Lennon, who is the short shorts-wearing Lt. Jim Dangle. Kerri Kenney-Silver plays the overly medicated Deputy Trudy Wiegel. Garant and Lennon wrote such box-office hits as *Night at the Museum*.

Even though reviews were bad, it isn't often that you get to see a mass masturbation scene in a general release flick.

 WHAT THE CRITICS SAID

"Comedy Central's *Cops* spoof gets promoted to a theatrical lark with a South Beach spin, but is handcuffed by an annoyingly contrived plot that keeps its zanier non-sequitur TV giggles in lockdown."
   Stephen Garrett
   Time Out New York

ROCK BOTTOM: GAY MEN AND METH

"Fuck Me Bareback," the Whacked-Out Demand from Crystal Heads

This is a chilling portrait of a community—in this case, New York's Chelsea District—in crisis. With an unflinching eye, this 61-minute docu by Jay Corcoran follows the journeys of seven gay men struggling with meth addiction and recovery.

It is set against a horrific backdrop of an emerging second wave of HIV infection, caused in large part by barebacking among crystal meth users. The docu captures the saga of these young men over a two-year period as they go from sex clubs to hospitals, and in some cases attend family gatherings.

The film delivers a powerful punch and doesn't hold back in its frank and honest portrait of crystal use, going from exciting, even glamorous highs, to devastating lows.

Meth addiction, according to the docu, can be blamed on many reasons—poor self-esteem, HIV burnout, internalized homophobia, and even intensely conflicted feelings about sex.

In one segment, a user is shown dying from drug use and diabetes. What is startling is the appearance of the subjects under the influence of crystal meth and the same men a few months later after freeing their systems of the substance.

The low point of the film is when one user describes in ghoulish detail the blatant signs of gonorrhea.

Perhaps the largest question confronted here is the price some of us pay for the pursuit of sensation.

 WHAT THE CRITICS SAID

"The bravado that a jolt of speed gives to men with shaky self-esteem in a still-homophobic culture is an element of its appeal. But as men describe the intensified and prolonged pleasure of sex with meth, you realize that it belongs to the same category of sensation-seeking as race-car driving, skydiving and gambling. A craving for delirious excitement may be hard-wired into the male psyche, and danger is a crucial component of whatever gratifies it. In a certain segment of gay society, sex is the competitive sport of choice."

Stephen Holden
The New York Times

Lucille Fay LeSueur
(the woman who became Joan Crawford)

ROME

A Historic, Half-Naked Story of Love, Ambition, Debauchery, & Betrayal

This excellent TV miniseries, a BBC-derived costume drama, drew a lot of gay viewers because of its sweeping sense of epic grandeur, cruelty, ambition, passion, an obsessive concern for the aesthetics of ancient Rome, and an unabashed showcasing of frequent male nudity. It includes graphic depictions of masters and slaves giving birth to a Roman Empire that would in time become a symbol for debauchery.

Nominated for two Golden Globes, and created through the united efforts of the teams that created both *Six Feet Under* and *The Sopranos*, it was crafted within the largest standing film set in the world, one that filled up five acres of a backlot at Cinecittà Studios. It is an action/drama centered around the final years of the reign of Julius Caesar and the events that immediately followed.

Ray Stevenson (Titus Pullo) and Kevin McKidd (Lucius Vorenus) star as two soldiers in the army of Caesar, as artfully depicted by Ciarán Hinds.

There are no rules about right or wrong, and soldiers develop their own personal code of morality as circumstances and their individual temperaments dictate. There is no disapproval of ladies who smoke hemp from Persia or men who fuck boy-ass either.

Of course, in terms of sheer flesh-peddling, nothing equaled Bob Guccione's quasi-porno, *Caligula* in 1979, where an actor didn't get cast unless he was well endowed. But *Rome* as a series is a hell of a lot better than the movies *Troy* with small-dicked Brad Pitt or *Alexander* with big-dicked Colin Farrell.

As a historic vehicle drenched with sweat, blood, and verisimilitude, we'd rate *Rome* up there with *Centennial* and *Roots*. *Rome* contains more than the typical Hollywood glitter that envelops most epics of the ancient world, and it's a long way more artful than any of Steve Reeves' gladiator films.

The depiction of the love affair/suicide of Antony and Cleopatra was, in the words of this long-time fan, riveting, as was the culmination of Servilia's chilly vendetta against Attia. And it's doubtful that any mother-son relationship could quite as poisonous as the one between Octavian and his magnificently self-involved mother, as played by Polly Walker.

Romans by Birth or by Treaty, left to right: *Cleopatra* (Lynsdey Marshal), *Mark Antony* (James Purefoy), suicidal ultra-aristocrat *Servilia of the Junii* (Lindsay Duncan), tragic *Niobe* (Indira Verma) with her husband, *Lucius Vorenus* (Kevin McKidd)

"The stories are full of sex, full frontal nudity (men and women), violence and good, old-fashioned drag (well, the women sure look like drag queens). The sex scenes don't shy away from much, and there are lots of men in barely there togas to ogle. The days before air conditioning never looked so enticing."
  Richard Hellstern
  Instinct

"Nevertheless, *Rome* isn't exactly Gibbon. Not for nothing is Dirty Harry's script doctor himself, John Milius, one of several executive producers. We are still talking about slave auctions, bloodbaths, bared breasts, battlefield rape, human footstools, and crucifixion as a handy means of torture when you're looking into the whereabouts of a stolen eagle standard."
  New York Magazine

Roman Holiday or *Mommie Dearest?*
Gaius Octavian (as played by Simon Woods, center), with his scheming mother, *Attia of the Julii* (Polly Walker) on extreme left.

RUNNING WITH SCISSORS
Scariest Portrait of a Mother Since Mommie Dearest

This is the most frightening depiction of motherhood since Faye Dunaway picked up that wire hanger.

Annette Bening, who has a large gay following, stars in this hilarious and poignant feature based on the memoirs of Augsten Burroughs. In the film she plays Deirdre, the mother who sends her son (Joseph Cross) to live with her oddball shrink, Dr. Finch (Brian Cox).

As always, Bening is brilliant as the deliciously mad bisexual mom. In the film, Deirdre has two female lovers, both played by amazing young actresses, Kristin Chenoweth and Gabrielle Union.

Nip/Tuck creator Ryan Murphy adapted and directed this tragic-comic memoir in which the young Burroughs lived with his closeted lesbian mother and an alcoholic father, played by Alec Baldwin.

The movie is so realistic that Burroughs was sued for defamation of character by the family featured in his memoir. One reviewer wrote, "After seeing the movie, you may side with the plaintiffs." Burroughs more or less depicted his adopted family like the Addams family on LSD, including Finch's profoundly depressed wife, Agnes (Jill Clayburgh) who snacks on dog kibble.

Neil (played by Joseph Fiennes) is a 33-year-old patient and adopted son of the family. He is a gay paranoid schizophrenic who immediately takes the virginity of young Augsten.

Playing the disturbed sisters are sex-mad Evan Rachel Wood as Natalie Finch and Gwyneth Paltrow as Hope Finch.

Paltrow plays the unsmiling sister as if she were still appearing in *The Royal Tenenbaums*. The adopted teenage daughter, Natalie, is recovering from an affair with a middle-aged married man. You can tell that Hope is a little off. She buries her cat, then later digs it up for stew meat. When hearing that the stew is feline, Joe's ad lib was "I don't eat pussy." Helmer Murphy kept the line in the final cut.

Dr. Finch himself thinks God is sending him messages through his bowel movements.

The question to ask here is can our young gay hero survive to come of age?

Joseph Fiennes

Gwyneth Paltrow

Alec Baldwin

"At what point was it decided that anyone with a car-wreck childhood could become an author? The rise of the confessional memoir has subjected readers to any number of torrid, true-life tales ending in redemption (and six-figure book deals), but Augusten Burrough's hilarious, profane contribution was a cut above the Mary Karrs and James Freys flooding the market."
David Fear
Time Out New York

"Annette Bening should earn an Oscar nomination for her fearless performance of the vain, flaky, deeply disturbed mother."
Todd Hill
Staten Island Advance

"The narrator is an adoring gay boy who loses his Auntie Mame-ish (and bipolar) mother to the seventies, an era in which loony-tune therapists counseled patients to act out their anger instead of learning to manage it."
David Edelstein
New York Magazine

"Pedophile Neil is practically a walking advertisement for the North American Man-Boy Love Association. Anyway, Augusten's budding sexuality is presented as the least of his problems. *Running With Scissors* gets a bit winded as it approaches the two-hour mark, but it's surprisingly nimble for a film that seems afraid to cut too deeply."
Lou Lumenick
New York Post

"Cross has a magically expressive face and provides a strong central presence to a film that might be tempted to meander through its nut-house environment."
Jack Mathews
New York Daily News

Annette Bening

We congratulate
ANNETTE BENING
on her designation by
Blood Moon as

RUNNER-UP FOR BEST ACTRESS (2007)

based on her work in
RUNNING WITH SCISSORS

SAINT OF 9/11

"We All Have Closets of One Kind or Another"

Narrated by Sir Ian McKellen, this 90-minute docu by helmer Glenn Holstein "stars," among other appearances, Bill and Hillary Rodham Clinton. In archival footage, Saint depicts the life of Father Mychal Judge, Chaplain, FDNY. In an inspiring portrait, the film traces the life of this celibate homosexual, a turbulent, restless, spiritual, and remarkable journey.

Everything this ecclesiastic did stemmed from his love for his fellow man. He was ministering to people with AIDS during a time when such victims were treated like lepers during the Middle Ages. His acts were often simple, including giving a warm coat to a homeless person on the streets of New York in winter.

After the 9/11 attack on the World Trade Center, he became famous. "He touched people in an ordinary, consistent way," said Brendan Fay, the co-producer of the film and a long-time friend of Judge's.

Gene Robinson, the first openly gay bishop in the Episcopal Church, claimed he identified with Judge.

The Irish-American priest, a recovering alcoholic and a confidant of tough, gritty firefighters, was a Franciscan friar. He chose to join his men within the North Tower rather than remaining on the sidelines. He died at the age of 68 after giving last rites to a fallen firefighter.

"He became celebrated for how he died," said critic Andrew Sullivan. "But there's so much more to him than that."

"Everything was all right until on location in Arizona. I had a four-page monologue, and because of my stage and radio background, I knew all the lines. We shot it in one take, and the crew applauded. Joan was in her trailer and heard the applause--and that started it. It made Joan mad, and *she* was the star of the picture."

-**Mercedes McCambridge**, on her
Johnny Guitar leading lady, Joan Crawford.

Chita Rivera

SAY UNCLE

When Is a Pedophile Not a Pedophile?

Most of us know actor Peter Paige from his portrayal of the witty, fashion-evolved Emmett on *Queer as Folk*. But whatever was he thinking when he made this inauspicious debut as a writer/director? Was he inspired by Michael Jackson . . . or what?

After his godson's parents wisely move to Japan, he develops an unhealthy obsession with children. After he loses his job as a telemarketer, he starts to hang out at playgrounds, even inviting young kids to his apartment.

He even advertises his services as a "nanny," although there are no takers. Small wonder. The Xeroxed babysitting flyers sport terrifying images of his pasty visage.

A homophobic mother (Kathy Najimy) organizes a lynch mob in Portland (Oregon) to deal with this suspicious character.

Frankly, we like Paige as the unapologetically queeny Emmett on *Queer as Folk* much better. But as David Ehrenstein asked in *The Advocate*: "How do you top *Queer as Folk*? With something even queerer, that's how."

 WHAT THE CRITICS SAID

"Laughless, pointless, and downright creepy, *Say Uncle* is a would-be-black comedy about a young gay man who is wrongly suspected of being a pedophile. *Say Uncle* argues unconvincingly that Paul—an artist who rebuffs romantic approaches by a co-worker—is emotionally stunted and misunderstood because of childhood trauma. Stay away."
Lou Lumenick
New York Post

"You'll be begging for mercy well before the end of this self-righteous, thoroughly unsavory 'farce' about a lonely gay man who—gosh darn it—can't seem to stop getting mistaken for a pedophile. Hmmm. Do you think it could have something to do with his odd habit of playing with strangers' children in public parks?"
Scott Foundas
Village Voice

"Because Paul is gay and well-meaning, we're meant to see him as a victim of reactionary politics. But ask yourself: If you saw an unknown, single man repeatedly approach kids in the park, would you be concerned? If so, you may not find Paul, and his unbalanced Peter Pan complex, quite as charming as Paige does."
Elizabeth Weitzman
New York Daily News

Kathy Najimy

Peter Paige

SCARY MOVIE 4
Tired Gay Jokes & Bodies Emptied of Their Waste

After four movies within this genre, we're starting to feel jaded. Is there any more humor left to wring from the pup tent of *Brokeback Mountain*, or has it been done to death, like the scatological jokes running through this *Scary Movie* franchise? Hasn't the entire world been convinced by now that Tom Cruise is the most heterosexual actor who ever lived? How else to explain that horrific pop culture moment when he made mincemeat of Oprah Winfrey's couch. His wigout performance on Oprah convinced us that Cruise has never come within 20 feet of another man's dick.

Of course, there are some chuckles at the expense of such celebrities as Leslie Nielsen (one of the usual suspects), but also the easy-to- satirize Dr. Phil, Carmen Electra, Charlie Sheen, and Shaquille O'Neal.

Series star Anna Faris is cast as dumb blonde Cindy Campbell who gets a job as nursemaid to an infirm elderly woman (Cloris Leachman). Craig Bierko appears as Tom Ryan, playing a divorced and working-class dad, who must, like Cruise in *War of the Worlds*, flee with his kids.

Series regular Regina Hall once again appears as Brenda Meeks. Since she's been killed in each prior *Scary* screening, this is indeed an amazing feat of serialized reincarnation

If you still get a belly laugh from ho-hum blows to the groin, information about what happens when someone overdoses on Viagra, C-list celebrities making asses of themselves, or even slapstick child abuse, then by all means rent the DVD.

 WHAT THE CRITICS SAID

"The *Scary Movie* series wants to be for horror and sci-fi what *Forbidden Broadway* is for theater: an ever-updated spoof of the most recent season. Too bad so many of the movies it tackles are already so feeble they hardly need sending up—which means the *Scary* franchise is forever overstaying its welcome."
Jami Bernard
New York Daily News

"There's not a lot of satire left in these films. Most of the jokes are just references to other movies, or rote ow-my-head! slap-stick violence, or a combination of both. Rarely is much fun had with genre conventions—as if that might be too sophisticated for an audience that finds humor enough in simply being reminded of the movies watched and songs heard since Scary Movie 3."
Dennis Harvey
Variety

"The trouble with Barbra [Streisand] is that she became a star long before she became an actress. Which is a pity, because if she learned her trade properly, she might become a competent actress instead of a freak attraction--like a boa constrictor."

Walter Matthau, who
co-starred with Babs in *Hello, Dolly!*

"When we commenced *On a Clear Day You Can See Forever,* I had the mistaken impression that I was the co-star. I was Miss Streisand's first leading man who can sing, even though this was her third musical. I thought she was my leading lady, a partner. I doubt I will choose to work again in Hollywood."

Yves Montand, referring to
Babs and his final American film

SEVEN VIRGINS

(7 VIRGENES)

Teen Machismo on Parade as Rebels Run Wild

Basically, this is a film about teenage rebellion that's set against the backdrop of the sweltering heat of an Andalusian summer in Seville. The title, *7 Virgins,* refers to an Andalusian superstition involving candles, a mirror and clairvoyance, a motif that appears throughout the film. Running for 86 minutes, this film from Spain—released as *7 Virgenes*—will delight chicken hawks drawn to juvenile delinquents. Tano (Juan José Ballesta), a teenager serving a sentence in a juvenile reform school, receives a 48-hour pass to attend his brother's wedding. The drama unfolds within a blue-collar neighborhood in the south of Spain.

Before his leave expires, Tano will witness the collapse of all things he has taken for granted in his life: His working-class neighborhood, his family, his friends, and his loved ones. The experience evolves into an odyssey along the road to growing up and becoming a man. At the San Sebastian Film Festival in 2005, Ballesta won as "Best Actor."

Directed by Alberto Rodríguez, who also co-wrote the screenplay, the movie casts non-professional actors, each selected at local high schools throughout Spain, as Tano's friends. The acting is surprisingly good—especially so, considering that these kids are non-actors. The character of Tano's comrade-in-crime, Richi (Jesus Carroza), is effectively played and his rich character is even more reckless than Tano as they commit petty thefts and engage in a lot of boozing and drug taking, even an attempted rape.

Variety claimed that *7 Virgins* is the best Spanish movie of its type since Fernando Leon's *Barrio* in 1998.

Gay audiences will wish that these boys were a little more queer, but, alas, they're not. Nonetheless, the film attracted large audiences of gays in Spain, a country that has become amazingly liberal in the post-Franco era, even allowing same-sex marriages.

 ## WHAT THE CRITICS SAID

"*7 Virgins* is a discouragingly senseless 48-hour journey into a world of teenage hooliganism and criminality in the company of a pair of amoral losers. The film's only point seems to be that one youth is self-aware while the other one isn't. The film has little commercial interest."
The Hollywood Reporter

"*Virgins* should snuggle up in plenty of fest beds, with art-house interest a certainty in Spanish-friendly territories. Dialogue is often the insubstantial, rat-a-tat vernacular of street kids wanting to be men, but reflective moments shatter the veneer of teen machismo to expose the fragility beneath."
Variety

A Scene from *7 Virgenes*

SHE'S THE MAN
Girls Can Do Anything Boys Can Do

When she learns that her high school is dropping its girls' soccer program, she-jock Viola Hastings (Amanda Bynes) decides to join the boys' team. And how does she do that? She disguises herself as her "twin" brother, Sebastian (James Kirk). She's aided by her stylist sidekick, Paul (Jonathan Sadowski, a dead ringer for Jude Law), who helps her butch it up. The film's original working title was *Walk Like a Man, Talk Like a Man.*

Her befuddled teammate is Duke (Channing Tatum), who's a real hunk. He wants Olivia (Laura Ramsey), a fellow schoolmate. But Olivia seems attracted to Sebastian/Viola, who develops a crush on Duke because he/she speaks with such sensitivity about women.

Stated another way, Duke wants Olivia who likes Sebastian who is really Viola whose brother is dating Monique (Alexandra Breckenridge), so she hates Olivia who's with Duke to make Sebastian jealous who is really Viola who's crushing on Duke who thinks she's a guy.

If this complicated plot sounds vaguely familiar, it's loosely based on Shakespeare's gender-bending *Twelfth Night*. And we mean *very* loosely based.

Bynes, of course, is the TV star of *What I Like About You.*   Elizabeth Weitzman of the *New York Daily News* got it right when she wrote: "As the Bard himself observed, 'some are born great, some achieve greatness and some have greatness thrust upon 'em.' Others should probably head back to TV, where greatness is optional." Or, put another way, he's a she and no great shakes.

Joel Siegel on ABC's *Good Morning America* claimed that Shakespeare ought to sue.

 ## WHAT THE CRITICS SAID

"The ensuing complications—romantic, social, sporty—are modeled on *Twelfth Night*, although the tone of the movie (hysterical peppiness) and style of acting (emphatic grotesquerie) are more suited to campy off-Broadway musicals, which is precisely where the director, Andy Fickman, hails from."
Nathan Lee
The New York Times

"Fickman mostly soft-pedals the play's homosexual panic, generating a comedy that lacks the verbal sophistication of its source and the sexual sophistication of its target audiences."
J.R. Jones
Chicago Reader

Gender-bending;
Amanda Bynes playing Sebastian (left) and Viola (right)

Above, Channing Tatum (left), with
Amanda Byrnes (right)

SHEM
Dallying With Men, Women & Drag Queens

This is a muddled stewpot with some sex (not hot) and kinkiness. Ash Newman, playing a teenage boy, Daniel, in Caroline Roboh's Shem, is very good looking—and at least that's something. One bright day in London, this bratty 19-year-old decides to abandon his two lovers—a mother-and-son combo. Incidentally, Mrs. Roboh, the scripter and producer, plays the older woman that Newman ditches.

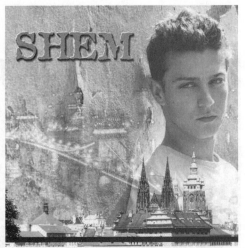

Quitting his job in advertising, he stops in to see his grandmother. This eccentric matriarch (Hadassah Hungar Diamant) sends Daniel on a wild goose chase to locate her father's grave. The search takes him through Paris, Berlin, Prague, Budapest, Belgrade, and Sofia.

The old lady's papa died in 1939, and she is eager to learn the whereabouts of his grave. In looking for it, our handsome but arrogant prick dallies with both sexes and some drag queens of unknown gender. One man blindfolds him and ties him up. "I'm not gay," he says to Daniel, "I like to play." Daniel seems ready to have sex with anybody, but turns down a trio of under-age girls he's presented with in a brothel in Sofia.

Our final verdict. Newman is a poor man's Jonathan Rhys-Meyers.

Yes, there are some night train hookups and bisexual disco dancing.

WHAT THE CRITICS SAID

"As a travelogue, Shem (which means 'name' in Hebrew) is pleasant. It just might send you packing for Eastern Europe. As a narrative, Shem, directed by Caroline Roboh, is a pointless hodge-podge with a finale that will leave viewers scratching their heads."
V.A. Musetto
New York Post

"Shem is a real shanda."
Time Out New York

"Daniel's looks may charm everyone who crosses his path, but he is like the movie: Most of the depth that does exist remains buried beneath the surface."
Laura Kern
The New York Times

"A bizarre hybrid between Euro erotic thriller and a parable of Jewish awakening."
Ken Fox
TV Guide

love and kisses

"How many Rocky sequels can he make?"
                    -Arnold Schwarzenegger,
                         on Sylvester Stallone

SHOCK TO THE SYSTEM
Film Noir Private Dick Goes Gay With Vanilla BF

In the wake of the release of *Brokeback Mountain,* Chad Allen, who plays Donald Strachey in this crime drama, told the press: "Until *Brokeback*, there was a huge fear or belief that you couldn't tell a story with a gay hero and have it make money. A well-made movie with a good story trumps everything. It's not just a victory for gay rights. It's a victory for humanity."

Though not totally satisfying as a thriller, *Shock to the System* is refreshing entertainment for gays. Writing under the pseudonym of Richard Stevenson, Richard Lipez launched the series with his 1981 novel, *Death Trick.* The mystery introduced Donald Strachey, a gay private investigator like Bogie in the 40s. He walks the mean streets of Albany, not New York City.

Shock to the System is the second Donald Strachey mystery to be adapted for film. The first of the series was *Third Man Out.*

Cast as Strachey's loving vanilla boyfriend (or husband) is Sebastian Spence, with Nelson Wong playing an enthusiastic assistant. Incidentally, our gay private eye makes his first big appearance bobbing up from his husband's lap.

The plot gets rolling when Strachey is hired by a nervous young man who promptly turns up dead.

Morgan Fairchild appears in a freakish cameo. Canuck helmer Ron Oliver (*Queer as Folk*) in this film noir cast Dr. Cornell (Michael Woods) as a shady type who runs a gay "reparative therapy" center.

A detour involves Stachey's first love, an Army buddy during the Gulf War. The subplot seems designed to poke fun at the stupid "don't-ask-don't-tell" policy.

We don't know what Dashiell Hammett or Raymond Chandler would have to say about bringing a gay twist to their old film noir genre.

Of course, some viewers wanted more sex in *Shock*, though there is some gay hanky panky and a steamy shower scene.

Even if you don't like the movie, gay viewers can enjoy that handful of naked football players in the shower.

 WHAT THE CRITICS SAID

"Filmmakers are aiming for a gay *noir.* Unfortunately, what they settle for is less Mickey Spillane than movie of the week. The lack of grittiness in this would-be hard-boiled thriller is underscored by the pre-naturally clean streets of 'Albany,' which look suspiciously safe and Canadian. Where film noir is often punch-drunk with a jab of snappy patter and a left hook of world-weary cynicism, *Shock* tries to clinch with understanding."
  Michael Ordoña
  Los Angeles Times

Above, left and right. Chad Allen

Above, left and center, Sebastian Spence; *right,* Chad Allen

SHORTBUS

Fresh-Faced Actors and Fetishists Perform with Their Genitals

In Cannes at the annual film festival, *Hedwig* creator John Cameron Mitchell insisted that all the orgasms in *Shortbus* be real—not faked.

We believe him too. In one of the opening scenes, a dude sucks himself off. We get to see that and even the jizz. It sure didn't look faked.

His *Shortbus*, perhaps the most provocative and controversial A-list film released in 2006, is a sexually explicit portrait of New York artists and flotsam/jetsam bohemians on a comic and cosmic quest for "connections."

One of the film's settings is a free-loving Manhattan salon where a hip crowd gathers to converse and share body fluids.

Justin Bond of the fabled Kiki & Herb cabaret act is the only big name star in this farce, and he delivers the real standout performance. He is the club's gay host who describes the venue as "just like the 1960s, except with less hope."

Among the chief characters in this candid sex tale is Sofia (Sook-Yin Lee), a sex therapist. Her big problem involves telling her husband Rob (Raphael Barker) that she's never had an orgasm.

Two lovers, James (Paul Dawson) and Jamie (P.J. DeBoy), bring in a third dude, Ceth (Jay Brannan), to spice up their relationship of five years. All this is being video-recorded by the voyeur, Caleb (Peter Stickles), in an apartment across the street.

Lindsay Beamish makes an appearance as Severin, a dominatrix, an artsy Midwesterner who disguises her insecurities and loneliness behind the whip of her adopted trade.

Now for the most provocative scene in the movie. It's not the sex but the appearance of an elderly gent who claims he was once the city's closeted mayor.

Did you know that New York once had a gay mayor? We forget his name.

The tagline for this shocker might be, "You're either on the bus, or you're off the bus," that rallying cry of 60s counterculture.

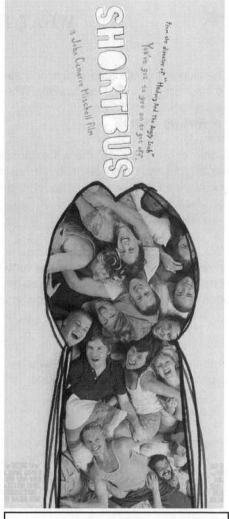

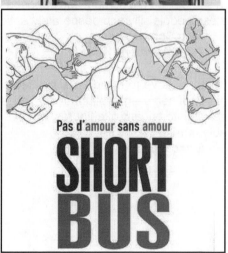

Pas d'amour sans amour

"By taking sex out of the Hollywood safe zone and exposing it to therapy-speak, Mitchell may be inadvertently killing its mystery. Where's the pleasure in that? But if there is such a thing as hardcore with a soft heart, this is it."
Rolling Stone

"Some viewers will call the whole business pornography, though it doesn't really qualify. The sex is blunt and enthusiastic, but arousing it ain't. In fact, when *Shortbus* arrives on DVD, viewers may be fast forwarding through the sex to get to the acting."
Jack Mathews
New York Daily News

"'We all get it in the end,' Bond sings during the film's closing moments. It's the perfect double entendre for a dreamy, deliciously dirty film that not only finds tremendous hope in the power of doing it till you're satisfied but also deeply mourns the fact that New Yorkers realize real death often looms much larger than *la petite mort*."
Melissa Anderson
Time Out New York

"And though Mitchell is wonderfully democratic in his openness to all sexual categories, it has to be said that his heterosexual men are the movie's least convincing, and sketchiest, figures."
David Ansen
Newsweek

"The participants demonstrate, as per the impish intentions of the man who invented the brilliant *Hedwig and the Angry Inch,* that inserting tab A into slot B is as unremarkable a daily activity as brushing one's teeth. Except maybe funnier, if that diddles your funny bone. It'd be dishonest not to disclose that it doesn't diddle mine, not the way Mitchell has in mind. If I'm going to see sex on the screen—as opposed to the brushing of teeth—I want something hotter. I find these people silly and desperately antic."
Lisa Schwarzbaum
Entertainment Weekly

"It takes nerve to make un-simulated sex boring, but John Cameron Mitchell has always had plenty of nerve—gumption, even. The 'actors' in *Shortbus* have fantastic bodies and twist themselves into origami-like figures, but every time they speak they say something utterly unbelievable or trite."
Isaac Guzman

SIDELINE SECRETS

Romance, Suspense & Secrets

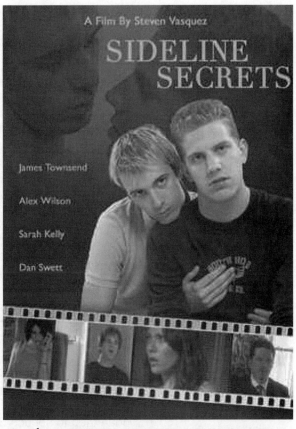

Call it 80 minutes of gay erotic drama.

It's far from the innocent film it first appears to be. It contains a bevy of taboos—child molestation, murder, street hustling, kidnapped boys, lesbianism. There's also a lot of frontal nudity among boys who look barely legal, but they're strangely not erotic, incapable of producing a hard-on even among the excessively horny.

Stephen Vasquez both directed and co-scripted this feature film with help from another writer, James Townsend, who also plays the lead character, a blond high schooler, Devon Tyler.

As the film begins, Devon seemingly has a nearly perfect life, with a girlfriend and middle-class parents who include a stepfather who works as a psychologist. Devon is about to graduate at the top of his class, but something is wrong. Perhaps it's the far and distant longing reflected in his eyes.

As he becomes more aware of his sexual identity, his girlfriend grows more overbearing. By this point in the film, the viewer has realized that this boyfriend/girlfriend team evokes "sisterhood" more than it does heterosexual passion.

Devon's mother seems to genuinely love her son, and perhaps his stepfather does too, but not in ways that are socially acceptable. Could there possibly be a hidden camera in Devon's bedroom, keeping a pictorial record of his frequent masturbation?

A new boy, Brian (Alex Wilson), enters the picture. He's even handsomer than the rather bland Devon and has far more charm and personal magnetism. As a sexual liaison develops between the two young men, Devon's life begins to unravel,

The stepfather kicks Devon out of the house when he learns of his homosexuality. (Despite his role as a psychologist, he doesn't seem to have much cool...what a hypocrite.) As the viewer begins to suspect, the psychologist doesn't object too strenuously to some white boy ass from time to time.

The melodrama, especially the violent conclusion, unfolds without conviction. The forced happy ending is just that . . . forced. Still the film is an amusement worth a momentary diversion, especially if you're sitting around with a group of gay friends and have had a drink or two.

Joan tried to seduce Bette, but not here in
What Ever Happened to Baby Jane? (1962)

THE SILVER SCREEN
COLOR ME LAVENDER

Spot the Closet Cases Within Golden Age Films—Randolph Scott & Cary Grant for Instance

Filmmaker Mark Rappaport brought us *Rock Hudson's Home Movies* in 1992. He did it again with this 100-minute docu that unearths gay highlights within dimly remembered films from the so-called Golden Age of Hollywood, when a certain kind of love dared not speak its name.

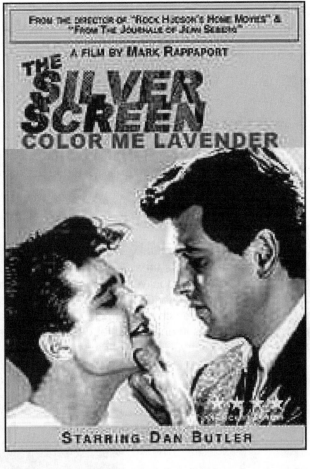

The film examines the various subterfuges that screenwriters and actors used to slyly depict "perverted" love. Between around 1930 up to the end of the 60s, this was done through the use of oblique references and double entendres which usually fooled the "uninitiated," but which were very clear to hipsters. By the end of the 60s, however, many members of the moviegoing public had become a lot better educated about what was coming Out of the Hollywood factory.

Rappaport himself wrote, directed, and edited this docu, using a narration by Dan Butler, described in the publicity material as an "outspoken gay actor." Butler, of course, is also known for playing the skirt-chasing womanizer on the hit sitcom *Frasier.*

Rappaport sees gay where only gays, not the general public, might see it. Were there really homosexual undercurrents between Bob Hope and Bing Crosby in all those Road pictures? Of course, they did kiss a few times, but presumably, whenever it happened, it was a mistake. The usual prissy character actors of the 30s are highlighted, including Franklin Pangborn, Edward Everett Horton, and Eric Blore.

Was Walter Brennan really gay when he played those grizzled old sidekicks to such macho stars as Humphrey Bogart, Gary Cooper, and John Wayne? Maybe he fell in love with these boys when they took out their dicks to piss together in the desert.

Film noir was riddled with gay and lesbian subcurrents, and scenes from that strange triangle of Lizabeth Scott, Wendell Corey, and John Hodiak in the 1945 *Desert Fury* do make a point. It's a treat to watch lavender undercurrents between Alain Delon and Jean Marais at the peak of their male beauty in films by Jean Cocteau (he was in love with Marais) and Luchino Visconti.

Two other suspects from the 1930s, "roomies" Randolph Scott and Cary Grant, are also identified. There's mention of a breakthrough film, the 1947 *Crossfire*, which was about a bigoted Army sergeant who kills a Jew. In the novel upon which the film was based, the victim was gay. But when they brought it to the screen, Hollywood decided it was better to designate a Jew as the victim instead of a homo.

Silver Screen is worth watching but *The Celluloid Closet* does it better.

WHAT THE CRITICS SAID

"Rappaport observes through Butler that the old films are rich with relationships, dialogue, glances and other bits of action susceptible to interpretation as being freighted with homosexuality. And when these moments are presented out of context, the assertion gains force. But at times, listening to the narration is like being in the company of adolescents who can find sexual innuendo anywhere."
Lawrence van Gelder
The New York Times

"*Silver Screen* is a sort of funky, cerebral twin to *The Celluloid Closet*, a cross between a sardonic grin and a master's thesis. Rappaport's manner of suggesting without asserting makes *The Silver Screen* so seductive. If he just came out and said that Walter Brennan was coming on to Gary Cooper, he'd instantly arouse skepticism, but by leaving out the final link, he forces his audience to become complicit in the process of making connections. What closes that final link is desire, and it's in engaging that desire that *Silver Screen* begins to seem less like history and more like poetry."
citypaper.net

Dan Butler

A SOAP

Danish Trannie Addicted to American Soaps

In Danish with English subtitles, Pernille Fischer Christensen's debut feature is not for everyone, but is a worthwhile diversion, especially for women.

Newly single Charlotte (Trine Dyrholm), in her 30s, moves into a decaying neighborhood in an unnamed Danish city. She has grown unfulfilled in her relationship with Kristian (Frank Thiel). It's good-bye b.f. and hello Veronica (David Dencik), her neighbor.

Veronica is an introverted transsexual dominatrix who prefers to keep the real world at a distance. "She" takes female hormones and is waiting gender-reassignment surgery. "Johns" pay for Veronica's skills in punishing them for being bad boys.

From this unlikely scenario, a relationship develops between Charlotte and Veronica. Before meeting Veronica, Charlotte engages in one-night stands and shows no interest in post-coital small talk. This suggests she has little interest in men, except for Veronica downstairs who was born Ulrik.

Kristian comes over one night and turns violent toward Charlotte, but Veronica rescues her. Could this be the beginning of a new friendship, even an intimate one? Incidentally, Veronica is addicted to American style soap operas—hence, the title of this flick.

Chapters of the movie are introduced by an announcer who asks, "Why is it so hard for her to find happiness?"

 WHAT THE CRITICS SAID

"At critical moments in their desperately lonely lives, Charlotte and Veronica rescue each other from harm, and their mutual acts of generosity seal a friendship deepened by their shared loneliness. But could such a friendship really flower into passion? Not likely."
Stephen Holden
The New York Times

"*Soap* flirts with Dogma 95 austerity, but really suggests what a daytime drama might be like if it were inhabited by actual human beings."
Don Avery
Time Out New York

"As common-or-garden realism, *Soap* works exceptionally well, handling what might sound like an outré setup with easy nonchalance. Pic's best moments are when its thesps seem to be doing the least acting—padding around their houses, watching TV, or talking casually—while complex feelings simmer just under the surface."
Russell Edwards
Variety

John Dall (left) and Farley Granger, both of whom were queer in real life, playing queer in *Rope* (1948). Hitchcock based this film, starring James Stewart, on the notorious Leopold and Loeb murder case that occurred in Chicago in 1924.

STAGESTRUCK:
GAY THEATER IN THE 20TH CENTURY
From Oscar Wilde to Tennessee Williams to Larry Kramer

Gay men, of course, have always been attracted to the theater where, or so it is said, entire worlds can be invented and the self reinvented.

That is exactly what happens in this three-part docu by David Jeffcock. The film shows how playwrights beginning with Oscar Wilde and going on to Noel Coward skewered society's mores, dressing up true stories of gay life in straight clothing. These two stately homos might be accused of inventing the language of camp.

As time went by and the theater became more implicit in its depiction of homosexuality, a whole new generation of play-

wrights emerged, including William Inge and Tennessee Williams, giving way in time to Edward Albee and Joe Orton, who gave way to Tony Kushner and Larry Kramer. In fact, Kramer and Kushner appear in this docu as themselves.

There are also interviews with Albee and Martin Sherman, as well as scenes from *Private Lives, Who's Afraid of Virginia Woolf?* and *Torch Song Trilogy*.

Madly in love with the theater, *Stagestruck* is not just for drama queens.

 WHAT THE CRITICS SAID

"The mid-twentieth century would see enormous success for gay playwrights like Terrence Rattigan and Tennessee Williams, but also a proliferation of work that portrayed homosexuality as corrupt and corrupting, with most gay characters either dead before the curtain rose or about to die before it fell. With Edward Albee, Joe Orton, and countless others, the modern, liberated gay stage illuminates the complexities of gay life, including the AIDS epidemic."
Mark Taylor

"Ronald Reagan doesn't dye his hair. He's just prematurely orange."

President Gerald Ford in 1974

"It's our own fault. We should have given him better parts."

Studio mogul **Jack Warner**,
on learning that Reagan had
been elected governor
of California

Rudolf Nureyev as Valentino

STARDUST: THE BETTE DAVIS STORY

Uncompromising, Peppery, Intractable, Monomaniacal, Tactless, Volatile, Disagreeable & Larger Than Life

Fasten your seat belts, as you're in for a bumpy ride in this TV bio first aired on Turner Classic Movies with narration by Susan Sarandon. Emmy-winning helmer, Peter Jones, along with Mark A. Catalena, pulled together this cigarette-twirling, ball-breaking homage to the great film diva, with Jones also doing the scripting.

They had unprecedented access to Davis's personal archives and were granted many original interviews, although it's hard to come up with a lot of new stuff about a woman whose life has already been so heavily investigated by biographers.

Stardust emerges as an excellent docu about one of the greatest stars of the so-called golden era. Davis herself would have rewritten that line as: "I was <u>the</u> greatest star—not <u>one</u> of the greatest."

In archival footage appear such characters as Bette's own Mommie Dearest, Ruthie Davis. We also get "memories" from B.D. Hyman, who wrote a tell-all book about her mother called *My Mother's Keeper*, seven years after Christina Crawford libeled Joan in her notorious portrait, *Mommie Dearest*. A relatively loving and charitable son, Michael Merrill, is also interviewed, admitting that Davis did take a drink or two on occasion.

The late Vincent Sherman, Davis's director and lover, also weighs in, along with Ellen Burstyn and Jane Fonda. In archival footage, George Arliss appears (he made *The Man Who Played God* with Bette in 1932). We're also treated to archival footage of Bette's boss, the dreaded Jack L. Warner.

The most stunning revelations—and told with obvious venom—come from Marion Richards, Davis's maid who married her boss's ex-husband, William Grant Sherry. She leaves the impression that Davis was implicated in the death of her second husband, Arthur Farnsworth, in 1943. The poor man died of head injuries, but from whom?

Davis's greatest triumphs are carefully documented, including her participation in William Wyler's *Jezebel* and the film that earned her first Oscar, *Dark Victory*, a role Garbo turned down. We also see Davis in *Now Voyager* (the two cigarette moon-and-stars thing), and in *The Little Foxes*, which Tallulah Bankhead had used previously as a vehicle for success on Broadway.

The directors could hardly leave out Bette Davis's crowning achievement, the role of Margo Channing in the 1950 *All About Eve*. Fox called Davis in at the last minute to take over the role of Margo. Originally, the studio had cast Claudette Colbert, who had to drop out because of a back injury. That year, Davis and Gloria Swanson, playing Norma Desmond in *Sunset Blvd.*, lost the Oscar to lesbian actress Judy Holliday in *Born Yesterday*. A shame, really. We only wish the Oscars could have been a tie that year between Ms. Channing and Ms. Desmond. Neither Swanson nor Davis had ever played such spectacular roles before, and, alas, never would again.

And, of course, we get *What Ever Happened to Baby Jane?* with her nemesis, Lady Crawford. Stardust reveals what we already know—that Bette Davis hated Joan Crawford. Yet they came together for a shooting schedule of only 21 days in *Baby Jane*, Joan's first picture in four years. Both were smart enough to know that they had to get along, and both of these fading stars needed a hit.

On learning of Joan's death, Bette said. "You should never say bad things about the dead. You should only say good. Joan Crawford is dead, good."

Aside from *All About Eve* or *Baby Jane*, what gay man can resist Bette's campy portrait of Rosa Moline in *Beyond the Forest* (1949)? It provided Davis impersonators with the immortal line, "WHAT A DUMP!"

Actually Davis was as big as the movies themselves and often bigger than many of her lesser efforts. Her life was stormy both on and off the screen. The docu attempts to deal with some myths, including the one that Davis was "never considered as a candidate in anybody's mind"—but her own—to play Scarlett O'Hara in *Gone With the Wind*.

Bette Davis died in France at the age of 81 in 1989 when the man she called "little Ronnie Reagan" was presiding over the Free World.

She did not live to see a certain biographer suggest she had a lesbian past.

 WHAT THE CRITICS SAID

"The gay sensibility is brought home by author James McCourt, Charles Busch, and a gem of a clip of Charles Pierce doing his famous impersonation. Trivia: Davis's tombstone reads, 'She did it the hard way.' This portrait of her tumultuous life certainly reflects that."
   Christopher Harrity
   The Advocate

"When *Stardust* isn't demonstrating what made Davis great, it is allowing her to speak for herself in television interviews with Dick Cavett, Jack Paar, Phil Donahue, and others. 'I never cared how I looked, as long as I looked like the character,' she said in one exchange."
   Anita Gates
   The New York Times

STONED
The Wild and Wicked World of Brian Jones

This movie extends the legend of Brian Jones. When historians record those glorious days of the 1960s, surely they will anoint Jones, the guitarist for the Rolling Stones, as "The Pied Piper of 1960s Hedonism." He deserves the title.

Officially, the 1969 death of Brian Jones was defined as an "accidental drowning under the influence of drugs and alcohol." His death electrified the world, and is still the subject of controversy. His body was found in the swimming pool of his country cottage.

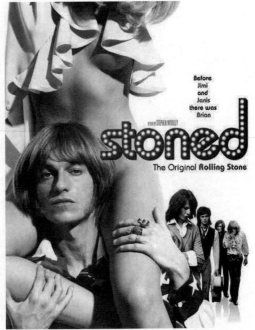

Rumors of foul play persist to this day, spawning three books and now this docu-drama, which runs for 102 minutes. Brian's building contractor reportedly confessed to the murder before he died in 1993, at least according to the film's producer and director, Stephen Woolley.

Lee Gregory plays the flamboyant Jones, and Paddy Considine is cast as Frank Thorogood, his assistant and possible murderer. The movie does not adequately explore the bisexual undertones of this relationship between the working class (and married) bloke and the dissipated, foppish rock star. There is a lot of tension between these two principals that seems to remain unresolved. Gay viewers would probably have appreciated more diss on the homosexuality of Jones.

Like Marilyn, Jones was "the blond one" who died young. MM might have left a beautiful memory, but the legacy of Jones is vague and blurred, especially in this docu. Historically, Jones is credited with founding the Rolling Stones in 1962, but was kicked out in 1969.

That Jones had talent is undisputed. That he was fucked up in the head is also undisputed. Woolley spent nearly 10 years investigating the death of the dead Stone, and thinks he's come up with the answer—that is, murder. With this docu, Woolley is making his directorial debut.

Jones was also unlucky in love with women. He was devastated when his great love, Anita Pallenberg (Monet Mazur), left him for Keith Richards.

Appearing only as shadowy figures are Keith Richards (Ben Whishaw) and Mick Jagger (Luke De Woolfson).

The film includes full frontal male and female nudity and frequent graphic sex. Naturally, there is constant drug use and profanity, plus the requisite violence as Brian beats the shit out of his girlfriend.

 WHAT THE CRITICS SAID

"*Stoned*, a fictionalized portrait of Jones' last days, goes over the same ground that's been covered in many other drug-and-orgy movies about celebrities, and with its low budget, unadventurous script and notable lack of any Stones' recordings, it has the look and feel of a TV movie. Still, *Stoned* carries a freaked-out buzz of nostalgia for the era when celebs willfully destroyed themselves for our amusement."

Kyle Smith
New York Post

Lee Gregory as rock star Brian Jones

SUN KISSED
Sexy, But Surreal & Oh Mama, That Garden Hose

When we stopped over in the Castro area of San Francisco in the summer of 2006, the most watched film among gay men was *Sun Kissed*, a drama/romance scripted and helmed by Patrick McGuinn. After sitting through this movie with its hallucinogenic plotline, the question might be asked—why?

The boys are beautiful, and the director doesn't believe in providing them with shirts. That's the good news. The bad news is this flick is hard to follow.

Teddy (John Ort) is a young writer who ventures to an isolated desert house owned by his professor in southeastern California. There he plans to write a novel.

Instead of undertaking that vast project, however, he becomes enthralled with a handsome and possibly bisexual caretaker, Leo (Gregory Marcel). Leo just might also be murderous. Teddy seduces the mysterious caretaker. Layers of memory and hallucinations unfold that intertwine the two studs, neither of whom is ashamed to show off his physical assets.

The two hotties like to battle each other with a garden hose.

You can file this bit of information under "Who cares?" Director McGuinn is the son of Roger of the Byrds. As a reviewer pointed out, someone must care about this biographical tidbit because the press material mentioned it repeatedly.

 WHAT THE CRITICS SAID

"When a movie aspires to be gay pornography, but can't even manage that, well, you know you've got a bad movie. The film, about five minutes' worth of plot stretched to more than an hour and a half, tells its thin tale with clumsy dialogue, clumsy editing and clumsy cinematography. At least it's consistent."
Neil Genzlinger
The New York Times

"The scenes of these super-hot guys hosing each other down to cool off will likely distract you long enough that you probably won't even care that the plot is hard to follow."
Instinct

ROSEANNE BARR (during her divorce): "Tom Arnold's penis is three inches long. Okay, I'll say four, 'cause we're trying to settle."

TOM ARNOLD (replying to Roseanne): "Even a 747 looks small when it lands in the Grand Canyon."

ROSEANNE (post-Tom): "I'm not upset about my divorce. I'm only upset I'm not a widow."

10 ATTITUDES

Romantic Tragic-Comedy Explores 10 Chances for Love

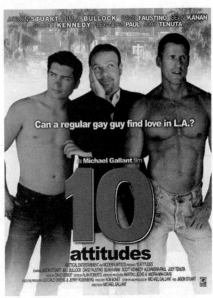

In a quick one-line summary, what is this film about? It's the story of a Jewish man who discovers that throughout the previous decade, his boyfriend has been cheating on him. Josh Stevens, as played by Jason Stuart, discovers his boyfriend, Lyle (Rusty Updegraff), getting head in his red Jaguar convertible from a boy ten years his junior. The tagline for the film is, "Can a regular gay guy find love in L.A."

Making his directorial debut with this low-budget quickie is Michael Gallant, who co-wrote the script with his leading man, Jason Stuart, not an unheard of situation. If you don't mind the grainy, poor quality of the film, you might have some fun with this flick.

Actor/comedian Stuart brings a certain pixie-like charm to the role of Josh, playing a "pushing 40" gay male who came to California from conservative Cleveland a decade earlier. With him was his significant other, Lyle, who adapts to the L.A. scenes more quickly than Josh, who isn't able to yank up his Midwestern values by the roots.

Devastated by the news that his lover is a back alley slut, Josh is comforted by his best friend, Brandon, as played by Christopher Cowen. Brandon persuades Josh that all he needs is a series of ten dates—hence, the title, *10 Attitudes*—to find Mr. Right or Prince Charming—take your choice. Consequently, Josh hits the Internet looking for love.

But first, he gets some fashion advice from the wildly flamboyant Tex, as played by Jim J. Bullock. Bullock was the voice of Queer Duck in Icebox.com's *Queer Duck* series. In 2005-06 he appeared as Wilbur Turnblad in the U.S. touring company production of *Hairspray*.

In an interview in 2004, he said, "I don't mind playing anything as long as it's work." Bullock is best known for the TV comedy series, *Too Close for Comfort*. He is also known for appearing on the *Jim J.*

and Tammy Faye Show, in which he told the world that the stricken evangelist used to survive just on chocolate cake and Diet coke.

Josh dreads dragging his paunch and his aging face into the shark-infested dating pool of West Hollywood, but he bravely ventures forth. Since the film is set in West Hollywood, the men he meets on his dates tend to be either hustler/actors or actor/hustlers. If not that, then an actor/waiter or a waiter/actor/hustler/druggie.

Everybody in town seems to be on the make, including a hunky salesman in a men's store willing to service Josh if he's got $200 bucks on him.

One of Josh's dates is Billy or "Attitude 3," actually David Faustino of *Married With Children* fame. Billy presents Josh with a proposal he just can't handle. Billy isn't looking for a boyfriend but rather a gay guy to serve as person number three in the threesome his girlfriend demands, as she's turned on by watching two men get it on.

Before the end of the film, Josh ends up kissing more than his share of frogs in his search for "the man of my dreams."

"Shot on video with no budget, *10 Attitudes* comes to a sudden conclusion with the kind of cinematic coincidence that makes it seem like the crew ran out of time and had to wrap things up that very afternoon. It's a clunky ending, but the journey to it is lighthearted enough to keep you interested in and amused by Josh's predicament. One mystery remains, however. If West Hollywood really is this bad, why are there so many people around to make so many movies about it? Why hasn't everyone just packed up and moved away?"

Don Willmott
Filmcritic.com

"While this film is in no way an award-winning film, and there are definitely no prize performances here, it is an enjoyable film. It is a film that touches on issues that impact everyone . . . NOT just the gay/lesbian community. Stronger performances from a few of the 'Attitudes,' a bit higher production value and a bit of script editing and this film would have entered the C range. Even at a C-, I'd say it's worth a view."

Richard Propes

Jason Stuart

THIS FILM IS NOT YET RATED
An Exposé About the American Movie Ratings Board

Would it surprise you that the notorious and much-despised Motion Picture Association of America, which rates films, includes a motley collection of straight "concerned parents," with opinions often provided by Catholic priests?

Almost any form of violence is acceptable, but gay sex is often deemed as "aberrational behavior." Except for *Brokeback Mountain*, nearly all indie films that feature some male/male action get an NC-17 rating, limiting their release and advertising. In many ways, helmer Kirby Dick makes U.S. censors look like the asses that Michael Moore made of the Bush family.

Some things are just too wild for the censors, including threesomes *(The Dreamers, American Psycho)*, oral sex *(Boys Don't Cry)* and "gay stuff" such as *Where the Truth Lies* and *Mysterious Skin*. Most filmmakers detest the MPAA, and with good reason.

Using archival footage, Dick has assembled an all-star cast with the likes of Pierce Brosnan, Richard Burton, Tom Cruise (that very heterosexual actor), Robert De Niro, Sandy Dennis, Michael Douglas, Jane Fonda, William Holden, Jeremy Irons, Jessica Lange, William H. Macy, Michael Pitt, George Segal, Kevin Spacey, Hilary Swank, Sharon Stone, Elizabeth Taylor, and Jon Voigt (Mr. *Midnight Cowboy* himself). Of course you expect John Waters to get into the act, but John Wayne?

 ## WHAT THE CRITICS SAID

"Kirby obviously has a soft spot in his heart for queer filmmakers, beginning his film with the travails Kimberly Peirce faced in releasing her Academy Award-winning *Boys Don't Cry*. He compares, for example, the sexual content of Peirce's film, which received an NC-17, with the hetero hominess of *American Pie*, which skated by with an R. The MPAA, which emerges in Kirby's film as a creature of the Hollywood studios, wraps itself in a cloak of morality. But like so much in the United States, what the MPAA presents as protecting children is much more about protecting profits. And it's clear that gay visibility on the silver screen suffers from Hollywood's greed."

Patrick Moore
The Advocate

389

"Back when Tab [Hunter] and Tony [Perkins] were real close, the story was that Tab told Tony, "Someday you'll make a fine actor." And Tony was supposed to have answered, "I already have. Several of them."

-Sal Mineo

Marilyn Monroe, Truman Capote

THIS FILTHY WORLD

John Waters' Torch Song: Trash as Art

"The first time I met Richard Simmons, I felt homophobic," John Waters confesses in this 90-minute docu. Helmer John Garlin brings us the fabulous world of this outrageous director. It was filmed over a two-night period at the Harry De Jur Playhouse on the Lower East Side of New York. And how lucky we are it was.

Even if you know Waters only through his Tony-winning musical, *Hairspray*, based on his 1988 film, you'll want to catch him "live" in this docu. After you do, we predict you'll go out and rent such notorious pictures by Waters as *Pink Flamingos* (1972) and *Polyester* (1981).

After all, Waters directed Tab Hunter in his comeback, and even introduced us to dog shit-eating Divine, the divine cross-dresser who defined the word slut.

Who but Waters could bring together a cast that in 2000 included Ricki Lake, Maggie Gyllenhaal, Melanie Griffith, and even Patricia Hearst for *Cecil B. Demented*.

Waters has a wonderful self-mocking style. He name-drops but in an amazingly kind way. He has a brilliant talent for delivering small, droll stories, and even lets us know that a fellow Baltimorean called him an "asshole."

    WHAT THE CRITICS SAID

"Those who think of the director, John Waters, only as a sicko, a wacko, a pervert, a psycho, a multi-fetishist, a deviant, a menace and/or a nut job will be surprised to discover, through *This Filthy World*, that he would also make an excellent dinner party guest. True, the other guests would need to have a tolerance for stories about singing rectums, but still, the guy is a raconteur of the first order."
Neil Genzlinger
The New York Times

"Zsa-Zsa Gabor is a cop socker."

Debbie Reynolds, after Gabor slapped a
Beverly Hills police officer.

"Is she making fun of *me* darling? Is that really nasty? I think she
looked better in her *old* movies."

Zsa Zsa, about Debbie

Are they or aren't they?

3 GUYS, 1 GIRL, 2 WEDDINGS

(3 GARÇONS, 1 FILLE, 2 MARRIAGES)

A New Look at the Boy-Wants-Boy-Who-Wants-Girl Theme

This 90-minute film is light, it's French, it's campy and somewhat stereotypical, and an amusing diversion. First released in France in 2004, and directed by first-time helmer Stéphane Clavier, it gives a slightly new twist to a time-tested theme, all the while inserting supportive comments about gay relationships and gay marriages. It's worth a look, and it's now available on Home Video, in French but with Spanish and English subtitles (take your pick).

Dan (Olivier Sitruk) and Laurent (Arnaud Giovaninetti) are best friends and roommates. Dan, a womanizer and professed "commitment-phobe," hosts a radio show called "Let's Talk Sex." And whereas Dan has a new girlfriend every week, Laurent is in love with his roomie. The plot thickens when Dan meets Miss Right, Camille (Julie Gayeet).

Laurent, horrified at the prospect of losing Dan, mournfully makes arrangements to move in a lesbian roommate "Sam" (Anne Azoulay). The insensitive Dan asks Laurent to be his best man at his wedding. As a reaction, Laurent steps up a campaign to scare Dan away from marriage. He sends Dan to meet Camille's parents, and even writes letters to Dan pretending to be an old girlfriend. He'll stop at nothing in his campaign to convert Dan from the straight-and-narrow path, even wearing Camille's wedding dress to a rally for legalizing gay marriages in France.

Hipper than her prospective groom, Camille is aware that Laurent has the hots for her husband-to-be, and encourages Dan to try gay sex as a means of determining if he's making the right choice between a male partner and a female bride.

The results are . . . . We can't really give away the plot, such as it is. But the ending includes two weddings, but you'll have to see the film to understand the significance of the title.

Many gay viewers have had to confront that "moment of truth" with a so-called straight roommate. If nothing else, this movie will remind us of that crucial turning point in our pasts--that is, if we want to be reminded.

 WHAT THE CRITICS SAID

"The story is fortunately executed in a fun way with clever twists and original turns that keep the movie from feeling formulaic. The plot moves along at a quick pace, and the soundtrack and editing give the film a lively *'Queer as Folk'* feel."
DVD Talk Review

"She likes men...I hear she never turns anything down except the bedcovers."

Mae West, referring to Jayne Mansfield

"If I look that good at sixty-four, I'll have no problems....[though] I think most of Miss West's curves now are from overeating."

Jayne Mansfield, referring to Mae West

300

A Gory Historical Drama with The World's Most Stunning Collection of Abs

Thousands of gay men, or so it is believed, will have viewed *300* before the end of its gory, well-publicized run. Although it contains a bit of sexuality and nudity, the reason *300* is on the Gay-Dar is because of the army of bare-chested men on voyeuristic display throughout the film. Talent scouts combed the world to find some of the most buffed actors ever to appear on camera.

The script calls for the male cast to spend the majority of their screen time showing their tits, as per Frank Miller's original graphic novel. To prepare themselves for the cameras as the best-trained and deadliest fighting force of the ancient world, the entire principal cast underwent a rigorous training regime for six weeks prior to shooting. The results are spectacular.

The 37-year-old Scottish actor, Gerard Butler, trained his body for eight months, six hours a day, to play the ultra-buffed King Leonidas. At one point Butler said he wished that he'd "never been born—I don't want to see another gym in my life." We know the actor from his role in *Phantom of the Opera*. He appears in *300* in a leather Speedo, which he fills out rather well.

The other Spartans on parade are certainly male beauties cast as holy warriors in their scarlet cloaks, loincloths, and sandals. Whether stuffed or the real thing, most of their leather pouches appear amply endowed. Did an actor have to be well hung to get cast as a Spartan?

The film is often a shot-for-shot adaptation of Frank Miller's comic book novel, similar to the film adaptation of *Sin City*, making extensive use of computer-generated imagery. The promo trailer for *300* was leaked onto the Internet on September 20, 2006, and gay men across the world were surfing the web for a look at those stout-hearted men on display.

Miller was inspired by the original 480 B.C. Battle of Thermopylae after viewing the 1962 film, *The 300 Spartans*, as a child. The Battle of Thermopylae was one of history's great last stands. Under King Leonidas, the Spartans bottled up the Persians in a narrow mountain pass by the sea—known as "The Gates of Hell"—and indeed it was. Their heroic defense for three days allowed other Greek forces to assemble, preventing a Persian takeover of the Hellenic lands—and thus, in effect, saving Western civilization.

If you remember from college history, the brave Spartans fought to the last man against the pagan Persian King Xerxes and his massive army from the east. The epic battle was the turning point in the Greco-Persian wars.

Zack Snyder, who helmed the 2004 remake of *Dawn of the Dead,* co-authored the screenplay with Kurt Johnstad and Michael B. Gordon. The whole film was shot in just 60 days, a bit less than it took to make another epic, Elizabeth Taylor's *Cleopatra*.

Violent death in the film is often choreographed as a ballet. Talk about heads rolling. More computer blood was used in this film than any other ever released. The decapitations are terribly stylized as necks virtually celebrate the liberation from their heads.

When the Persians warn the brave Spartans that their arrows will blot out the sun, the warrior heroes counter that they will fight in the shade. The director blasts the screen with some of the gaudiest, giddiest computer-generated effects seen in any post-millennium film.

The Persian king is played by Rodrigo Santoro. As Xerxes, he would definitely fit the bill of one of

Arnold Schwarzenegger's "girly men." One columnist thought the traveling throne of the god-king evoked "a louche Brazilian Gay Pride carnival float."

If you can take your eyes off those bare-chested hunks, you might enjoy the performance of Lena Headey as Queen Gorgo. She's the best thespian in the film and virtually the only woman. With beauty and confidence, she dominates the screen with a radiant femininity, and appears to have more balls than her adversary, Dominic West, cast as the evil Theron.

Headey is known for her roles in *Imagine Me & You* and in *The Brothers Grimm*. Before the director offered her the role of the queen, he considered both Sienna Miller and Silvia Colloca.

When the film opened across the nation, many seats were filled with both (straight) black men who liked the appeal of action movies and gay men who appreciate the Adonis-like beauty of many of the actors. In some screenings, members of these diverse groups cat-called to each other. Even in a New York's Chelsea district theater, the word "faggot" was frequently heard within the audience. This mixed audience enabled this bloody, ultra-violent film to take in a staggering $70 million in three days, the largest March opening ever. The movie was shot for a modest budget of $60 million.

Although it had been a commercial disappointment in the United States, *Troy*, starring another buffed star, Brad Pitt, earned nearly $500 million worldwide at the box office. *Troy* was released by Warner Brothers, as was *300*. Once again the Warner friars have a hit.

Like most Hollywood epics about actual historical events, scriptwriters took liberties—call it bloody license in the case of *300*. Actually 7,000 Greeks, not just the 300 Spartans, rallied to block the Persian invasion.

Xerxes is depicted as an effeminate madman, with a lot of body piercing, even though there is no historic evidence to support this caricature. In the movie, a Spartan hunchback is promised some good fucking if he betrays his comrades, which he does. Historically, the Spartans were indeed betrayed, but by a Malian Greek, not by a Spartan.

The film even inspired editorials across the nation, David Kahane asking in the *New York Post* if it contained "blatant homophobia"? In the film, it is suggested that the Athenians were boy-lovers, the Spartans manly men, fighting Oriental voluptuaries. Kahane even posed the provocative question: "Is *300* an ode to Riefenstahllian fascist militarism?"

The radical Islamic government in Iran blasted the blockbuster, asserting that the United States, through the film's worldwide release, had launched a cultural war against the Persians (read that "Iranians"). In a front-page article, the newspaper, *Ayandeh-No*, declared that the movie spreads the lie that Iran "has long been the source of evil, and modern Iran's ancestors are ugly, murderous savages."

The film's helmer, Snyder, has denied that *300* carries any hidden message. Even so, right-wingers in the United States denounced the film, claiming it was an attack on President Bush because it depicts the Spartan king as waging an illegal war.

Although some saw an anti-Bush subtext in the film, other viewers saw just the opposite—the story of a brave Western leader defying the barbarians of the East. What do we feel is the true message of the film as conceived by its Hollywood producers? Simply put, "Buy a god damn ticket!"

"The only way this bunch of refugees from a Village People show can whup our heroes is by dangling some dubious hookers in front of a horny hunchback who makes Quasimodo look like Tom Cruise."
National Review Online

"Possibly nowhere outside of gay porn have so many broad shoulders, bulging biceps and ripped torsos been seen on screen as in *300*, a fact that will generate a certain bonus audience of its own; it's not even certain Steve Reeves, the original Hercules, would have made the grade here."
Todd McCarthy
Variety

"*300* is about as violent as *Apocalypto* and twice as stupid. Devotees of the pectoral, deltoid and other fine muscle groups will find much to savor. The Persians, pioneers in the art of facial piercing, have vastly greater numbers—including ninjas, dervishes, elephants, a charging rhino and an angry bald giant—but the Spartans have superior health clubs and electrolysis facilities. In time, *300* may find its cultural niche as an object of camp derision, like the sword-and-sandals epics of an earlier, pre-computer-generated imagery age. At present, though, its muscle-bound, grunting, self-seriousness is more tiresome than entertaining. Go tell the Spartans, whoever they are, to stay home and watch wrestling. Much butchery, some lechery."
A.O. Scott
The New York Times

"The filmmakers deny any intentional [modern day] parallels, and I couldn't find one. Dick Cheney may be a bit like Xerxes and Bush a bit like Leonidas. But the Greek and Persian kings like to fight; Bush and Cheney just like to watch."
Jack Mathews
New York Daily News

"Sparta's king, Leonidas, who sounds like he grew up in the Glasgow section of Sparta, is told by a messenger that Persia's king, Xerxes, demands tribute—a token gift. There's no shame in diplomacy, but Leonidas goes berserk because he heard that the Athenians, those 'philosophers and boy-lovers,' didn't pay. Then he punts the messenger down a well. That crack about boy-love becomes central when we meet Xerxes. He's modeling the latest in earrings, dog collars, lipstick and eyeliner, like an 8-foot Ru-Paul. It's hard to escape the idea that Leonidas is a king who just doesn't like queens."
Kyle Smith
New York Post

"When the Spartans, pumped like linebackers leaving the weight room, go out to fight, they wear nothing but leather codpieces and red capes; they die clutching one another's hands. The Persians go one better. Their king, Xerxes, an epicene seven-footer with a shaved head and what looks like a gold-lamé thong, lounges on cushions in his court, surrounded by aroused lesbians intertwined and writhing like snakes in a basket. *300* is perhaps the nuttiest film ever to become an enormous box-office hit."
The New Yorker

Gay iconic drag?

3 NEEDLES
Three Tales of Ignorance, Greed, Fear & Superstition

This sometimes frustrating Canadian film examines the AIDS epidemic within three countries--South Africa, China, and Canada--on three different continents. Ironically, the word AIDS is never heard in the film.

Thom Fitzgerald, who gave us *The Hanging Garden* in 1997 and *Beefcake* in 1998, directed and wrote the film. In spite of all the actors and crew, it remains his personal baby. Fitzgerald was nominated for outstanding direction in a feature film from the Directors Guild of Canada.

The trilogy tells the story of a novice nun in South Africa; a black marketer in China, and an HIV-positive porn star in Canada. This three-in-one film provides very different perspectives on the struggle against AIDS. Each one of the trilogies turns on some kind of O. Henry-esque surprise.

If you speak English, Mandarin, Xhosi, French, and Afrikaans, you'll enjoy the movie more, as all five languages are used.

A grim prologue launches the film with a tribal initiation rite in which African boys are led into a forest and circumcised to mark their passage into manhood. As a trivia note, many of the Pondo and Xhosi people of Africa cast in *3 Needles* had never seen a movie in their lives. Of all the African myths about AIDS, none is more terrifying and destructive than the superstition that a man can rid himself of HIV by having unprotected sex with a virgin.

At the beginning of the first section, the porn actor Shawn Ashmore, playing Denys, schemes to pass his mandatory blood test. In the second part, a young nun, Chloë Sevigny as Sister Clara, makes a personal sacrifice for the benefit of a South African village. In rural China, in part three, a black-market operative, Lucy Liu, cast as Jin Ping, posing as a government-sanctioned blood drawer, jeopardizes an entire village's safety.

The Canadian plot mimics the 1998 scandal that focused on real-life straight porn star, Marc Wallace. Denys' on-screen life as a porno star ends when it's discovered he's been faking negative HIV test results.

Also appearing in the film is one of the greatest broads on the screen today, Stockard Channing, as Olive Cowie, delivering an Oscar-worthy performance as Denys' mother. Stockard's character works as a waitress who's facing the prospect of long-term care for her son, a second-rate porn actor. She develops a plan to escape her luckless hardship by investing her savings into an upgraded life insurance policy. She deliberately exposes herself to a fatal disease, then sells her life insurance for a settlement worth millions.

Is this dark melodrama or scathing farce? As she slings coffee or fucks a stranger in a strip club, Channing plays to both tragedy and humor. The film's sharp socio-political rancor comes bursting from the screen only when Fitzgerald turns the words bitter and sweet into one word—bittersweet.

One of our favorites, Olympia Dukakis, playing a nun, Sister Hilde, delivers the film's benediction, a rather rambling and eccentric message from the Great Beyond. Dukakis' lofty, morally quizzical monologue tries, effectively or not, to connect the film's dots.

In a statement to the press, the director, Fitzgerald, says *3 Needles* is "about transformation. Each character sacrifices one seemingly insignificant belief about themselves, only to feel their entire identity unravel. It exemplifies the challenges of simple people trying to seek education from an indifferent regime."

The movie is in the style of *Babel* with overlapping stories but without one unifying theme other than AIDS itself. The drama is actually three separate, sequentially told stories. To sum up, this is a well-meaning misfire.

Left to right. Shawn Ashmore, Chloe Sevigny, Lucy Liu, and Stockard Channing

WHAT THE CRITICS SAID

"Had it taken a more hard-headed approach, *3 Needles* might have been to the AIDS epidemic what *Traffic* was to drug trade."
Stephen Holden
The New York Times

"Inside even the most snarky, sugar-free-Red-Bull-and-vodka soaked man, there is a soft, gooey, compassionate center just waiting to have a cathartic cinematic wake-up call. On World AIDS Day, *3 Needles* will slap the shit out of anyone who thinks the pandemic is over. A stellar cast of Hollywood A-listers and indigenous actors brings an authentic integrity (and a touch of humor) to a subject we're all too aware of in our community, but one that is easily forgotten."
Instinct

"In terms of simple provocation, nothing in this melodramatic mosaic of global suffering comes close to matching director Thom Fitzgerald's press kit prediction that 'the AIDS pandemic will be seen in retrospect as much more significant than the ongoing jihad.' A film about THAT could be compelling, this one is merely content to suggest, cleverly and often, that it recognizes far more than we ever could the pain and cruelty of disease."
Rob Nelson
The Village Voice

"It sometimes produces moments of unexpected power. It also produces a bizarre and fatally uneven movie, veering from black comedy to utter stupidity to maudlin religiosity, which seems to have been made in total defiance of both narrative conventions and emotional logic."
Andrew O'Hehir
Salon.com

TIME TO LEAVE
(LE TEMPS QUI RESTE)

Life Is Over Too Soon and Never Complete

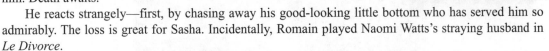

The talented French filmmaker, François Ozon, returns with *Le Temps Qui Reste.* It's a companion piece to *Under the Sand*, a haunting examination of bereavement and grief, starring the magnificent Charlotte Rampling. In some respects, *Under the Sand* was a cinematic precursor to Joan Didion's *Year of Magical Thinking*.

As the film opens, Romain (Melvil Poupaud) is a good-looking man, 31, living in Paris and working as a fashion photographer. Seemingly, he enjoys the good life, aided in no small part by his delicate, slim, and almost child-like boyfriend, Sasha (as played by the German-born actor Christian Sengewald), who is an obvious bottom.

Then Romain is given a diagnosis of brain cancer. There is no hope for him. Death awaits.

He reacts strangely—first, by chasing away his good-looking little bottom who has served him so admirably. The loss is great for Sasha. Incidentally, Romain played Naomi Watts's straying husband in *Le Divorce*.

He rejects treatment and decides to face death from his tumor on his own terms. He lashes out at his pregnant sister, but does not tell her of his illness. He is also uncommunicative to his loving and supporting parents.

However, he does confide in his grandmother, played by that national French treasure, Jeanne Moreau. When she asks him why he is confiding in her, he tells her. "Because you're like me, you'll be dying soon." Without his lover, he wanders aimlessly. The leather bar in this movie seems left over from the set of that notorious flick, *Cruising*.

The film takes a detour when Romain has a chance encounter with a roadside waitress played by Valeria Bruni-Tedeschi. Although in love with her husband, she can't have a child with him. With her husband's consent—in fact, he joins them in bed—Romain impregnates the woman. It's his chance to bring one life into the world as he is leaving it. It's a rather tender portrait of a *ménage à trois*.

Some critics found *Time to Leave* a "gay variation on a Douglas Sirk melodrama."

In France, the gay scenes in the movie didn't threaten the populace and make them run wild in the streets. *Brokeback Mountain* didn't create a scandal in Paris. However, in Hong Kong the *South China Morning Post* ran a picture of Poupaud and his character's boyfriend, as played by Sengewald. It created a scandal, as dozens of readers called in to cancel their subscriptions, claiming that they were offended by such "filth."

 WHAT THE CRITICS SAID

"*Time to Leave* just might be Ozon's best work yet. He tackles a sensitive, off-putting subject with a dignity that will put viewers at ease. Poupaud connects as the dying man. Anyone familiar with Ozon's work knows that he loves shots of the beach. It's no surprise then that his *Time to Leave* opens and closes on the beach."
V.A. Musetto
New York Post

Above, the real Oscar Wilde and the real Bosie at
Oxford in 1893.
Below, actors Stephen Fry and Jude Law as they
appeared in *Wilde* in 1997.

TWO DRIFTERS
(ODETE)

Looking for Love, Lost in Dreaming

In Portuguese with English subtitles, this 101-minute film contains sex, nudity, violence, and profanity. Otherwise, you wouldn't want to bother with it. Its helmer and co-scripter was João Pedro Rodrigues, the Portuguese filmmaker who made a debut in 2002 with his highly acclaimed feature, *O Fantasma*, that hardcore tale of a libidinous garbage man who enthralled movie certain audiences.

In many ways, *Two Drifters* is less dirty but even more perverse. Its plot, which includes transmigration of souls, is easy to parody.

The plot? Here goes: Pedro (João Carreira) and Rui (Nuno Gil) kiss after a dinner celebrating their first anniversary as a united couple. The two men exchange rings inscribed with the words, "Two Drifters," the lyric from "Moon River."

Pedro dies en route home in a car crash. The story then switches to another pair of very different lovers—Odete (Ana Cristina de Oliveira) and Alberto (Carloto Cotta). They split over her desire to have a child.

Back to Pedro's funeral. Odete lives in the building of the deceased, and she attends the wake, stealing a ring from the dead man, a last gift from Rui. At the gravesite, she behaves hysterically. Later, with Pedro's ring on her finger, she insists she's carrying the dead man's child. In one scene, Odete returns to the cemetery on a rainy night. On Pedro's grave, she cries out to the dead body: "Fuck me! Fuck me!"

Rui, deep in grief, drinks too much and sees Pedro's apparition. While wondering who this crazy chick (Odete) is, Rui cruises for anonymous sex.

Odete begins to push around an empty baby carriage. Rui gets simplistic and rather silly advice from a friend: "Pedro is dead, but you're very much alive."

 WHAT THE CRITICS SAID

"*Two Drifters* concludes with an unforgettable episode that is at once strangely perverse and also quite beautiful. No matter what one thinks of the rest of this unusual, striking film, the ending will haunt viewers. Like *O Fantasma*, *Two Drifters* gets under one's skin and stays there for days."
Gary Kramer
Gay City News

"The feat of *Two Drifters* is to advance a contradiction—Odete is overtaken by madness; Odete is overtaken by Pedro—and refuses to resolve it, spinning the two possibilities around the axis of Rui's sadness. Neither sentimental nor cruel, yet touching and trenchant, the movie sustains a profound ambivalence right up to the final shot. With a doozy of a provocation—a happy ending like no other—Mr. Rodrigues explains nothing while clarifying what's really at stake here: grappling with loss, transcending through love."
Nathan Lee
The New York Times

João Carreira

Ana Cristina de Oliveira

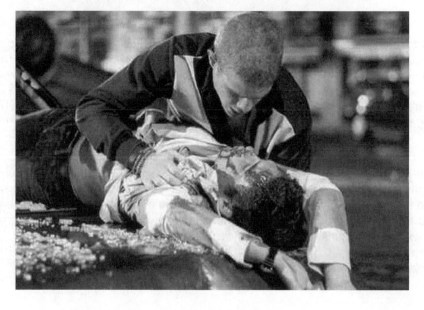

TYING THE KNOT

The Union That's Dividing America

Jim de Sève gets nearly all the credit for this docu about same-sex marriages. He directed it, produced it, and edited most of it.

Extremely relevant, highly entertaining, and utterly humanist, it's a critically acclaimed film festival favorite which poignantly explores one of today's hottest political issues. Along with abortion, right-wing America is enraged about gay marriage. This film is about gay people who want to marry and those who are hell-bent on stopping them.

The movie asks the question, "If you lost the one you love, how would it feel to have your love placed on trial?" It cites the case of a bank robber's bullet ending the life of cop Lois Marrero. Her wife of 13 years, Mickie, discovers a police department willing to accept the lesbian relationship of the two women, but unwilling to release Lois' pension. An Oklahoma rancher, Sam, loses his husband of 25 years. But cousins of the deceased challenge the dead man's will and move to evict Sam from his home.

As Mickie and Sam take up battle stations to defend their lives, *Tying the Knot* digs deep into the past and present to discover the meaning of marriage today, focusing on such key issues as rights, privilege, and love.

There are the usual suspects, including right-wing politicos and interviews with gay activists. Some of the best archival footage features gay hippies storming the Manhattan marriage bureau in 1971.

 WHAT THE CRITICS SAID

"Wrenching and skillful."
   Stephen Holden
   The New York Times

"Packs a wallop!"
   Max Goldberg
   San Francisco Bay Guardian

"Brilliant. A potent call to arms."
   Gerald Peary
   The Boston Phoenix

"It seems to me that when you reach the kind of acclaim that she's reached and can do whatever you want to do, you should be a little more magnanimous and a little less of a @^%&."

Cher, referring to Madonna

"I think Madonna called Cher a @^%&. once, but I'm sure she meant it in the nicest possible way."

Liz Rosenberg, publicist for both Cher and Madonna

"It was like being in a blender with an alligator."

Director Peter Bogdanovich, on working with Cher

"He thinks the frigging director is God."

Cher, on working with Peter Bogdanovich in *Mask*

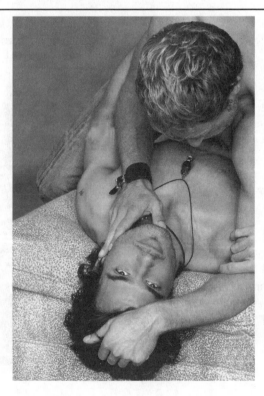

Antonio Sabato Jr. and a co-star posing for the camera

UNCUT

The Longest Filmed Shot of a Penis Ever Recorded

Gay men don't need this film to tell them what they already know: That cock is king. The 75-minute film—in Italian with English subtitles—is uncut, as is the penis of its star, Ciccio (Franco Trentalance), a repugnant ladies' man recovering from a fractured pelvis. The accident involved one of the women in his life.

Uncut holds the dubious Guinness world record for containing the longest filmed shot of a penis ever recorded. Gionata Zarantonello, both the director and writer, definitely believes in aiming the camera at crotch level. There is more here than Ciccio's uncut dick but not much. A randy male nurse. Pubic hair shaving. A vacuum. Chocolate sauce. Even a murder investigation.

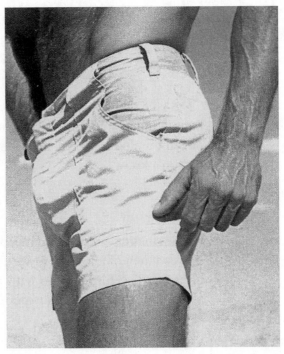

 ## WHAT THE CRITICS SAID

"Fans of uncut Italians expecting hard 'n' heavy action should stay home and rent the latest Falcon extravaganza instead. *Uncut* eschews porn for art and becomes a literal realization of the idea that man is driven by his cock in all facets of love, life and passion—a symbolic synecdoche of his part representing his whole."
Justin Ocean

"Uncompromised, uninterrupted, uncircumcised . . . possibly the weirdest sexploitation movie stunt of all time."
The Miami Herald

"*Uncut* ogles its subject while limp and erect, and while being shaved, fondled, placed in an enlargement apparatus, doused in candle wax and dabbed with Chanel No. 5, all of which is accompanied by the efforts of its owner to lure one of his prior conquests over for some physical therapy. Explicit as it is, *Uncut* explains little about men or their members."
Nathan Lee
The New York Times

"The face that [Doris Day] shows the world--smiling, only talking good, happy, tuned into God--as far as I'm concerned that's just a mask. I haven't a clue as to what's underneath. Doris is just about the remotest person I know."

Doris Day's co-star **Kirk Douglas**

"Kirk Douglas was civil to me, and that's about all. But then, Kirk never makes much of an effort toward anyone else. He's pretty wrapped up in himself. The film I made with Kirk, *Young Man with a Horn,* was one of the few utterly joyless experiences I had in films."

Doris Day

"Of all the people I performed with, I got to know Cary Grant least of all. He is a completely private person, totally reserved, and there is no way into him. Very distant."

Doris Day

"Oh yes, Miss Day...nice girl. Good singer...a good comedienne."

Cary Grant

THE UNDERMINER

"Friend" as Urban Predator of the Psyche

Based on a book by Mike Albo and Virginia Hefferman, Todd Downing's film reveals the insidious tactics of the quintessential New York "underminer," a master of passive aggression who throws his victim into a spiral of self-doubt and hopelessness every time he sees him. Albo plays both the role of the underminer and undermined, leaving one to wonder just how much of the underminer comes from within.

When *The Underminer* was published in 2005, he received critical acclaim. *The New York Times* called Albo "the ultimate satirist of the downtown New York social landscape, and Ron Rosenbaum (see below) proclaimed *The Underminer* as "Raid for the roaches of the soul."

Helmer Downing makes films that appeal to both gay and straight audiences at festivals. His short films, ranging from *Dirty Baby Does Fire Island* to *Jeffrey's Hollywood Screen Test*, have been profiled in press ranging from *Film Comment* to porno mags. He was recently named one of the "Six Best Directors You've Never Heard Of" by *SHOUT* magazine.

THE UNDERMINER

A NOVEL

THE BEST FRIEND WHO CASUALLY DESTROYS YOUR LIFE

MIKE ALBO

WITH VIRGINIA HEFFERNAN

 WHAT THE CRITICS SAID

"*The Underminer* is a compressed comic classic of New York, a kind of anti-E.B. White fable that focuses on the one unavoidable character everyone in New York runs into, a "friend" bred out of an unstable fusion of ambition and envy, of *Schadenfreude* and *Fluckschmerz*. (You know the former, the joy of the failure of others. The latter may be less familiar: Sadness at the success of others.) Add a strain of something very American: Oblivious self-congratulation. Fold in an arsenal of barbed compliments, faux flattery, and paranoia-inducing praise, and you've got The Underminer, a defining figure of our age, alas."
 Ron Rosenbaum

Judith Anderson, hot for
Joan Fontaine in *Rebecca* (1940)

UNITED 93

Common Passengers Showing Uncommon Valor

This is a docudrama about the Newark-to-San Francisco flight that crashed in a Pennsylvania field after passengers tried to retake it from its 9/11 hijackers. Directed by Paul Greengrass with disturbing images, it's an excellent film but almost unbearable to watch.

But what is such a film doing in a gay and lesbian film guide? If one remembers, stories leaked out that one of the ring leaders of the brave souls who led the final desperate attempt to save their lives was gay.

The filmmaker doesn't deal openly with the passenger's gayness, because it has nothing really to do with the plot. The gay man is not really identified as such. However, across America, homosexual men with their gay radar at the film's premiere determined who the gay passenger was. We don't want to tell you, but suggest that you'll have fun figuring it out yourself. The director left many clues.

The final, horrifying minutes inside flight 93, which had to be fictionalized, of course, are some of the most hideous we've ever seen on the screen. Perhaps the tragedy

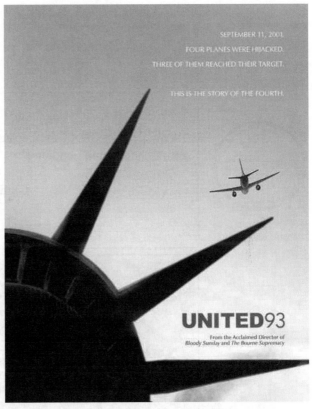

of the incident could have been prevented. Even before 93 left the ground in Boston, controllers were reporting losing contact with two of their planes. That alone should have sent a signal that hijackers were busy going about their dirty business.

As much as we hate to admit it, considering how we loathe them, the actors chosen to play Islamofascists were brilliantly cast as a band of suicidal religious fanatics. And imagine—some religious nuts living in America have stated publicly that they think same-sex marriage will mark the end of Western civilization as we know it.

If nothing else, the film shows us that the potential for extraordinary acts lies within each of us.

 ## WHAT THE CRITICS SAID

"*United 93,* written and directed with bruising brilliance and healing compassion, is a monumental achievement. There's not an ounce of bull in this movie's 111 minutes. Greengrass captures the staggering horror of that 91-minute flight and how courage emerged from chaos. Far from being exploitive, the effect is inspiring: This is the best of us."

Peter Travers
Rolling Stone

"We called her Miss Cute because of all the cute tricks she pulled to get all the attention on herself."

Gladys Knight, referring to Diana Ross

V FOR VENDETTA

Graphic Novel Lost in Translation

The year is 2020 and a totalitarian government is ruling England, its symbol a modified crucifix. Its slogan is "Strength Through Unity, Unity Through Faith." The action takes place after a series of devastating terrorist attacks.

The avenger (Hugo Weaving) is known only as V. Like a lurking Phantom of the Opera in a Guy Fawkes mask, he conducts guerilla warfare against the government. When he rescues a normal young woman, Evey (Natalie Portman), these two citizens unite, wanting to put an end to this fascist state.

V wins Evey's confidence because he rescues her from a life-and-death situation. V not only does that, but he ignites a revolution when he detonates two London landmarks and takes over the government-controlled airwaves, urging his fellow citizens to rise up against tyranny and oppression.

V is out to restore individuality and reclaim freedom for the people, even at the expense of their happiness. The movie suggests that a future totalitarian state might repress not just homosexuality, but Islam, too.

Millions of movie fans identified with V, who can be defined either as a terrorist or a freedom fighter, depending on your point of view. Many fans who flocked to the movie were enthralled by the graphic novel of the same name by Alan Moore. Moore disassociated himself from the movie and had his name removed from the credits.

The producers, the Wachhowski brothers, were clearly hoping they had another *Matrix* on their hands. But they did not achieve that dream.

 WHAT THE CRITICS SAID

"Helmed by James Mcteigue, pic suffers from many of same problems as last two installations of producers Andy and Larry Wachowski's *Matrix* franchise: Indigestible dialogue, pacing difficulties, and too much pseudo-philosophical info."
Leslie Felperin
Variety

"The film may spark interesting debates—about the nature of terrorism and governments, about the inalienable right of artists to shock and provoke—but what we're dealing with is a lackluster comic-book movie that thinks terrorist is a synonym for revolutionary. The movie plays like a clumsy assault on post-9/11 paranoia. It references 'America's war,' uses imagery direct from Abu Ghraib, and contains dialogue likely to offend anyone who's not, say, a suicide bomber."
Jeff Giles
Newsweek

Natalie Portman

Hugo Weaving

VACATIONLAND

Growing Up Gay on the Seedy Side of Bangor, Maine

Todd Verow strikes again. For more on this underground cult filmmaker, see this edition's reviews of *All Star* or *Bulldog in the Whitehouse*. For his micro-budgeted *Vacationland*, the young helmer drew upon his own experiences of growing up gay in Bangor, Maine.

This is far from being a perfect film—in fact, it's heavily flawed—yet in some compelling way it's eminently watchable. Although drawn from Verow's real-life experiences, many of the characters and situations have been altered "to protect the guilty."

Directed by Verow, who co-authored the script along with Jim Dwyer, *Vacationland* casts Brad Hallowell as Joe (presumably the stand-in for the director himself).

The young man lives with his single mom, Cathy (Jennifer Mallett), and his older sister, Theresa (Hilary Mann) in the notorious Capehart slum projects in Bangor. At the Capehart projects, where young boys grow up fast, there is always something happening such as a woman smothering her baby because she believes he's the anti-Christ. Along with another boy, Joe was molested when he was ten years old but never told anyone about it.

As they work together at a rundown mall next to the projects, Joe and Theresa bond in their joint dream. He wants to go to college, and she wants to wing her way to sample the glorious life of Los Angeles. They have no money and must scheme to get some to achieve their dreams.

Hallowell is an engaging actor but looks close to being 30 years old than he does a 17-year-old closeted high school senior. Theresa is a compelling detour in the film, and we almost applaud her as she robs her boss, turns a trick, and gets on that plane singing "California, Here I Come."

Meanwhile, Joe is falling for super-hottie, Andrew, his best friend, as engagingly played by a handsome hunk, Gregory J. Lucas.

The downside of Andrew is that he is a compulsive shoplifter even though he is the school football star. After a drunken night, Joe and Andrew get it on, but their love is complicated by Andrew's manipulative girlfriend, Mandy (Jennifer Stackpole), who doesn't want to lose those powerful inches that have been pounding into her.

When not pursuing Andrew, Joe likes to hang out in toilets in search of such adventures as letting strange men play with his leg hair. He also fools around with his French teacher, Nathan Johnson, blackmailing the man into assisting him with his application to the Rhode Island School of Design.

Joe also answers a personal ad, taking a job as a "houseboy-model" to an unattractive old man, Victor (Charles Ard), who lives in a studio loft above the local opera house.

Joe's life is complicated by the emergence of an old nemesis, Tim (Michael Dion), who shares a violent past with the young man. But we're giving away too much of the plot.

Even though intriguing in part, this sexual burlesque ends on a sour note with a muddled, violent conclusion. See for yourself. There was a lot of potential here, but much of it got stifled in subplots not adequately developed.

"Too bad the title, *Another Gay Movie*, is already in use; it would have worked nicely for *Vacationland*, a generic coming-of-age movie whose arrival on the scene suggests that the audience for gay indie clunkers is inexhaustible."
Nathan Lee
The New York Times

"The film aspires to the splendor of *The Living End* and *Totally Fucked Up*, stuffed as it is with every queer small-town cliché the movies have ever seen, but Verow's passion and talent, unlike Gregg Araki's, is not equal to his ambition."
Ed Gonzalez
Slant Magazine

"Vacationland remains marred by sluggish script and Verow's inability to either direct actors or cast ones whose thesping ability matches their good looks. Cast, apart from Charles Ard, all look like they're in their 20s rather than teens. Tech package sucks."
Leslie Felperin
Variety

"A cluttered assemblage of low-budget gay-cinema hooks—go-go dancing, nude modeling, sexual blackmail, bathroom-stall cruising—Todd Verow's overstuffed *Vacationland* promises more than it delivers in just about every sense."
Joshua Land

"Yet another gay teenage movie opens, this one a hackneyed coming-out tale rife with angst, violence and bare backsides. Considering the number of films under indie director-writer Todd Verow's belt, there's no excuse for the poor performances, leaden pacing and nearly inaudible sound (which, given the lame dialogue, is perhaps a good thing)."
Time Out New York

WALK IN THE LIGHT

Tales from a Black & Gay Church in Los Angeles

A grassroots church movement was founded in 1982 by the Rev. Carl Bean. Openly accepting of homosexuality, the Unity Fellowship Church set out to show that "Gay Christian" is not an oxymoron.

Walk in the Light explores the lives of people who yearn for a relationship with God but are turned away from traditional churches. Revealing the impact of intolerance and demonstrating the power of self-love, the film explores the lives of three individuals who attend Unity Fellowship church. The mother church, which later branched-out to San Diego, lies in a gritty section of South Central Los Angeles. Intimate footage and lively gospel music provide the backdrop to a film about struggling to accept others and one's self.

The present pastor of the church, Rev. Charles Lanier, once said, "I began to realize that I was gay as a little boy, but I always loved church. I wanted to be a good little Christian, and so in listening to the teachings, the one subject that they always talk about is homosexuality, and those are the worst sinners, and God does not love them. Subsequently, I started drinking and using marijuana at about 13: Anything to escape the self-hatred that had begun to grow inside of me for not being able to accept my feelings." Eventually he discovered Unity Fellowship Church and his real healing began.

Worshippers depicted in the film include Cookie, a transgender female. "At Unity, I feel like I'm fighting for something," she said. An ex-marine and the biological father of two, Cookie always felt her identity was not that of a man. After years of self-denial, Cookie decided to continue her life as a woman.

On the other hand, Claire is more troubled. She wants to be with her partner, Bridget, but her conviction that she will go to hell for being a lesbian haunts the relationship. Coming from a conservative Christian background, Claire faces constant condemnation of her sexual orientation by her mother. "I feel like I'm living for other people, I'm living for my family," Claire said. In contrast, Bridget's family is tolerant of homosexuality but their church preaches that gays will go to hell. Together, Bridget and Claire confront Bridget's family about their church's views, and attend Unity Fellowship Church for the first time.

"To the girls back home, Guy Madison's pecs symbolized what Betty Grable's legs did to the guys overseas, and Henry Willson [the casting couch agent] had little difficulty turning the 21-year-old sailor into the fan magazine's World War II poster boy. A raw, essentially incompetent performer, Madison presented a *tabula rasa* that made him the consummate model, especially if photographed in his navy uniform, or, as Henry suggested, in equally rugged attire, whether it be a white T-shirt and jeans, or shirtless, his chest covered with hair in some shots, as smooth and glabrous as a baby's behind in others."

Author **Robert Hofler**

This page: Four photos of Gay icon and 1940s heartthrob, Guy Madison

A WALK INTO THE SEA
The Whipping Boy for Warhol's Sadism

If you got off on *Factory Girl*, a semi-fictionalized feature on the ill-fated Edie Sedgwick, you might be up for seeing the story of another ill-fated Andy Warhol favorite, Danny Williams. "Who in hell was Danny Williams?" you might legitimately ask.

Among his other credentials, Danny was Warhol's lover. He was not a very sexy guy, standing about five feet ten. He was nice looking rather than beautiful--a bit chunky, but not unpleasantly so.

In 1965, soon after he and Warhol met, Danny moved into Warhol's home on Lexington Avenue. As Warhol biographer, Victor Bockris, relates, "Soon Danny was wearing the same boat-neck striped shirts Andy and Edie were wearing and regularly accompanying Warhol on their social rounds. However, after two months, the relationship broke down."

At one point in a restaurant on Christopher Street in Greenwich Village, Danny jumped up from the table and pulled off Warhol's wig. Friends at the table got a rare chance to see Warhol bald before he grabbed the wig from Danny and plopped it back onto his head.

Danny moved into Warhol's Factory after he got kicked out of Warhol's home. He slept there throughout most of 1966, having set up a workshop for himself. He knew how to work the lights and record sound.

Like Edie, Danny transformed himself from a Harvard preppie into an addict, his hair becoming matted and stringy, his skin looking ghostly. According to Bockris, Danny became the Factory's whipping boy, and Warhol constantly screamed at him.

An observer at the time, Henry Geldzahler, summed up the Danny/Warhol relationship this way: "Andy was a voyeur-sadist and he needed exhibitionist-masochists in order to fulfill both halves of his destiny. And it's obvious that an exhibitionist-masochist is not going to last very long."

Such was the case with Danny. In July of 1966 Danny showed up at the house of his grandmother, Nadia Williams, who appears as herself in the docu. He borrowed her auto for a drive to the ocean "to get some fresh air." He never came back. His disappearance remains a mystery to this day.

Like Norman Maine in *A Star is Born* (played by James Mason) opposite Judy Garland, Danny did drive to the ocean. Once there, he stripped off his clothing, leaving the apparel in a neat pile by the vehicle. He apparently jumped into the sea and drowned. Presumably, he was washed out to sea where he might have become a shark's dinner.

When Warhol was informed of Danny's death, he said, "Oh, I don't care. What a pain in the ass Danny was. He was just an amphetamine addict!" He spent no time mourning his former lover.

The docu was directed by Esther B. Robinson, who was the niece of Danny. If you look quickly, you can see Edie Sedgwick herself in a clip from one of Danny's movies.

Robinson has assembled an impressive list of interviewees to tell Danny's story, including director Paul Morrissey. Many of the subjects appear in archive footage. The famous filmmaker, Albert Maysles, tells how the 21-year-old Danny worked on his early films, including *Showman* in 1963 and *What's Happening! The Beatles in the U.S.A.* in 1964.

The 16mm black-and-white short, *Factory*, is shown in its entirely in this docu. In addition to Edie and Warhol, Danny captures Billy Name on film as well, as well as Velvet Underground member John Cale. The subjects contradict each other, helmer Morrissey dismissing Danny, who wins praise from—say, photographer Nat Finkelstein.

Over the years, virtually everyone connected with Warhol's Factory has come up with wildly different accounts of what actually happened there.

Even though it's a docu on his life, at the end of the film, Danny Williams remains an enigmatic figure. Except for some film work he left behind, there only remains this docu, a few photos, and some distant memories.

 WHAT THE CRITICS SAID

"Even allowing for the fact that *A Walk Into the Sea* is a sober-sided docu, and *Factory Girl* a sensationalist, semi-fictionalized feature, both depict the Factory's milieu as a vicious circle, where creativity was indeed fostered but rivalries could turn poisonous, presided over by the fickle Warhol himself. Both films illustrate how Warhol made a habit of elevating favorites such as Danny Williams, and then tossing them aside."
Leslie Felperin
Variety

"Andy Warhol is the only genius I've ever known with an IQ of 60."

Gore Vidal

ANDY WARHOL: A DOCUMENTARY FILM

A Voyeur with a Voracious Appetite for Fame

First, the bad news for anyone suffering from Attention Deficit Disorder. This portrait of the artist, Andy Warhol, is 4 hours long—so be duly warned. Is there anyone alive who doesn't know who Warhol (1928-1987) was? Artist, filmmaker, photographer, writer, publisher, interviewer, model, actor, businessman, fashion consultant, set designer, TV show host, rock choreographer, record producer, gourmet, jet-setter, trendsetter, dog lover, and modern dancer. Dare we add homosexual? Warhol, of course, became the leading exponent of Pop Art, the artist who gave us those silk-screen portraits of Marilyn Monroe, Elizabeth Taylor, and Elvis Presley that still hang in our bathrooms, sometimes directly imprinted on our shower curtains.

The film assures us that Warhol was the greatest artist of the second half of the 20th century, the first part of that century going to Pablo Picasso, of course.

Ric Burns was both the director and co-author (along with James Sanders). The helmer told the press that it was a hard sell raising money for his documentary. Previously he'd done docus on Eugene O'Neill, the playwright, and on Ansel Adams, the photographer. "People hate Andy and they love him," Burns said in an interview with *The New York Times*.

"Warhol is the American dream, but in the minds of corporations it could be the American nightmare," said Donald Rosenfeld, who produced the film with Daniel Wolf. "He's peculiar looking—not of this world." Wolf added a footnote: "Warhol was branded as this gay, weird, party-going genius—and not the great artist he should have been known as."

Burns blended interviews with archival footage. Narration by Laurie Anderson is a bit too reverent when a more dispassionate tone might have been called for.

Paul Morrissey, who wrote and directed such Warhol-produced films as *Trash, Heat*, and *Flesh*, is barely mentioned in the movie. Yet in some respects those films, starring superstud Joe Dallesandro, form one of Warhol's most enduring legacies.

The docu traces Warhol from his origins on the seedy side of Pittsburgh, where he was poor, physically frail, and very effeminate. He was forced to share a bed with his two brothers. When he finally did reach New York, he met Truman Capote, sensing a kindred spirit.

Ever since he'd seen the notoriously fey portrait of Capote on the book jacket of his first novel, *Other Voices, Other Rooms*, Warhol became obsessed with the writer and even stalked him. Capote rejected Warhol's overtures of friendship. When not stalking Capote, Warhol delivered his early commercial artwork in a brown paper bag, his colleagues mocking him as "Raggedy Andy."

To record his drama, the filmmakers rounded up all the usual suspects, including Warhol's best biographer, Wayne Koestenbaum. They even tracked down Warhol's brother, John Warhola. Warhola was Andy's original name. A typesetter at a magazine where the artist was working accidentally dropped the final "A."

Warhol liked his revised name and stuck with it for the rest of his life.

Like a one-man Collyer Brothers, Warhol left a vast trail of documentation, even dinner invitations and fan mail. If we have any criticism at all, it's that the praise in the film is a bit too effusive. How many times do we need to hear that Warhol was a genius?

After exploring Warhol's early attempts at commercial art in the Big Apple, the second half of the docu turns to The Factory, both its 47th Street and Union Square locations. Peopled with hustlers, drug addicts, wannabees, "superstars," and drag queens, The Factory's opening party in 1964—or so it was said—was "the night the 60s were born."

In the drugged out bliss of The Factory, films were made, and art, music, and even dance were presented. It was here that Warhol created such alleged masterpieces as *The Chelsea Girls*. It was also here that that man-hating crackpot, Valerie Solanas, shot Warhol. She'd convinced herself that the artist had conspired with her publisher to steal her ideas. As Warhol recovered, his business was generating a cool million a year for him before he died of medical malfeasance in 1987. He was an unripe 58.

Although Warhol with his blotched skin, bulbous nose, and early hair loss concealed by bad wigs gained international fame, he never achieved his childhood dream of becoming Shirley Temple. He didn't even achieve his adult dream of becoming Marilyn Monroe.

 # WHAT THE CRITICS SAID

"Andy Warhol had a reputation for shallowness and superficiality; his assembly-line paintings and artless movies were initially received as elaborate put-ons. But in Andy Warhol, director Ric Burns parades a legion of critics, biographers, and former acolytes who attribute unexpectedly profound meanings to his deceptive *oeuvre*. A four-hour running time may seem unduly long, but Andy Warhol, like its enigmatic subject, is never boring."
Tom Beer
Time Out New York

"Before Madonna and Paris Hilton, there was Warhol. But to assume, as some still do, that Warhol's vision was nihilistic and steeped in irony is to look only at the chilly industrialized surfaces of art that sprang from a passionate, quasi-religious workshop of pop culture and its icons."
Stephen Holden
The New York Times

"One misses the voices of Lou Reed and John Cale, Rauschenberg or the critics who pegged the soup cans a vulgar joke. There's little sense of what Warhol had to overcome in the art establishment—or how he helped create a new art establishment—or the state of mind of individuals who rode a Warhol wave through the 60s."
Variety

"Even with 240 minutes at his disposal, director Ric Burns can't quite decode the enigma that was Andy Warhol. Nevertheless, his epic examination of the artist is consistently compelling and required viewing for anyone remotely interested in pop culture. We need all four hours, and even more, to understand the man who so prophetically divided the world into 15-minute increments."
The New York Daily News

Fifteen Minutes of Fame

Thanks to new documentary, plus the recent release of *Factory Girl* and *Walk Into the Sea*, and now a book, we seem to be in the midst of an Andy Warhol renaissance. Of course, Warhol has never gone out of style. Nor has he ever become forgotten.

Andy Warhol Screen Tests: The Films of Andy Warhol, Catalogue Raisonné, Volume One, was recently published by Abrams, priced at $60 per copy. Grace Hendris in the *New York Post*, suggested that these screen tests "might just be Warhol's greatest work of art," although encased in a book with an academic title that "sounds about as interesting as paste."

Warhol began filming his living portraits in 1963, asking each of his subjects, from Dennis Hopper to Susan Sontag, to sit still for three minutes in front of the camera. Over a period of two years, he filmed 472 of these living portraits.

Even Bob Dylan and Salvador Dalí agreed to a sitting. Of course, these are famous subjects. Some of the names in the tests have been assigned to the dustbin of history, including Warhol's friend, Willard Maas, whose troubled marriage reportedly was the inspiration for Edward Albee's *Who's Afraid of Virginia Woolf?*

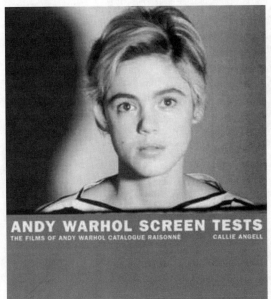

Although not as revealing as the actual film clips, the catalogue provides a series of still photographs of Warhol's subjects, who range from drag queens to socialites. There is the occasional famous face but mostly the artist's subjects were unknown. Biographical blurbs provide information about who they were. Sometimes a bio is quite tantalizing, as in the case of Freddy Herko who "danced out the window" of John Dodd's fifth-floor apartment."

If nothing else, this book reveals that Warhol thought nothing was more fascinating than the human face, and in the case of poet Allen Ginsberg, a close friend of Warhol's, that might be true.

MARVELOUS MAE

WITH AFFECTION, WE DEDICATE THIS PAGE TO THE MEMORY OF MAE WEST.

THE ENDURING ALLURE OF VAUDEVILLE

Upper left and bottom left: Mae West.

Upper right: Which of the bodies on the cover of *Muscle Magazine* belongs to Mae West?

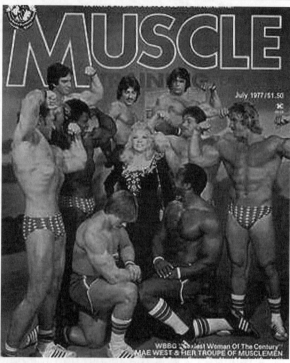

Special Feature
Marvelous Mae

Left:
Entertainer Rosemarie Ballard impersonating Mae West.

Below:
Sofa, designed by Salvador Dalí, inspired by Mae West's lips.

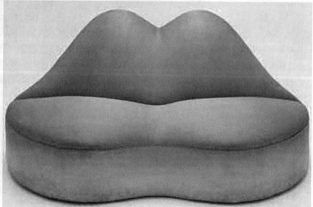

424

WEDDING WARS
Gay People Across the U.S. Go on Strike

"Oh, my God," shouted one viewer. "Uncle Jessie kissing another man and with passion!" The reference was to John Stamos, always with the top buttons of his shirt unfastened, who became world famous playing his role on *Full House*, the TV sitcom in which three men raise a family in San Francisco. "I love John like he's the sister I never had," said *Full House* co-star Bob Saget.

Not only with *Wedding Wars*, but on the stage, Stamos is taking chances. He appeared bare-chested (at long last) in the stage version of *Cabaret*, playing the pansexual role of the emcee. With nipples sparkling and in full lipstick with a bow-tie between his naked breasts, "Uncle Jesse" both wowed and shocked audiences in the role Joel Grey made famous and won the Best Supporting Actor Oscar for his attention-grabbing characterization in the 1972 film that starred Liza Minnelli, of course.

Stamos said his character in Cabaret "would have sex with a squirrel if he had a chance—and he probably did." He learned to "push the boundaries" in *Cabaret* and was prepared to play gay in *Wedding Wars*, where he was cast as a likable gay rights activist.

In the role he tackles the delicate issue of same-sex marriage but with light humor. Stamos as Shel Grandy takes up the issue of gay marriage after his brother—played by *Grey's Anatomy* Eric Dane (as Ben)—becomes engaged to the daughter of a conservative governor, Conrad Welling (James Brolin), whom we never refer to as Mr. Barbra Streisand.

The film was directed by Jim Fall, who married his own boyfriend on the set in Halifax, Canada.

Wedding Wars asks the question: "What would happen if every gay person in America suddenly went on strike?" An argument between the two brothers inadvertently triggers the strike, and it's up to the siblings to solve their differences before the entire country is shut down.

John Stamos

MARLENE DIETRICH (1901-1992)

Is this the real Marlene or a drag queen?
Actually, it's the real, high-camp thing,
Ms. Dietrich as she appeared in
Rancho Notorious in 1952.
Although the picture bombed with the general
public, a lot of gay men went to see it.

WHISPERING MOON

(DAS FLUSTERN DES MONDES)

Something Strange This Way Comes

If you like a movie about hoaxes, exposés, young love, poisonous tree frogs, and a lot more, wander into the mind of writer/director Michael Satzinger who helmed this 97-minute Austrian entry. Dominik Hartl, Julian Stampfer, and Liane Wagner star in this film which tries to push the borders of conventional movie photography.

Playful, subversive, and scintillating, *Whispering Moon* is visually stunning, like nothing you've probably seen before. It blends media, narratives, and skin to tell "a story about storytelling."

Jannis and his mute lover, Patrick, are a pair of young techno rebels living in the not-too-distant future, a world of conspiracy and paranoia. These two boys set up surveillance cameras at a circus that may—or may not—be raising poisonous frogs to kill politicians.

Might the frog conspiracy also involve Mo, a young woman who lives with the circus and suffers from Xeroderma pigmentosa, a malady of the skin which forces her to live by night and avoid all ultraviolet light? Such people are often called "Children of the Moon."

The movie blends traditional film, digital video, computer graphics, and animation, allowing the main character to stop the action and make changes to the story at will.

Audiences are likely to be frustrated, even confused, but perhaps enraptured by the antics on screen.

The film is in German with English subtitles.

  WHAT THE CRITICS SAID

"*Whispering Moon*, a unique Austrian entry, is an offbeat, visually striking film in which the characters at times reinvent the action. The story concerns two cute teen lovers who hatch a plan that backfires. As the film opens, one boy is being interrogated, describing how he and his lover tried to manipulate the truth for their own advantage. *Whispering Moon* is rather manipulative as well, carrying viewers through a series of episodes that may or may not be true."
Gary M. Kramer

AUSTRIAN AESTHETICS:
Scenes from *Das flustern des mondes*

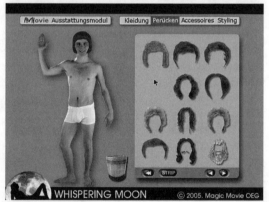

THE WHORE'S SON

(HURENSOHN)

And What Does Your Mama Do for a Living?

This Austrian film, in German with English subtitles, was the creation of co-scripter and director Michael Sturminger, who is vaguely Fassbinder-ish. In fact, the movie was photographed by Fassbinder's former collaborator, Jürgen Jürges. Its running time of 85 minutes treats us to a parade of sex, violence, and profanity, all that good old stuff. The results, however, are not always successful.

Sturminger dusts off another coming-of-age plot. Opening with a flashback, the teenager star of the movie, Ozren (Stanislav Lisnic), has just confessed that he's killed his beautiful mother, Silvija (Chulpan Khamatova). When their native Yugoslavia descended into civil wars in the 1980s, mother and son had fled to Vienna.

Orzen at age 3 is played by Gabriel Usein; at age 8 by Emanuel Usein. In spite of the parade of "johns" in her life, Silvija tells the older Orzen (Stanislav) that she is a waitress.

As the film progresses Silvija moves out of their modest digs, getting her son a job in the brothel being run by a madam downstairs. The teenager's curiosity leads to tragedy.

In spite of everything, she's still your mom.

The Whore's Son

 WHAT THE CRITICS SAID

"Austrian director Michael Sturminger's debut feature creates a visually evocative environment in which to explore some significant themes, from religious repression to Freudian guilt. But our teen protagonist never develops a personality beyond his reactions to Mom's profession, and the movie might have made a greater impact if it focused less upon the whore, and more on the son."

New York Daily News

"Bruce [Willis] used to moon us all the time. He had a very hairy bottom but was always concerned with the thinning hair on his head. One day I suggested he might get a transplant from his [bottom] to his head. At least that kept him from mooning us for several weeks."

Cybill Shepherd

430

WILD TIGERS I HAVE KNOWN

A Wrenching But Occasionally Lyrical Depiction of Sexual Anguish

Cam Archer, previously known as director of some respected music videos, both directed and scripted this feature film, with Gus Van Sant serving as one of the executive directors. It's a coming-of-age story, with Malcolm Stumpf playing the misfit kid, Logan.

Logan pines for the hunky loner, Rodeo (Patrick White), in the co-starring role. The gay 13-year-old Stumpf decides to act on his attraction to the older boy by disguising himself as a girl. In the film, he learns to cope with his newfound sexuality and his unrequited love for the cool kid in school.

The film fails in many ways, but it's momentarily intriguing if you've got nothing better to do one night. The cast, however, is admirable, including Fairuza Balk as Logan's mom. Max Paradise appears as Joey, Tom Gilroy playing the school principal.

There is something to admire in Archer's attempt to turn a yearning for rough trade into something lyrical and feminine.

 ## WHAT THE CRITICS SAID

"Two high school wrestlers grapple on a fuzzed-out TV screen. A pubescent boy in sunglasses masturbates in a luridly red room. That same lad, wearing lipstick and blond wig, stares into a cracked mirror. Cam Archer's feature debut offers a stunning opening triptych that's a virtual pomo-homo filmography, skipping from the pixilated New Queer Cinema of Sadie Benning to Kenneth Anger's colorful cryptography and Andy Warhol's narcissistic *Drag City* in two cuts."
David Fear
Time Out New York

"Encouraged by the older boy's attentions, Logan develops a female alter ego he calls Leah, one bold enough to call Rodeo in the middle of the night and come on to him in a way Logan himself could hardly muster."
Kyle Buchanan
The Advocate

Marilyn Monroe and drag queens, Tony Curtis
and Jack Lemmon in *Some Like It Hot* (1959)

WRESTLING WITH ANGELS:
PLAYWRIGHT TONY KUSHNER

The Devil Behind *Angels in America*

The scripter and helmer Freida Lee Mock is known mainly for her Oscar-winning *Maya Lin*. Released in 1995, it documented the design process and controversies associated with the Vietnam War Memorial in Washington, D.C. Taking on a biography of the playwright, Tony Kushner, however, proved too daunting a challenge.

By now every gay man in America, and even most straights, know who Kushner is. He's the left-leaning gay political activist who won a Pulitzer Prize for his sweeping stage epic, *Angels in America*, his play about AIDS during the Reagan era.

To appreciate Mock's 98-minute docu on Kushner, it's best to have already seen the Mike Nichols-directed HBO movie version of Kushner's visionary play. Mock's docu highlights the participation of Nichols, Diane Sawyer, Meryl Streep, and Emma Thompson, even including some archival footage of the latter in her role as an archangel.

Mock's docu is divided into three parts, a structure equivalent to that of one of Kushner's three-act plays. Act I, "As a Citizen of the World," focuses on Kushner as activist. He discusses his play, *Homebody/Kabul*, about a middle-class, middle-aged English woman's obsession with Afghanistan. Like a prophet, Kushner wrote this play before 9/11.

Act II, "Mama, I'm a Homosexual," is obviously a reflection of his his own coming-out saga, including aspects of his involvement in the gay rights movement. At the age of 6, Kushner, who was born and reared in Lake Charles, Louisiana, knew he was gay.

Interviewed at Lake Charles on his 80th birthday, Kushner's father talks about his son's homosexuality. William Kushner admits that he would have been "ashamed to have had Tchaikovsky as a son." But time has mellowed him, and now he seems to be content to have a thoroughly out-of-the-closet Tchaikovsky as a son.

Act III, "Collective Action to Overcome Injustice," delves into Kushner's Jewish heritage, and includes scenes from his play on Jewish immigration, *Why Should It Be Easy When It Can Be Hard*?

Kushner is also depicted working on *Caroline, or Change*, his musical collaboration with composer Jeanine Tesori.

The most touching moment in the film involve's Kushner's collaboration with artist/writer/producer Maurice Sendak ("The Picasso of children's books") on an adaptation of *Brundibar*, a musical originally performed by children in Nazi death camps.

There is not enough attention devoted to Kushner's private life, though there is some, including insights into his marriage to his lover, Mark Harris. But gay marriage is not really addressed. We would have liked to have known more about the Harris/Kushner relationship. Instead we get an appearance by gay guru Larry Kramer.

Regrettably, the film concludes in 2004 before Kushner began work on his controversial script for Steven Spielberg's film *Munich*.

 # WHAT THE CRITICS SAID

"*Wrestling With Angels* is best approached as an admiring portrait of a likable, creative power-house at mid-career. No disapproving voices interrupt the stream of praise for his politics and his art. Mr. Kushner's place in the history of American theater, and American culture in general, is left unexamined. These are subjects well worth exploring in another, deeper film."
Stephen Holden
The New York Times

"Freida Lee Mock's adulatory portrait makes for pleasant viewing—but should it? Her subject is a professional rabble-rouser, an intellect determined to provoke a sleeping world into action. But what about the controversies his plays inspire? Kushner's work is honest; his biography should be, too."
Elizabeth Weitzman
New York Daily News

"Mock didn't find room for any of the many critics who accuse Kushner of being an anti-Zionist."
Lou Lumenick
New York Post

Emma Thompson descending from Heaven
in *Angels in America*

A YEAR WITHOUT LOVE *(Un Año Sin Amor)*

A Writer Dying of AIDS Searches for Human Interaction in the Hospitals and Sex Clubs of Buenos Aires

In Spanish with English subtitles, this is the debut feature of Anahi Berneri, an Argentine director.

Pablo (Juan Minujin) descends the steps to a gay porn theater for a night of protected sex since he is HIV-positive. When not doing that, and to support himself, he gives private French lessons to teenage girls and takes out personal ads that read, "30, 5'8", 140, HIV-positive, big cock."

He is a solitary poet living in a cramped Buenos Aires apartment with his childlike aunt, Mimi Ardu.

Pablo likes not only the dark confines of the porn theater, but the pain-centered rituals of an S&M club, where he becomes fascinated by Martin (Van de Couter), a rugged young leather top, who engages him in, among others, phone play. Remember that bathtub scene in *Pillow Talk* with Doris Day and Rock Hudson? Bemeri brings a 21st-century—and very gay—twist to the cliché. In split-screen sex dialogue, we hear:

"I'm your slave, sir."

"Lick my boots!"

The film was based on the diaries of the real-life Pablo Peréz, who is listed as the co-scripter.

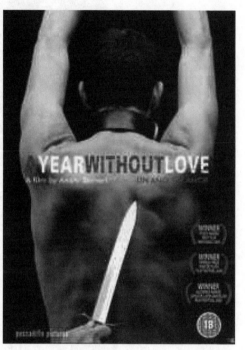

WHAT THE CRITICS SAID

"Whereas so much contemporary gay cinema peddles pseudo-campy humor or bland soft-core eroticism, Berneri's film, with its washed-out palette and desultory pacing, is unafraid to name loneliness as a fact of gay—make that human—existence. *A Year Without Love* is as bleak as its title promises, but it never feels less than honest."

Tom Beer
Time Out New York

"The striking film tells a sharp and sexy story of one gay man's steady climb to dignity and fulfillment against great odds. The film represents a breath of fresh air in its transfiguration of narrative convention, illustrating a gay life laced with irony and grace with resourcefulness and love."

Shannon Kelley
The Advocate

"The S-and-M activities Pablo dabbles in aren't particularly hard core, or impassioned, even, like those, say, of Bob Flanagan, whose similar quest for finding pleasure in physical pain while fighting a debilitating disease was documented in the 1997 film *Sick*. In fact, Pablo, looking numb and inexpressive, seems to be in it more for the companionship."

Laura Kern
The New York Times

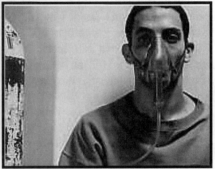

Three views of actor Juan Minujin.

THE YOUNG, THE GAY & THE RESTLESS
Gay Spoof of Soapy TV Dramas

Spoofs are difficult to pull off, especially when you're satirizing daytime TV soaps. These programs are almost spoofs of themselves. Nonetheless, Joe Castro, who wrote and directed this picture, sticks his toes into waters that have turned scalding for so many other helmers and scripters.

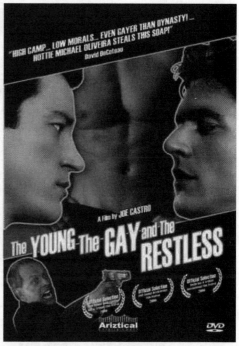

The action, such as it is, spins around the household of Victoria Gaylord, an heiress who looks like a drag queen on a bad hair day. She throws a party at which she is stricken with a heart attack but refuses to go to the hospital.

There are various greedy children hovering in the distance, eager to grab her millions. But a handsome doctor and a mysterious black nurse appear.

The doctor, it seems, though flirting with a gay man, has previously played stud duty to Victoria, who has named him as the executor of her will. The black girl may be Victoria's daughter.

There's a lackluster husband, Mr. Gaylord, hovering about. He has given blow-jobs to all the boys—his sons or otherwise—when they were teenagers. It seems his secret habit involves sucking young dick.

There's the buffed stud married to one of Victoria's daughters. She accuses him of homophobia because he's always complaining about being hit upon by other guys. He spends most of his time staring at his image in the mirror. He's later accused of standing nude in front of the full-length mirror while he masturbates. We just know that secretively he wants to plug boy-ass and is just pretending he's straight. After all, Tennessee Williams told that story in his play, *Cat on a Hot Tin Roof,* back in the 50s, when Paul Newman wouldn't fuck Elizabeth Taylor.

Three men, plus one Asian girl, are after one hottie, and there's a possible four-way relationship brewing on the horizon.

The homophobic stud has a beautiful wife who is actually in love with her brother. To avoid another incest issue, helmer Castro suggests that as adopted children they didn't have the same biological parents—hence, it's okay if they bang each other. Naturally, however, Mr. Gaylord long ago molested this "son" as well as the homophobic stud.

As the plot unfolds, no viewer will care if Victoria dies or not. She's one of the most unsympathetic characters played on film.

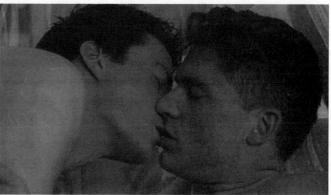

For most gay men, the big question is will the homophobic, buffed "straight" bi finally come out of the closet and start plugging gay men—or at least one gay man. We don't have to give away the plot to tell you that 99 and 9/10 percent of gay men watching this flick will know the answer to that. We've all lived this scene in real life, some of us more than once, so we know the answer.

Montgomery Clift and Elizabeth Taylor facing
gay truth in *Suddenly, Last Summer* (1959)

ZEROPHILIA
Being a Woman Doesn't Make You Any Less of a Man

This 90-minute film, written and directed by Martin Curland, has a strange premise. Its star, Luke (Taylor Handley), can self-transform from male to female as circumstances dictate.

As a male, he's a real hottie with his Titian curls and lickable tits. Luke has a rare chromosomal disorder, allowing him to switch back and forth between genders. Although he's doing well as a man, the plot gets complicated when he develops a crush on a beautiful man.

This screwy romantic comedy and sexual fantasy raises a question. What if a man, who turns into a woman when he's aroused, meets a woman who turns into a man when she's aroused. That is a hell of a lot to ponder. Call this the oddest romantic comedy of the year. One critic likened it to "American Pie on Crack."

His girl form, Luca (Marieh Delfino), is adept in her role. The plot thickens when Luke/Luca meets the dazzling Michelle (Rebecca Mozo), and Luca meets Michelle's hunky brother, Max (Kyle Schmid). Talk about gender confusion. The funniest scene is when Luke sprouts breasts during a romantic dinner date with Michelle.

Cast as Luke's best friends, Dustin Seavey, as Keenan, and Alison Folland, as Janine, deliver keen, upbeat performances.

    WHAT THE CRITICS SAID

"The movie is fresh, suspenseful and lovely to look at, thanks to a fine cast of young hotties. And its final twist will leave you cheering."
Beth Greenfield
Time Out New York

"Unrated pic features enough nudity to entice the frat-house set, while putting it out of the reach of slumber party auds. Amid deliberately campy situations and sophomoric jokes, *Zerophilia* offers a disarmingly sweet lesson about learning to identify with the opposite gender."
Peter Debruge
Variety

"A novel teenage comedy with an astute understanding of adolescent sexual confusion and the nebulous nature of desire, *Zerophilia* suggests an elastic view of gender that's alternately gleeful and terrifying."
Jeannette Catsoulis
The New York Times

Taylor Handley, Rebecca Mozo

Zoo
The Love That Dare Not Speak Its Name

In high school vocabulary we learned the words "francophile," and "pedophile," but "zoophile" was strangely missing. This beautifully photographed semi-docu, set in the U.S. Northwest, aims to remedy our ignorance . . . and does so exceedingly well.

Helmed and co-scripted by Robinson Devor, it tells the strange story of a Seattle man who died as a result of an "unusual encounter" with an Arabian stallion. The death of the Boeing executive made headlines across America. He died from a perforated colon after having sex with a horse.

Zoophiles found an unwitting ally in right-wing talking head, Rush Limbaugh. He suggested in an audio clip, "How in the world can this happen without consent?"

A hit at the Sundance Film Festival, this is a semi-docu in that it is a re-enactment of the true-to-life tale in 2005. It's a sort of blurring of the line between narrative and documentary storytelling. Abandoned by fellow zoophiles at an emergency room in rural Washington, the victim eventually died from internal injuries. The investigation into his death uncovered a nearby horse farm that hid a dark sexual secret. Tapes, including one entitled BIG DICK, were discovered at the farm. The zoophiles communicated with each other over the Internet, arranging various gatherings at this remote farm.

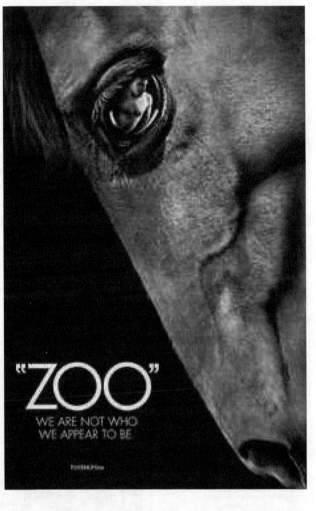

The film, in spite of its subject matter, is not lurid. In fact, it rather gently exposes this hidden subculture in America by presenting both a compassionate portrait and one that is subdued to the point of being almost poetic.

As David Ansen of *Newsweek* so accurately put it, "Zoo is transfixing and eerily beautiful, creating a dreamlike, elliptical reverie that neither condemns nor condones what it explores."

Never has bestiality been shown in such an elegant, eerily lyrical way. It sure beats all those big-dog-fucking-putas in Tijuana bestiality films brought back over the porous border with Mexico. No major film about horseplay was quite like this one. At the time of the death of the victim, 45-year-old Kenneth Pinyan, bestiality was not a crime in Washington State. So no charges were filed against the zoophiles exposed. It is now illegal, however.

Of his pioneering effort with *Zoo*, the director said, "these are totally uncharted waters. It's been happening for thousands of years, with very little study or attention. Is it cruel? God, I love animals, and I'd hate to think something was happening that was hurting them. But we kill and eat them, too."

"What was once a water-cooler punch line becomes a gorgeously shot, impressionistic portrait of the hidden corners of human sexuality—still the great unknown."
Michael Koresky
Interview

"'Nothing sexual ever happened until I gained their trust and they gained mine,' says one zoophile of his animal friends—a common enough averment from pedophiles."
Melissa Anderson
Time Out New York

"When Devor turns his camera on the world, it's as though he is seeing everything for the first time, whether it's the city lights of Seattle shining like diamonds under an evening sky or the unspoiled natural vistas of rural Washington."
Scott Foundas
Variety

"Horsey movies--and the concept of what it really means to ride a horse--have come a long way since *National Velvet* and *My Friend Flicka.*"
Animal rights activist **Aubrey Donohue**

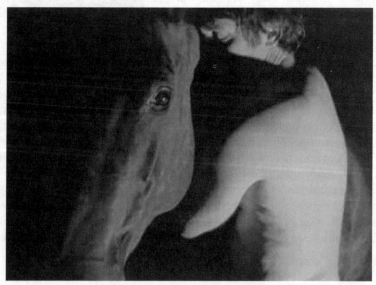

443

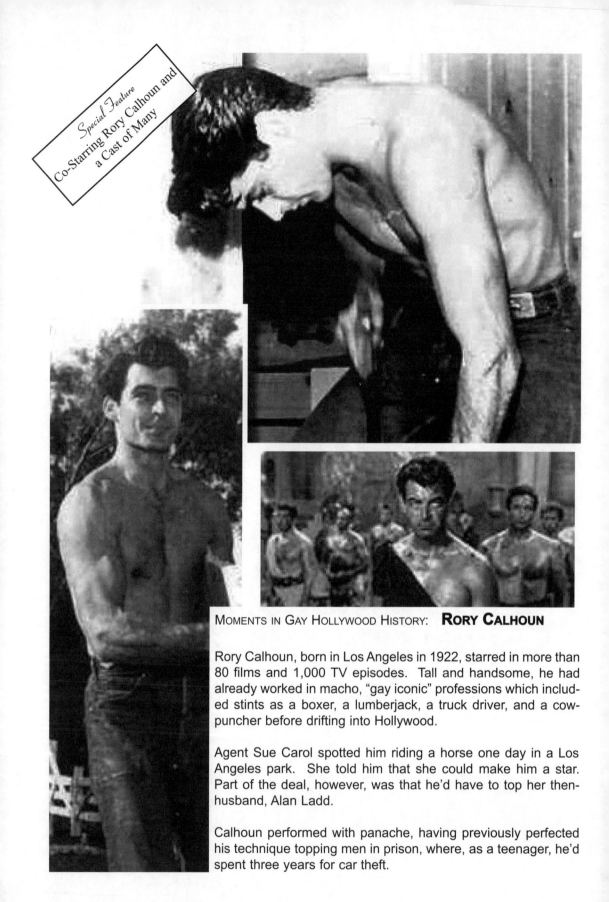

MOMENTS IN GAY HOLLYWOOD HISTORY: **RORY CALHOUN**

Rory Calhoun, born in Los Angeles in 1922, starred in more than 80 films and 1,000 TV episodes. Tall and handsome, he had already worked in macho, "gay iconic" professions which included stints as a boxer, a lumberjack, a truck driver, and a cowpuncher before drifting into Hollywood.

Agent Sue Carol spotted him riding a horse one day in a Los Angeles park. She told him that she could make him a star. Part of the deal, however, was that he'd have to top her then-husband, Alan Ladd.

Calhoun performed with panache, having previously perfected his technique topping men in prison, where, as a teenager, he'd spent three years for car theft.

"Sometimes, it's a good idea to keep your shorts on."
Fatherly advice from the editors at Blood Moon

Finally--
Part Three

Short Gay Films

Short, low-budget gay and lesbian films need recognition too.

Here's Blood Moon's take on a crop of recent shorties, many of which run for less than 30 minutes each.

ASSWAX

Going Where the Sun Don't Shine

In this short by David Burns, the naked ass is dehaired in a wax job. The video depicts the process of a professional ass wax. And, yes, Virginia, the damn thing hurts.

The ass waxer explains that the pain is good, and he giggles as his client screams in pain. The client is like a surgical patient, his body no longer entirely his own. Two cameras focus front and back on the client's face and his ass. His balls are revealed, but not much else. But we do see that ass in close-up. Once hairy, it emerges at the end as smooth as a baby's butt.

BEYOND LOVELY

Can't a Ghost Get a Table Dance?

What about this for a plotline for a 10-minute short? Lovely, as played by Guinevere Turner, is a struggling psychic who is contacted by "Bruce B.," an ambitious gay spirit bent on fulfilling his earthy desire for a TV show. Incidentally Bruce B. is played by Vaginal Davis. Yes, the correct spelling is indeed Vaginal.

Written and directed by Hilary Goldberg, this quirky little movie premiered at the San Francisco International LGBT Film Festival.

Goldberg has a poetic soul, and tours the nation performing not only as a poet but "a word artist." She's also a director of photography and has edited several short films. Her most intriguing character to date is obviously Bruce B., who has such a need for success for his TV show that he was and is oblivious to his own death.

As Lovely, Guinevere Turner has a real screen presence that captivated Goldberg. "She is a muse, and she inspires me to write characters that I want to see her play—and the camera has a mad crush on her. In *Beyond Lovely*, it was really fun to watch her tap into this innocent, playful side, and because she's beautiful you don't expect such brilliant comedic timing, so it is extra funny."

If you get off on Goldberg and her work, and that of Turner, you might want to catch *In the Spotlight*, coming soon. In it, Turner goes Gemini, playing twins. She'll scare the shit out of you—one twin loves you and the other wants to kill you.

BLACK BEULAHS & RAPE FOR WHO I AM

The Unexplored Gay Sub-Culture of Soweto

In South African slang, "Beulah" is gay slang for beautiful or fabulous. The director, Fanney Tsimong, follows three of his black gay male friends in homophobic Soweto to discover how they integrate their sexuality into a community that does not view their lifestyle favorably.

Running for 48 minutes, the film focuses on a trio that includes DK, a businessman who owns a funeral parlor; Chiz, a bodybuilder, and Somizi, a choreographer and entertainer. They defy societal expectations to live their lives as they see them. Their struggles with the reality of homosexuality in a hostile clime is a rather engrossing and remarkable experience. Taking on the largely unexamined Soweto gay scene, the film is a pioneering documentary. At festivals, it was usually shown immediately before or after *Rape For Who I Am,* another docu that covers the hidden world of the African lesbian. In it, we see first-hand how lesbians face daily injustice because of their sexuality. Homosexuality, of course, is Africa's last great taboo, and in some parts of South Africa homophobia is "expressed" through targeted rape of black lesbians. We meet Keba, Mary, and Bathini, all of whom were raped because of their sexual orientation. *Rape For Who I Am,* as written and directed by Lovinsa Kavuma, tells their horrid story.

(above) Three hot Beulahs from Soweto
(below) Lovinsa Kavuma, writer/director, *Rape for Who I Am*

BOYS BRIEFS 4

Six Short Films About Guys Who Sell It

We're not usually drawn to multiple films from different helmers on one DVD, finding the programs most often uneven—both in direction and acting. The 110-minute *Boys Briefs 4* is no exception, culled from films as far afield as France or New Zealand.

Some of these flicks feel like college assignments in film school; others are more forceful in their punch. It's hit-and-miss. The only element that ties this international anthology together—in both French and English—is that *Briefs* depicts young men who sell their dicks on the open market.

The best film in the collection is called *Into the Night*, written by Cath Moore and directed by Tony Krawitz. It depicts a late middle-aged man, Marcus (Bryan Marshall), who picks up a reasonably attractive teenaged hustler, Damien (Sam Barlow), who eerily resembles his dead son.

The tense relationship between the john and the hustler is depicted with verisimilitude, including brief violence. There is realism here when the hustler offers to suck off the john but won't let him fuck him in the ass. The tenderest moment occurs when the hustler is taking a bath in a large tub, and the older man comes in to scrub his back, much like he probably did with his own son, with whom he might have had an incestuous obsession.

The other good film in the collection is called *Build*, which was written and directed by Greg Atkins, who cast himself as Crete, a student of architecture at the University of Toronto. This is a compelling drama about a young hustler whose secret life catches up with him. He quits his studies to support his alcoholic mother and, in so doing, meets another seasoned, opportunistic hustler.

The Paris of Bastian Schweitzer is evoked in *Gigolo*, which documents Euro-trash through the eyes of a petulant Algerian rent boy given to interior monologues. This good-looking Arab, Karim (Salim Kechiouche), whores himself to both men and women of the jet set. His plight is that of countless other young Arab boys caught up in a hostile, indifferent France, as evoked by the super-rich, middle-aged, and surgically enhanced blonde (Amanda Lear). The helmer, Schweitzer, sees Paris like a perfume commercial.

A Canadian entry, Armen Kazazian's *Gold* tells the story of an aging artist (P.J. Lazic) losing his eyesight. He employs a drug-addicted hustler, Billy (Aron Tager), to paint his paintings for him in a mutual quest for salvation. The wealthy artist takes delight in humiliating Billy as he instructs him in exceedingly precise fashion in painting. An incident sends Billy back to hustling on the streets, which ultimately climaxes in a test of his character.

In Mary Feuer's *Rock Bottom,* John Militello stars as Billy, an overweight freelance writer who picks up a wiry hustler, Jason (Timothy Lee DePriest), on Santa Monica Boulevard. Jason gets high on drugs, but, even so, there are sometimes tender moments depicted in this emerging relationship between an ill-matched duo of the night.

The real bore of the collection is called *Boy*, written and directed by Welby Ings. It's the story of Sam (Jesse Lee), a toilet-sharpened hustler who lives in a small town in New Zealand. The best thing about the film is a coterie of crusty old character actors who appear as in a time warp from the 1950s. Sam discovers the truth behind a hit-and-run accident, putting his own life in jeopardy.

If you attend a theater showing *Boys Briefs 4* (or, more likely, if you see it on DVD), know that the road it travels is a long way from the trail blazed by *My Own Private Idaho*.

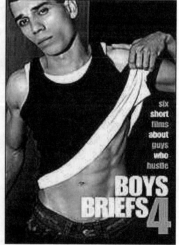

448

THE BRIDGE

Asylum Heartbreak for Two Gay Lovers

This short drama runs for only 8 minutes, but it's rather moving, suggesting director George Barbakadze has greater stuff in him. The Sydney helmer was the winner of the City of Melbourne Emerging Filmmaker Award for Best Australian Queer Short Film.

Glen Upton as Luka and Andy Cunningham as Niko star as a gay couple in Georgia (the former colony of the USSR). Their dream is to flee their homophobic homeland to the relative security of a more liberal Australia. They eagerly await a response to their visa applications. Regrettably, only one of them gets a visa for Australia. The other is left behind to face a lonely life.

COLORBLIND

When Is a Man Really Straight?

In this short, Peter (Danny Feigelson) plays it straight. But is he really? His so-called girlfriend is called "she'll do for now."

In a bleached blonde performance, Pamela Randolph as Amy is very effective as the girlfriend. She's the type of bosomy woman that could turn straight men gay. A supporting role is played by the couple's drug dealer buddy, Rich Sienko, who keeps the unloving couple supplied with pot.

The opening scene is effective when Peter wakes up in bed with his girlfriend, Amy. It's obvious that he's disgusted with her. He's also upset by the noise the movers are making. They are moving in a new neighbor who will change Peter's life.

On the stairs, Peter is rather hostile when he confronts a gay Latino male hottie, referred to only as "X." Perhaps X-Man. Peter is initially hostile to X, but perhaps it is only to disguise his attraction.

As Amy grows more disgusting to Peter, he flees to the shower where he jacks off while images of X float through his brain. Without showing his hard-on, the scene is so realistic that you think Peter is actually masturbating. Perhaps he was.

By this point, gay male viewers know what is going to happen—call it inevitable. The final scenes explain the reason for the title.

The film was written, produced, and directed by Apollo Oliva, who shows a talent for revealing suppressed feelings on screen. *Colorblind* marks Oliva's directorial debut in film.

CONTEMPLATING EMILY
Lesbian Love Where East Meets West

Contemplating Emily, a 15-minute film, is a poetic treatment of a feature-length screenplay of the same name that tells the East-meets-West love story of a young Taiwanese poet and her New York City English teacher. The story is a romantic comedy—*Kissing Jessica Stein* meets *Lost in Translation* dashed with *Brokeback Mountain*. It explores the complexities of discovering and eventually accepting lesbian love, as catalyzed by the poetry of Emily Dickinson

In the short film, scenes from the feature script were shot on 16mm. They were then artificially book-ended with digitally shot scenes from the feature to give the highlighted material some structure. While the short helps to introduce the principal characters, storyline, and nature of the screenplay, it only lightly touches on the potential grandeur of the piece.

The film stars three talented performers—Sarah E. Shively as Elizabeth Richards, Kathy Shao-Lin Lee as Lulu Yao, and Clove Galilee as Emily Dickinson.

Clove Galilee as Emily Dickinson

450

CREMMATE: MUFFY

We'll Never Look at Coffee the Same Way Again!

This 3-minute video was directed by Diane Wilkins, depicting the lives of a cat-loving lesbian couple. They are changed forever as they discover CremMate non-dairy coffee creamer. And just when we thought every subject for film had been used up.

"The couple really love their cat. In the morning at their kitchen table, they sip coffee from matching cat mugs while sitting under a cat clock in front of knickknack shelves dripping with kitty statuettes. They wear cat T-shirts and drive to work in their car with a license plate that reads: "I (heart) Cats." When an unfortunate driveway incident occurs, Dona and Susan come up with a creative solution to memorializing their beloved pet."

The above-noted comment about this film was made at the 2006 New York LGBT Film Festival by Shella Lambert.

DAVY AND STU

Adolescent Romance & Forbidden Love

This is a short, a drama/romance of two very different Scottish lads who meet each day after school at a nearby peat bog. Director Soman Chainani cast Nicholas Cutro as Stu and Travis Walters as Davy in this 13-minute color short. Based on Anton Dudley's award-winning play, *Davy & Stu* is a heart-wrenching look at the intensity of adolescent romance and forbidden love.

First Out

A Collection of Award-Winning Gay-Theme Shorts

Running for 65 minutes, *First Out* presents five very different gay themed shorts. The first in the series, *Is One of You Eddie?* stars Robbie Laughlin of *Queer Eye for the Straight Guy* and *Another Gay Movie*. Stereotypes are challenged as four reasonably attractive but rather girly men in West Hollywood look disapprovingly upon their upstairs neighbor, the roughcut and very butch Eddie.

Suddenly, a charismatically beautiful man appears in their midst, looking for Eddie to give him a massage. After the hunk's rave review of Eddie's talented hands following an in-depth massage, the men at their outdoor lunch begin to re-evaluate this Eddie number.

The spookiest entry is *The Neighborly Thing,* a chilling tale about a gay man's overzealous obsession with his upstairs neighbor. When he encounters a young street couple inhabiting his neighbor's apartment, his territory is threatened. He introduces himself to them, causing an imminent—and possibly deadly—confrontation. Michael Simon and Samantha Light star in this one.

Meet Joe Gay is a multi-media docu in which 27-year-old gay filmmaker, Benjamin Morgan, attempts to understand why he's single and what it takes to maintain a successful relationship.

A Good Son won the Jury Prize for Best Short at the Philadelphia International Gay Lesbian Film Festival. It tells of a chance encounter between two teenage boys, leading to a turning point in their lives.

Finally, in the short, *Different*, Justin has a secret: He's straight. In the parallel universe of Liberty High School, gay is the norm. Homecoming is only days away. The film stars Ben Hogestyn, the first openly gay character on *General Hospital.*

Gay

Hardships Gay Teens Face in High School

Brandon Yanovsky produced and directed this 10-minute short, addressing the problems many gay teens face in going to high school. He used both gay and straight teens to discuss this dilemma, but claimed that "very few people wanted to be interviewed." Apparently, students feared they would be criticized or labeled as gay if they appeared in a docu about homosexuality, even if introduced as straight. Such is the stigma.

Both young men and women frankly discuss such problems as alienation, name calling, bullying, and religion, among other topics. Some of them who have been called queer reveal their hurt and anguish, which takes place on a daily basis, at least when they're in school.

But these teens also face the same hostility out of school. One lesbian student related what happened to her on a date with another girl. A straight boy approached her date, grabbed his crotch, and suggested something to the effect that a plugging from his dick would cure "the chick" forever of her lesbianism.

Don't expect a lot of action. The docu consists mostly of filmed segments of the teens' talk. We can only applaud the bravery of such teens as Colin Holtzinger, Greg Robinson, and Michelle Meadows for talking so openly about the problems gays face.

GUY 101
Human Sexuality on the Internet

Directed by Ian W. Gouldstone, this 9-minute short held its premiere at the New York Lesbian and Gay Film Festival in June of 2006. The film has been screened in both Europe (Paris) and the States (Miami and Nashville) with great success.

Gouldstone, a filmmaker and designer, shot the piece as a graduation assignment from the Royal College of Art in London.

In a tagline, it's about a man who hears a tale about a hitchhiker from the other side of the Internet. The film uses computer desktop icons and Internet image searches to tell a story that subtly but powerfully challenges our ideas of Internet safety, freedom, and human sexuality.

HIS NAME IS COSMO
Two Lesbians Give Sex Toys a Shot

This 18-minute short explores the sexual hang-ups of Laurie and Nancy, a 20-something couple who decide it's time to give sex toys a try. Laurie is Laura Terruso, who also wrote and co-produced the film. Nancy is Nicole Opper who both directed *His Name Is Cosmo* and co-produced it. The film represents Laura's screenwriting debut.

Laurie is a quirky and endearing lesbian who yearns to push the bedroom boundaries with her other half, the grounded and slightly insecure Nancy. She is skeptical yet willing to try out these new games, though she quickly discovers they are not for her.

The tension escalates as Laurie develops an unhealthy fixation that lets her imagination run wild, resulting in absurd fantasy sequences involving a life-sized phallus.

Enter a fictitious fairy godmother, portrayed by comedienne, Julie Goldman who was the only openly lesbian character on HBO's *The Sopranos*. She also toured Australia with the hit, *Puppetry of the Penis*.

The exaggerated dialogue and screwball sketches in this "sex comedy without the sex" draws us into Laurie's laughable inner conflict right up until the final moment, when an unusual compromise is reached between the two lovers.

IF YOU LIVED HERE, YOU'D BE HOME BY NOW

A Short Film About the Afterglow

This Israeli film, written and directed by Tamar Glezerman, is one of the best we've seen about two lesbians who have broken up but still share the same apartment. Obviously this is done for economic reasons, not desire.

For some reason, Shira has left her love relationship with Noa, but she is still hanging out in the Tel Aviv apartment. Noa just wants her out of the house so she can get on with her life.

The principal players, Maya Sarfati and Hila Meckier, are two talented and attractive actresses. The inevitable problems arise, including who owns possession of the living room, which the women don't want to share at the same time. The biggest problem arises when Shira brings over a female trick for some fun and games, much to Noa's annoyance . . . and obvious jealousy.

The film is not to be confused with a same-named TV drama from 2006 called *If You Lived Here, You'd Be Home Now*, a US film directed by Peter Lauer that was the pilot for a TV series about a group of people from different backgrounds who live in a temporary housing complex in Los Angeles.

LOVE IS BLIND

Sparks Fly & So Do the Bullets

Both comical and poignant, Peter Pizzi is an independent filmmaker to watch. He works mainly with digital video, his shorts dealing with issues of sexuality, gender, and identity.

Love Is Blind, one of his latest works, runs for 9 minutes and in that time deals with the age-old adage that forms the title of the movie. The question asked is this: Just why do we make the choices we make in love?

Betty in the film is a girl out of luck and out of love. The role is played by Michelle Tea, a well-known novelist and poet from San Francisco. She is at wits end with her rock star girlfriend.

Along comes Lucy, a renegade, a firecracker, a whisky-belting tart who can curse like a sailor. She's also legally blind. When Betty and Lucy meet, sparks fly. But also the bullets!

MAN SEEKING MAN *(Mies Etsii Miestä)*

Son Gets Groped as Dad Mistakes Him for a Hustler

In this 12-minute Finnish short, a mistaken identity farce is created by helmer and scripter Matti Harju. Seppo (Asko Sahlman) is a man in his 50s who places an ad for a man in the personals. Kale (Jussi Lehtonen) is 25 years old and has not seen dear ol' dad in 20 years.

He decides to have a reunion with him and comes to his hometown after calling his mother to get his father's address. Waiting for the arrival of his hot date, Seppo thinks Kale is the man of his dreams when he arrives at his apartment.

After all these years, he does not recognize his son. At one point dad strips completely nude and confronts his startled son. That's one full frontal we wish we'd never witnessed. He doesn't know that Kale is his son until the gay man (Markus Karekallas) arrives at the door in answer to the ad MAN SEEKING MAN.

MY HUSTLER BOYFRIEND

Tarty White Bitch Raves About Her BF's 10" Dick

Director Peter Pizzi is having some fun with us in this short. A white whore, who looks like "she" was designed to give blow-jobs, raves about why she likes her hustler boyfriend. She claims he even taught her how to climax even though he had bad breath. Ben McCoy stars as a sassy tranny.

We get to meet this hottie, a black man who deals drugs on the side when he's not selling his big dick. There is one shot where we get to see him in a sex pouch, which he does indeed seem to fill out. Cedric Harper plays the urban thug.

With *My Hustler Boyfriend,* Pizzi is indeed taking a walk on the seedy side of life.

All this short needs now is for Pat Robertson to show it on the 700 Club as a docu about what homosexuals are really like and why they were responsible for the destruction of the World Trade Center.

QUEER EYE FOR THE HOMELESS GUY

"Hysterical . . . I Peed in My Pants!"

That review came from the director's best friend. When you check this short out, see if you can control your urine. With its title, even the dimmest bulb will get the idea the short was inspired by the reality TV program, *Queer Eye for the Straight Guy* . . . and so it was.

It's a send-up of America's obsession with the make-over phenomenon. As social satire, it hits the mark.

Helmer Joshua Stern is to blame for this outrageous spoof. Stern chose the cast with skill. If called upon, each actor could play a demonic queen.

Stern was also the scripter on the project. Perhaps his wife said it all: "This film is to cinema what bad breath was to our first date!"

SHORT FILMS OF CHARLES LUM
Voyeurism, Fetishism, & a Dog's Life

Charles Lum of New York is a photographer and filmmaker who studied at The Art Institute of Chicago. His weird, weird world is contained on one video with a collection of some of his most provocative shorts: *Pissies Not Sissies; Dog Eat Dog, Overdue Conversation*, and the rather, bizarre *Sex Manic*.

Pissies Not Sissies was the first installation of a trilogy exploring the International Mister Leather Contest, the largest gathering of leather S&M devotees in the world. The camera follows the IML Boys as they navigate the contest, the hotel, and the theme parties. The camera even goes into the contest men's room to raise questions of performance, embarrassment, desire, and voyeurism in a shocking display of fetishism.

Dog Eat Dog is another installment of the leather trilogy. In this short, you meet "Sparky," the feral star of this dog-and-pony show. Let's say no more.

The shortest of the shorts, *Sex Manic* runs for only 5 minutes. Its subject is HIV disclosure laws.

Overdue Conversation is longer, running for 9 minutes and dealing with sex, responsibility, and HIV. Lum spoke of this confrontational work that addresses AIDS with a new tactic. "*Overdue Conversation* de-objectifies the documentary interview by triangulating the audience between two video perspectives. Eliminating camera crew and cross cutting, the subjects/objects and audience become split-screen equals as participants, witness, and editors in a candid video confrontation over sexual truthfulness. Placed between the players, the camcorder/audience can scrutinize deceptions and decisions made on issues concerning personal vs. public freedoms, privacy, HIV disclosure, legal accountability, and sexual dynamics."

Charles Lum

SOLITUDE
Fantasies & Nightmares of a Lonely Man

With no dialogue and with black-and-white surreal images, *Solitude* is an 8-minute experimental film. It leaves the viewer with a deep sense of having experienced the materialization of loneliness, even when depicting masturbatory fantasies.

This is a very personal work, having been scripted and helmed by Jesus M. Rodriguez, who is from Venezuela but living now in Los Angeles. He shot his first horror movies when he was only 13. He first gained notice with his short film, *Lucy & Ricky*, an official selection of the Sundance Film Festival in 2003.

Solitude is his third short film to date, and is his most daring, including underwater scenes shot by Peter Zuccarini.

STILL
Young Man's Self-Discovery, Love, & Reconnection with Dad

Kenny Santana, reviewing films for *The Jakarta Post*, was a bit taken aback by some of the subjects in this festival of shorts. Santana wrote: "Naked bodies, a scene from a gay sauna, or a transvestite tale in Paris, are not things you would normally expect to see on an Indonesian screen."

One of those shorts is *Still,* directed by 25-year-old Lucky Kuswandi and shot in Los Angeles when Lucky was in his final year of studies.

In *Still*, a gay teenager Guy (Jason Woo), is detached from his surroundings. He runs away from home to escape the stillness of his life. He has little purpose and is desperate for a human connection, even a substitute for love.

Love is something he never receives from his distant father. Guy takes the train to a beach town and checks into a dilapidated motel. Leaving the motel, he wanders the barely alive streets aimlessly cruising through life's clichés only to find discomfort and disillusionment.

Bored and lonely, he seeks solace through the only means with which he is familiar and capable: Sex with strangers. He finds himself in a bathhouse, depicted as a series of long, dark hallways filled with other desperate, lost men. He meets an older man (Keith Jennings) who wants to care for him. The older man wraps Guy in a tight but tender embrace, but this exhausts him. It reminds him of his own father's possessive dominance, and his resistance and emotional pain force him to confront that ominous figure which has been haunting him.

In the end, Guy is transported to a dream-like encounter with his father (Brett C. Shim) on a cold, deserted beach. Guy finally has to make the choice in taking the laborious first step to close the distance between them, and face the trouble he has been trying to elude.

THANKS FOR CALLING, BABY
A Young Woman and a Father with AIDS

Since she was reared by two lesbians and a gay man, filmmaker Zia Florence Anger knows her subject well. Her film runs for less than 4 minutes, but it has power and a punch.

In the short, a young woman examines her relationship with father and confronts the AIDS drugs that keep him alive. Shot using a Bolex on 16mm film, it was edited to include footage of Anger's somewhat bizarre childhood.

THANKSGIVING

Who's the Turkey in This One?

This short, whose tagline is "Meat, Online," is a psycho-sexual thriller involving Tom (as played by the film's writer, Neal Utterback), and his (unnamed) boyfriend, who's briefly portrayed by the film's director, Joe LaRue. Released in 2007, it begins harmlessly enough when the moderately annoying boyfriend leaves on a trip for a week, and Tom is left to his own (obsessive and sexual) devices for Thanksgiving.

Within a few minutes' of boyfriend's departure, Tom begins surfing the web for sex. He ignores an 8-incher and opts for a self-proclaimed 9-incher, as played by Vincent De Paul, a hot and genuinely charismatic actor whose feature films have recently included, among others, *Contadora Is for Lovers*. Vincent (playing Tucker), portrays himself as a beautiful piece of manmeat with 9 inches. Through the phone, Vince tells Tom, "I want to devour you."

If only Tom had listened.

Soonafter, Tom opens his door to discover that Tucker is everything he promised he was in the ad. Except for one thing. He lied. He's not 9 inches, but more like 10. Tom giggles, claiming that no one lies down, only up. He admits to 6 inches . . . well, maybe 5½, perhaps 5¼.

Tucker doesn't seem particularly concerned with measurements, and begins to get down and dirty with Tom.

Flash forward. After sex, Tom finds himself tied up—"a little tight." Tucker warns that "piggies don't talk" and tapes his mouth shut. Tucker then starts kicking Tom, beating up on him, and dragging his screaming, tied-up body down a long hallway in a way that the viewer is keenly aware isn't consensual.

We won't give the final scene away, which is one of the most frightening within any gay short we've seen this year. As the film ends, we realize that Tom got those 10 inches plus a lot more than he bargained for!

TO HOLD A HEART

A Not-So-Chance Encounter at a Gym

In this 13-minute short, two men, separated by decades in age and thousands of miles in home and culture, meet in a gym. At a glacial pace, an intense bond of intimacy and trust develops.

Helmer Michael Wallin, of his own film, asks: "Can this be love? Sex, if it happens at all, may just be icing on the cake. Touch, physical contact, affection . . . to feel alive, to feel engaged, to feel understood."

Roland Barthes plays the older man who falls for the hot young (Japanese) man, as played by Taro Masuschio, who consistently wears baggy red shorts during his workouts.

The helmer explores the halting development and awkward moments of a courtship that takes place over nearly a year. Barthes longs to touch the boy but can't, except for a perfunctory squeeze of the knee or a goodbye hug.

Trailer For a Remake of Gore Vidal's *Caligula*

CALIGULA: *I hear you have a taste for little boys. Is that not so?*
CHAEREA: *No, Caesar, big boys.*

Gay director Francesco Vezzoli made this 5-minute short inspired by the notorious 1979 film, *Caligula*, written by Gore Vidal, who sued to get his name removed from the credits.

It starred such big names as Malcolm McDowell, Helen Mirren, Peter O'Toole, Adriana Asti, and even John Gielgud ("my first porno movie").

Its director, Tinto Brass, in collaboration with *Penthouse* publisher Bob Guccione, later added hardcore porno scenes to Vidal's original script, none of which involved or portrayed the A-list main cast members. There are various versions still out there of this '79 film, ranging from the heavily truncated 90-minute edition to the legendary 160-minute hardcore version which leaves nothing to the imagination.

Into this simmering hotbed of cinematic controversy came Vezzoli, a 34-year-old artist from Milan, who lined up Helen Mirren once again, along with such stars as Karen Black and Benicio Del Toro, for the creation of a fake promotional short. The togas in the short were designed by Donatella Versace. An imperial-looking Vidal appears as himself, asking and responding, "Who needs a remake of *Caligula*? Everyone."

One of the many ironies associated with this trailer is that there is, and probably never will be, a remake of Gore Vidal's *Caligula*. But perhaps therein lies part of the charm.

The trailer was filmed at a neo-Roman villa on Sunset Boulevard in Los Angeles. Vezzoli himself appears in a cameo, playing a mad Roman emperor who sleeps with his sister and presides over a bevy of ambisexual extras. Courtney Love even made a brief appearances, and men and women interchanged their roles freely.

One might ask why was such a short ever made? Nonetheless, when it premiered at the Venice Biennale, the work, which was custom-made specifically for that event, became the hottest ticket there.

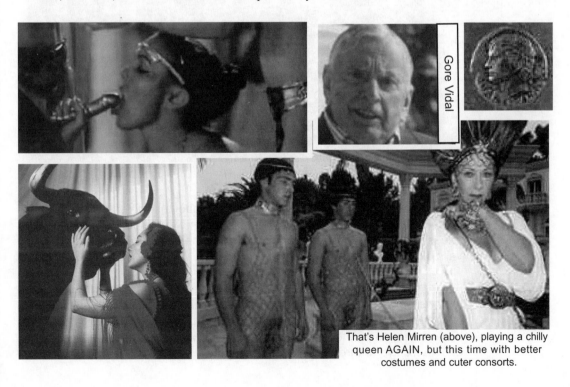

Gore Vidal

That's Helen Mirren (above), playing a chilly queen AGAIN, but this time with better costumes and cuter consorts.

MOMENTS IN GAY HOLLYWOOD HISTORY

Some moviegoers thought Guy Madison (left, above) and ultra-macho Robert Mitchum (right, above), were playing a love scene in this scene from the 1946 release of *Till the End of Time*. It was one of the first films to address the travails of veterans in post-World War II America.

Its director, Edward Dmytryk, told friends that "Guy fell in love with Bob when they were pissing at a urinal at a military base in San Diego. Bob didn't agree to go the whole route, but let Guy fellate him." Dmytryk went on to say, "When he was a teenaged hood, Bob told me he often let guys on the road go down on him for two or three dollars."

Here it is, folks, what you've all been waiting for:

Mirror, Mirror on the Wall, who's the hottest of them all?

HOLLYWOOD'S HOTTEST HOTTIES

For their courage in their interpretation of gay-sensitive roles, and with recognition of their intelligence and their talent, we extend sincere thanks to the actors celebrated within this honorary roster of hotties.

Then we'll respectfully continue with these heartfelt compliments:

WOOF! WOW! OINK! HAI CARUMBA! MAMASITA! PITTER-PATTER! AND VA-VA-VA-VOOM!

BRANDON

" I believe that we are all one on the inside, despite our outward differences, and this is something I brought to the role. Superman should unite people. As far as the person I am in the world, I just intend on being positive, and ready to learn from the experiences that life brings me. "

Brandon James Routh

Born: October 9, 1979
Birthplace: Des Moines, Iowa
www.BrandonRouth.com

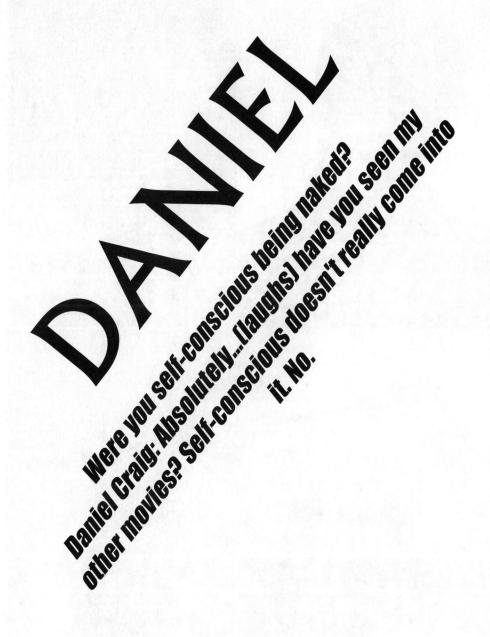

DANIEL

Were you self-conscious being naked?

Daniel Craig: Absolutely...[laughs] have you seen my other movies? Self-conscious doesn't really come into it. No.

Daniel Wroughton Craig

Born: March 2, 1968
Birthplace: Cheshire, England
www.danielcraig.fan-sites.org

465

JUSTIN

"I used to think I actually was Batman."

Justin Randall
Timberlake

Born: January 31, 1981
Birthplace: Memphis, Tennessee
www.officialjustintimberlake.com

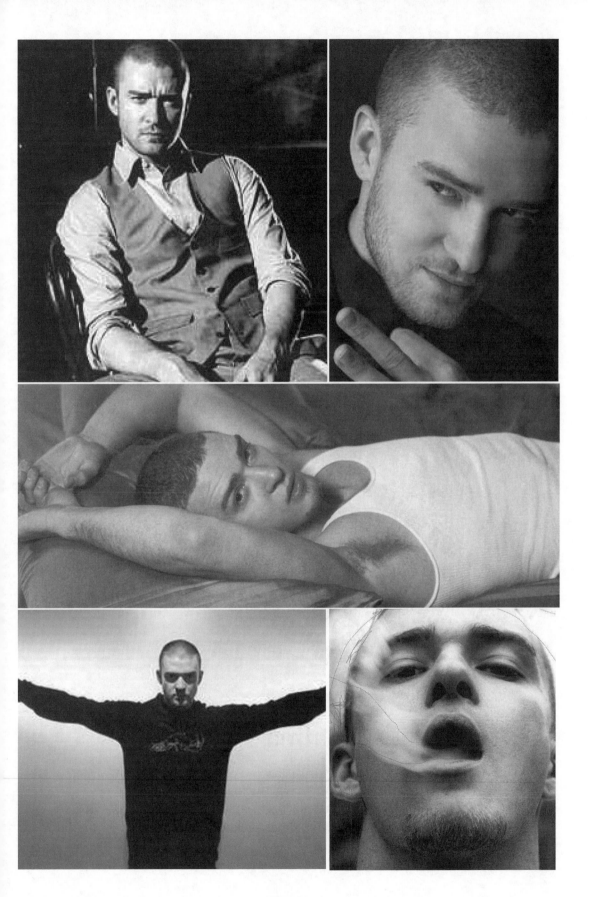

SALMA

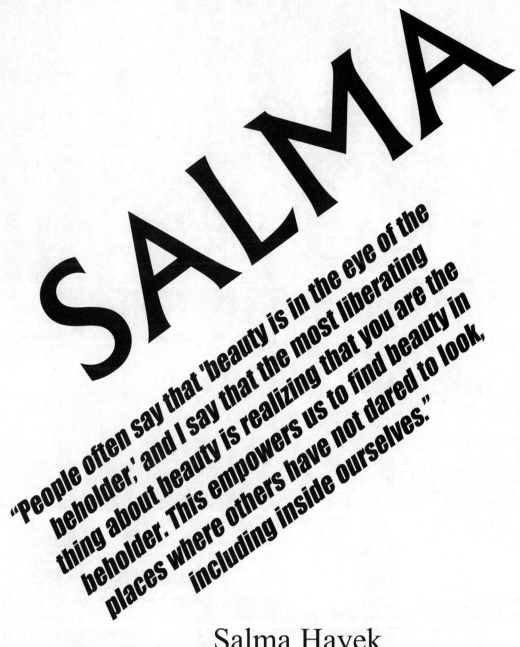

"People often say that 'beauty is in the eye of the beholder,' and I say that the most liberating thing about beauty is realizing that you are the beholder. This empowers us to find beauty in places where others have not dared to look, including inside ourselves."

Salma Hayek

Born: September 2, 1966
Birthplace: Coatzacoalcos, Veracruz, Mexico
www.salmahayekonline.com

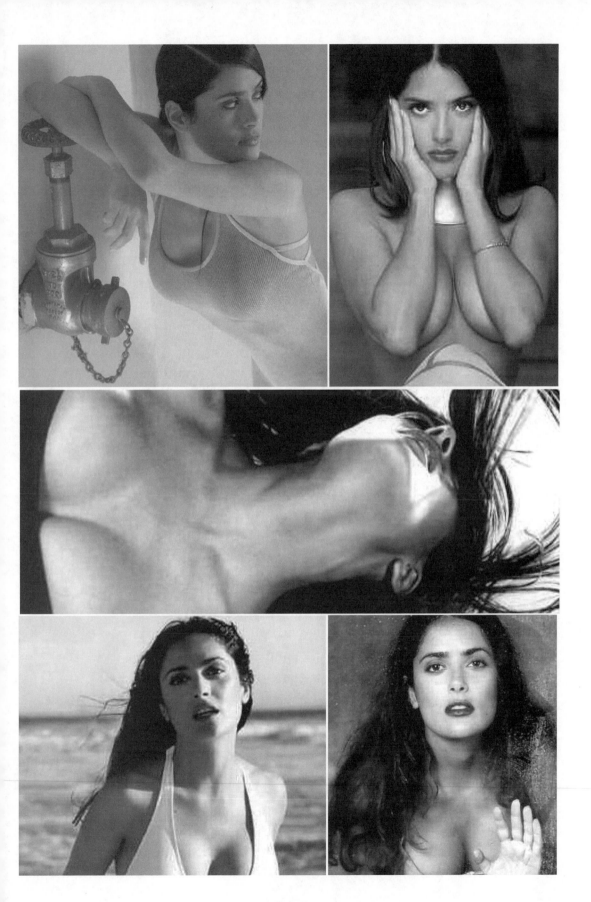

469

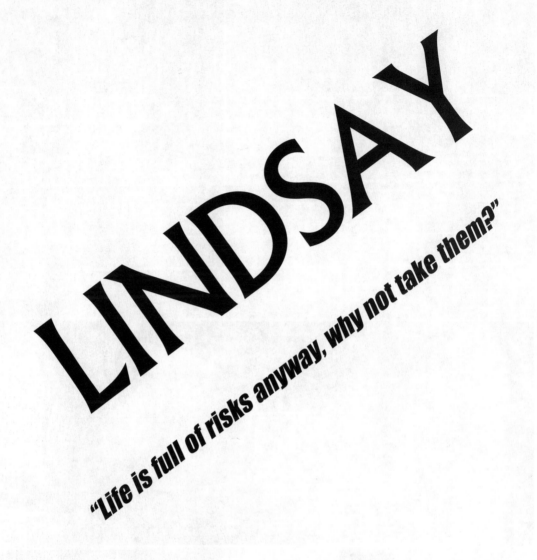

LINDSAY

"Life is full of risks anyway, why not take them?"

Lindsay Dee Lohan

Born: July 2, 1986
Birthplace: New York City, NY
www.llrocks.com

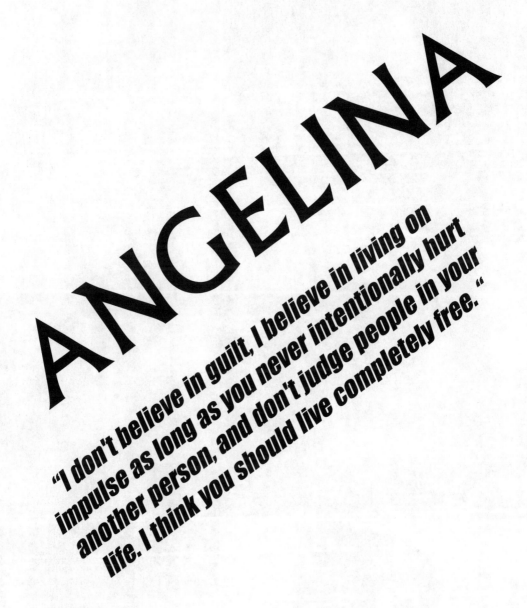

ANGELINA

"I don't believe in guilt, I believe in living on impulse as long as you never intentionally hurt another person, and don't judge people in your life. I think you should live completely free."

Angelina Jolie

Born: June 4, 1975
Birthplace: Los Angeles, CA
www.angelinafan.com

Before he became Governor Schwarzenegger of California, the Austrian bodybuilder was known to casting directors in 1970 as "Arnold Strong" for his appearance in the low-budget horror, *Hercules in New York* (aka *Hercules Goes Bananas*).

The film revealed an impressively sculpted body and the fact that its owner could not act or speak English.

A decade later, the same actor, now speaking English and known as Arnold Schwarzenegger, portrayed Miklos (Mickey) Hargitay, the Hungarian-born bodybuilder who was the former lover of Mae West, the husband of Jayne Mansfield, and the father of Mariska Hargitay, a talented actress best known as detective Olivia Benson in about 200 recent episodes of *Law and Order*. Where was Mickey being portrayed? In the 1980 biopic, *The Jayne Mansfield Story*.

Mickey was alive at the time to review Arnold's performance. His verdict? In a word, "inept—I could have played myself so much better. I'd even be great as Arnold in the story of *his* life. Instead of faking an Austrian accent, I could have played him as a Hungarian. After all, my country is directly next door to his."

Photos, beginning upper left and moving clockwise:
Mickey Hargitay, his wife, Jayne Mansfield, Mickey and Jayne together, Arnold as Conan the Barbarian, and Arnold in *Hercules in New York.*

474

The Secret Life of
HUMPHREY BOGART
THE EARLY YEARS (1899-1931)   BY DARWIN PORTER

The Secret Life of
Humphrey Bogart
The Early Years
(1899 - 1931)
Darwin Porter

This myth-shattering biography gives a controversial CLOSEUP of a young, hot and horny Bogart pre-Casablanca, pre-Bacall, pre-African Queen Revealing for the first time what was under the trench coat of history's most famous movie star

Loaded with information once suppressed by the Hollywood studios, this is the most revealing book ever written about the undercover lives of movie stars during the 1930s. Learn what America's most visible male star was doing during his mysterious early years on Broadway and in Hollywood at the dawn of the Talkies--details that Bogie worked hard to suppress during his later years with Bacall.

The subject of more than 80 radio interviews by its author, and widely covered by both the tabloids and the mainstream press, it's based on never-before-published memoirs, letters, diaries, and interviews from men and women who either loved Bogie or who wanted him to burn in hell. No wonder Bogie, in later life, usually avoided talking about his early years.

Serialized in three parts by Britain's *Mail on Sunday*, with some of its revelations flashed around the world, it demonstrates that Hollywood's Golden Age stars were human, highly sexed, and at least when they were with other Hollywood insiders, remarkably indiscreet.

"This biography has had us pondering as to how to handle its revelations within a town so protective of its own...This biography of Bogart's early years is exceptionally well-written."
JOHN AUSTIN, *HOLLYWOOD INSIDE*

"In this new biography, we learn about how Bogart struggled for stardom in the "anything goes" era of the Roaring 20s."   ***THE GLOBE***

"Porter's book uncovers scandals within the entertainment industry of the 1920s and 1930s, when publicists from the movie studios deliberately twisted and suppressed inconvenient details about the lives of their emerging stars."

TURNER CLASSIC MOVIE NEWS

"This biography brilliantly portrays a slice of time: In this case, the scandal-soaked days of Prohibition, when a frequently hung-over Bogie operated somwhat like a blank sheet of paper on which other actors, many of them infamous, were able to design their lives. The book is beautifully written."

LAURENCE HAZELL, PhD. University of Durham (UK)

527 pages, with an index and at least 60 vintage photos.
ISBN 0-9668030-5-1   **SOFTCOVER**   **$16.95**

HOWARD HUGHES: HELL'S ANGEL
AMERICA'S NOTORIOUS BISEXUAL BILLIONAIRE
THE SECRET LIFE OF THE U.S. EMPEROR

by Darwin Porter

A rigorously researched, highly entertaining hardcover. **ISBN 0-9748118-1-5**. $26.95

814 pages, plus 175 vintage photos

Howard Hughes: Hell's Angel

America's Notorious Bisexual Billionaire
Exposed for the First Time
BY DARWIN PORTER

As serialized by London's
Mail on Sunday,
this book is about the Hollywood
intrigue, and the Hollywood
debauchery of
Howard Hughes
and the A-list legends
who participated.

Researched over a period of 40
years, it's a stormingly good read
about *Who* and *What*
money can buy.

FOREWORD MAGAZINE'S
Book of the Year
AWARD
FINALIST

**Outrageous Fortune
Tragic Greed**

It's All Here!

"Thanks to Darwin Porter's biography of Howard Hughes, we'll never be able to look at the old pin-ups in quite the same way"

THE LONDON TIMES

"Darwin Porter grew up in the midst of Hollywood Royalty. his access to film industy insiders and other Hughes confidantes supplied him with the resources he needed to create a portrait that both corroborates what other Hughes biographies have divulged and go them one better."

FOREWORD MAGAZINE

"According to a new biography by Darwin Porter, Hughes's attitude toward sex, like the Emperor Caligula, was selfish at best and at its worst, sadistic. He was obsessed with controlling his lovers and, although he had a pathological fear of relationships and marriage, he proposed to countless women, often at the same time. Only three people successfully resisted Hughes's persistent advances: Elizabeth Taylor, Jean Simmons, and Joan Crawford. Of the three, it was Crawford who most succinctly revealed her reasons for refusing Hughes's advances, "I adore homosexuals, but not in my bed after midnight."

THE SUNDAY EXPRESS LONDON)

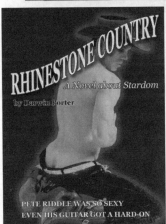

RHINESTONE COUNTRY   by Darwin Porter

A provocative but tender portrait of America's country-western music industry. Sweeping across the racial and sexual landscapes of the Deep South, it takes a hard look at closeted lives south of the Mason-Dixon line and the destructive aspects of fame.

"A sexual kick in the groin. High-adrenaline love, violence, and betrayal. A riveting show-biz tale of fame and lust."
-Tyrone Maxwell

FROM THE GEORGIA LITERARY ASSOCIATION
ISBN 0-9668030-3-5 PAPERBACK $15.95

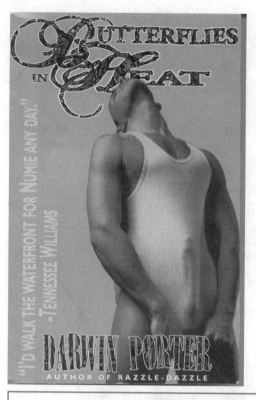

From the Georgia Literary Association, in cooperation with the Florida Literary Association, a reprint of the bestselling cult classic.

ISBN 1-877978-95-7. Paperback $12.95

BUTTERFLIES IN HEAT

THE RENAISSANCE OF A CULT CLASSIC--
ONE OF THE BEST-SELLING GLBT NOVELS OF ALL TIME.

A study in malevolence, vendetta, morbid fascination, and redemption. One of the very few pop novels ever praised by Tennessee Williams ("I'd walk the waterfront for Numie any day...."), it was the inspiration for the original character of the male prostitute as portrayed by Jon Voight in *Midnight Cowboy*. Its hero is blond god Numie Chase, an unlucky hustler with flesh to sell.

"Darwin Porter writes with an incredible understanding of the milieu--hot enough to singe the wings off any butterfly."

James Kirkwood, co-author, *A Chorus Line*

"How does Darwin Porter's garden grow? Only in the moonlight, and only at midnight, when man-eating vegetation in any color but green bursts into full bloom to devour the latest offerings."

James Leo Herlihy, author of *MIDNIGHT COWBOY*

"Not since I saw Tennessee Williams's first Broadway play have I experienced such a compelling American writer."

Greta Keller

BLOOD MOON

AN EROTIC THRILLER

*"**Blood Moon** is like reading Anaïs Nin on Viagra
with a bump of crystal meth."*

Eugene Raymond

Set within the glittery and sometimes tawdry context of South Florida, this is the abridged version of Darwin Porter's most successful erotic thriller. It's about love, psychosis, sexual obsession, pornography, power, and religious fanaticism in America today. Its title (and sales record) inspired our choice of **Blood Moon Productions** as the name of our publishing house after its reorganization in 2003. And because of recent revelations about the links between the regime of George W. Bush and the Saudi oil empire, its plot and many of its then-shocking premises (originally published in an expanded edition in 1999) now seem almost clairvoyant. **Its ending reveals what really happens when the moon turns to blood.**

"Rose Phillips, ***Blood Moon***'s charismatic and deviant evangelist, and her uncontrollable gay son, Shelley, were surely written in hell." **Buddy Hamilton**

"***Blood Moon*** reads like *Dynasty* on steroids. A compelling psycho-sexual adventure of three beautiful men meeting on the fast road to hell." **Kathryn Cobb**

FROM THE GEORGIA LITERARY ASSOCIATION. NOW IN ITS THIRD PRINTING
ISBN 0-9668030-4-3   PAPERBACK $10.99

This is the book
that satirized THE BOOK
that changed the face of tourism in Savannah
for all time.

MIDNIGHT IN SAVANNAH

BY DARWIN PORTER   ISBN 09668030-1-9   Paperback   **$14.95**

This is the more explicit and more entertaining alternative to John Berendt's Savannah-based *Midnight in the Garden of Good and Evil*. Decadent but insightful, it's a saga of corruption, greed, sexual tension, and murder that gets down and dirty in the Deep Old South.

For more than a year after its publication in 2000, this was was the best-selling GLBT novel in Georgia and the Carolinas. If you're gay and southern, or if you've ever felt either traumatized or eroticized south of the Mason-Dixon Line, you should probably read this book.

"In Darwin Porter's Midnight, *both Lavender Morgan ("At 72, the world's oldest courtesan") and Tipper Zelda ("an obese, fading chanteuse taunted as "the black widow,") purchase lust from sexually conflicted young men with drop-dead faces, chiseled bodies, and genetically gifted crotches. These women once relied on their physicality to steal the hearts and fortunes of the world's richest and most powerful men. Now, as they slide closer every day to joining the corpses of their former husbands, these once-beautiful women must depend, in a perverse twist of fate, on sexual outlaws for* le petit mort. *And to survive, the hustlers must idle their personal dreams while struggling to cajole what they need from a sexual liaison they detest. Mendacity reigns, Perversity in extremis. Physical beauty as living hell. CAT ON A HOT TIN ROOF'S Big Daddy must be spinning in his grave right now."*

EUGENE RAYMOND

In Hollywood at the Dawn of the Talkies,
most of the sins were never shown on screen

Hollywood's Silent Closet

**A Scandalous Info-Novel Where
90% of Everything in It is True**

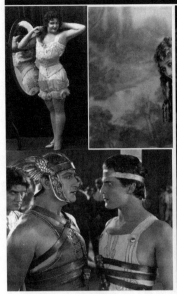

Hollywood's Silent Closet

by Darwin Porter

"A brilliant primer for the <u>Who's Who</u> of early Hollywood
Intricately researched by entertainment columnist Darwin Porter,
this is the most realistic account ever written about sex,
murder, blackmail, and degradation in early Hollywood."
Gay Times (London)

A banquet of information about the pansexual intrigues of Hollywood between 1919 and
1926, compiled from eyewitness interviews with men and women, all of them insiders, who
flourished in its midst. Not for the timid, it names names, and doesn't spare the guilty...

If you believe, like Truman Capote, that the literary treatment of gossip will become the
literature of the 21st century, then you will love this book.

**From the Georgia Literary Association
(an affiliate of Blood Moon Productions)**

ISBN 0966-8030-2-7   Trade paperback   746 pages   60 vintage photos. $24.95

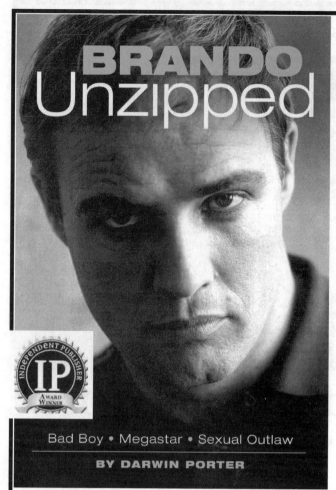

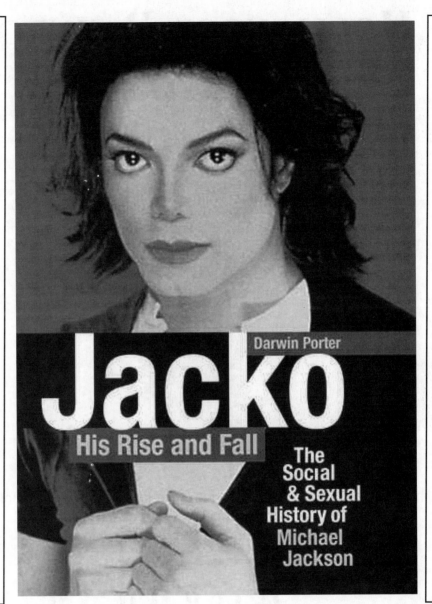